Exploring
Big South Fork
National River and
Recreation Area

Todd S. Campbell
and Kym Rouse Campbell

FALCON®

GUILFORD, CONNECTICUT
HELENA, MONTANA
AN IMPRINT OF THE GLOBE PEQUOT PRESS

TSC: To my nephews, Ross and Ian Campbell, who exemplify our next generation of explorers and conservationists.

KRC: To my grandparents, Dorothy and the late Fred Rouse, who instilled in me a love and respect for the outdoors, taught me many ways to enjoy it, and always told me I could do anything.

A FALCON GUIDE®

Copyright © 2002 by The Globe Pequot Press
All rights reserved. No part of this book may be reproduced or transmitted in any form by any means, electronic or mechanical, including photocopying and recording, or by any information storage and retrieval system, except as may be expressly permitted by the 1976 Copyright Act or by the publisher. Requests for permission should be made in writing to The Globe Pequot Press, P.O. Box 480, Guilford, Connecticut 06437.

Falcon and FalconGuide are registered trademarks of The Globe Pequot Press.

Text design: Nancy Freeborn
Maps created by Chris Salcedo; © The Globe Pequot Press
Photos: Todd S. Campbell

Library of Congress Cataloging-In-Publication Data
Campbell, Todd S.
    Exploring Big South Fork National River and Recreation Area / Todd S.
Campbell and Kym Rouse Campbell.—1st ed.
        p. cm. — (A Falcon guide)
    Includes bibliographical references.
    ISBN 0-7627-1090-X
        1. Outdoor recreation—Big South Fork National River and Recreation Area
(Tenn. and Ky.)—Guidebooks. 2. Trails—Big South Fork National River and
Recreation Area (Tenn. and Ky.)—Guidebooks. 3. Big South Fork National River
and Recreation Area (Tenn. and Ky.)—Guidebooks. I. Campbell, Kym Rouse.
II. Title. III. Series.

GV191.42.K4 C36 2002
917.68'71—dc21

                                                        2002021514

♻ Text pages printed on recycled paper.
Manufactured in the United States of America
First Edition/First Printing

Contents

Mt. Helen, Honey Creek, and Rugby Areas

Floating the Big South Fork and Its Tributaries

Directory of Maps

Preface

We had mixed feelings writing an exploring guide about a place that hardly anyone knows about. Even though we can see the Great Smoky Mountains National Park (GSMNP) from our small farm outside Maryville, Tennessee, we prefer the quiet solitude of the Big South Fork National River and Recreation Area (NRRA) for outdoor activities. We hope that the Big South Fork NRRA, which has been in existence for less than thirty years and receives fewer than 900,000 visitors a year, never becomes as popular as the GSMNP. No matter how you choose to explore the Big South Fork NRRA, it is rare to see a lot of people, even though it is located within a day's drive from about anywhere in the East.

With gorges hundreds of feet deep and other spectacular natural features, the Big South Fork NRRA is like a small Grand Canyon covered with eastern forests. Since it's a reclaimed wilderness, the land is covered with second-growth forest. Old roads and abandoned railbeds criss-cross the area; abandoned coal mines, oil wells, and natural gas wells can be found; and cemeteries and man-made structures still stand. However, you will not find more spectacular scenery and natural architecture anywhere east of the Rocky Mountains.

The Big South Fork NRRA has something for everyone. It offers outstanding day-hiking, backpacking, horseback riding, mountain biking, rock climbing, canoe camping, and some of the best white-water rafting and kayaking in the East. The Big South Fork NRRA is also a great place to picnic, swim, hunt, and fish.

We have been coming to the Big South Fork NRRA regularly since 1994, and we hiked, biked, and horseback rode literally hundreds of miles to arrive at the various combinations of loop trails in this book. We also white-water rafted or canoed every wonderful mile of the Big South Fork River. We hope this guide will help you have many wonderful adventures in the Big South Fork NRRA. Happy trails!

Acknowledgments

Many people helped us make this book what it is. First of all, we sincerely thank Superintendent Reed E. Detring and his staff at the Big South Fork NRRA for their help and support, including, but not limited to Tom Blount, Ron Cornelius, Tom Des Jean, Sue Duncan, John Fischer, Frank Graham, Sue Jennings, Wally Linder, Steve Seven, and Chris Stubbs. Special thanks to Robert Emmott for providing long-term housing in trade for a reptile and amphibian survey. Extra special thanks to Howard Ray Duncan and Brenda Deaver, who tirelessly conveyed their vast knowledge of the area to us during numerous phone calls and constant badgering. Finally, thanks to Senator Howard Baker Jr., Brenda Deaver, Howard Ray Duncan, Arthur McDade, Russ Manning, and Jo Anna Smith—the authors of previous trail guides—for paving the way.

Many people provided support, accommodations, and information and reviewed drafts of various chapters. We thank Gretta and Billie Gene York of Bandy Creek Stables; Tim Line, William Shealy, Sandra Walker, Pat "Weenie Roller" Greene, and Keith Garnes of Charit Creek Lodge; Sheltowee Trace Outfitters (including "Mean Jean" and "Papa Smurf"); Mark Jordan of the Big South Fork Scenic Railway; Harold Koger of Barthell; Dawn Strunk of the Stearns Museum; Barbara Sedivi and Kathy Lockhart of Sweet Kreations Gift Shoppe & Fudgery and Big South Fork Motor Lodge; Barbara Stagg and Amy Barnes of Historic Rugby; Linda Brooks Jones of Grey Gables; Gary Matthews and Darrell Lewallen of Zenith Stables; and Dallas Stults and the volunteers of Breakaway. We thank our friends Kathy Kalisek, Ashley Kissick, Karen Clark, Joanne Grimes, Debby Lashley, and Lucy Scanlon. Earth Traverse Outfitters kept Todd's Gary Fisher Super-Caliber working flawlessly. Our horses, Cinnamon and Dakota, faithfully carried us over many hundreds of miles of trails and proudly finished every endurance ride they started. We thank our editors Peggy O'Neill-McLeod, Erin Turner, and Josh Rosenberg for their tireless work. Finally, we thank Kym's sister, Debby (Cheyenne) Rouse, for telling us about the book request.

Map Legend

FEATURES

Roads and Trails

Interstate

Miscellaneous Roads (Paved)

Gravel Road

Unimproved Roads

Selected Route

Utilities

Railroad Tracks

Boundary Lines

Park Boundary

State Boundary

Water Bodies

River/Creek

Lakes/Large Rivers

Land Features

Cliffs

Islands

Meadow

SYMBOLS

Roads

Interstate   5   55   555

U.S. Highways   5   55   555

State Roads   5   55   555

Nat'l. Park Route   5   55

Forest Roads   41   416   4165

Cities

Capitol   Large   Small   Street Grid

Miscellaneous

Airport	✕	Trailhead	T
Bike Trail	⮷	Visitor Info	?
Bridge	⩥	Waterfalls	∬
Bus Stop	🚌	Overlook	◘
Campground	▲	Park Entrance	◇
Cave/Rock House	⌒●	Parking	P
Cemetery	†	Pass/Gap	⊖)(
Climbing Area	◐	Picnic	🛉
Church	⊥	Portage	⥀
Dining	🍴	Post office	✉
Golf Course	🚩	Ranger Station	◿
Hiking trail	🚶	Rapids	≋
Hospital	H	Rest room	🚻
Library	L	School	🎓
Lodging	🛏	Skiing	⚠
Mine	✕	Spring	○—
Mountain / Peak	▲	Stadium	🏟
Structures	■		
Connection	C		

Map 1—Location of the Big South Fork NRRA in KY/TN

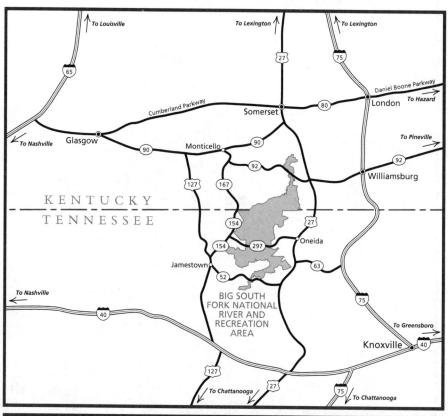

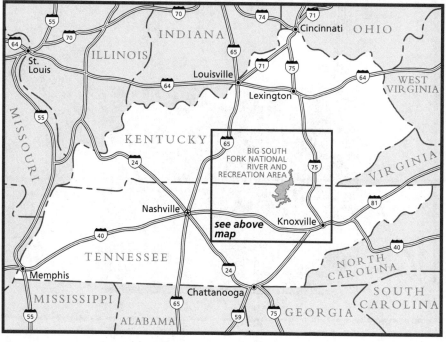

Map 2—Locations of Trailheads, River Access Points, Picnic Areas, and Campgrounds

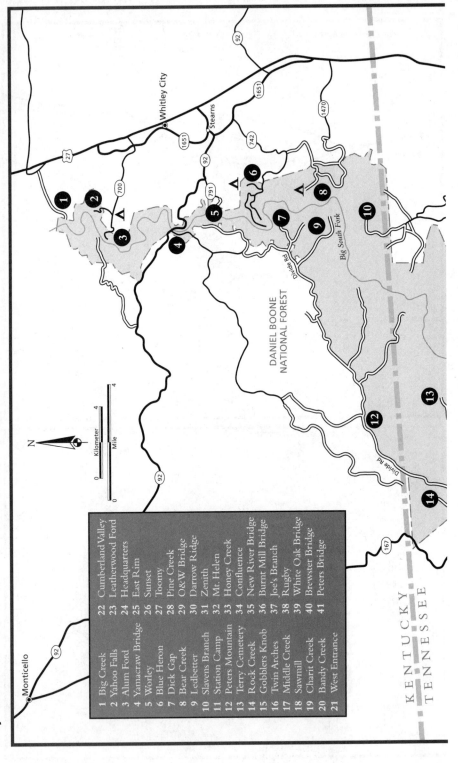

1 Big Creek
2 Yahoo Falls
3 Alum Ford
4 Yamacraw Bridge
5 Worley
6 Blue Heron
7 Dick Gap
8 Bear Creek
9 Ledbetter
10 Slavens Branch
11 Station Camp
12 Peters Mountain
13 Terry Cemetery
14 Rock Creek
15 Gobblers Knob
16 Twin Arches
17 Middle Creek
18 Sawmill
19 Charit Creek
20 Bandy Creek
21 West Entrance
22 Cumberland Valley
23 Leatherwood Ford
24 Headquarters
25 East Rim
26 Sunset
27 Toomy
28 Pine Creek
29 O&W Bridge
30 Darrow Ridge
31 Zenith
32 Mt. Helen
33 Honey Creek
34 Confluence
35 New River Bridge
36 Burnt Mill Bridge
37 Joe's Branch
38 Rugby
39 White Oak Bridge
40 Brewster Bridge
41 Peters Bridge

DANIEL BOONE
NATIONAL FOREST

KENTUCKY
TENNESSEE

Monticello

Whitley City

Stearns

Big South Fork

Divide Rd

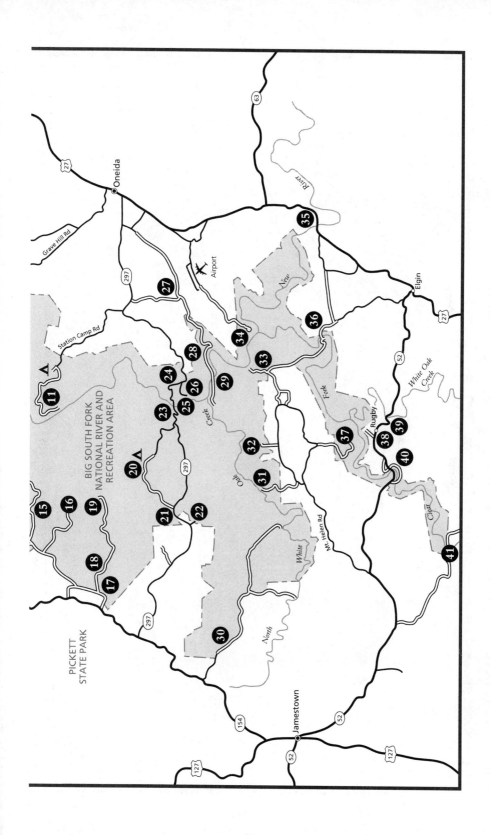

Map 3—Trail Locator Map (by trail number)

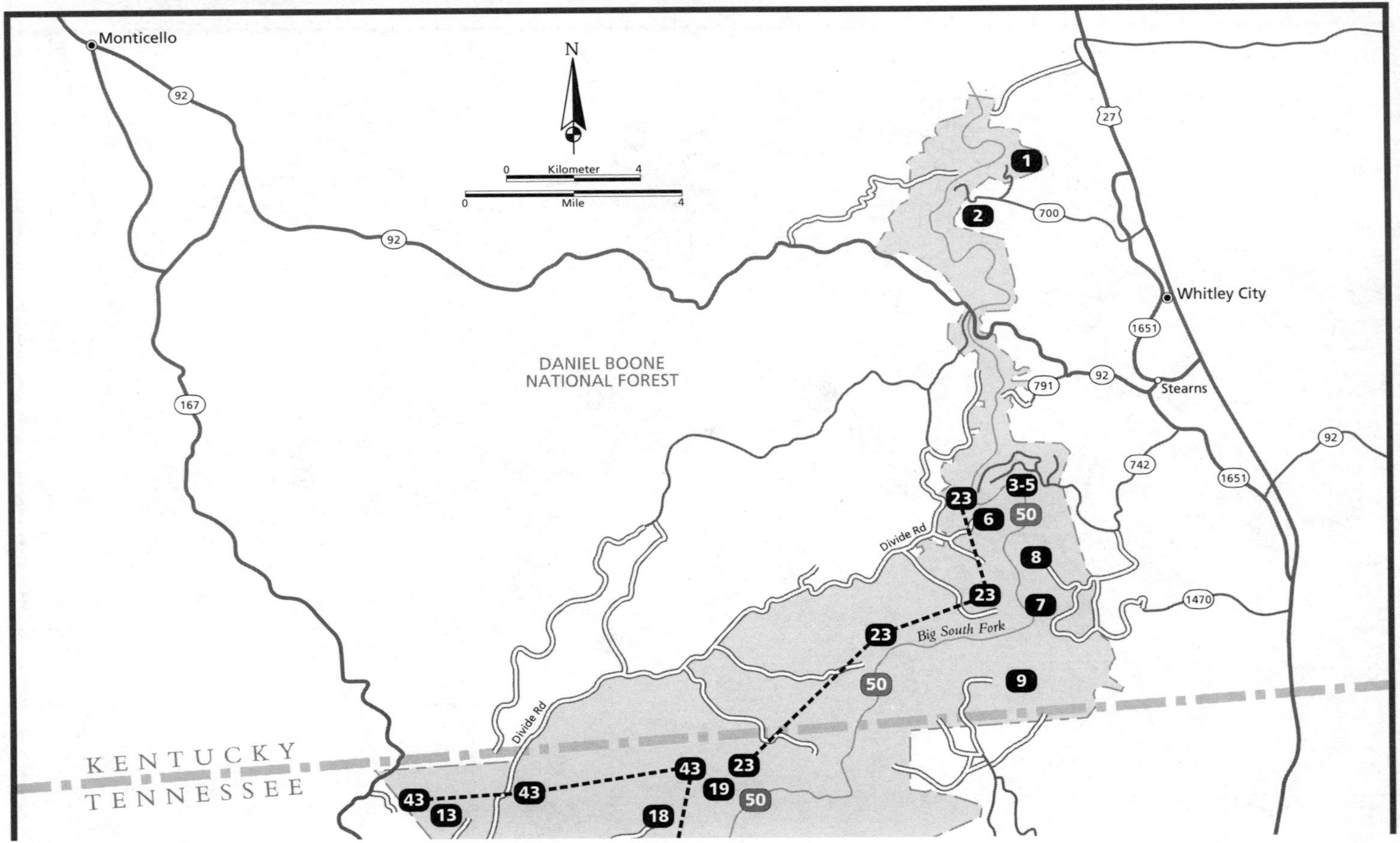

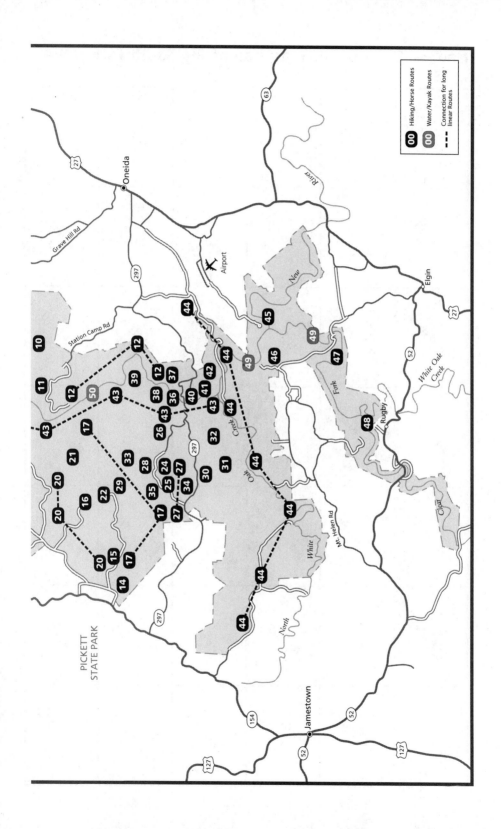

PICKETT
STATE PARK

Oneida

Grave Hill Rd

Station Camp Rd

Airport

Elgin

Rugby

White Oak
Creek

Jamestown

Hiking/Horse Routes
Water/Kayak Routes
Connection for long
linear Routes

Map 4—USGS Quadrangle Map of Big South Fork NRRA

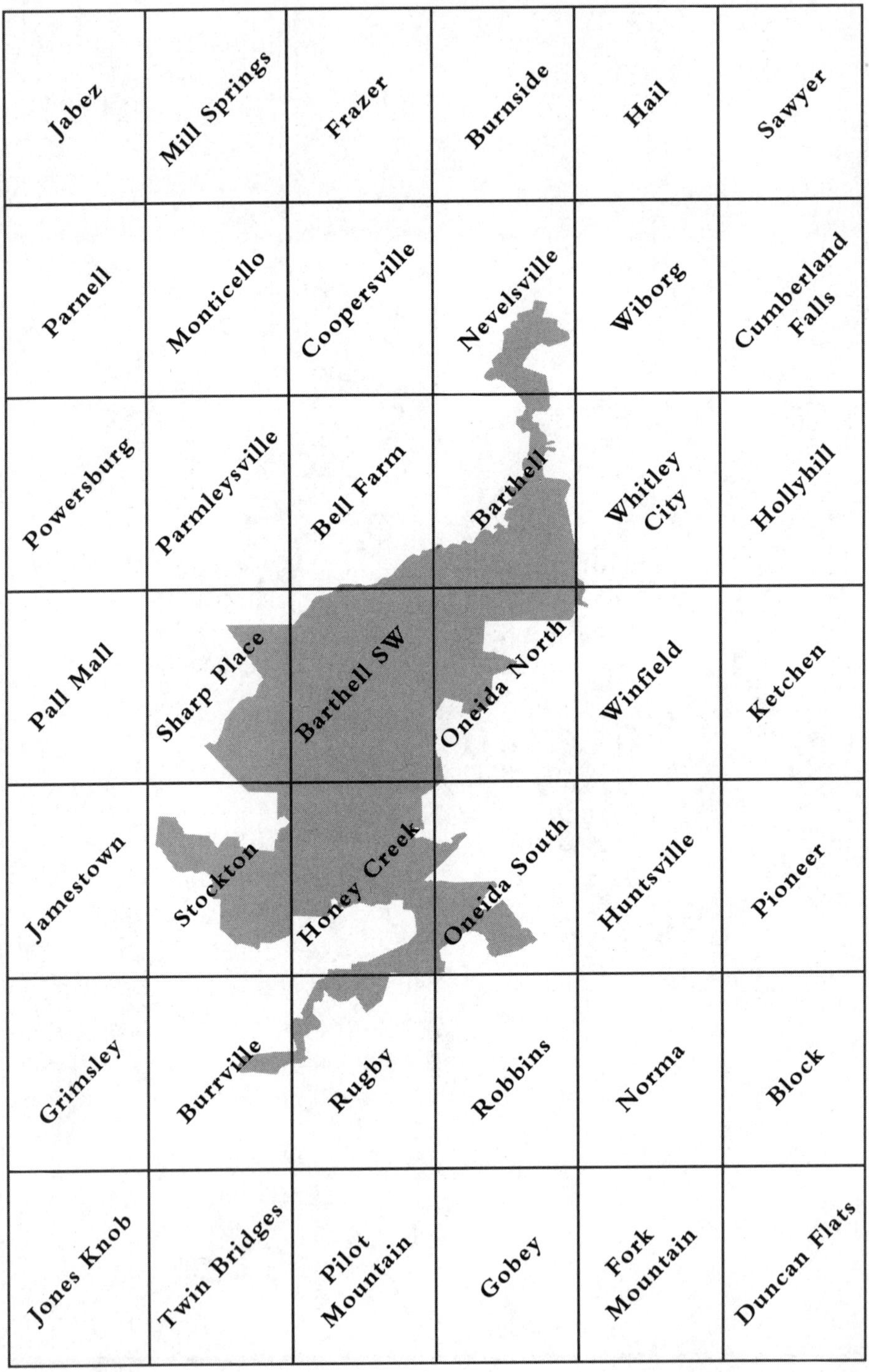

Jabez	Mill Springs	Frazer	Burnside	Hail	Sawyer
Parnell	Monticello	Coopersville	Nevelsville	Wiborg	Cumberland Falls
Powersburg	Parmleysville	Bell Farm	Barthell	Whitley City	Hollyhill
Pall Mall	Sharp Place	Barthell SW	Oneida North	Winfield	Ketchen
Jamestown	Stockton	Honey Creek	Oneida South	Huntsville	Pioneer
Grimsley	Burrville	Rugby	Robbins	Norma	Block
Jones Knob	Twin Bridges	Pilot Mountain	Gobey	Fork Mountain	Duncan Flats

Introduction to the Big South Fork National River and Recreation Area

The Big South Fork of the Cumberland River begins at the confluence of the New River and the Clear Fork in Scott County, Tennessee, and flows north into McCreary County, Kentucky. It cuts through rocks more than 250 million years old on the Cumberland Plateau. The Big South Fork River drains about 1,400 square miles of some of the most primitive and isolated land in the eastern United States. It is one of only a few rivers in the United States designated by Congress as a National River because of its historical significance as well as its wild and scenic beauty.

Creation of a National River and Recreation Area

The Big South Fork is one of the few rivers in the eastern United States that has not been dammed for flood control or hydroelectric power generation—but not for lack of trying. In the late 1920s the Tennessee Electric Power Company (TEPCO) proposed building a dam to produce hydroelectric power at the confluence of the New River and Clear Fork. TEPCO sold out during the Great Depression to the newly created Tennessee Valley Authority (TVA), which was also interested in damming the Big South Fork, and the U.S. Army Corps of Engineers (USACOE) first proposed to dam the river at Devil's Jump Rapids in Kentucky in 1933. This dam would have been the highest dam in the eastern United States and would have flooded the river gorge all the way into the Clear Fork and New River Gorges in Tennessee. Tennessee politicians tried for years to get approval from Congress to authorize construction of the dam. Five times during the 1960s the U.S. Senate voted to fund the project, but each time the House of Representatives refused to agree.

View from O&W Overlook

The fight to preserve the area was led by the Tennessee Citizens for Wilderness Planning (TCWP), a local conservation group led by Liane Russell. In 1968 the Big South Fork was excluded from both the Tennessee Scenic Rivers Bill and the National Wild and Scenic Rivers Bill. However, the threat of development convinced many people that the Big South Fork area needed permanent protection. Many alternative federal designations were proposed, including national park, national forest, national recreation area, and scenic river.

The Big South Fork Coalition, formed by the TCWP, worked with former Senator Howard Baker, Jr., to introduce legislation in 1972 creating a combination national river and recreation area as part of a water resources bill. For reasons that had nothing to do with the Big South Fork, President Nixon vetoed the bill. However, this delay allowed the bill to be rewritten so that management of the area would be turned over to the National Park Service (NPS), after the area was established by the USACOE.

The Big South Fork NRRA was authorized and funded by Congress on March 7, 1974. Approximately 123,000 acres of the Big South Fork drainage basin are located within its boundaries and include portions of Fentress, Morgan, and Scott Counties in Tennessee and McCreary County, Kentucky. It includes the gorge and rim areas of the Clear Fork, New, and Big South Fork Rivers.

The USACOE purchased land, built visitor facilities, and developed trails as funding became available. In November 1990 Congress authorized the transfer of the Big South Fork NRRA to the NPS, which is responsible for further land purchases (approximately 119,000 acres as of this writing) and development.

The 17,372-acre Pickett State Park and Forest is adjacent to the western edge of the Big South Fork NRRA in Tennessee. This neighboring park contains many scenic, botanical, and geological wonders.

The Geology of the Big South Fork
Rock Formations of the Cumberland Plateau

An important chapter in the story of Earth's early history is told in the sedimentary rocks of the Big South Fork region. It is a tale of deposition, uplift, and subsequent erosion, exposing strata deposited 280 to 320 million years ago (mya) in the Pennsylvanian and Mississippian Epochs of the Carboniferous Period, near the end of the Paleozoic Era. The defining characteristic of rock layers from this period is an alternating sequence of nonmarine and marine origins: from coarse alluvial sediments eroded from uplands, to veins of coal formed in vast swamps, to limestones formed in the shallow seas. The Cumberland Plateau is a subregion of the Appalachian Plateau, a long shelf of sedimentary rock that runs from Alabama to New York. The layers have not been folded or buckled by tectonic activity, so they reveal the sequence in which they were deposited. The oldest exposure in the area is the Pennington Formation, a Mississippian limestone deposited in shallow, inland seas around 320 mya. This fine, white stratum is composed of calcium carbonate left over from the shells of diverse marine organisms. It was covered in the Pennsylvanian Epoch (about 300 mya) by alternating sandstones, shales, and coals of the Beattyville Shale Member, the lowest (oldest) strata of the Lee Formation. Sandstone looks like concrete but, unlike its unnatural counterpart, is highly vulnerable to erosion by water and wind. Fine silts form shale, a fragile, smooth gray rock that is often found fractured into wafer-thin layers.

Interspersed between the shales and sandstones are veins of coal, a type of rock composed mainly of carbon. Coal seams were formed over the course of millions of years, as remains of plants and animals in swampy areas were covered by thick layers of sandstone and shale. These heavy layers compressed the underlying organic materials into coal, oil, and/or natural gas deposits, depending on local conditions. Subsequent erosion of the surrounding layers resulted in the discovery of these burnable materials and altered the course of human history, for better and for worse.

The youngest stratum is the Rockcastle Conglomerate Member of the Lee Formation, deposited during the late Pennsylvanian, about 280 mya. This tough stratum caps the plateau, seen prominently as massive sandstone bluffs lining the river gorge and huge boulders that tumble or gradually slide down the gorge slopes and litter the river and its tributaries. Some exposures contain embedded quartz pebbles, rounded by the action of faster moving water—the fossilized remains of ancient sandbars or creekbeds. Other exposures have interesting honeycomb or wavy formations, formed by differential erosion of sandstones of different hardness, with iron ore deposits being the most resistant.

The Cumberland Plateau Past and Present

During the Carboniferous Period, deposition was the underlying geological theme. The area we now know as Kentucky and Tennessee was a vast, relatively flat area of alluvial plains and tropical lowlands blanketed by rich coal swamps with a diverse array of seedless vascular plants. Large treelike forms such as *Lepidodendron*, which attained a height of more than 100 feet, dominated the terrain and formed much of our coal deposits. Huge fossils of these can be found in areas higher on the Cumberland Plateau in Anderson County. Smaller treelike forms such as *Calamites* (about 20 feet tall) were also present.

During this time many invertebrate groups (e.g., trilobites, crinoids, and brachiopods) reached their greatest level of abundance and diversity. Like the early plants, their fossilized forms are found on the Cumberland Plateau but are relatively rare in strata within the NRRA. This was a pivotal time in Earth's history, as it marked the emergence of terrestrial vertebrates: Anthracosaurs, Temnospondyls, Cotylosaurs, Captorhinomorphs, Synapsids, Diapsids, and other colorfully named aquatic, amphibious, and crocodile-like forms.

Recent geological events in this region are driven by the ubiquitous force of gravity. The strata forming the plateau were uplifted by tectonic activity and came to rest between 1,000 and 2,000 feet above sea level. A slight northerly tilt caused water to run off toward the north. The Big South Fork River cuts into the plateau as it flows northward to the Cumberland River. The rock strata are now visible only because of the uplift and subsequent erosion of the Cumberland Plateau by numerous waterways, including the Big South Fork River.

If gravity is the most influential force on Earth, water is the most influential substance. Not only does life revolve around water, it dissolves the geological strata over which it flows and carries the suspended materials downstream, only to be redeposited elsewhere. Water also expands when it freezes, chipping away at the rock surface like a chisel. As a result of erosion, the Cumberland Plateau is characterized by mesas and ridges capped with resistant sandstone. Steep canyons formed by the relatively rapid downcutting action of streams have narrow or poorly developed floodplains, if they have any floodplain at all.

Small tributaries drain the plateau, starting as surface runoff and groundwater bubbling from springs at the base of the sandstone bluffs lining the gorge. They pick up steam and cut steep, narrow ravines into the gorge slope, eroding their gorges upstream in a process called head-cut erosion. Waterfalls lie on the very front line of head-cut erosion, where water cuts its way upstream into the side of the gorge.

Rock shelters and arches are formed by differential erosion and weathering of the sandstones, shales, and coals of the valley walls. The freeze-thaw cycle causes large slabs to fall from beneath the more resistant strata, forming first the roof of a rock house. An arch can be formed if water and ice open up a window in the roof of a rock house. Or, slabs can fall from both sides of a narrow ridge, eventually meeting in the middle, forming an arch.

Rapids are formed just downstream of the confluences of major and minor tributaries. As water and plants erode rock and boulders crash down the gorge slope, they are naturally broken down into finer materials. On the side slopes and in waterways below, rocks are tumbling and grinding, chipping one another into smaller and smaller pieces. At the point where a major tributary empties into the main river channel, its water slows, allowing materials to drop out of the water column. This is how most rapids, riffles, and shoals are created. Coal is lighter than sandstone, so it sorts out of the water column differently than sandstone rocks, leaving shoals of coal pebbles washed smooth by the action of water.

History of the People and Their Effects on the Big South Fork NRRA

Humans have occupied the Big South Fork area for at least 13,000 years. Archaeological evidence suggests that hunting parties occupied the area on a seasonal basis and hunted bison, bear, elk, white-tailed deer, and wild turkey. They developed pottery, gathered nuts and berries, and harvested fish and shellfish from the river. The Big South Fork area remained a hunting ground as Native American cultures appeared and declined and as the climate, forests, and types of animals hunted changed. However, the lack of broad, fertile river valleys discouraged permanent settlement.

Thousands of rock shelters along the bluffs of the Big South Fork River and its tributaries are now protected by law due to their archaeological significance. They provided dry, protected, convenient campsites for the early inhabitants. Unfortunately, by the time the Big South Fork NRRA was created, amateur collectors had destroyed much of the ancient archaeological and recent historical record.

Rock shelters were also used by "longhunters" who came into the area during the late 1700s. The name comes either from the fact that their hunting trips were long both in time and distance or because of the long rifles they carried. Daniel Boone was the most famous longhunter. In the fall groups of hunters would leave their homes in North Carolina and Virginia and travel to base camps in the area that is now Tennessee and Kentucky, including the Big South Fork area. Hunters would return home with their bounty after a winter of hunting and trapping.

When people living along the eastern seaboard eventually began to follow the major migration routes west, some longhunters returned to settle in the area, as did Revolutionary War veterans who received land grants as compensation for their services. Forced treaties with the Cherokees opened the Big South Fork area to white settlement. The early settlers, mostly of English and Scotch-Irish descent, first lived in rock shelters then built pole cabins with mud floors; eventually they built log cabins. Rock shelters were also used to hold livestock, as storage, as schools—even as hideaways for moonshine stills.

The longhunters continued to hunt the ridges and valleys while their descendants cleared the narrow bottomlands to farm, but the transition to farming was gradual. These hardy and independent subsistence farmers were able to survive by growing corn, wheat, flax, and cotton; raising food in large gardens; raising chickens and bees, maintaining free-ranging cows, sheep, and hogs; and hunting and trapping. They tanned hides; made shoes, clothing, and household linens; produced gunpowder, bullets, tar, turpentine, and lime; and made wagons, furniture, and tools. Fish did not seem to be an important food resource, probably because people were so busy tending to their farms and gardens. However, fishing was a recreational activity that provided a special treat.

Saltpeter, or potassium nitrate, an essential ingredient in gunpowder, was mined from sandstone rock shelters and bluffs for the War of 1812 and the Civil War. This is the fluffy, white-gray powder covering the floor of many rock shelters. The miners collected the rock, debris, and soil from the rock shelters after blasting the walls and placed everything in large vats. Saltpeter crystals were formed by pouring boiling water over the material in the vats and then filtering the liquid.

In 1818 Marcus Huling and Andrew Zimmerman struck oil on land in the Big South Fork area leased from Martin Beaty and started the first commercial oil well in the United States. They were actually after salt, which was used as a preservative before the days of refrigeration. Unfortunately for Huling and Zimmerman, oil at the time was virtually worthless, getting the oil out of the area was extremely difficult, and the public was outraged by the pollution caused by the "devil's tar." Before searching for salt in other locations, Marcus Huling sold oil to makers of patent medicines, liniments, and other cure-alls in the United States and Europe.

The communities that developed along the Big South Fork and its larger tributaries were very isolated; each settlement usually occupied a particular watershed. Larger settlements were established along Laurel Crossing Branch, Rock Creek, and Bear Creek in Kentucky and Williams, Station Camp, Parch Corn, and No Business Creeks in Tennessee. No Business Creek supposedly got its name when a couple first tried to settle there; the wife said that they had no business leaving home and no business trying to stay there. Names of other creeks in the area (Difficulty, Lonesome, and Troublesome) give an idea of how difficult life was for the early white settlers in the Big South Fork area.

Because of its many rapids, the Big South Fork was not navigable and was a barrier to transportation and commerce. Contact with the outside world occurred by socializing with families that lived in neighboring valleys or through infrequent trips out of the gorges and valleys over very difficult wagon roads. The isolated way of life in the Big South Fork area was interrupted during the Civil War. Although Tennessee joined the Confederacy, it was the last state to secede and the first to return; the Big South Fork area, along with the state of Kentucky, remained with the Union. Scott County even seceded from the state of Tennessee and became the Independent State of Scott. Since there were few plantations (and few slaves) in mountainous East Tennessee, there was little interest in fighting for the rights of plantation owners in the South to own slaves. Many men left to join the Union army; others stayed and formed a Home Guard to fight guerrilla attacks by Confederate sympathizers from Fentress and Pickett Counties. During the attacks, food and livestock were taken, and civilians were often killed. Whatever could not be taken was often destroyed. Some families who left during the conflict permanently lost their land.

Later settlers pushed into the Big South Fork area from the southern end of the Cumberland Plateau. The colony of Rugby, which we describe in a later chapter, was established by English immigrants in 1880. German immigrants started the planned community of Allardt.

The Big South Fork NRRA contains late examples of building types that have long since disappeared from elsewhere in Tennessee and Kentucky. Forms of construction that generally stopped being used during the nineteenth century were still being used in the area as late as 1930. Local architecture often involved adding on to existing structures and using what-

Log home at Clara Sue Blevins Farm

ever materials were available. You can visit some of the old farmsteads, including log cabins, barns, and other structures, while exploring the Big South Fork NRRA. They include the Charit Creek Lodge, the Oscar Blevins Farm Site, the Clara Sue Blevins Site, and the John Litton/General Slaven Farm.

There are numerous cemeteries located throughout the Big South Fork NRRA. Larger cemeteries include the Katie Blevins, Hattie Blevins, Terry, and Slaven Cemeteries. Many small cemeteries, consisting of only one or just a few gravesites, are also scattered throughout the NRRA.

Completion of the Southern Railway between Cincinnati and Monroe, Louisiana, in 1880 marked the beginning of the intensive commercial exploitation of timber and coal in the area. People and equipment could be brought in, and coal and lumber could be shipped out. Several short-line railroads were built to haul timber and coal to the Southern Railway. The area was almost completely deforested by independent loggers and lumber companies as logging continued until the 1950s.

Coal mining never totally dominated the economy of the Big South Fork area as it did in eastern Kentucky and West Virginia. The Stearns Coal and Lumber Company, founded in 1902, was the largest company in the region. The company owned more than 200,000 acres in the Big South Fork area and had the greatest social and economic impact on the area. It treated its employees well, paid decent wages, and used state-of-the-art mining technology. The company produced one million tons of coal and 18 million board feet of lumber during its peak year of 1929. It employed approximately 2,000 miners and several hundred loggers, mostly local folks. The remains of the various railways, Stearns, the Blue Heron Mining Community, and the Barthell Mining Camp are reminders of this part of the history of the Big South Fork area.

Coal mines in the Tennessee portion of the Big South Fork area were operated by individuals. Although coal mining did occur in other locations, most independent operations occurred along North White Oak Creek. The Tennessee Stave and Lumber Company (later changed to Tennessee Lumber and Coal Company) was the largest logging operation in the Tennessee portion of the Big South Fork area; it reached peak production in 1929 and declined rapidly thereafter. There were also many smaller independent logging operations.

Coal mining, which peaked during the 1920s, the railroads, and logging brought many people to the area. The coal and timber industries began to decline as the resources became depleted and the Great Depression reduced demand. Labor unrest was another factor. The decline halted briefly during World War II, which energized the economy, but most mining operations had ended by the 1950s. Coal company towns, mining camps, lumber mills, and railroads slowly disappeared. Rural schools, country stores, and post offices also closed. Unpaved roads, which were not car-friendly to begin with, were allowed to deteriorate. Many people left the isolated area to work in defense plants up North, but some residents of the river gorge area moved to the surrounding tableland communities.

Most of the Big South Fork area was left to recover and heal in peace. However, with the exception of the river gorge area, monitored oil and gas production is allowed within the NRRA. Approximately 300 oil and gas wells are located within NRRA boundaries. By the time the Big South Fork NRRA was authorized in 1974, only about forty households of year-round residents, primarily subsistence farmers, lived within the proposed boundaries. Past land use practices, recent conservation and restoration efforts, and current attitudes and activities in the NRRA and surrounding areas have shaped and will continue to shape the region's ecology.

Ecology of the Big South Fork Area

The Big South Fork NRRA lies in the mixed mesophytic forest zone of the eastern deciduous forest region, a forest that once covered much of North America east of the ninety-eighth parallel. Growing on geological features exposed for millions of years, this is the oldest forest type on the continent. Despite extensive logging, coal mining, oil and natural gas exploration, and agricultural operations, this wonderful natural area is recovering nicely and is well along a trajectory toward becoming a regionally significant natural area.

Even the "virgin forests" of Great Smoky Mountains National Park and Joyce Kilmer Memorial Forest look nothing like they did originally—the dominant tree species has been completely eliminated! The once-grand American chestnut exists only as small shrubs due to chestnut blight, a fungus accidentally imported from Asia in the 1800s. Attempts are being made to breed fungal resistance into American chestnuts. Scott State Forest is conducting experiments on this species in a field along Duncan Hollow Trail.

More than anything else in the NRRA, you may notice that the upland plateau forests have suffered extensive damage, temporarily knocking back the growth that has accrued since the plateau was stripped of its trees. First, a winter storm in 1998 dropped heavy, wet snow that snapped many hardwoods and pines like toothpicks. Second, recent outbreaks of southern pine beetles have left patches of standing-dead pines all over the Southeast. This native insect occurs naturally in pine stands throughout the South, but trees under stress are susceptible to beetle outbreaks. The 1998 storm damage and three years of drought and mild winters between 1998 and 2000 triggered its worst outbreak since the 1960s. Once pine beetles infest a tree, it will surely die. The natural cycle of outbreak is five to seven years, with predators, parasites, disease, and weather keeping the beetles in check. In 2001 the National Park Service removed many damaged trees around public use areas and cut them up for firewood; other areas were left to recover on their own. Please heed the signs that warn you of the dangers of falling trees.

There have also been a number of fires in the NRRA, with three bad fires in 2000. Fire is a natural and important component of many ecosystems, but a combination of fire suppression starting in the 1940s, the winter storm of 1998, and the southern pine beetle made conditions ripe for fires that spread to the crowns of trees and killed them. Some plant communities—such as the pine forests that have filled in drier areas in this region—would not exist without periodic fire, but that is not the case for the eastern deciduous forest.

Coal Mining and Acid Mine Drainage

Extensive surface and deep coal mining in the Big South Fork River watershed has left permanent scars on the landscape and many streams contaminated with acid mine drainage. During the coal mining process, low-grade coals and bedrock layers surrounding coal beds are excavated and piled on the edge of the mine site. In these "spoil piles," weathering processes are accelerated, and minerals are subject to oxidation, dissolution, and transport in runoff from the site. In the Big South Fork area, coal contains medium to high levels of sulfur, and the sulfur in the coal and the surrounding bedrock reacts with water to create acid mine drainage that runs into the streams. In the eastern United States, coal mines that were closed fifteen to twenty years ago are still contaminating the environment; at some sites, acid mine drainage has continued for more than fifty years after the mines were closed. Streams are particularly vulnerable to direct discharges of acid mine drainage after storms, but the slow seepage of contaminated ground water is also a serious threat.

Unfortunately, polluted and silt-laden runoff from numerous coal mines enters tributaries in the Big South Fork watershed. Severely polluted streams include Bear Creek, Roaring Paunch Creek, and Rock Creek downstream from the confluence with White Oak Creek. The New River, Pine Creek, Puncheoncamp Fork of Williams Creek, and White Oak Creek are considered moderately polluted. Clear Fork, North White Oak Creek, Williams Creek, and Laurel Fork of North White Oak Creek are considered slightly polluted by mine drainage. Waters from these streams flow into the Big South Fork River, reducing the diversity of plants and animals in the river, eliminating habitat for several species of endangered plants and animals, and ultimately degrading the beauty of the river and the recreational value of the NRRA.

The restoration of polluted streams within the boundaries of the Big South Fork NRRA will take a long time and will be expensive. The NPS is working with a number of other agencies to restore the water quality of streams. Since most of the Big South Fork River watershed is outside the boundaries of the NRRA and activities outside the NRRA affect the water quality within it, the NPS is also collaborating with many other agencies to reclaim sites outside NRRA boundaries.

Exotic Species

Settlers planted nonnative vegetation at many of the historical sites in the Big South Fork. Most are not spreading into natural areas and some non-invasive species, such as apple trees, are maintained or even planted as part of the restoration of historical sites. However, some species are invasive and are spreading from these sites. Although some may smell pretty (e.g., honeysuckle), many of these species completely overgrow native vegetation, stealing their light and soil nutrients and completely altering the habitat and, in turn, affecting native animals.

Hogs were imported long ago, and settlers hunted them in many areas. As in some other national parks, like the GSMNP, feral hogs are wreaking havoc on the forest floor by rooting for grubs and roots with their noses and digging and stomping with their hooves. You will notice considerable damage, mostly in riparian and floodplain habitats where there are large wallows.

Dogwood anthracnose, beech bark fungus, and exotic insects already threaten plants in areas to the north, and the threat to the Big South Fork looms on the horizon. The worst threat of all may be the hemlock wooly adelgid, which would likely cause the demise of the primeval hemlock forests on the gorge slopes within about five years of its arrival.

Habitats and Species in the Big South Fork NRRA

Despite past impacts, ecologically the Big South Fork NRRA is a truly wonderful place. With 102 genera of native woody plants, it rivals the Great Smoky Mountains in woody plant diversity. We recognize eight general habitat types in the Big South Fork NRRA. Since water flows downhill, we describe them from plateau to river, as follows:

Upland Plateau

This habitat is found along most ridgelines above 1,200 feet in elevation, and nearly all the roads and trails on the plateau run through this forest type. Forest composition varies with soil type and depth, time since logging or other disturbances, and many other factors, so you will notice a number of different subtypes of this habitat.

Along the very tops of ridgelines, a vast mixture of tree species includes white, black, red, pin, and chestnut oak. Maples are abundant, as are buckeye, hickory, and American holly, and Virginia, shortleaf, and white pine to a lesser extent. Most disturbed habitats, including homesites, cemeteries, and farm fields, generally occur on the upland plateau, often on the tops of narrow ridgelines. In these areas you can expect to see pasture grasses, cultivated crops, fruit trees, ornamental plants, and a number of exotic invasive species, such as multiflora rose, tree of heaven, silk tree, honeysuckle, and possibly kudzu. Deer and turkey disappeared from the area in the early 1900s due to logging but were restocked from nearby sources.

There are very few natural ponds in the Big South Fork—most are oxbows in creek and river floodplains—but there are a number of ponds on the plateau, most constructed by settlers and more recent residents as water sources for livestock. Despite their artificial nature, stock ponds provide lots of wildlife viewing opportunities, and the visitor center pond is a fantastic example. Red-winged blackbirds construct their nests in the cattails in spring, and the staccato peep of spring peepers is very loud on spring evenings. Large choruses of bullfrogs and green frogs sing during the summer months: The former is recognized by the classic "jug-o-rum" call; the latter goes "doink," like a loose banjo string. The beautiful trill of the gray tree frog can also be heard on most summer nights. You might catch a glimpse of a large northern water snake (not poisonous) searching for prey among the cattails in the evening. Gather up the kids and bring a flashlight to the pond after dark!

Gorge Rim

The driest sites on the Cumberland Plateau occur on the thinnest soils near the plateau edges and are dominated by stands of Virginia and shortleaf pine, with American holly and witch hazel in the understory. Mountain laurel, three species of blueberry, and green briar usually form a thicket less than waist-high, making the forest open and parklike. Closer to bluff lines and at nearly every overlook, interesting lichen communities grow on exposed sandstone. Lichens are symbiotic associations between algae and fungi. Many different plants grow here, and butterflies are generally abundant at these sites. Eastern fence lizards can be found on nearly every sandstone outcrop, and most overlooks have a fence lizard sentinel or two. You are likely to hear pine warblers and rufous-sided towhees in this habitat on the gorge rim.

Because plants are growing on extremely thin soil or directly on the rock surface, this habitat is extremely fragile. Please do not wander from the trail or overlook platform. Even limited foot travel kills fragile lichens and disturbs the thin soil on which other plants depend. This is followed by severe erosion and exposure of bare sandstone, leading to heavier foot traffic, more erosion, and so on, until the plant community is completely eliminated. This damage is especially evident at Angel Falls Overlook and on the top of Twin Arches.

Sandstone Bluffs and Rock Houses

A number of interesting plants are found in the unique cool and damp microclimates formed by these geological features. Along with some rare flowering plants, liverworts, ferns, and sphagnum and other mosses can all be found at the base of large rock walls and in rock houses. The narrow cracks make great homes for cave crickets, spiders, millipedes, mice, and chipmunks. Organ-pipe mud dauber wasps are found on nearly every rock face and historical building.

The cone-shaped depressions under rock shelters with sandy substrates are the traps constructed by ant lion larvae. These clever little monsters have long mandibles they use to fling sand skyward out of their hole as they carve a circular pathway down into the earth. Eventually they form a cone-shaped hole with an edge that is not so steep that it collapses, but steep enough that if an ant steps over the lip, the slope will collapse and the ant will plummet to the bottom of the hole and the waiting larva. As adults, ant lions look somewhat like dragonflies but do not fly nearly as well. The soft sand beneath sandstone bluffs is also very good for finding animal tracks.

These unique habitats are also great for amphibians. Longtail, slimy, and zig-zag salamanders can be seen in cracks of wet walls (drip-walls) and overhangs, and the green salamander is found on drier walls. Aquatic salamanders such as the mountain dusky, northern dusky, spring, red, and four-toed and their tiny, gilled larvae are often found in the splash pools of waterfalls and under rocks and sphagnum moss beneath rock houses from which water flows. To see these critters during the day, you will need to bring a flashlight to look in cracks. Night hikes around these geological features are very interesting—a whole different suite of critters emerges, and your flashlight will reveal many surprises!

Gorge Slopes

The gorge slopes consist of colluvial soil, which slowly flows downhill. Boulders break off the cliff faces and tumble all the way to the river below. This opens gaps in the densely canopied slope forest below, allowing light-loving plants to gain a foothold and augmenting local plant diversity. Also, there is a distinct difference in the plant communities on north-facing and south-facing slopes due to their very different sunlight regimes. North-facing slopes tend to contain mesic species, such as hemlock and tulip poplar, while south-facing slopes are dominated by white oak and pine and other species that like sunny, dry, hot conditions.

Cicada-killer wasps are extremely large and can be seen flying over the forest floor and through the trees like jet fighters. They are looking for cicadas—the forest insect whose loud buzzing song signals the onset of summer—to lay eggs upon. Slopes covered in boulder fields are great habitat for small mammals and the snakes that eat them. If you flip any logs or rocks, make sure you flip them back to their original position, or the moisture regime will change and their home will no longer be livable. The slope forest is home to numerous birds, the most common being the red-eyed vireo and hooded warbler.

Headwaters, Waterfalls, and Creeks

Creeks often begin as springs or drip-walls or flow directly out of rock houses. These headwaters may stop flowing during dry times. As creeks build, they flow over flat sandstone shelves and erode their valleys in a process called head-cut erosion. This creates the beautiful waterfalls you can see in nearly any area of the NRRA. As the headwater streams plunge over the gorge slopes and join other small waterways, they pick up velocity and volume and carry more material and larger rocks. Larval and adult salamanders, water striders, mayflies, stoneflies, caddis flies, and crayfish are common denizens of headwater and larger creeks.

Riparian and Aquatic Habitats

The riparian zone along the Big South Fork River and its larger tributaries is probably the richest habitat type in the NRRA. It is the most dynamic, with flooding ("tides") and scouring. If you do not have the chance to witness the spectacle of a spring flood firsthand from one of the many bridges in the area, evidence of high water can be found hanging high in trees along any of the riverside trails. The building-sized boulders that seem to be standing in the forest in the middle of nowhere along Leatherwood Ford Loop, Angel Falls Trail, River Trail East, Alum-Yahoo Loop, and many other trails deep in the gorge are remnants of the rock walls above. The Appalachian region is known as a hotbed of aquatic diversity. Many fish and aquatic invertebrates are found only here, and more mussels are found in this region than anywhere else on Earth.

Oxbow lakes are small depressions created by the slow, serpentine-like movements of creeks and rivers. Rivers eventually meander back onto themselves and connect with other curved channels, leaving a depression shaped like a hairpin curve called an oxbow lake. A number of small oxbow ponds are found along the Big South Fork River and smaller waterways. Because they provide standing water, these are natural breeding sites for many amphibians.

The waters of Lake Cumberland are regulated at around 730 feet in elevation. The river just below (north of) Blue Heron is under the influence of this reservoir.

Black Bear Reintroduction Program

Black bears once inhabited the Big South Fork region and were found throughout Tennessee and Kentucky, but they disappeared from the area in the late 1800s/early 1900s because of overhunting and resource exploitation. In the late 1980s interest in bringing the black bear back to the Cumberland Plateau grew, and studies were initiated to determine the feasibility of reintroducing black bears into the Big South Fork NRRA and the Daniel Boone National Forest (DBNF). The experimental release of black bears was approved in the fall of 1995. During 1996 and 1997, female bears were transferred from the GSMNP and placed in remote areas of the Big South Fork NRRA. They were fitted with radio-transmitter collars for close monitoring. Some bears have been killed by vehicles; others have left the area. Newborn bear cubs were found with two of the radio-collared females in February 1999 and the winter of 2001. Bears in the Big South Fork NRRA weigh more than those in other nearby populations, an indicator that the bears are doing well in their new home. However, to establish a permanent, viable population, supplemental stocking of black bears will be necessary. The estimated bear population in the Big South Fork NRRA and surrounding public lands is between fifteen and twenty. Monitoring of bears will continue for the next several years. The decision to supplement the bear population with relocated bears will depend on further environmental assessment, funding, and public review. To minimize nuisance bear behavior and human-bear interaction, bear-proof trash cans have replaced old trash containers in many areas. Over the next few years, all the garbage cans in the Big South Fork NRRA will be replaced with animal-proof receptacles.

How to Use This Book

The purpose of this book is to introduce you to the best of the Big South Fork NRRA. However, the NPS General Management Plan (GMP), which includes a detailed Roads and Trails Management Plan (RTMP), was only in draft form as of this writing, and public comments were still being submitted. Thus, we only present information about activities and trails that are fun, safe, and already sanctioned or proposed by the NRRA and/or likely to survive the GMP review process based on extensive NPS input in summer 2001.

You should not have to spend time fumbling through our book to piece together a bunch of individual trail segments to make a decent half-day loop or epic journey. Instead, we present you with a suite of complete hiking, mountain biking, and horseback riding adventures. Some are really short but still warrant their own chapter, some are just long enough for weekend warriors, and others are long enough to challenge trained athletes. There are no marginal adventures in this book, so just pick one and go! We adopted a "loop mentality" whenever possible so that you experience something new around every bend.

Trail Chapters

Individual trail chapters are designed so that you can easily choose and efficiently plan your adventure, and include the following information:

Type of trail: The official uses of the trail (hiking, biking, horseback riding, or multiuse).

Type of adventure: What to expect from this trail or activity, in a nutshell.

Total distance: For loop trails, we include distances for the loop itself and all suggested side trips (or spurs) to overlooks, arches, or rock houses. For linear trails we present either one-way or round-trip mileage, depending on how the trail is normally used.

Rapids below the O&W Railroad Bridge

Difficulty: In subjectively rating trail difficulty, we took four things into account: (1) total distance, (2) elevation change, (3) overall and most difficult grades and slopes, and (4) overall trail condition (i.e. how sandy, muddy, rocky, slippery, or dangerous the trail may be under a wide range of weather conditions). Thus, a short trail might be difficult if it were extremely steep and rocky, whereas a 6-mile hike might be easy if it lies along a flat, solid road. Categories are **Very Easy, Easy, Moderate, Strenuous,** and **Very Strenuous.** These are highly subjective categories, but in general, Very Easy and Easy trails will accommodate small children and sometimes even injured or handicapped folks, whereas Strenuous and Very Strenuous trails should be tackled only by fit individuals (and their mounts) with some outdoors experience. As of this writing, we know of no individual trails that we would consider Very Strenuous and very few that are Strenuous, but we make suggestions connecting a few Moderate or Strenuous trails in a single trip, so you might find yourself in that zone!

Time required: A rough estimate or range of time that it should reasonably take a physically fit person between sixteen and fifty years of age, or a reasonably fit horse, to complete a given adventure. Photographers, biologists, geologists, and history buffs will probably take more time, and athletes in training will (hopefully) take less.

Special concerns: This points out safety problems, including road crossings or sections shared with roads or other types of users, dangerous bluffs, unprotected overlooks, loose or slippery rocks, mine shafts, potential flooding, dry or hot conditions, and questionable water sources.

Water availability: A subjective category meant to help you plan your horseback ride, bike ride, or backpacking trip, this is the availability of water for people, horses, and dogs. Our categories are **None, Poor** (you need to bring water for the whole trip, or plan to do without); **Fair** (water is present but sparse, so bring some extra water in case); **Adequate** (sources are regular but far enough apart that your horse should drink at each crossing; planning may be required for backpacking and even day hikes); **Good** (sources are abundant and regular, but some might be seasonally dry); and **Abundant** (sources are abundant, regular, and permanent).

Scenic value: A subjective rating of the overall aesthetic value of the habitats and geological features along the trail. The categories are **Poor** (no geological features, lots of clear-cuts, southern pine beetle, and/or storm damage and/or streams badly damaged by acid mine drainage); **Fair** (few geological features, forest with isolated damage, and/or stream damage evident); **Good** (healthy forest with minimal damage, some large geological features, and/or historical sites); **Excellent** (healthy forest and streams, good overlooks, extensive geological features, and/or interesting historical sites); and **Spectacular** (mature forest, grand vistas, immense geological features, and/or significant historical sites).

USGS maps: Lists the U.S. Geological Survey (USGS) 7.5-minute series quadrangle maps for the entire trail. (Map 4 on page xvi shows the USGS map coverage for the entire NRRA.)

Best starting point: Our suggested starting point, based on considerable experience in the park. There are always other ways to do things, but these have survived the test of time—and park ranger scrutiny.

Overview: The first paragraph usually summarizes the most interesting biological, geological, historical, and/or archaeological features you will encounter during your adventure. The second paragraph provides an overview of important connections and side trips.

Finding the trailhead(s): Refers to the "Local Directions" section in The Basics chapter for the trailhead of choice, and to the map(s) you should follow.

Trail description: We used a "hybrid" trail description, a punch-list of mileposts with paragraph-style descriptions of the sections between. We included all trail intersections, water crossings, major hazards or points of potential confusion, and the most interesting biological, geological, historical, and archaeological features, accurate to 0.1 mile. Some trails have mileages in reverse (in parentheses), mostly to help you make connections easier. Minor connecting trails are discussed briefly in the chapter(s) for which they apply.

Trail profile: A graphical representation of the vertical aspect of your trip, from start to finish, following our suggested start/end points and direction of travel from left to right. Keep in mind that the horizontal scale is in miles while the vertical scale is in feet; this exaggerates the vertical but makes the plots readable. A "C" on the profile denotes a connection to another trail.

Trails To Avoid

We left certain trails out of this book because they were in the planning stage, closed, unsafe, impassable, difficult to find, located mostly outside the

NRRA, or within areas of abysmal scenic value. You may see them listed in other books and on NPS pamphlets, DBNF trail guides or maps, and commercially available maps, but we strongly suggest avoiding them. Always consult a park ranger if you are in doubt about a trail.

- **Sheltowee Trace** (multiuse)
- **Long Trail** (multiuse)
- **Cub Branch Trail** (multiuse)
- **Trails around Peters Mountain Trailhead** (multiuse)
- **River Trail West** (horseback riding and mountain biking)
- **Fork Ridge Trail** (multiuse)
- **John Muir Trail, southern portion** (hiking only)
- **Gar Blevins Trail** (multiuse)
- **O&W Overlook** (multiuse)
- **Mt. Helen "Prototype" Trail** (multiuse)

How to Get Here

The Big South Fork NRRA straddles the Kentucky-Tennessee border within a triangle formed by Lexington, Kentucky, and Nashville and Knoxville, Tennessee (see Map 1 on page xi). More precisely, it lies generally within a rectangle formed by Monticello and Whitley City, Kentucky, and Jamestown and Oneida, Tennessee. I–40 and I–75 are the major access routes.

From the east (Asheville), take I–40 to I–75 in Knoxville, and read on. From the south (Knoxville, Chattanooga, or Atlanta), take I–75 northbound to the Huntsville/Oneida/TN 63 exit. Go west on TN 63 (Howard Baker Memorial Highway) for 21 miles, passing through Huntsville, turn right (north) on U.S. 27, and drive another seven miles to Oneida. At the first stoplight in Oneida, turn left (west) on TN 297 and follow the signs, or flip to local directions below to reach the main Tennessee areas of the Big South Fork NRRA. To reach the Kentucky end of the NRRA, keep going north through Oneida on U.S. 27 and flip to our local directions. To reach the southern parts of the NRRA, turn left (south) off TN 63 onto U.S. 27 and flip to our local directions. For an alternate way to U.S. 27 from west of Knoxville on I–40, take TN 62 (in Oak Ridge) to its intersection with U.S. 27 in Wartburg, or simply get on U.S. 27 at the Harriman exit.

Warning: When you enter the NRRA from the east using U.S. 27 and TN 297, you must cross the river gorge to reach the Bandy Creek area on 13 percent grades and hairpin turns going both uphill and downhill. Visitors pulling campers and horse trailers or driving large RVs should consider entering the NRRA from the west using U.S. 127. It may add to your travel time but it is safer and might be worth it in brakes and transmission service. From I–40, take the Jamestown/Crossville/U.S. 127 exit about 40 miles west of Knoxville. Turn north on U.S. 127 and drive 36 miles to Jamestown, pass through town, and turn northeast on TN 154 about 2 miles north of town. You will reach the intersection with TN 297 about 12 miles from Jamestown. Turn right to drive TN 297 to the Bandy Creek area, or flip to our local directions to reach other locations.

From the west (Nashville or Memphis), take I–40 east, exit at the Jamestown/Monterey exit on TN 62, and drive east for 16 miles to the intersection with U.S. 127 at Clarkrange. Turn left (north) onto U.S. 127 and drive 18 miles to Jamestown, pass through town, and turn northeast on TN 154 about 2 miles north of town. Turn right to drive TN 297 into the NRRA to the Bandy Creek area, or flip to our local directions to reach other locations. To get to the Kentucky end of the NRRA from this intersection, it is probably faster to take TN 297 to U.S. 27 in Oneida.

From the north (Lexington, Louisville, or Cincinnati), take I–75 southbound, exit at the Williamsburg/KY 92 exit, and take KY 92 west to U.S. 27. Turn south on U.S. 27 and flip to our directions to areas in the Kentucky portion of the NRRA, or continue south to Oneida, drive through town, and take TN 297 west to reach the Tennessee portion of the NRRA.

Local Directions

To ease the usual conflicts between two or more people trying to reach one spot, and to help with through-hiking and river-float shuttles, we provide detailed local directions to the visitor centers, headquarters, main trailheads, campgrounds, overlooks, river access points, and major historical and cultural attractions, all in one place. We used the most direct routes from the nearest cities or intersections of major roads mentioned in the directions above (Map 1). Locations are listed from north to south and referenced to the numbered locations on Map 2. Individual trail maps are also mentioned, when applicable.

1. **Big Creek River Access:** From Oneida, go north on U.S. 27 for about 23 miles (or about 3.5 miles north of KY 700) and turn left (west) on Wyborg Loop Road. The street sign may be down, so look for the turn across from Howard's Mill and the Flat Rock Baptist Church. Check the miles on your odometer at U.S. 27. Cross the railroad tracks, swing north, pass Harley Coffee Road on your left at 0.4 mile, and turn left on Tom Roberts Road at 0.6 mile. Go west on this roughly paved road, stay left at the Y at 0.8 mile, and at 1.1 miles go left on Big Creek Road, a gravel road near a farmhouse at the end of the paved road. At 3.1 miles you will reach the intersection of FR 663 and FR 663A (signs may be down). Go right on FR 663, the narrower

The Big Creek access on Lake Cumberland

of the two roads, plunge into the river gorge on switchbacks, and enter the NRRA at 3.6 miles. The boat ramp, which is very steep, is about 3.8 miles from U.S. 27 (see Map 2).

2. **Yahoo Falls Picnic Area and Trailhead:** From the intersection of U.S. 27 and KY 92 near Stearns (at a stoplight about 16 miles north of Oneida), go north another 3.3 miles and turn left (west) on KY 700 just north of Whitley City. Cross the railroad tracks and KY 1651 at Marshes Siding about 0.5 mile from U.S. 27, wind your way through a residential area, and reach the intersection of the road leading to Yahoo Falls Scenic Area about 4 miles from U.S. 27. Turn right (north), and drive 1.5 miles down to the Yahoo Falls Scenic Area (see Map 5). The hiking trailhead is on the north end of the picnic area near the bathroom.

3. **Alum Ford Campground, Trailhead, and River Access:** From the intersection of U.S. 27 and KY 92 just east of Stearns (at a stoplight about 16 miles north of Oneida), go north another 3.3 miles and turn left (west) on KY 700 just north of Whitley City. Cross the railroad tracks and KY 1651 at Marshes Siding, about 0.5 mile from U.S. 27, wind your way through a residential area, and reach the intersection

of the road leading to Yahoo Falls Picnic Area about 4 miles from U.S. 27. Continue straight (west) for 1.5 miles down into the river gorge. The road eventually turns to gravel. The campground, boat ramp, parking area, and trailhead lie at the end of the road, about 5.5 miles from where you turned off U.S. 27 (see Map 6).

4. **Yamacraw Bridge Trailhead and River Access:** Take KY 92 west through Stearns and continue another 5.3 miles through a residential area, down into the river gorge, and turn right into the Yamacraw Day Use Area just before Yamacraw Bridge, the large concrete bridge that crosses the river (see Map 6). Follow the gravel road left and go under the bridge. The launch on the east side of the river is primitive, but you can also access the river on the west side of Yamacraw Bridge by turning south onto KY 1361. Look immediately to your left for a concrete slab leading down to the river on the south side of the bridge.

5. **Worley River Access:** From the intersection of U.S. 27 and KY 92 near Stearns, take KY 92 west, through Stearns, toward Yamacraw Bridge. About 1.8 miles west of Stearns (or 3.5 miles east of Yamacraw Bridge), turn left (south) at Smith Town on KY 791, a paved road (see Map 2). Proceed southwest on KY 791 for about 1.4 miles and make a sharp right turn at a fork in the road (still paved). About 0.2 mile after that, turn right on a gravel road (no sign) that plunges steeply into the gorge, leading to the old Worley Mine. This road may be a problem for 2WD vehicles during certain times of the year. About 0.5 mile after turning onto the gravel road, you will enter the NRRA and, shortly after that, reach an intersection. A right turn leads directly down to the river, but the road is steep and muddy and passage may require a 4WD vehicle. Straight ahead you will find a small parking area that is passable in 2WD vehicles but elevated well above the river.

From the elevated parking area, you can reach the river via a long flight of concrete stairs. This hand-launch on the Big South Fork River is difficult to reach by car and difficult to launch a boat from. The road down to the river is rough and eroded and sometimes muddy, so a 4WD vehicle is recommended. You may not even be able to get near the river on this road. Also, as of this writing it did not appear to be safe to leave a vehicle here. We recommend launching or loading at Blue Heron or Yamacraw Bridge instead.

6. **Stearns Visitor Center and Historical Area, Big South Fork Scenic Railway, Blue Heron Campground, Overlooks, Trailheads, Mine 18, River Access, and Barthell Mining Camp:** From Oneida drive about 16 miles north on U.S. 27 and look for a stoplight at the intersection of U.S. 27 and KY 92 west, just east of Stearns. Turn west on KY 92 and look for the Stearns Visitor Center on your right (north) after only 0.2 mile. To reach historical Stearns and the Big South Fork Scenic Railway, keep going west past the visitor center for another 0.8 mile, cross the bridge over the Big South Fork Scenic Railroad, and turn right just after the bridge.

To reach the Blue Heron area, continue past Stearns on KY 92 and turn left (south) on KY 1651 near the U.S. Post Office and Big South Fork Motor Lodge. Proceed another 1.1 miles to KY 742 at Revelo, turn right (west), and follow the brown signs all the way to the NRRA. About 3.2 miles from Revelo, you will pass the turn to Bear Creek. Continue straight on KY 742 for another 2.2 miles and look for the entrance to Blue Heron Campground on your right. The campground lies at the end of this entrance road, about 0.6 mile from KY 742. Continue past the campground entrance road to reach the overlooks, mine, and river access. Only 0.5 mile past the campground entrance, you will reach a fork in the road. The left fork, sometimes called Overlook Road, takes you past the upper Blue Heron Trailhead, then on to the trailheads for Devil's Jump and Blue Heron Overlooks, 1.2 and 1.5 miles, respectively, from the fork. The right fork takes you down into the gorge past Barthell Mining Camp, a gravel entrance on your right about 0.6 mile past the fork. About 2.1 miles farther down into the gorge, you will reach the Blue Heron Mine area, the lower trailhead for Blue Heron Loop (see Map 7).

The hand-launch lies at the end of the large parking area south of the Blue Heron Mine and coal tipple. The launch is only about 200 feet from your vehicle at the end of a wide gravel footpath that leads down a slight grade to the river. There is plenty of parking, nice rest rooms, outside showers, picnic tables, barbeque grills, and even a snack bar.

7. **Dick Gap Trailhead:** Follow our directions to Yamacraw Bridge. Just west of the bridge, turn left (south) on KY 1363 and drive along the

river; stay left at a fork and continue along Rock Creek. About 0.7 mile from the fork, turn left (south) on Devils Creek Road and cross Rock Creek on a new bridge. The road is gravel from here on. After passing Koger Arch on your left, stay right at an intersection about 1.6 miles from the bridge; descend steeply on a gravel road, following the NRRA boundary. In another 1.1 miles, turn left at Beech Grove Church, stay left at another fork, and follow this road to its end at Dick Gap Overlook Trailhead (see Map 7).

8. **Bear Creek Equestrian Campground, Trailhead, Overlook, and River Access:** From the intersection of U.S. 27 and KY 92 just east of Stearns (at a stoplight about 16 miles north of Oneida), go west on KY 92 for 1.2 miles, passing the Stearns Visitor Center and Big South Fork Scenic Railway, to the intersection of KY 1651 at the post office and Big South Fork Motor Lodge. Turn left (south) on KY 1651, and go another 1.1 miles to KY 742 at Revelo. Turn right (west) and proceed for another 3.2 miles to the intersection with Ross Road, and turn left (south) toward the Bear Creek area. In another 2 miles you reach a four-way intersection and the roads all turn to gravel. Go straight through the intersection. About 0.4 mile farther on your right, you will reach the access road to Bear Creek Equestrian Campground, which lies at the end of the road about 0.7 mile from this intersection. Split Bow Arch is another mile south of the campground entrance road, Bear Creek Overlook is 0.2 mile south of Split Bow Arch, and Bear Creek Equestrian Trailhead is about 0.2 mile south of the overlook (see Map 8).

For a shorter but rougher route from Oneida, take U.S. 27 north for about 13 miles to Mount Pleasant Road (KY 1470); check your odometer and turn left (west) and cross the railroad tracks. Cross Roaring Paunch Creek in about 2.9 miles. The road turns to gravel in another 0.5 mile and gets fairly rough. After another 2.1 miles, stay left at an intersection and enter the NRRA. The equestrian trailhead is on the left in another 1.3 miles, or a total of 6.8 miles from U.S. 27. The overlook is 0.2 mile north of the trailhead; Split Bow Arch is 0.2 mile north of the trailhead. The campground access road is another mile north of the arch, and the campground lies at the end of the road about 0.7 mile from this intersection.

To launch your boat here, you must hike down a steep gravel road to the gauging station at the confluence of Bear Creek and the Big

South Fork River (see Trail 8). The trail is steep, so you might want to consider launching at Blue Heron instead.

9. **Ledbetter Trailhead:** Follow directions to Yamacraw Bridge. Just west of the bridge, turn left (south) on KY 1363 and drive along the river; stay left at a fork and continue along Rock Creek. About 0.7 mile from the fork, turn left (south) on Devils Creek Road and cross over Rock Creek on a new bridge. The road is gravel from here on. After passing Koger Arch on your left, stay right at an intersection about 1.6 miles from the bridge; descend steeply on a gravel road, following the NRRA boundary. In another 1.1 miles, stay right at Beech Grove Church. In another mile, turn left on the road that leads to Ledbetter Trailhead. The trailhead is a grassy parking area on your left about 1.5 miles down this road (see Map 16).

10. **Slavens Branch Trailhead:** Drive to Oneida on U.S. 27. In the middle of town, just south of the strip malls and fast-food restaurants, look for the stoplight at a four-way intersection with Main Street heading east and Litton Road heading west. Go west on Litton Road for 0.2 mile and go left on Grave Hill Road. About 2 miles from that intersection, Big Ridge Road splits off Grave Hill Road. You can take either road because they rejoin in about 5 miles, but Grave Hill Road is slightly shorter and takes you past Tally Ho Stables. Just past the point where the two roads rejoin, you will reach Foster Crossroads, passing Willie Boyt Road on your right and Rob Watson Road on your left, then reach the Crossroads Church, which lies in the fork between Cliff Terry Road (left) and Little Bill Slaven Road (right). Go right on Little Bill Slaven Road, which changes to gravel here; pass by some farms, and enter the NRRA (and Kentucky) in about 0.8 mile. Pass Huling Branch Road on your left in another 1 mile. About 0.5 mile farther, look right for the Slavens Branch Trailhead, a large gravel parking area skirted by hitching posts (see Map 8). Little Bill Slaven Road ends at a gate another 0.5 mile northeast of the new trailhead, but there is very little room to park or turn a horse trailer around there; park at the trailhead.

11. **Station Camp Equestrian Trailhead, Campground, and River Access:** Take TN 297 to Station Camp Road at the old Terry and Terry Store, about 5.2 miles west of Oneida and about 7.5 miles east of Leatherwood Ford. From the store turn north on Station Camp

Road; enter the NRRA in about 5.6 miles, and reach the right (north) turn for Station Camp Campground and Equestrian Trailhead after about 6 miles. For boaters, hikers, and bikers wanting to get down to the river at Station Camp, drive past the campground on the gravel road and head down into the gorge; pass Chimney Rocks on your left at a sharp turn, and reach Station Camp Crossing about 4 miles from the campground (see Map 9). River access is by hand-launch on a slow section of the Big South Fork River that is suitable for canoes, kayaks, rafts, and even small Jon-boats but is often very muddy. There is plenty of parking and portable toilets. Horse trailers are not allowed to proceed into the gorge on this road. There are a few places to turn around just past Station Camp Campground.

12. **Peters Mountain Trailhead:** From the intersection of TN 297 and TN 154 at Sharp Place (about 10 miles east of Jamestown or 6.5 miles west of the NRRA), turn north on TN 154. After about 1.9 miles, turn right (east) onto Divide Road (gravel). Stay on Divide Road, passing Fork Ridge Road and Twin Arches Road, and continue straight through the intersection at Three Forks on Divide Road (the middle prong of Three Forks). Peters Mountain Trailhead is on the right about 6 miles past Three Forks, or about 11 miles from TN 154 (see Map 16).

13. **Terry Cemetery Trailhead:** Follow our directions to Gobblers Knob Trailhead (#15 below), which is on Terry Cemetery Road (see Map 11). From Gobblers Knob Trailhead, continue east on Terry Cemetery Road for about 3.6 miles, passing Hatfield Ridge Trail and the Pennington-Watson Cemetery, to the end of the road at Terry Cemetery (see Maps 11 and 14). There is a large grassy parking area just past (east of) Terry Cemetery with plenty of room to turn around.

14. **Rock Creek Trailhead:** From the intersection of TN 297 and TN 154 at Sharp Place (about 10 miles east of Jamestown or 6.5 miles west of the NRRA), turn north on TN 154. After about 1.9 miles, turn east onto Divide Road (gravel). Stay on Divide Road for about 4.9 miles, passing Middle Creek Hiking Trailhead, Fork Ridge Road, some lesser gravel roads, and Twin Arches Road, and take the left-most fork at a three-way intersection called Three Forks. From Three Forks, continue generally north for about 1.4 miles to Hattie Blevins Cemetery; park under the trees in the small parking area across from the cemetery (see Map 11).

15. **Gobblers Knob Equestrian Trailhead:** From the intersection of TN 297 and TN 154 at Sharp Place (about 10 miles east of Jamestown or 6.5 miles west of the NRRA), turn north on TN 154. After about 1.9 miles, turn east onto Divide Road (gravel). Stay on Divide Road for about 5 miles, passing Fork Ridge Road and Twin Arches Road; turn right on Terry Cemetery Road, the right-most fork at a three-way intersection (Three Forks). Gobblers Knob Equestrian Trailhead is a large gravel parking area rimmed with hitching posts on the left side of the road just over a mile past Three Forks (see Map 15).

16. **Twin Arches Picnic Area and Trailhead:** From the intersection of TN 297 and TN 154 at Sharp Place (about 10 miles east of Jamestown or 6.5 miles west of the NRRA), turn north on TN 154. After about 1.9 miles, turn east onto Divide Road (gravel). Stay on Divide Road for about 3.8 miles, passing Middle Creek Hiking Trailhead, Fork Ridge Road, and a number of lesser gravel roads; turn right (east) on Twin Arches Road, and proceed 2.1 miles to the large gravel parking area end of the road (see Map 12).

17. **Middle Creek Hiking and Equestrian Trailheads:** From the intersection of TN 297 and TN 154 at Sharp Place (about 10 miles east of Jamestown or 6.5 miles west of the NRRA), turn north on TN 154. After about 1.9 miles, turn right (east) onto Divide Road (gravel). About 0.7 mile from that intersection, look to your right for Middle Creek Hiking Trailhead. To reach Middle Creek Equestrian Trailhead, continue about 0.3 mile past Middle Creek Hiking Trailhead and turn right (east) on Fork Ridge Road. Middle Creek Equestrian Trailhead is a large gravel parking area on your left about 0.6 mile down Fork Ridge Road (see Map 12).

18. **Sawmill Trailhead:** Continue about 0.5 mile past the Middle Creek Equestrian Trailhead (#17 above) to the grassy area on the left (north) side of Fork Ridge Road (see Map 12).

19. **Charit Creek Equestrian and Hiking Trailheads:** Follow the directions to Middle Creek Equestrian Trailhead (#17 above), but proceed another 0.5 mile east on Fork Ridge Road to Sawmill Trailhead; continue past Sawmill Trailhead for another 3.4 miles to the Charit Creek Equestrian Trailhead, a large gravel parking area on your left under some massive power lines. Charit Creek Hiking Trailhead lies another 0.4 mile past the Charit Creek Equestrian Trailhead on the north end

of a large gravel parking area on the left at the very end of Fork Ridge Road (see Map 12).

20. **Bandy Creek Visitor Center, Campground, Stables, and Trailheads:** From Oneida drive west on TN 297; pass through the river gorge, and turn right on Bandy Creek Road. From Jamestown drive northeast on TN 154; turn east on TN 297, then turn left on Bandy Creek Road about 4 miles after entering the NRRA (just before plunging into the river gorge). About 1.7 miles from TN 297, you will find Bandy Creek Visitor Center and Bandy Creek Stables on the left (south) side of the road and Bandy Creek Campground on the right (north) side. To reach the Bandy Creek Hiking and Equestrian Trailheads, continue west on Bandy Creek Road for 0.2 mile and look for a paved access road leading to a rest room building and parking area on the left (south) side of Bandy Creek Road, just before Bandy Creek Road turns to gravel. The hiking trailhead is west of the rest rooms; the equestrian trailhead is located another 0.1 mile farther south at the end of the access road (see Maps 13, 17, 18, and 19).

21. **West Entrance Trailhead:** From Oneida take TN 297 west to Leatherwood Ford; continue another 5 miles west, and look on the right for the gravel parking area just before you reach the western terminus of Bandy Creek Road (gravel). From Jamestown take TN 154 east to TN 297; turn right (east), and go another 6.5 miles, looking left for the trailhead. From the Bandy Creek area, go west for 3.2 miles on Bandy Creek Road (gravel) until it intersects with TN 297; look for the trailhead on your left, just east of the intersection (see Map 17).

22. **Cumberland Valley Trailhead:** From the Bandy Creek area, head west on TN 297. About 1 mile from the West Entrance Trailhead, turn left (south) on a gravel road near a store and proceed about 0.3 mile to the loop parking area. From Jamestown go east on TN 154, then turn east on TN 297; go 5.5 miles to the intersection mentioned above (see Map 19).

23. **Leatherwood Ford Trailhead, Boardwalk, Picnic Area, and River Access:** Take TN 297 down into the river gorge and turn into the paved parking area near the Leatherwood Ford Bridge abutment on the east side of the Big South Fork River (see Map 20). TN 297 crosses the river about 12 miles west of Oneida and about 10 miles east of the TN 154/TN 297 intersection.

This is the most popular raft, canoe, and kayak launch on the Big South Fork River and generally where you meet Sheltowee Trace Outfitters before their guided river trips. The hand-launch lies at the bottom of a short flight of stairs on the east side of the river below the gazebo. There is plenty of parking, a large covered gazebo, roomy rest rooms with big benches, outdoor showers, outdoor changing stalls, a river gauge, picnic tables, and barbeque grills.

24. **Big South Fork NRRA Headquarters, Resource Management, Maintenance, and Law Enforcement Offices:** From Oneida go west on TN 297 into the NRRA, and look for the headquarters complex about 0.3 mile from the entrance. From Jamestown take TN 154 to TN 297 east; proceed through the river gorge, and look for the headquarters complex just after coming out of the gorge at the top of the plateau (see Map 20).

25. **East Rim Overlook Trailhead:** Follow the directions to the Big South Fork Headquarters area (#24 above); turn west on the paved road to East Rim Overlook (there should be a big sign), and drive to the loop parking area at the end of the road (see Map 20).

26. **Sunset Trailhead:** Take TN 297 to the park headquarters area. Sunset Trailhead is on the road to East Rim Overlook (#24 above), about 0.2 mile after you turn off of TN 297 (see Map 20).

27. **Toomy Trailhead:** The gravel road running southwest from Oneida along Pine Creek is level but potholed, so from Oneida you can also take TN 297 west for about 4.5 miles to Toomy Road. From the west, Toomy Road is about 0.6 mile east of the intersection of TN 297 and Station Camp Road at the Terry and Terry Store. Turn south on Toomy Road and go 2.2 miles to Toomy, which consists of some oil tanks at a T intersection with the O&W Railroad Grade on the north bank of Pine Creek (see Map 21). Toomy Road is steep, eroded, and often washboarded where it drops into Pine Creek Gorge, but a 2WD vehicle will get you there under most circumstances.

28. **Pine Creek River Access:** Follow directions to the Toomy Trailhead (#27). From the Toomy Trailhead, drive west along Pine Creek, crossing it twice on narrow wood bridges, and enter the NRRA on the O&W Railroad Grade (see Map 21). About 2.9 miles from Toomy, on a right-handed curve, you will pass through a narrow spot where a ridge was blasted to accommodate the O&W Railroad Grade, and

emerge in the Big South Fork River Gorge. Immediately after the narrow spot, you will notice a small parking spot between some rocks. Just after that, a gate and a gravel trail lead down to the river on the left. Parking is limited to a few vehicles. From here you must hike down to the river, but the trail is short, well groomed, and not too steep. It provides good access to the river for rafts, canoes, and kayaks.

29. **O&W Railroad Grade, Bridge, Trailhead, and River Access:** Follow directions to Toomy Trailhead, then Pine Creek River Access (#27 and #28 above). From the Pine Creek River Access, continue on the O&W Railroad Grade for another 1.8 miles to the O&W Railroad Bridge (see Map 21). There is plenty of parking on the east side of the bridge. In 2001 you could safely cross this bridge with your vehicle and continue for another 1.2 miles on the ever-narrowing, increasingly potholed railroad grade, past a number of campsites, to a point where the grade fords North White Oak Creek. However, the NPS was considering blocking vehicle access at the bridge, so consult a park ranger before you make plans. If you can proceed past the bridge, be careful if you do not have a 4WD vehicle; there is little room to turn around, and the path gets even worse near the creek ford. Park in one of the roadside campsites and walk to the ford from there, or you will probably have to back out. If you are able to ford the creek and continue on the O&W Railroad Grade along North White Oak Creek, flip to Trail 44.

Access to the Big South Fork River for light rafts, canoes, and kayaks is directly below the O&W Railroad Bridge. You must hike down a long, steep flight of stairs on the east side of the bridge and launch your boat wherever you can find a good spot. There is plenty of parking on the east side of the bridge near the stairs.

30. **Darrow Ridge Trailhead:** From the intersection of TN 154 and TN 297, go south on TN 154 for about 3 miles; turn left (east) on Darrow Ridge Road (see Map 21). Proceed 1 mile to the trailhead on the left (north) side of the road, just after it turns to gravel.

31. **Zenith Picnic Area, Trailhead, and River Access:** From Jamestown, Oneida, or the south on U.S. 27, get on TN 52 and proceed to Mt. Helen Road, which is about 6.3 miles west of Rugby and about 11 miles east of Jamestown. Turn on Mt. Helen Road; proceed northeast for about 4.9 miles, then turn left on Old Mt. Helen Road

at the A. J. Garrett Grocery. About 0.2 mile after that intersection, turn left (north) on Zenith Road (gravel) and plunge down into the gorge for about 1.5 miles to the old Zenith Mine area at North White Oak Creek. As of August 2001, parking was limited and there were no picnic tables, rest rooms, or other facilities. Zenith Stables and Campground lies about a mile down Cole Place, a gravel road on the south side of the intersection at A. J. Garrett Grocery. The hand-launch provides easy access to North White Oak Creek for small rafts, canoes, and kayaks.

32. **Mt. Helen Trailhead:** From Jamestown, Oneida, or the south on U.S. 27, get on TN 52 and proceed to Mt. Helen Road, which is about 6.3 miles west of Rugby and about 11 miles east of Jamestown. Turn on Mt. Helen Road; proceed northeast for about 4.9 miles, then turn left on Old Mt. Helen Road at the A. J. Garrett Grocery. Pass Zenith Road about 0.3 mile from the intersection; continue on Old Mt. Helen Road for another 1.6 miles, and turn left (north) on the Mt. Helen Trailhead access road. The trailhead is about 0.8 mile off Old Mt. Helen Road, but was not developed as of Spring 2002. Zenith Stables and Campground lies about a mile down Cole Place, a gravel road on the south side of the Old Mt. Helen Road intersection at A. J. Garrett Grocery.

33. **Honey Creek Trailhead and Overlook:** From any location except Zenith, first follow directions to Burnt Mill Bridge (#36). From Burnt Mill Bridge continue west over the bridge and climb out of the gorge; after about 3.3 miles you will reach an intersection with the gravel road leading west to Mt. Helen Road. Stay right (north) and look for Honey Creek Trailhead immediately north of this intersection (see Map 22). To reach the Honey Creek Overlook directly, continue past the trailhead for about 0.8 mile to the large, newly paved parking area at the end of the road.

From Zenith turn left (east) on Mt. Helen Road and go 3.3 miles to an intersection with a gravel road on a sharp right-hand curve; stay left on the gravel road, proceed another 1.9 miles to an intersection, and turn left (north). The trailhead is immediately north of this intersection, and the overlook is another 0.8 mile past the trailhead.

34. **Confluence Trailhead and River Access:** From U.S. 27 turn west onto Niggs Creek Road, which is about 2.4 miles south of Oneida or

4.2 miles north of the intersection of U.S. 27 and TN 63 at Huntsville. Cross over the railroad tracks and immediately turn left (south) on Helenwood Road; proceed southwest for 1 mile and turn right (west) on Airport Road. Continue west for another 1.1 miles, turning left off the pavement onto the gravel road that heads south of the airport. Proceed another 2.8 miles, with the Scott County Airport on your right, to a fork in the road. Turn left and proceed about another mile, in which you will enter the Big South Fork NRRA; pass the Dewey-Phillips Cemetery on your right, then reach a gravel parking area in a loop drive at the end of the road (see Map 21). It should take less than fifteen minutes to get to this trailhead from U.S. 27. The launch lies at the end of a 0.6-mile downhill trek, but the trail is wide and often used for launching even large river rafts.

35. **New River Bridge River Access:** This bridge is located on U.S. 27, about 2.5 miles south of the intersection of U.S. 27 and TN 63 at Huntsville, or about 7 miles north of the intersection of U.S. 27 and TN 52 at Elgin (see Map 2). The hand-launch on the northeast side of this bridge provides relatively easy access for rafts, canoes, and kayaks and is the only access point for the New River.

36. **Burnt Mill Bridge Picnic Area, Trailhead, and River Access:** From the north (Oneida or TN 63), take U.S. 27 south; turn right on a paved road about 0.5 mile after crossing the New River Bridge, and proceed west for about 1.5 miles to an intersection at Mountain View. Turn right (north) at the intersection and go 1 block north; turn left (west) at the Mountain View Church, and continue west for 2 miles to another intersection at Crossroads Church. Turn right (north) on the narrow, paved road. Soon after the intersection, the pavement ends; stay left at a fork, then drop into Clear Fork Gorge on switchbacks and reach Burnt Mill Bridge, about 0.8 mile from the Crossroads Church intersection (see Map 22). Hold your breath as you cross this old, creaky bridge, which has a weight limit of four tons (we think two is pushing it). This historical bridge is slated for replacement, but traffic will not be stopped. Cross the bridge (traveling west), and look for the gravel parking lot and boat launch on the left (south) side of the road immediately after the bridge. As of this writing, there were picnic tables, garbage cans, and portable toilets near the launch.

From the south take U.S. 27 to Elgin and turn left (west). About 0.4 mile west of that intersection, turn right (north) on West Robbins

Road (paved). From this intersection, proceed north for 3.4 miles to the four-way intersection at Crossroads Church; go straight through the intersection, and follow the above directions to the bridge. If you are coming from the west (Jamestown or elsewhere), take TN 52 east and make the left (north) turn on West Robbins Road about 6.5 miles east of Rugby. The hand-launch provides direct access for rafts, canoes, and kayaks.

37. **Joe's Branch:** Follow the directions to Zenith (#31 above), but before the turn to Zenith, turn right on Cole Place (gravel) and proceed about 1.5 miles to a gravel road intersection at Mt. Helen Church. Turn right (south) and proceed another 2 miles to the end of the road at Joe's Branch (see Map 23), a grassy area with a few picnic tables and a fire pit.

38. **Rugby Visitor Center, Trailhead, and River Access:** Take TN 52 to the town of Rugby, which is about 7 miles west of U.S. 27 at Elgin and 17.5 miles east of Jamestown. The visitor center is in the middle of town on the south side of the road. The town is described in detail in the Historic Rugby chapter. In the next couple of years, TN 52 will probably be rerouted to divert the heavy traffic (i.e., coal and lumber trucks) around Rugby. To reach the Rugby Trailhead from the Rugby Visitor Center, drive 0.3 mile west on TN 52 and look for a road on your right (north) called Laurel Dale Cemetery Road. Take this road to where it dead-ends at a loop drive at Laurel Dale Cemetery, and look for the small parking area on the northwest corner of the loop (see Map 23). To access the Clear Fork, hike 0.4 mile downhill (about 200 vertical feet) on the Meeting of the Waters Trail to the Gentleman's Swimming Hole.

39. **White Oak Bridge River Access:** This bridge is on TN 52 about 6 miles west of U.S. 27 at Elgin and about 1 mile east of Rugby. For river access turn north off TN 52 just west of the bridge, and park on the short road leading to the old White Oak Bridge. The primitive launch lies on the northwest corner of the new TN 52 bridge (see Map 23). From there you must carry your boat down below the new bridge on a faint trail on the north side of its western causeway.

40. **Brewster Bridge Overlook, Picnic Area, and River Access:** Take TN 52 to the new Brewster Bridge, about 2.2 miles west of Rugby or about 15 miles east of Jamestown. Stop briefly at the scenic overlook (the new bridge itself) to catch a glimpse of Clear Fork, which lies

more than 200 feet below. To reach the picnic area and river access, turn about 0.3 mile west of the new bridge at a sign indicating a picnic area (see Map 2). From there proceed 0.8 mile down into the gorge to the small picnic area, 0.2 mile farther to the old bridge, and another 0.2 mile to the roomy river access parking area under the surrealistically high Brewster Bridge. The hand-launch lies a short distance past the Brewster Bridge Picnic Area and Old Brewster Bridge, on the south side of a large asphalt parking area directly underneath the new bridge. It provides easy access to Clear Fork for rafts, canoes, and kayaks.

41. **Peters Ford Bridge, Picnic Area, and River Access:** Take TN 52 to Peters Ford Road, a well-signed intersection about 12 miles west of Rugby or about 8.5 miles east of Jamestown. Turn south and descend steadily to Peters Ford Bridge, which is about 4.6 miles from TN 52. Cross the bridge and look for the picnic area and launch ramp immediately east of Clear Fork on the right, or south side, of the road (see Map 2). Access to the river is by a gravel hand-launch that lies near the east end of Peters Bridge on the south side of the road, below the Peters Bridge Picnic Area. The approach and launch ramp are eroded but provide easy access to Clear Fork for rafts, canoes, and kayaks.

Weather

Moist, hot summers and mild winters are typical for the Big South Fork NRRA. The Cumberland Plateau usually has milder temperatures and higher annual precipitation than the adjoining parts of Kentucky and Tennessee. Temperatures in the NRRA are usually about 5°F (3°C) lower than those in Knoxville, Tennessee, and nights are usually cool, even during summer. The average temperature on the Cumberland Plateau is 55°F (13°C), with yearly extremes ranging from -6°F (-21°C) to above 99°F (37°C). The highest temperatures occur during July and August; the lowest occur in January and February. During winter, temperatures may not rise above freezing for several days. Temperatures can vary as much as 5°F from the bottom of the gorge to the plateau. Moist air from the Gulf Coast is brought into the area by the south/southwest prevailing winds. The average annual precipitation is 50 to 55 inches (127 to 140 cm). Flooding is most common from December through March, but flash flooding can be caused by summer thunderstorms. Snowfall averages 15 to 17 inches (38 to 43 cm) a year, but it rarely stays on the ground longer than a few days. Thousands and thousands of trees in the Big South Fork NRRA were uprooted and broken as a result of a heavy snowstorm that dropped 18 to 24 inches (46 to 61 cm) of wet snow in February 1998; you can still see the damage caused by this unusual storm in many parts of the NRRA. A lack of rain during the fall of 2000 caused more than 6,500 acres to be burned by wildfires.

Safety and Etiquette on Land and Water
All Users

Telephones are located at both visitor centers, Bandy Creek and Blue Heron Campgrounds, Bandy Creek Stables, Station Camp and Bear Creek Horse Camps, Leatherwood Ford, and the Blue Heron Mining Community. A list of emergency phone numbers and addresses is included in the appendix. Cell phones are useless within the gorges and valleys, and do not always work on the plateau. Never rely on a cell phone to get you out of a bind or as a replacement for safety equipment.

Plan ahead and be prepared for the worst. Gain as much knowledge as you can about the trail or the water before you start out. Always carry at least a knife, flashlight (with extra batteries), first aid kit, topo map, compass, poncho or raincoat, and insect repellent. We recommend carrying at least the National Geographic Trails Illustrated topo map for the Big South Fork NRRA with you; it can be purchased from the visitor centers as well as from many other area stores. Know the weather forecast, and be prepared for rapid changes, especially in spring and fall. Bring plenty of food (including treats for your horses or dog) and water. Wear proper clothing and footwear (good hiking boots when climbing in and out of the gorges, etc.). Know how to use your equipment, and know its limitations! Use only the trails that are open to your type of use. Do not hike, ride, or boat alone. If you are alone, tell someone exactly where you are going and when you expect to return in case you have a problem or get lost. In fact, no matter how many in your group, always file your adventure plan with someone. Stick to your plan once you are out on the trail or on the water.

Dogs must be on a leash at all times, even in the backcountry. Do not allow your dog to harass wildlife or be a nuisance to others, who may not find your pet so adorable.

Bikers, horseback riders, and all-terrain vehicle (ATV) and trail bike users: *Always* wear an approved safety helmet. It can prevent serious injuries—it may even save your life.

Travel within your fitness level and that of your horse or dog as well. Before you start out on the trail or on the water (actually, you should do this before you even leave home), check and service all of your equipment. Double-check your equipment (bike brakes, saddle girth, etc.) before each steep descent.

Be aware that you may encounter other users. Always look ahead. Slow down around corners and any blind spots on trails. When approaching another user from the rear, yell out "hello" as soon as you are close enough to make them aware of your presence (and to alert your horse). If you want to pass, ask if it is OK, and tell them which side you want to pass on.

Horseback riders have the right-of-way over *all* other users because they are aboard a large animal with an instinct to flee, and do not have ultimate control over their horse. Hikers should yield to horseback riders. Bikers should yield to both horseback riders and hikers. Vehicles (including off-road) should yield to all other users. Downhill users should yield to uphill users. Always be courteous and thank others for yielding the trail.

When meeting horses on the trail, *stop*, step, or pullover to the side of the trail, speak in a normal but soft voice, and do not make sudden movements. Shut down your engine if in or on a vehicle. Assume that you will encounter riders of different skill levels and horses with different levels of training. Horses that see vehicles, bikes, or hikers with large backpacks sometimes think they are dangerous and may shy or try to run away. If you are not sure what to do, ask the rider. Do not attempt to pet horses without asking first.

In addition to packing out everything you brought with you (including cigarette butts and gum wrappers!), please try to pack out any litter that you find, within reason; tell a park ranger about any large items you find. Back-country campers should go over their campsite one last time to be sure it is free of garbage and the fire is completely out. Do not leave unburned garbage in your fire pit for someone else to deal with.

Stay on designated trails and *never* shortcut switchbacks. This causes erosion, which damages the main trail as well as adjacent trail areas. To preserve the tread, travel on the uphill side of the trail. If possible, avoid wet or muddy trails. If you cannot avoid a wet or muddy area, walk or ride *through* the area, instead of going around it. Most of the time, the trail surface is hard, which is why it holds water. Bypassing muddy areas damages areas adjacent to the trail, makes the muddy area larger, and puts you in harm's way (poison ivy, snakes, etc.).

In the summer of 2000, the NPS marked trail corridors at the Big South Fork River crossings at Station Camp and Big Island fords to protect the unique, endangered fish and mussel species. These corridors were marked to minimize the area of river bottom disturbed by the crushing and churning action of horses' hooves, as well as other disturbances. *Please* help protect our endangered species by staying within the marked route in a single file line when crossing the river. Signs have been placed at both crossings explaining the trail corridors. These crossings may be closed to horses in the future, so check with a park ranger before making plans.

Hunting is permitted in the Big South Fork NRRA during regular Tennessee and Kentucky seasons. Check with the visitor centers, and be familiar with the different hunting season schedules. Wear blaze orange and make lots of noise (talking, singing, bells) if on the trail during hunting season. Since most hunters are active during dawn and dusk and usually stake out less traveled areas, being on well-used trails during the middle of the day is recommended. Hunters are most numerous during the first few days and weekends of the various hunting seasons, so schedule your activities accordingly. We recommend staying off the trails during big-game (deer) muzzleloader and gun hunting seasons (late fall/early winter).

If you plan on fishing and hunting in the Big South Fork NRRA, make sure you are familiar with state regulations, as well as NRRA rules. Anglers and hunters should have a valid license if required (see the Picnicking, Swimming, Fishing, and Hunting Adventures chapter). Collecting mussels is prohibited. Report any fishing or hunting violations (see appendix).

A bad southern pine beetle outbreak in 1999 and 2000 has left thousands of standing dead pine trees all over the NRRA, especially on the plateau. Branches and whole trees regularly fall to the ground. Be aware of your surroundings by sight and sound as the warning signs everywhere indicate.

Never enter old mine tunnels; use extreme caution at overlooks, cliff tops, and bluffs; and do not climb on waterfalls. Some of these activities are against park regulations, and *all* are dangerous. Do not pick or collect plants or rocks, and do not disturb historic or archeological sites.

Never cross high water. A good rule to follow: Don't cross if you can't see the bottom. Contact a park ranger at one of the visitor centers to find out about water levels.

Be aware of lightning associated with thunderstorms, usually in the spring and summer. Lightning travels far ahead of a storm so if you see or hear a thunderstorm approaching, seek shelter immediately and wait for the storm to pass. Don't get caught on or in the water; on top of a mountain or on an exposed ridge; under large, solitary trees; or in the open. Seek shelter in a low-lying area such as a dense stand of small trees. Stay away from anything metal that attracts lightning. Get off your horse or bike, place both feet on the ground, and assume a crouched position. Everyone in a group should stay about 50 feet apart.

Always keep your group together, letting the slowest person set the pace. Don't panic if you get lost. Check your topo map, and take a reading with your compass. If you can, backtrack to the last point where you knew that you were still on the trail. If you can't find familiar ground, stop and stay where you are. Since someone is expecting your return, they will send help when you don't.

Be aware of hazards caused by ice and snow and associated weather. Hypothermia, which can be fatal, is always a threat while on the water and during cold and wet weather. Water, especially flowing water, does not have to be very cold to suck the heat out of your body. Know the symptoms of hypothermia, how to prevent it, and, if necessary, how to treat it.

Bring/drink plenty of water during the warmer months to prevent heat stress and dehydration. Rather than carry a bunch of water in big bottles, bring a filter and a few smaller bottles so that you can guzzle water all day! Check out our trail descriptions to be sure there will be enough water along the trail, and pack accordingly. Avoid strenuous activity during the hottest part of the day. Know the signs of heat stress and dehydration and how to treat for them. Never drink water from any spring, creek, stream, river, lake, or pond unless you treat it first. It may contain harmful parasites, such as giardia, which causes severe intestinal infections. Boil the water for two minutes, use water purification tablets, or use a water filter. If you do treat and drink water, flowing water is recommended over stagnant water. Also, no matter how thirsty you are, do not drink even filtered water from creeks with lots of white, yellow, or red slime or other coating on rocks. This indicates the creek still suffers from the effects of acid mine drainage.

Do not consume alcoholic beverages while on the trail or on the water. Drinking alcohol while on horseback is illegal, and alcohol is prohibited in the Kentucky portion of the Big South Fork NRRA.

If you encounter wildlife, stop and wait for the animal to get out of your way. Observe wildlife from a distance. *Never* disturb, feed, or chase wildlife. When camping, store all food so that it is inaccessible to wildlife.

Black bears have been reintroduced into the Big South Fork NRRA. If you do encounter a bear, which is unlikely, don't overreact. Consider yourself lucky and enjoy the experience! If you encounter a bear, back off and wait for the bear to move on; a bear will usually try to avoid you. *Never* place yourself between a mother and her cubs; female bears are fiercely protective. If you come upon a cub, the mother is probably close by; back off and wait for them to move on. *Never* turn and run, which could cause the bear to chase you. *Never* approach, chase, harass, feed, or leave food for a bear. If a bear approaches, try to scare it off by making lots of noise.

Bears that learn that people are a source of food lose their natural fear of humans, become dangerous, and often have to be killed. Please don't be part of the problem. *Never* leave unattended food (including bird, pet, and horse feed) or garbage outside. When backcountry camping, place all of your food and anything with strong odors (toothpaste, soap, etc.) in a bag and hang high enough on a rope (at least 10 feet high) between two trees, on a large branch, or on a leaning tree (at least 4 feet from) so bears cannot reach it. *Never* cook or store food in or near your tent in the backcountry.

Two poisonous snakes, the northern copperhead and the timber rattlesnake, live in the Big South Fork NRRA. Both are nocturnal hunters, so always use a flashlight when walking around in the woods at night. Snakes are just as interested in avoiding you as you are of avoiding them, and "attack" large animals and humans merely to defend themselves. Be aware of your surroundings, and always watch where you put your hands and feet. Do not step over a log lying on the ground; rather, step onto the log first, then step down. Do not approach, harass, or disturb a snake, and *never* attempt to kill any snake—ironically, this is the leading cause of snake bite! If you do encounter a poisonous snake, back off and wait for it to move on, or go around it. If you find a snake in a campground, do not broadcast the fact to everyone, because it increases their risk. Simply tell a park ranger or campground host, who will remove it from the area. In addition to being cool animals, snakes are an integral part of the Big South Fork ecosystem, and *all* wildlife, including snakes, is protected within the NRRA.

In the unlikely event that someone is bitten by a snake, stay calm and seek medical treatment as soon as possible. Most actual snake bites are "dry" (no venom injected), and most successful injections are intramuscular, so the venom usually spreads slowly. Treat the victim for shock by keeping them calm, warm, and comfortable. Treatment methods are controversial, but most agree on a few important issues: Immobilize the bite area, and wash it with clean water. Remove any jewelry or clothing from the affected area, because swelling will occur. Regarding "snakebite kits," *never* "cut and suck," because it will only traumatize the wound and cause the venom to spread faster! *Never* use a tourniquet or anything else that halts blood flow. Many have suggested wrapping the area around and just above the bite with an Ace bandage to slow lymph flow, so our snake bite kit is nothing more than a big Ace bandage. Finally, do not try to capture or kill the snake (it may bite again), but do try to remember what the snake looked like so that you can describe it to park/medical personnel.

Yellow jackets nest on the ground in holes and can be a problem on the trail between June and September. Those at the back of the group are most at risk of being stung. If you get into a nest, yell "bees!" to the rest of your group, and run or ride as fast as you can until the yellow jackets are no longer chasing you. Hikers, bikers, or riders that have not yet gone by the nest may want to choose an alternate route if possible or wait awhile until the yellow jackets settle back down. Allergic reactions can be life threatening, so those sensitive or allergic to bee stings should *always* carry a bee sting kit.

Mosquitoes; black, deer, and horse flies; gnats; and red bugs (chiggers) can be a problem during the warm months. To avoid chiggers (which you won't notice until later), never sit directly on the ground or a log. In addition, spray your legs with repellant or tuck your pants inside your socks when walking through the woods and open fields. Be very conscious of checking for ticks and keeping them off of you since they transmit Rocky Mountain spotted fever and Lyme disease. Wear light-colored clothing and inspect yourself often. Wear long pants and tuck your pant legs inside your socks, or spray your shoes, socks, and pants with a tick repellent. Always check yourself at the end of the day. Look closely, because some ticks are no bigger than the head of a pin! If a tick has become attached to you, grasp the tick with tweezers as close to the skin as possible and pull slowly until it releases. Avoid mashing the tick or breaking it off. See a doctor immediately if a rash or fever develops.

Poison ivy is very abundant in the NRRA, and can cause a nasty skin rash. If you don't know what it looks like, ask a park ranger. Avoid brushing against it and watch where you put your hands since it grows up trees (it is one of the fuzzy vines you see plastered to many tree trunks—the other is Virginia creeper). Simply stay on the trail to avoid contact!

Horseback Riders

Make sure you or one rider in your group has a first aid kit for horses. You should carry an Easyboot or two in case your horse loses a shoe. It is also a good idea to carry a few items, such as duct tape, wire, nylon cord, leather strings or rawhide, leatherman tool or knife, pliers, and hoof pick, to make repairs on the trail.

As part of your horse's training program, get them used to other horses, backpacks, bikes, and vehicles (including off-road vehicles such as ATVs) and anything else you think you may encounter on a multi-user trail.

Make sure all riders are mounted and ready before you ride off. If you are leading, find out the experience level of the riders before you start. Keep your group small; split up the group into slow and fast riders. Make sure you ask if it is OK before you pick up the pace so that you do not catch someone off guard. Call out to the riders behind you if you encounter an obstacle or another trail user.

Pass *all* other users at a walk, including other horseback riders. Not only is passing at a fast pace rude, but you could place the user you are passing or yourself in danger. If someone wants to pass you, stop and let them. Horses are big animals and can be intimidating from the ground. If it appears that another user is not going to yield to you or appears unfamiliar with horses, politely ask the person to stop—and be sure to thank them as you pass. Always give the horses around you enough room, especially if they are unfamiliar. Alert others if your horse kicks, or ride in the rear of the group. Stop before any crossing (road, bridge, river) to make sure all the horses in your group cross together. Separating a horse from the group can place the rider in extreme danger. If it is extremely steep (up or down) or rocky, do your horse a favor—get off and walk. Do not hesitate to get off and lead your horse through any dangerous areas, such as narrow areas or large obstacles.

When tying your horse, never tie using the reins, and always use a quick-release knot. Where available, tie your horse to hitching posts; otherwise, tie using cross-ties or picket lines for safety and to prevent tree damage. Never tie horses within 100 feet of waterbodies or campsites. Scatter manure and smooth out places where horses have been tied.

Know the availability of water on the trail for your horse (check our trail descriptions), especially during warm weather. Know the signs of heat stress and dehydration, what to do to prevent them, and how to treat them. Avoid riding hard during the heat of the day, and encourage your horse to drink as often and as much as it wants. Do not water horses in areas that cannot be easily accessed without damaging the environment (springs, small creeks). When stopping to water horses, make sure *all* have finished drinking before moving on (a thirsty horse usually won't drink if it thinks it's getting left behind). Even if your horse does not want a drink, stop at all available water to make sure that all the horses in your group that want a drink have an opportunity to drink.

Mountain Bikers

On bike-only trails, travel in the suggested direction, which is clockwise on Collier Ridge Loop and Duncan Hollow Loop. This will help minimize nasty head-on collisions.

Some of the downhill trail sections are incredibly steep, so watch your speed. Loose gravel, large boulders, deep mud, or all of these hazards are just about guaranteed on sections going into and out of the river gorge. Creek crossings can be slippery, so dismount.

Boaters

You are required by law to wear a personal flotation device on all waterways in the NRRA, regardless of the type of watercraft. *Always* wear an approved life jacket and helmet (in white water). Do not attempt to float sections of the river that are beyond your level of experience. Make sure your boat is properly equipped, including appropriate safety equipment. Scout all major rapids. Make sure throw-ropes have been set up and that everything is tied down and secure before running rapids. Portage high rapids, waterfalls, logjams, and other flow-through hazards.

Since your first-aid kit will likely be the only medical support you'll have for many hours, make sure it is waterproof and complete. Bring a safety (or thermal) blanket, or at least a small tarp, on your trip because hypothermia can be a terribly sneaky killer when water is involved. Better yet, a neoprene wet suit of any thickness is highly effective for holding heat and provides flotation as well. Bring some extra food with you even on the shortest of trips—you never know what might happen. Because many of the waterways in the NRRA are very remote, you will not be able to just walk out periodically and get supplies. Make a checklist and check it twice. Store all gear in secure waterproof containers.

If your boat flips, hang on, and get on the upstream side. Lie on your back with your feet pointed downstream and arms out to your side. Let go of your boat only if you have to, but stay on the upstream side. Never try to stand in fast water. Wait until you are in a calm section to retrieve your boat.

On- and Off-Road Drivers

Wear your seat belt! Do not use excessive speed. Unless indicated otherwise, the speed limit is 35 miles per hour on paved roads and 25 miles per hour on gravel roads. Approach intersections with caution. Off-road vehicles and even 2-wheel drive vehicles venturing onto unpaved roads should have repair tools, a fire extinguisher, jumper cables, tow strap, winch, shovel or similar tool, jack and tire iron, and spare tire.

To our knowledge, all the portions of old logging roads and other access roads that lie on the very steep slopes of the gorge between the plateau and the river or its tributaries were closed to off-road vehicles as of this writing. *Never* go around a blocked gate, enter a restricted area, or drive on a trail not approved for off-road vehicle use, just because you see tracks of others. Those tracks may be from park rangers, trail crews, surveyors, volunteers, or other folks that have permission to travel in these areas. Many of the trails once opened for off-road vehicle use could be closed in the near future, so always check with a park ranger for updates before you plan an off-road trip.

History of the Charit Creek Lodge and Area Towns

Charit Creek Lodge

Charit Creek Lodge is the only lodge within the boundaries of the Big South Fork NRRA. The lodge is located in a picturesque valley bordered on the north by Hatfield Ridge and on the south by Fork Ridge at the confluence of Station Camp and Charit Creeks. The only way to get there is to hike, bike, or ride your horse (refer to local directions to the Charit Creek Lodge trailheads and the Charit Creek Lodge Trails [Trail #22]). In addition to the fun you'll have getting there, the lodge makes a great base camp for additional hiking, mountain biking, horseback riding, and hunting. There is nothing like sitting in a rocking chair on the porch of one of the cabins after a day outdoors and a hearty meal, watching fireflies, gazing at a sky full of stars, and listening to the night sounds and the water. It is the perfect place to clear your mind!

Charit Creek was named in memory of a young girl named Charity who lived here during the 1920s; she drowned in the creek during a flash flood. The valley of Station Camp Creek has provided shelter to travelers since the Native American hunting camps. By 1850, 126 people—longhunters and their descendants—had settled in the valley on subsistence farms along Station Camp Creek, which flows in front of the lodge. Station Camp still had a post office in 1930, but today a few small cemeteries and the old cabin and outbuildings at Charit Creek Lodge are all that remain of the community.

The main lodge structure is listed on the National Register of Historic Places. The oldest part of the main lodge structure, built around 1816, is the one-room log cabin with a chimney that makes up the far west part of the lodge. An addition to the cabin, with the chimney in the middle forming a saddlebag house, was added later; it was made of rough-hewn logs, indicating that it may have been built by someone else. The cabin may have been the homeplace of Jonathan Blevins, one of the earliest settlers of the region. He moved into the Scott County area of Tennessee between 1850 and 1860. He either lived at the site of the lodge or farther down the creek near where he is buried.

John Blevins, Jonathan Blevins's great-grandson also lived at Charit Creek. He and his son, Oscar, built the four-crib barn of hemlock and oak logs, located near the lodge, around 1920 to 1930 following the design of an original barn that had burned. They also built the corncrib located in front of the lodge, the blacksmith shop behind the lodge, and a smoke house, which has been converted into the bathhouse. Even though the buildings were constructed during the 1920s, they were constructed in a style that had not been used in other areas since the nineteenth century. The four-crib barn, corncrib, and blacksmith shop are also listed on the National Register of Historic Places.

Around 1963, the Phillipses, the last family to live at the homesite in the late 1950s, sold it to Joe Simpson. The site was modified to become the Parch Corn Hunting Lodge or "Hog Farm" (Russian wild boar were introduced for hunting), which Joe Simpson operated until 1982 when the lodge was bought by the USACOE for the NRRA. Joe Simpson brought in logs from other cabins in the area to create the two smaller cabins that now serve as bunkhouses. One cabin (now the far bunkhouse) from up Station

Charit Creek Lodge

Camp Creek belonged to Jacob Blevins, Jr. (Jake); the other from down the creek belonged to Appalonia Slaven and Ellen and Daniel Blevins. Joe Simpson used logs from a house he found in Slagle Hollow, Kentucky, to build the east end of the main lodge building. The lodge, renamed the Charit Creek Lodge when it became part of the Big South Fork NRRA, was operated as a youth hostel from 1987 through 1989 before it was open to the general public.

Historic Rugby

Historic Rugby borders the southern boundary of the Big South Fork NRRA. Visiting Rugby, one of the most authentically preserved historic villages in America, is well worth your time. (See "Local Directions.")

The colony of Rugby was established in 1880 by Thomas Hughes—an English author, educator, and social reformer—for the younger sons of English gentry, who were traditionally excluded from any family inheritance. Artisans, tradesman, and farming families were also welcome to join the cooperative, class-free colony. Rugby grew to a maximum population of 350, but by 1900 only a few families occupied the colony. The reasons Rugby did not succeed are many and include mismanagement, land title problems, soil that was not as fertile as anticipated, disease, severe weather, and a railroad spur that never was built. One of the most significant reasons the colony failed was that the colonists were not equipped to be farmers (no manual labor experience) or prepared for rural life in such an isolated location. By 1900 many went back to England or moved to cities such as Chattanooga and Knoxville; others were absorbed into the local population.

Though Rugby declined, it was never completely deserted. Individual residents struggled for many decades to keep the heritage alive, caring for the buildings and lands. However, Rugby was virtually abandoned in the isolation of the Cumberland Plateau for decades until Brian L. Stagg came along during the 1960s. Stagg, who studied local East Tennessee history and was interested in preserving the remaining buildings at Rugby, helped form the Rugby Restoration Association, now called Historic Rugby, Inc. The nonprofit organization is run by a volunteer board; Barbara Stagg, Brian's sister, is the director. The entire original Rugby townsite (about 1,000 acres) is listed on the National Register of Historic Places.

Twenty buildings of this would-be Utopia still stand. Several of Rugby's remaining buildings are open to the public, and daily tours are conducted from February 1 through December 31, excluding major holidays. Information and guided tours are available from the visitor center, located in the former schoolhouse (see appendix). The visitor center has an excellent interpretive exhibit, including a video; allow about an hour to see the exhibit. Site admission includes the interpretive exhibit and a guided tour.

The guided tour, which begins at the schoolhouse visitor center and takes about an hour, includes the Thomas Hughes Public Library, the Christ Church Episcopal, and Kingstone Lisle, founder Thomas Hughes's house. The Thomas Hughes Library, which was specifically designed to preserve books (special venting, no heat, windows located so that the sun never shines on books), is the most interesting building to visit. It opened in 1882 and has 7,000 books, printed from 1687 to 1899, which were undisturbed for decades. The church has been continuously used for worship since 1887 and contains all its early furnishings and fixtures. Kingstone Lisle is furnished with many original Rugby pieces and reveals a lot about early life in Rugby.

Many annual events are held at Historic Rugby, including the Annual Festival of British and Appalachian Culture in May and the Annual Rugby Pilgrimage in August. Historic Rugby offers a wide variety of traditional craft workshops. Check with the visitor center or Web site for schedules (see appendix).

Historic Rugby, Inc., continues to restore, preserve, and protect this unique historic site and has developed a Master Plan for future development. Their latest project is the restoration of Uffington House, the home of Thomas Hughes's mother and niece.

Historic Stearns, Barthell, Blue Heron Mine, and the Big South Fork Scenic Railway

In 1902 Stearns Coal and Lumber Company built the town of Stearns, Kentucky, as its headquarters for mining and logging operations. We recommend spending a day or two in this historical area on the north end of the NRRA (directions on page 27). You should at least ride the old K&T Railroad from Stearns to Barthell Mining Camp and Blue Heron Mining Community on the Big South Fork Scenic Railway and visit the McCreary County Museum. The Whistle Stop Cafe and the Stearns Restaurant have great food and are located in the historic district with some interesting shops. Overnight accommodations are available at the Barthell Mining Camp, Big South Fork Motor Lodge, and/or Blue Heron Campground.

Board the Big South Fork Scenic Railway, an authorized NPS

concessionaire, at the newly restored freight warehouse in Stearns. The trains run on a regular schedule from May through October and on a less frequent schedule in April and November. Round-trip times vary for different trains and include varying times spent in Barthell and/or Blue Heron. Call or check the railway's Web site for schedules, fares, and other details (see appendix). Tickets are sold on a first-come, first-served basis, and group rates are available. The train fare includes admission to the train, Barthell (even if you choose to drive there later), Blue Heron, and the McCreary County Museum.

A great bluegrass band will usually serenade you before the train departs, at Barthell, and at the Blue Heron Mining Community. The trains, with open-air cars, pass through lush forest, hugging cliffs and following Roaring Paunch Creek, and descend 600 feet in 5 miles into the Big South Fork River Gorge to Barthell and the Blue Heron Mining Community. At Barthell you can take a tour of the many reconstructed buildings; visit a museum, coal mine opening, and moonshine still; shop for antiques, pottery, and crafts; eat excellent country cooking; be entertained; and much more. While the train is stopped at Blue Heron Mining Community, you can visit the restored coal tipple, the tram bridge that spans 975 feet over the Big South Fork River, and the main Mine 18 entrance. The most interesting features are the interpretive displays and ghost structures, which have oral history exhibits. There is a gift shop, snack bar with a very limited menu, picnic area, and rest rooms. You can also drive to Barthell (about twenty minutes from Stearns) so that you have plenty of time to see it and/or can spend the night.

Barthell was the first of eighteen mining camps established by the Stearns Coal and Lumber Company in 1902. It was abandoned and torn down in 1952 but has been reconstructed as it looked in the early 1900s by the Koger family. It is located 7 miles west of Stearns (see directions to the Blue Heron Area in "Local Directions" section) and is open April through December. Overnight lodging is available in one- and two-bedroom miner's cabins. We highly recommend a visit and, better yet, a stay to experience the serenity, culture, and history of the mining camp.

Blue Heron was the last camp to be developed by the Stearns Coal and Lumber Company. Hundreds of people lived and worked in this isolated community. Blue Heron was the Stearns Coal and Lumber Company's brand name for an intermediate grade of coal. The Blue Heron Mine (Mine 18) operated from 1938 to 1962 using state-of-the-art technology. The Stearns Coal and Lumber Company built the Blue Heron Tipple in 1937

Big South Fork Scenic Railway at Barthell

and operated it until the mid-1960s. The tipple, an engineering wonder in its time, is a giant sorting machine that separated coal into various commercial grades (sizes) using conveyors and vibrating grids.

When the Blue Heron Mining Community was re-created in the 1980s as an interpretive center, there were no original buildings left; open metal shells of buildings were constructed on the approximate sites of several of the original buildings. At each of these ghost structures, along with viewing exhibits, interesting recorded recollections of some of the people that lived and worked in Blue Heron can be heard. The tipple was also restored and stabilized, and the tram bridge provides access to hiking trails on the west side of the Big South Fork. A virtual tour of the Blue Heron Mining Community, including listening to some of the past residents, can be taken at www.nps.gov/biso/bheron.htm.

Back at Stearns you have a number of options to continue on your historical tour of the area. The unique McCreary County Museum is located in the old Stearns Coal and Lumber Company's office building, which was built in 1907. The museum highlights the area's history from the Native American and pioneer era though the boom times of the coal and lumber industries. The museum is open Tuesday through Sunday from mid-April through October.

Camping and Horses

Supplies and Essentials

We recommend either purchasing all your supplies in your hometown before your visit or stocking up on everything in Oneida, Jamestown, Whitley City, or Williamsburg. The closest grocery stores to the Big South Fork NRRA are located in Oneida, Jamestown, and Whitley City.

Make sure you have enough ice before you enter the Big South Fork NRRA, especially if you plan on arriving late. Ice can be purchased from the Bandy Creek Visitor Center only when it is open.

There are many convenience stores in the Big South Fork area in case you forgot something, need to pick up some essentials, or get some gas. We do not recommend entering the Big South Fork NRRA without having plenty of gas in your vehicle, especially if you plan on driving around a lot once you get here, since gas stations are not exactly down the street. Entering from the north, east, or south, gas stations with regular operating hours are located along KY 92, U.S. 27 in Oneida, and TN 52. From the west, make sure you get gas before you pass Jamestown or turn off of U.S. 127.

Bandy Creek Campground, the largest developed fee campground within the Big South Fork NRRA, is open year-round. It is located north of TN 297 (Leatherwood Ford Road) on the west side of the river gorge adjacent to the Bandy Creek Visitor Center in Tennessee. A large sign on TN 297 directs you to the road that leads to the campground. The campground has one hundred developed sites with water and electrical hookups, fifty tent sites, and two large group sites (no electrical hookups) with cooking shelters. The group sites must be reserved in advance and are for groups of at least twenty-five people. Bathhouses with hot-water showers are conveniently located throughout the campground. Adjacent to the campground are a swimming pool (fee required, open Memorial Day through Labor Day), volleyball court, playground, and dump station. Reservations, which are not required but recommended, can be made for campsites from April 1 through October 31 up to five months in advance (see appendix). From April through October, campers without reservations are also welcome first-come, first-served, but we recommend calling ahead to check site availability. The rest of the year, camping is on a first-come, first-served basis.

The Blue Heron Campground, located within the Kentucky portion of the Big South Fork NRRA, has forty-five sites with water and electrical hookups, a modern rest room with hot showers, and a dump station. The campsites will accommodate RVs up to 35 feet long. This campground is open April through November. Reservations, which are recommended, can be made for campsites from April 1 through October 31 up to five months in advance (see appendix). During November campsites are available on a first-come, first-served basis, with self-registration.

Primitive camping is available for a small fee at Alum Ford in the north end of the NRRA in Kentucky. This campground is open year-round, has no water or electricity, and is not for RVs. There are eight sites with tables, grills, and pit toilets. For a daily or annual fee, boats can be launched from the ramp located directly below the campground.

Backcountry camping is allowed throughout the Big South Fork NRRA, except in places designated as noncamping areas and within the yellow safety zones surrounding the Bandy Creek and Blue Heron Campgrounds. Backcountry permits are required for overnight stays and can be purchased from the visitor centers and the Bandy Creek Campground entrance station and after hours at many vendors outside the NRRA (annaul permit available). You may camp just about anywhere, with the following exceptions: You must camp at least 25 feet from dirt or gravel roads, trails, rock shelters, caves, cemeteries, grave sites, major historical and geological sites or structures, and the gorge rim; at least 100 feet from paved roads and streams; and at least 200 feet from and out of view of developed parking areas. Camping is not permitted at developed parking areas. Only dead and downed trees may be used for firewood, and chain saws cannot be used to cut firewood. Practice zero-impact techniques. Bury your waste at least 6 inches deep and at least 100 feet away from water sources, campsites, and trails. Horses should be tied some distance away from your campsite using a picket line (never tied directly to trees) at least 100 feet from any water source. Canoe camping is allowed within the river floodplain. A complete list of backcountry camping rules and regulations can be obtained from the visitor centers.

Special Equestrian Campgrounds

Two excellent fee campgrounds within the Big South Fork NRRA, operated by an authorized NPS concessionaire, have been specifically built to provide accommodations for horse and rider. Station Camp Horse Camp has twenty-four campsites and is located on Station Camp Road off TN 297 west of Oneida, Tennessee. Bear Creek Horse Camp, with twenty-three campsites, is west of Stearns, Kentucky. All the campsites at both horse camps, which accommodate up to six persons, have tables, grills, water and electrical hookups, and uncovered, metal tie-out stalls for four horses. Each horse camp has modern rest rooms with hot showers. Both campgrounds are open year-round, and pick-up and shuttle services as well as catering (for groups of at least six persons) are available. Contact the concessionaire for information and reservations, which are highly recommended (see appendix).

Bandy Creek Stables

When you bring your horse to the Big South Fork NRRA, you can keep it at Bandy Creek Stables, an authorized NPS concession managed by the wonderful York family, and camp at Bandy Creek Campground. The campground and stables are about a quarter mile from each other, within easy biking/walking/driving distance. The stables make a great base location for exploring the Big South Fork NRRA on horseback, since many great, diverse trails can be accessed from the stables.

Bandy Creek Stables offers fifty-four 10-by-10-foot stalls in barns that are cleaned daily while you're out riding. Sheltered and unsheltered tie-out stalls are also available when the barns are full. Make your reservations early (see appendix; they prefer reservations made by telephone), since the stables get busier every year. The stables are often full, especially during the popular spring and fall months. Proof of a current negative Coggins test is required and must be presented to the management before horses are unloaded. Halters must be removed from stabled horses. Registration and fee collection is at the tack shop located in the middle of the complex, which also sells snacks and many other things you may need. Hay, grain, and firewood can be purchased.

Bandy Creek Stables also offers gentle, surefooted horses and experienced, certified guides to take you on beautiful, exciting trail rides. We highly recommend going on a trail ride if you don't have your own horse;

it is a great way to see the Big South Fork NRRA! One-hour, two-and-a-half-hour (Jacks Ridge Loop), four-hour (to Leatherwood Overlook and back; bring a snack), all-day (to Charit Creek Lodge and back, lunch included), and customized overnight rides (including lodging and meals at Charit Creek Lodge) are available. Riders must be at least six years old; the maximum weight limit is 300 pounds. Rides can be customized to fit your needs. Hayrides are available on Friday and Saturday nights from Memorial Day through Labor Day. Reservations are recommended for all rides.

Other Permitted Horseback Riding Outfitters

If you don't have your own horse, two outfitters are permitted by the NPS to lead guided horseback trips into the Big South Fork NRRA. Southeast Pack Trips, Inc., is located on TN 297, 4 miles east of the junction of TN 297 and TN 154 just outside the Big South Fork NRRA. They provide everything from one-hour trips to customized overnight camping trips. All trips are customized to meet the needs of the particular group and are guided by experienced wranglers. Trips are available 365 days a year. Advanced reservations are required for overnight trips and recommended for all rides; group rates are available.

Tally Ho Stables is located on Grave Hill Road (Main Street at intersection with U.S. 27) northwest of Oneida. (See directions to the Slavens Branch Trailhead.) They offer one-hour, two-hour, half-day, and all-day trail rides. Guide service is available for those who have their own horses, and custom group rates are available. Guided hunting packages are also available. In addition, one-day, three-day, and family-fun equestrian camps are offered each year. Camp Tally Ho is an equestrian youth camp that teaches children from age eight to fifteen about horses, trail riding, camping, outdoor skills, safety, and good horsemanship. The appendix contains contact information for both outfitters.

Yahoo Falls and Alum Ford Areas

1 Yahoo Falls Scenic Area Trails

TYPE OF TRAIL: Hiking only.

TYPE OF ADVENTURE: Short hike on interconnected trails below and above a high waterfall.

TOTAL DISTANCE: 3.5 miles.

DIFFICULTY: Easy.

TIME REQUIRED: 2 hours.

SPECIAL CONCERNS: Unprotected overlooks, steep stairs, rock-hopping, and creek crossings.

WATER AVAILABILITY: Abundant on trail and at trailhead.

SCENIC VALUE: Spectacular: mature riparian forest, high free-falling waterfall, multiple overlooks, and diverse wildlife and wildflowers.

USGS MAP: Nevelsville.

BEST STARTING POINT: Yahoo Falls Trailhead.

Overview: The Yahoo Creek watershed was last logged in the 1920s, so the forest embodies the late stages of recovery of riparian forests in the Big South Fork River Gorge; this is what other area watersheds will look like in a few decades. Surrounded by high rock walls and canopied by massive hemlock, tulip poplar, beech, and white pine, Yahoo Creek Gorge is dark, cool, and damp, even at midday. You will be exposed to a diverse community of ferns, fungi, mosses, wildflowers, trees, insects, spiders, millipedes, fish, amphibians (at least six species of salamanders!), reptiles, birds, and mammals. Bring a flashlight to look in cracks and under ledges for critters.

This is one of the best short hikes in the NRRA. Three short, interconnected loops take you into the gorge and to five ledges overlooking the gorge. One loop leads to the base of Yahoo Falls, a 113-foot free-falling waterfall that is the highest in the NRRA and all of Kentucky, and three ledges overlooking the falls. Because the falls face west, the best lighting for photos is in the afternoon. Another trail takes you below the falls and along the southeast bank of Lake Cumberland but also puts you on two ledges

Map 5—Yahoo Falls Scenic Area

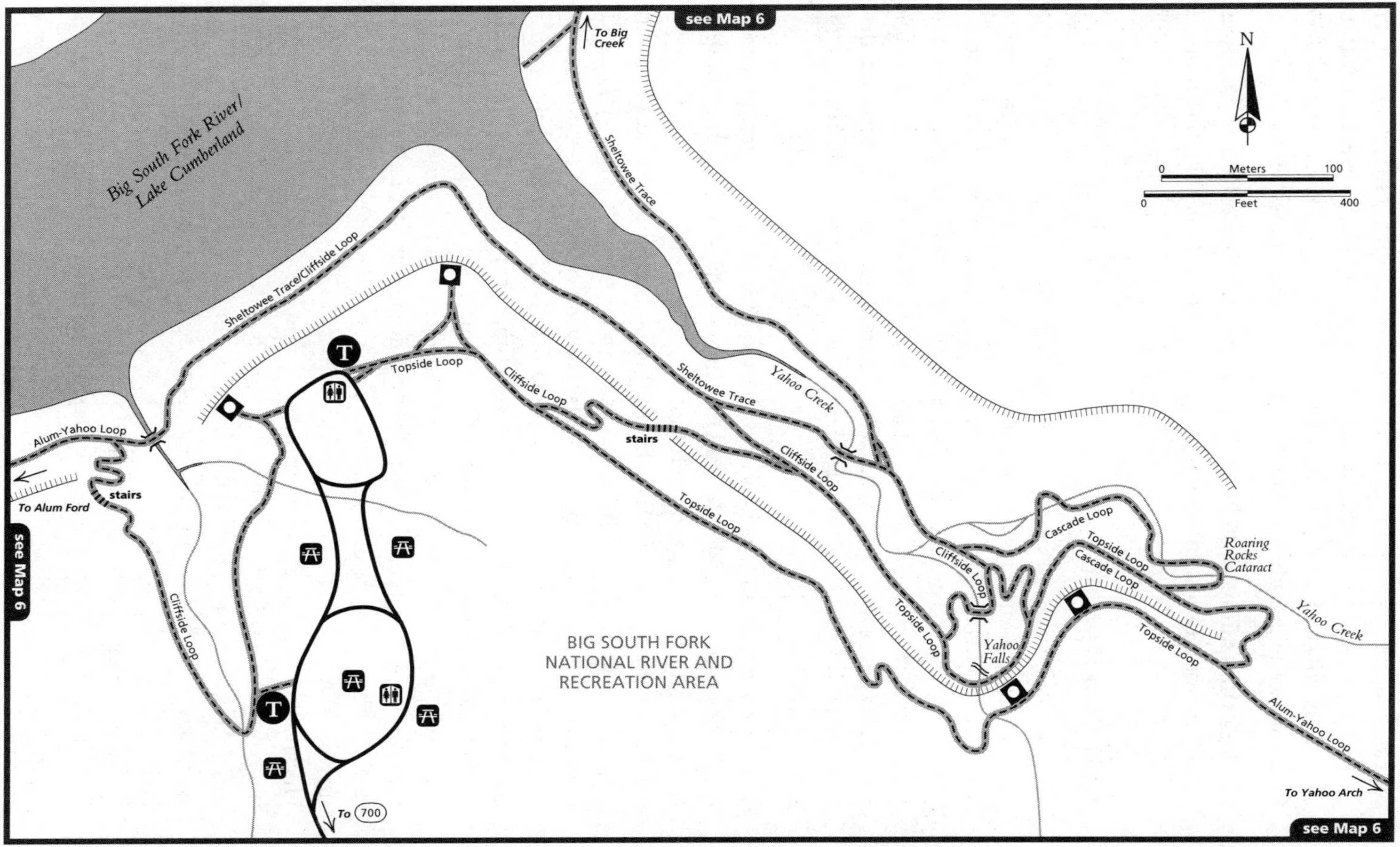

N

Meters
Feet
100
400
0
0

see Map 6

To Big Creek

Sheltowee Trace

Yahoo Creek

Roaring Rocks Cataract

Yahoo Creek

Cascade Loop

Topside Loop

Cascade Loop

Topside Loop

Alum-Yahoo Loop

To Yahoo Arch

see Map 6

Yahoo Falls

Cliffside Loop

Topside Loop

Sheltowee Trace

Cliffside Loop

stairs

Topside Loop

BIG SOUTH FORK
NATIONAL RIVER AND
RECREATION AREA

Cliffside Loop

Topside Loop

Sheltowee Trace/Cliffside Loop

T

To 700

T

Alum-Yahoo Loop

Cliffside Loop

stairs

To Alum Ford

see Map 6

Big South Fork River/
Lake Cumberland

overlooking the lake, with spectacular views of the misty gorge in the morning or glowing, red-orange sandstone bluffs in the evening. A third trail takes you to Roaring Rock Cataract—a deep, dark section of Yahoo Creek where it cascades down boulders into clear plunge pools.

Finding the trailhead: Follow directions to the Yahoo Falls Scenic Area. Of the two trailheads, the one on the northeast end near the rest rooms is better.

Trail Descriptions

We do not formally describe these trails mile by mile. Rather, we provide general descriptions of the trails and their intersections, present a good map, and send you on your way. These loops overlap in many places, so the mileage figures are not additive. You will probably walk only about 3 miles unless you have to backtrack—a likely prospect, but no big deal. If you find yourself walking north or south along Lake Cumberland for more than about ten minutes or encounter Yahoo Arch you have wandered outside the scenic area.

Topside Loop (1.2 miles; yellow arrowhead blazes) heads east from the trailhead along with the Cliffside Trail (green arrowheads). After the interpretive sign, narrow trails on the left (north) lead to a grand view of the upper reaches of Lake Cumberland. The staggering beauty of this lake is deceptive. The dam that tamed this river lies more than 30 miles away as the crow flies, quieting more than twice as many curvy miles of beautiful riparian habitat. As beautiful and fun as they may be, reservoirs do not harbor the diversity—and generally do not even support the same kinds of aquatic species—as do free-flowing rivers. For example, darters, tiny members of the perch family, sit lizardlike on the river bottom in fast-flowing riffles and runways between pools and wait for aquatic insects to tumble past. Once flowing waterways are changed into reservoirs, however, darters no longer survive. You still may see them in runways and riffles upstream of the Blue Heron Area and in isolated tributaries flowing into Lake Cumberland (including Yahoo Creek). The entire Big South Fork River Gorge below was slated for flooding behind a dam near the Blue Heron Mine but was saved when the gorge and surrounding plateau were incorporated into the NRRA.

To go counterclockwise on this loop (the better way), stay right at the fork on the trail with only yellow blazes. The left fork takes you clockwise on a common Topside/Cliffside section down below the falls, where you will be shortly. After some curves, there is a ledge overlooking Yahoo Falls on your left. Rock-hop across the small tributary creek that flows along the sandstone caprock and plunges over the ledge forming Yahoo Falls, and stop at two more overlooks on your left. You are on the very front lines of head-cut erosion, where water cuts its way upstream into the side of the gorge. However, the caprock is more resistant to erosion than are the underlying strata, which are eaten away at a faster rate by the powerful erosive action of water plunging over the ever-heightening waterfall. Stay left at the next intersection, Alum-Yahoo Loop (Trail 2), a long trail leading southeast up to Yahoo Arch and beyond. After making a gentle left-hand turn and descending below the bluffline, you will join the Cascade Loop on your right; stay straight ahead along the base of the bluffs to go down under the falls. You can always come back and do Cascade Loop. At Yahoo Falls the trail "crosses" the creek on the talus slope behind—actually beneath— the free-falling column of water, and rock steps allow you to get down near the plunge pool. Words to describe this magical area are hard to find. To finish this loop, continue northwest on the section in common with Topside and Cliffside Loops, and climb the metal staircase leading up the bluff wall to the trailhead.

Cliffside Loop (1.2 miles, green arrowhead blazes) heads east from the trailhead along with the Topside Trail (yellow arrowheads). After the interpretive sign, narrow trails on the left (north) lead to an overlook of Lake Cumberland (see above). Return to the trail and continue east. The left fork takes you down a steep metal staircase affixed to the bluff wall, then upstream along Yahoo Creek in probably the most wonderful forest in the area. At a fork, Cliffside Loop turns left and crosses a bridge well below Yahoo Falls. You should visit the falls first, then come back to this intersection. Cross the bridge, and stay left at the intersection with another trail leading up to the base of the falls; stay left again at the intersection with Cascade Loop (with blue arrowheads), and rock-hop across Yahoo Creek just upstream of its confluence with the tributary that forms Yahoo Falls. At the next intersection, you will notice turtle blazes of the Sheltowee Trace leading both left and right. Stay left to start the common section of Cliffside Loop and Sheltowee Trace, and cross a wood bridge, now with Yahoo Creek on your right (north), which eventually reaches the level of Lake Cumberland. Veer gradually left, heading southwest as you enter the Big South Fork River Gorge below the overlooks, which are perched on the sheer sandstone walls above your left shoulder. Just after crossing a wood bridge over a steep, bouldery tributary, Cliffside Loop leaves the Sheltowee Trace on your left (southeast) and climbs very steeply up switchbacks, steps, then stairs. The trail follows and crosses a small creek in a forest of huge beech, hemlock, and tulip poplar and reaches the Yahoo Falls Picnic Area. You can enter the parking area here, but first continue to another spectacular overlook on the very northern tip of the bluffs overlooking Lake Cumberland.

Cascade Trail (1.1 miles, blue arrowhead blazes) can only be reached from the other loop trails. It connects with Cliffside Trail near the confluence of Yahoo Creek and the small tributary housing Yahoo Falls and connects with Topside Loop just around the bend from its connection with Alum-Yahoo Loop. Going clockwise, the wiggly trail brings you to Roaring Rock Cataract after fording Yahoo Creek three times, so if the creek is up, you may have to forgo this loop. However, you can still reach the cataract by hiking counterclockwise from where this loop intersects Topside Loop. In the cataract—a deep chasm filled with huge boulders over which Yahoo Creek tumbles—some rock-hopping will be required. Some of the crossings require squeezing through low cracks between rocks and will be unsafe or impossible during high water. Do *not* hike this trail during or after a rain storm.

2 Alum-Yahoo Loop

TYPE OF TRAIL: Hiking only.

TYPE OF ADVENTURE: Day hike or short backpack loop from river to plateau and back.

TOTAL DISTANCE: 10.4 miles.

DIFFICULTY: Strenuous.

TIME REQUIRED: Full day (day hike) or two days (backpacking).

SPECIAL CONCERNS: Paved road crossing, exposed cliffs, other user types in DBNF.

WATER AVAILABILITY: Abundant on trail and at trailhead.

SCENIC VALUE: Spectacular: mature forest, high waterfall, two arches, four overlooks.

Map 6—Alum-Yahoo Loop

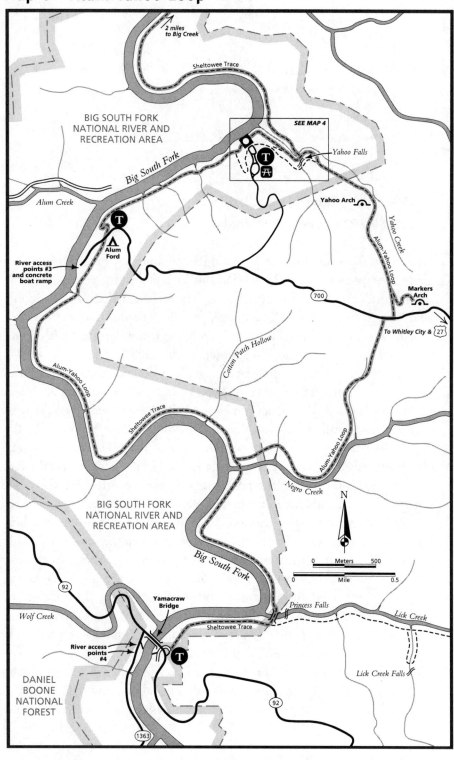

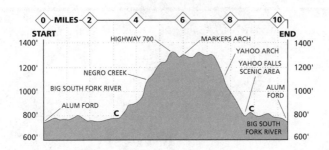

USGS MAPS: Nevelsville and Barthell.

BEST STARTING POINT: Alum Ford or Yahoo Falls Trailhead.

Overview: If you are looking for a moderately long day hike with spectacular scenery, this is a great loop. Half this loop lies on the east bank of the Big South Fork River on the Sheltowee Trace, named after Daniel Boone, who was given the name "Sheltowee," or "Big Turtle," by the Shawnee Indians who captured him in 1778. During the winter he spent with them, he gained their respect and was adopted by the tribe.

After a steep climb to the plateau, the loop follows narrow ridgelines where arches form. Yahoo Arch is a young arch, while Markers Arch is a narrow bridge formed long ago. In Yahoo Falls Scenic Area (Trail 1), three different short trails take you above and below 113-foot Yahoo Falls, the highest free-falling water in the NRRA and Kentucky. Trees in the Yahoo Creek watershed are perhaps the oldest in the NRRA. Side trails take you to two ledges overlooking the falls and two others overlooking the quiet waters of Lake Cumberland, where the river has been tamed.

Although you can access this loop from at least three locations, day hikers should start at Alum Ford Trailhead and travel counterclockwise. This puts you on a beautiful part of the river in the morning, with light shining down the river corridor in one section. You suffer the climb to the less scenic plateau portion of the trail during the middle of the day. The sun bathes you in warm afternoon light during your visit to Markers Arch, Yahoo Arch, and Yahoo Falls (which face west) and the last 2 miles along the river. Plus, you get to swim at the end of the hike!

If you plan to backpack this loop, the trail mileages are better distributed by starting at Yahoo Falls Trailhead. This allows you to do half the loop each day and camp on the river, regardless of which direction you travel. Although you can also park at Yamacraw Bridge and access this loop via a 3-mile (one-way) section of the Sheltowee Trace, vehicle security is questionable at the bridge, so we advise against it. Backpackers can (and should) add that flat section to this loop (see mile 3.3) and camp in a wonderful location along the river or at Princess Falls—a great 17-mile adventure! You can also connect with the Sheltowee Trace to the north, leaving the loop at Yahoo Falls. We took the liberty of adding the 1-mile side trip to Markers Arch to this otherwise 9.4-mile loop.

Finding the trailhead: Follow directions to Alum Ford and see Map C. If you are using Yahoo Falls Trailhead, start description at mile 8.3.

Trail Description

From the boat ramp parking area at Alum Ford, walk back up the road, turn right into Alum Ford Campground on the Sheltowee Trace (marked with blue turtle blazes), and head southwest through the campground. Stay on the campground road and follow the turtles into a nice beech and tulip poplar forest. A lone, wedge-shaped boulder sticking up into the canopy is a sign of the scenery to come. The trail remains perched well above river level, and you will not hear rushing water along this trail because the river loses its free-flowing character as it enters Lake Cumberland. This makes it easy to hear birds, which are numerous in this lush riparian forest. Among other species, we usually hear wood thrushes, white- and red-eyed vireos, yellow-billed cuckoos, pileated woodpeckers, chickadees, Carolina wrens, white-breasted nuthatches, brown creepers, and black-throated green, yellow, and hooded warblers.

For the next few miles you will be elevated above the river but periodically cross small creeks draining steep ravines that cut their way eastward into the plateau. Most of these creeks are reliable sources of drinking water, but use your filter. Moss-covered sandstone boulders with embedded quartzite pebbles are fossilized remains of ancient sandbars or creekbeds. The forest is old and diverse, with tulip poplar, beech, hemlock, sweetgum, hickory, chestnut oak, and white oak on the gorge slope and sycamore and river birch in the riparian zone near the river. Some impressive beech trees show the telltale workings of a sapsucker, a woodpecker that drills sap wells in horizontal, dotted-line patterns, as if tiny gangsters strafed them with machine-gun fire. This entire stretch of trail is great for wildflower photographers. The understory is open, indicative of a more mature forest, and the forest floor is covered with mayapple, pawpaw, Solomon's seal, trillium, and many others. If you look closely, you may see five-lined skinks basking on logs and bug-sized American toadlets hopping across the trail. The forest floor is littered with a large number of tree trunks in various stages of decay, essential habitat for arthropods, salamanders, and small mammals.

At a spot called Fishtrap Hollow, the river makes a hairpin turn, the floodplain becomes wider, and the trail swings left (east) over a rocky saddle at the southern tip of a ridge. On the other side of the saddle, the trail continues northeast, high above the river on its outside bank. You may notice a dramatic "bathtub effect" in the river—a zone of bare mud between the forest and river indicating the difference between the regulated high and low of Lake Cumberland.

2.0 After passing an old sandstone chimney, a faint trail on your right leads to Cotton Patch Shelter, a pavilion overlooking the river that is a nice camping spot for backpackers. Climb steeply away from the river, pass some rock outcrops, and turn left up into a small, bifurcated creek valley where water runs along a sandstone wall with some good critter cracks and nice coal seams. After returning to the river, you will be walking along the outside bend of the river on a steep slope.

2.9 After turning away from the river into the ravine of Cotton Patch Creek, pass through a crack created by large rocks leaning against each other, marked DANGEROUS. Climb a short flight of stairs and a ladder over the rocks, then cross Cotton Patch Creek. About 50 feet after passing through the crack you will notice a faint trail leading directly down to the creek, a cool, dark place where you may see northern dusky and longtail salamanders. After the creek crossing there are some gigantic beech and hemlock trees among some impressive oaks and tulip poplars on the gorge slope; you can see a long, high sandstone wall looming above. On your right, notice the water ponded behind a building-sized rock with a convex surface on its uphill side. These types of temporary water sources provide fishless breeding sites for frogs, toads, newts, and spotted salamanders.

3.3 Just after the gorge opens up into the Negro Creek watershed, look for a trail intersection with signs directing you left (east) to Yahoo Arch in 4 miles. A large camp lies just below this intersection, beneath sycamores and river birch at a terrace on the river. The site may be underwater during floods, and the water will likely be muddy from boat wakes eroding the muddy shoreline, but it is a nice site when dry.

You can continue straight (south), cross Negro Creek on a bridge, and do a side trip on the Sheltowee Trace, reaching Yamacraw Bridge in another 3 miles (see Map 6). If you are staying overnight or just want to see more of the river corridor, we recommend hiking at least some of this beautiful trail, which lies on a nearly flat and easy-to-follow tram road along the river. For backpackers there are numerous campsites along Lick Creek Trail and a particularly beautiful one near the plunge pool at the base of Princess Falls, a waterfall that plunges over a wide shelf on Lick Creek just outside the NRRA boundary. Princess Falls is only about 2 miles away and well worth the trip. The campsite, 1.2 miles from Yamacraw Bridge, may be occupied, but there are other places to camp within earshot of the falls.

To continue the loop, head east of the rocky intersection, climb up the back sides of some boulders, and pass some low bluffs and rock shelters. In a few minutes you will be walking along the north slope of the steep ravine of Negro Creek under some massive hemlock and beech. The next 2 miles are entirely uphill, so filter some extra water, guzzle a bunch, and filter some more. You will cross an old logging road a few times during a steep climb on switchbacks, head into a tiny hemlock drainage, then exit the NRRA and enter DBNF, where the trees are obviously smaller. The trail blazes will be white triangles until you reach Yahoo Creek. After crossing another tiny dry tributary, the trail flattens out at the top of a southeast-facing slope high above Negro Creek, overlooking the hemlock forest below. You may encounter lots of blackberry bushes in an area damaged by the 1998 winter storm. The trail swings north, with Negro Creek on your right (east) becoming narrower as you head into the upper reaches of its headwaters. After crossing Negro Creek, your last water source for a while, make your final ascent up a short flight of stairs cut in the limestone to a grassy area at the southern tip of a ridge. Near the top you will find a really nice campsite with a commanding view of the valley below, but no close water source.

5.3 Enter a power line right-of-way and climb a short flight of sandstone steps leading up to an access road—the hottest and least scenic part of the trail—and pass an open area on your left, which was burned shortly before summer 2000.

5.5 Reach KY 700 at a sign indicating that you were on Negro Creek Trail and are about to start Yahoo Arch Trail, the Forest Service names for these trails. Turn right (east) and walk about 100 feet down the road; reenter the woods at the opening on your left, and head north along a narrow, dry ridge covered with Virginia pine, shortleaf pine, and maple—a forest clearly in the early stages of post-logging succession. The dense canopy of these small trees will shade you even during the hottest part of the day, except in the patches of trees damaged by southern pine beetles (see ecology chapter).

5.6 Markers Arch, a narrow, "mature" arch with a nearly 60-foot span, lies about 0.5 mile down the spur trail on your right and is worth a visit.

6.6 Back at the loop, turn right (north). A sign indicates that you are walking Yahoo Arch Trail 602, with the arch and falls 1 and 2 miles ahead, respectively. Ascend a knob covered with Virginia pine, blueberry, and lots of greenbriar. Listen for downy and hairy woodpeckers.

7.3 Start the descent into the gorge through a shortleaf pine forest damaged by southern pine beetles. Veer east and skirt the side of the ridge. Descend on stairs, pass a nice rock shelter, then descend a few switchbacks in a forest of obviously different, older trees.

7.6 Reach Yahoo Arch, which looks like a deep, dark rock shelter. Its roof is splitting away from the ridge, so it is really an arch in the making. Pictures of this west-facing arch-shelter are best taken in afternoon light. Large beech, hemlock, and oak loom above you a short distance past the arch. From here to the river, the trees get larger and larger. Continue descending into the Yahoo Creek watershed on switchbacks and reach Yahoo Creek at red arrowhead blazes, a sign that you are back in BSFN-RRA.

8.3 Reach a fork at the Topside Loop of the Yahoo Falls Scenic Area (Trail 1), blazed with yellow arrowheads. A trip to Yahoo Falls and the Lake Cumberland overlooks is highly recommended. This is simply the best forest and waterfall in the region and should not be missed.

From your current position, the most direct route to see the falls from below and get back on the Sheltowee Trace without getting lost is to turn right on Topside Loop (yellow blazes) and follow it (combined with blue blazes for a short section) to a point underneath the falls on its north side. After visiting the falls, head west on the yellow trail and get on Cliffside Loop (green blazes), which will eventually be shared with the Sheltowee Trace (turtle blazes). If you have time, take Cliffside and Topside Trails up the metal stairs on the bluff face and visit the overlooks, only a few tenths of a mile away, for views of the upper reaches of Lake Cumberland. From the overlook return to the Sheltowee Trace on the Cliffside Trail (green) to continue the Alum-Yahoo Loop. If you have the time, take a short side trip along the river north of Yahoo Creek on the Trace, marvel at some massive bluffs, and return to this spot. (If this is confusing, flip back to Trail 1 for a description and map of the area.)

8.7 After visiting the Yahoo Falls area, continue on the loop—making certain you are on the trail with green arrowhead and turtle blazes, with Yahoo Creek—on your right (north). Back on the green trail and Sheltowee Trace, Yahoo Creek eventually reaches the level of Lake Cumberland. Veer gradually left, heading southwest as you enter the river gorge below Yahoo Overlook, which is perched on the sheer sandstone walls above you. There is a great campsite below these bluffs at the confluence of the river and Yahoo Creek.

8.8 Cross a wood bridge over a steep, rocky tributary. Just afterward, Cliffside Loop (green) leaves the Trace on your left (southeast) and climbs very steeply up to the Yahoo Falls Picnic Area on switchbacks, then stairs. From here to Alum Ford, the trail is simply the Sheltowee Trace and Alum-Yahoo Loop. As the floodplain widens, you will be greeted by building-sized boulders standing alone in the forest and cross three more creeks draining steep head-cut ravines, some with rock shelters and drip-walls.

10.4 Cross KY 700 and head to your vehicle at Alum Ford—after a swim, of course.

Blue Heron Area

TYPE OF TRAIL: Hiking (paved, but too steep for wheelchair access).

TYPE OF ADVENTURE: Short visit to one of the best overlooks in the NRRA, or a rock climbing or rappelling adventure on a massive vertical wall near the overlook.

TOTAL DISTANCE: 0.6 mile (round-trip).

DIFFICULTY: Very Easy.

TIME REQUIRED: At least 30 minutes.

SPECIAL CONCERNS: Side trails lead to some very dangerous cliffs, so watch children closely.

WATER AVAILABILITY: None available on the trail, at the overlook, or at the trailhead.

SCENIC VALUE: Spectacular.

USGS MAP: Barthell.

BEST STARTING POINT: Blue Heron Overlook Trailhead.

Overview: This paved trail is a bit longer than the one leading to Devil's Jump Overlook (Trail 4), but the walk is really nice. The view at the overlook is grand, especially in the early morning and at sunset, and ranges from about 40 to 180 degrees (generally southeast). The view to the west is almost completely obscured by a Virginia pine forest, so visit the nearby Devil's Jump Overlook if you are itching to photograph the gorge beneath a spectacular sunset sky from a more westward-facing overlook. Devil's Jump Overlook is visible on the top of the bluff line to the east. Park rangers sometimes conduct interpretive programs at these overlooks, so check with a park ranger at the Kentucky Visitor Center at Stearns, or ask the Blue Heron Campground host.

This overlook consists of paving stones, rock seats, and a covered gazebo perched atop a sheer rock wall at about 1,160 feet. It is completely surrounded by a low fence. The river lies more than 400 feet below at about 735 feet. Almost directly below your position, Devil's Jump, a dangerous rapid, is actually closer to this overlook than to its namesake overlook to the east but cannot be seen through the trees.

Map 7—Blue Heron Area

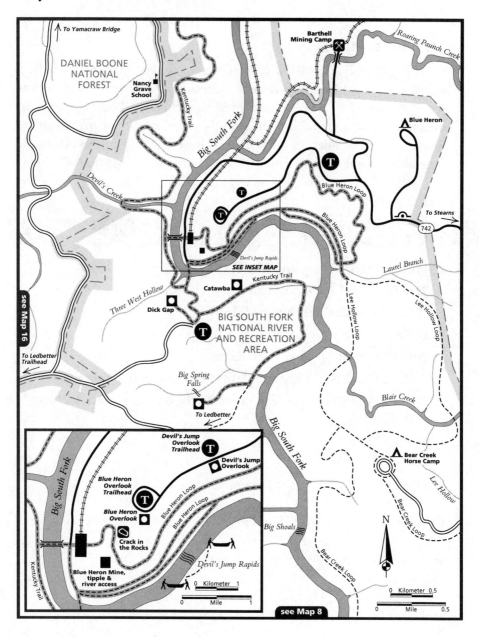

To Yamacraw Bridge

DANIEL BOONE NATIONAL FOREST

Nancy Grave School

Kentucky Trail

Big South Fork

Devil's Creek

Barthell Mining Camp

Roaring Paunch Creek

Blue Heron

Blue Heron Loop

Blue Heron Loop

To Stearns

742

Laurel Branch

Lee Hollow Loop

Lee Hollow Loop

Devil's Jump Rapids

SEE INSET MAP

see Map 16

Three West Hollow

Catawba

Dick Gap

Kentucky Trail

BIG SOUTH FORK NATIONAL RIVER AND RECREATION AREA

To Ledbetter Trailhead

Big Spring Falls

To Ledbetter

Blair Creek

Big South Fork

Bear Creek Horse Camp

Lee Hollow

Bear Creek Loop

Bear Creek Loop

N

Devil's Jump Overlook Trailhead

Devil's Jump Overlook

Blue Heron Overlook Trailhead

Blue Heron Overlook

Blue Heron Loop

Blue Heron Loop

Crack in the Rocks

Big Shoals

Blue Heron Mine, tipple & river access

Kentucky Trail

Big South Fork

Devil's Jump Rapids

0   Kilometer   1
0   Mile   1

see Map 8

0   Kilometer   0.5
0   Mile   0.5

Finding the trailhead: Follow directions to the Blue Heron Area and see Map 7.

Trail Description

From parking area, walk 0.3 mile straight south on the paved trail that leads directly to the overlook. **Caution:** A number of dirt side trails lead to some very dangerous cliffs, so be sure to watch your children. These dirt trails are used to access the climbing walls near this overlook. If you are a climber, please review the rules and regulations about climbing in the NRRA. In general, you cannot climb within 100 feet of developed overlooks.

4 Devil's Jump Overlook

TYPE OF TRAIL: Hiking and wheelchair accessible.

TYPE OF ADVENTURE: Short visit to a developed overlook.

TOTAL DISTANCE: A few hundred feet.

DIFFICULTY: Very Easy.

TIME REQUIRED: At least 15 minutes.

SPECIAL CONCERNS: A side trail leads to some very dangerous cliffs.

WATER AVAILABILITY: None available on the trail, at the overlook, or at the trailhead.

SCENIC VALUE: Spectacular.

USGS MAP: Barthell.

BEST STARTING POINT: Devil's Jump Overlook Trailhead.

Overview: The short, paved trail to this overlook is an absolute must-do if you are anywhere near the Blue Heron area. The deck of the overlook lies at about 1,140 feet of elevation. With its water level at about 735 feet of elevation, the Big South Fork lies more than 400 feet below. The panoramic southward view, ranging from about 50 to 270 degrees, is probably the best of all the overlooks in the NRRA. The view is staggering at any time of day, but early morning, sunset, and just after storms are particularly nice times. Look for eastern fence lizards on the rocks at the overlook.

Finding the trailhead: Follow directions to the Blue Heron Area and see Map 7.

Devil's Jump Overlook

Trail Description

Simply head east or west from your car on the paved switchbacks that lead directly to the overlook. This trail is wheelchair-friendly, but the overlook platform lies well below the elevation of your car, so be certain that you can make the return trip or bring someone to push you back to your car. The overlook is a massive wood platform perched atop a sheer rock wall, with a narrow pavilion to keep you out of the rain. The platform is completely surrounded by a low metal fence, but you can stick a camera lens through the openings. **Caution:** One dirt side-trail leads to a very dangerous cliff wall, so watch your children.

Directly west from the overlook, you can make out Devil's Jump Rapids. Although it looks like nothing more than a little riffle flowing through some river cobble from your viewpoint, it is really a large, dangerous chute of water that flows between three massive, building-sized boulders. The scale will be obvious if you can see any people on the river, a rare occurrence. If you are on your way down to the Blue Heron Mining Community, simply take a short hike on Blue Heron Loop (Trail 5) to Devil's Jump to see what we mean. On the north side of the river directly below and to your left, the forest that was cleared for mining operations is now recovering.

(For a history of the Blue Heron Mining Community, see the History of Charit Creek Lodge and Area Towns chapter.) On a less serious note, if you look south and really stretch your imagination, you might see a huge frog face, peering back at you from the gorge wall on the south side of the river.

5 Blue Heron Loop

TYPE OF TRAIL: Hiking only.

TYPE OF ADVENTURE: River-to-rim trek, including two overlooks, a historical area, and a swimming hole.

TOTAL DISTANCE: 6.4 miles.

DIFFICULTY: Moderate.

TIME REQUIRED: Half day.

SPECIAL CONCERNS: Stairs and ladders, dangerous bluff edges, dangerous rapids.

WATER AVAILABILITY: Adequate on trail; abundant at trailhead.

SCENIC VALUE: Spectacular: mature riparian forest, two great overlooks, and an interesting historical site; recovering from severe mining impacts.

USGS MAP: Barthell.

BEST STARTING POINT: Blue Heron Mining Community.

Overview: This wonderful trail brings you to "Cracks-in-the-Rock," a cool geological feature, the two best overlooks, and a Class IV rapids. We start and end the loop at Mine 18, more often called Blue Heron Mine, a coal mine in operation from the late 1930s to the early 1960s. Unfortunately, with coal mining comes severe ecological impacts. You will witness the full range of mining-related impacts along this trail, including slag heaps and acid mine drainage. You will witness the remarkable recovery the gorge has made since mining ceased only about thirty years ago. The Stearns Coal and Lumber Company logged the Big South Fork watershed from north to south, so the forests between here and the Yahoo Falls area have had the longest time to recover. For the most part, however, the forest is still recovering, but you will find some fairly large trees along the river and possibly some isolated uncut beech in steep ravines.

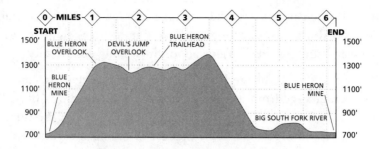

You can start this trail from Blue Heron Loop Trailhead (the "official" trailhead), Blue Heron Overlook (Trail 3), Devil's Jump Overlook (Trail 4), or Blue Heron Campground—all on the plateau. However, we think this trail is much better if you start in the gorge and learn about the history of Mine 18 before becoming weary from the hike. Then make the steep climb to the plateau and visit the overlooks before plunging back into the gorge and ending the hike with a swim in the river below Devil's Jump or at River Access #14.

Finding the trailhead: Follow directions to the Blue Heron Mine (and see Map 7) and park near the tipple, where tall trees will shade your vehicle in the afternoon. If you prefer to start from the plateau at any of the other entry points, simply flip to them in the description below.

Trail Description

We start from the Mine 18 tipple and go clockwise but also provide mileages in reverse (parentheses).

0.0 (6.4) A tour of the mine area will probably take at least thirty minutes. We cover some of the history of the Blue Heron Mining Community in the History chapter, but you will learn much more from the on-site displays, oral histories, and pictures. First visit the interesting displays near the Big South Fork Scenic Railway depot. After the depot, check out the tipple structure and the incredible view from its tram bridge, which spans the river high above the sycamores that line its banks. Then walk east toward the hillside and turn left (north) on the paved walkway to visit the mine shaft entrance and the ghost buildings equipped with speakers that broadcast oral histories told by the folks that lived in the area and worked in the mine. Keep walking north on the paved trail.

0.2 (6.2) At a hairpin curve, Blue Heron Loop leaves the paved trail on your left (north), becomes a singletrack dirt trail, veers right (east), and steeply ascends the forested hillside above the mining community.

0.6 (5.8) Enter Cracks-in-the-Rock and climb up one staircase and down another, then emerge from its cool climate at a west-facing bluffline. The crack makes a window through a narrow spine at the end of the ridge line below Blue Heron Overlook. This popular climbing area has forty-two established routes but so few bolts (fixtures to help climbers climb) that we could not even find one when we were there in 2001. Hopefully, such ethical behavior on the part of climbers will continue. This is a great place for photographers. A shaft of light shines directly down the crack at around 2:00 P.M. in the summer—easily captured on film by kicking up a little dust. The western exposure makes this spot really nice in the afternoon; and the other side of this wraparound wall is lit in morning.

After the cracks, continue north along the base of the bluffs above a slope covered with large hemlock and beech and climb a long, wood staircase nestled in a gap in the bluff. At a sharp right turn in the trail, a faint trail on the left leads to an unprotected overlook at the top of the climbing wall, providing a view of the Blue Heron Mining Community. The two best overlooks in the entire NRRA lie just ahead of you, so make this one a low priority unless you are a climber. The rock ledge is very dangerous, so stay at least one person-length from the edge, and watch children carefully.

0.8 (5.6) The trail on your left marked with blue arrowhead blazes leads to Blue Heron Overlook (Trail 3), a protected rock platform with a wood gazebo overlooking the river gorge. Back on the trail, continue along the base of a bluff above your left shoulder.

1.2 (5.2) Reach the paved parking area for Devil's Jump Overlook (Trail 4), a protected wood platform with a canopy, and arguably the best overlook in the NRRA. You will probably hear eastern fence lizards scurrying around on the rocks and in leaf litter behind the overlook. Blue Heron Loop exits the paved path on the left and heads generally northeast on a fairly level singletrack trail in a mixed forest with hardwoods and Virginia, shortleaf, and white pine. The numerous dead pines were damaged by southern pine beetles, a native insect that undergoes outbreaks periodically (see our ecology section). For more than 2 miles, the trail lies between the bluff edge and the paved access road leading to the overlooks.

2.0 (4.4) A short path on your left leads out to Blue Heron Loop Trailhead. Stay right.

2.9 (3.5) Ascend a long flight of wood stairs to Mine 18 Road (paved); immediately turn right at the top. Stay on the same side of the road, and hike along the edge of the right-of-way until the trail reenters the woods.

3.8 (2.6) After crossing a few wood bridges, you will find an access road leading out to Mine 18 Road and eventually Blue Heron Campground. Stay right (southeast) on the old dirt roadbed and plummet into the gorge along a narrow, rocky spine; descend gradually at first, then steeply, passing under a sandstone overhang and turning on switchbacks. During your descent to the river, watch as the forest changes from dry Virginia pine habitat to mixed forest, to hemlock, beech, and poplar, and eventually to riparian species: sweetgum, sycamore, and river birch.

4.6 (1.8) Complete the descent on some long, wood staircases, landing on the horse trail just north of Laurel Branch. Turn right (north) and follow the red arrowhead blazes. You can also hike back to Mine 18 on Laurel Branch Trail (described in Trail 8), just one of the many mining tram roads in the area. It lacks rails and ties but is still black with coal dust and extremely muddy. For the next 1.8 miles, the hiking trail crosses the horse trail a few times, but both lead directly to Mine 18. You will be walking along the river all the way back to the mine site, with the horse trail mostly on your right. You will be sharing a short section of the trail with horses, so remember your trail etiquette.

5.6 (0.8) Rejoin the horse trail, but in a few minutes turn left off the tram and descend stairs into a reclaimed mine slag site. The trail descends into a bottomland hardwood forest and passes some oxbows of the river shadowed by large poplar, beech, and hemlock. The hiking trail passes through a few more reclaimed mine sites, evident by the young planted pine trees and unnatural, eroded slopes. You will also hop across two creeks showing the effects of acid mine drainage and pass a small impoundment on the right side of the trail, likely incidental to the construction of the tram road, but possibly there to mitigate damage to water quality.

6.0 (0.4) A number of trails lead down to the rocky area around Devil's Jump—a dangerous, Class IV rapids—below which are some of the best swimming holes on the river.

Under no circumstances should you swim above this narrow, triangular chute on the other side of the channel (near the southeast bank) between three humongous boulders that have been undercut by the erosive force of water, trapping logs and debris underwater. If you were to be sucked into this chute from upstream, you also would likely become trapped. This chute is difficult to see from certain places on your side of the river. If you have any doubts about where you are, walk downstream until you are certain you are below the chute. Below Devil's Jump, the water is calm and clear in the deep pools, and there are some sandy banks with good access to the river. This area is also a popular fishing spot, so be considerate of others. Do not swim if the water is high and muddy. It is generally difficult to rock-hop to the mine area along the river, so after your swim climb back up to the trail and turn left. You will be dry by the time you get to your vehicle.

6.3 (0.1) Reach a series of horse hitching posts on your right. Horses are not allowed past this point. Avoid startling sleeping or freshly mounted horses; make your presence known with a whistle or a "hello." The snack shop is just ahead but is open only when the train has brought visitors to the mine. However, there is a soda machine and a drinking fountain that you can access after hours.

6.4 (0.0) You're back at the parking area under the coal tipple.

6 Dick Gap Overlook Trail

TYPE OF TRAIL: Hiking only.

TYPE OF ADVENTURE: A short hike to a great overlook or a connection to other trails.

TOTAL DISTANCE: 0.6 mile (round-trip).

DIFFICULTY: Easy.

TIME REQUIRED: 30 to 60 minutes.

SPECIAL CONCERNS: Dangerous drop-off near overlook.

WATER AVAILABILITY: None on trail or at trailhead.

SCENIC VALUE: Excellent: grand overlook of river gorge and coal tipple at Blue Heron.

USGS MAP: Barthell.

BEST STARTING POINT: Dick Gap Overlook Trailhead.

Overview: This overlook provides a spectacular view of the V-shaped Big South Fork River Gorge, the Blue Heron Mining Community and its tipple tram crossing high over the river, and Devil's Jump Rapids. It consists of a railed wood platform perched atop a tall sandstone bluff at the very northern tip of a spine sticking out into the gorge. Some great side trips are possible as well.

Catawba Overlook, another great vista, is easily reached from this trailhead by walking east on the Kentucky Trail (Trail 23) for just under a mile. Big Springs Falls, a spectacular free-falling waterfall, is about 2 miles down the same trail. Simply follow the description for the Kentucky Trail backward from its intersection with Dick Gap Overlook at mile 18.1. If you are in the Blue Heron area and want to take photographs from this great vantage point, it will probably take you longer to drive over than to hike across the river and climb the short, but steep trail up the gorge slope to the overlook (also described in the Kentucky Trail chapter). However, if the river is running high, cross the river on the tipple bridge and turn south on the Kentucky Trail (see Map 7).

Finding the trailhead: Follow directions to Dick Gap Overlook Trailhead and see Map 7.

View from Dick Gap Overlook, showing Blue Heron tipple

Trail Description

From the trailhead parking area, hike north on the wide gravel trail along a narrow ridge covered in Virginia pine, mountain laurel, and blueberry. After only 0.3 mile, you will enter an open area and reach Dick Gap Overlook. The Blue Heron Mining Community and coal tipple are directly north of you. Devil's Jump Rapids lies to the east and far below your position. Three West Hollow is the tributary ravine directly west of you. Please do not trample the sensitive vegetation on either side of the wood platform to reach the sandstone ledge, which is covered with plants and leaf litter and is extremely dangerous. The platform provides a safer and less obstructed view of the gorge.

Bear Creek Area

7 Bear Creek Overlook Trail and Split Bow Arch Loop

TYPE OF TRAIL: Hiking only.

TYPE OF ADVENTURE: Short hike to a grand gorge overlook and an interesting sandstone arch.

TOTAL DISTANCE: 1.2 miles.

DIFFICULTY: Easy.

TIME REQUIRED: 1 to 2 hours.

SPECIAL CONCERNS: Stairs under the arch, potentially dangerous spots near both overlooks.

WATER AVAILABILITY: None on trails or at trailhead.

SCENIC VALUE: Spectacular: panoramic gorge overlook and significant arch.

USGS MAP: Barthell.

BEST STARTING POINTS: Bear Creek Overlook Trailhead.

Overview: These two short loop trails are great by themselves but together make a nice combination of experiences. The 0.3-mile trail (one-way) to Bear Creek Overlook is flat and easy, and the overlook affords a spectacular westward view into probably the most remote areas of the river gorge. This is truly a great place to watch the sunset after a long ride and a hearty meal. Sunrise is also fantastic, with morning fog rising off the moist valley below. Sometimes clouds fill the gorge to its rim. You may hear fence lizards scrambling in the Virginia pine, blueberry, and mountain laurel behind you and rufous-sided towhees and pine warblers singing from trees on the rim. A visit on a clear, dark or moonlit night will be truly unforgettable, and we have never had a daytime nap interrupted at this rarely used overlook. The 0.6-mile Split Bow Arch Loop is also easy (unless stairs are a problem), and forms a loop below and above a wonderful sandstone arch.

Finding the trailheads: Follow directions to Bear Creek Overlook Trail-

Map 8—Bear Creek and Slavens Branch Areas

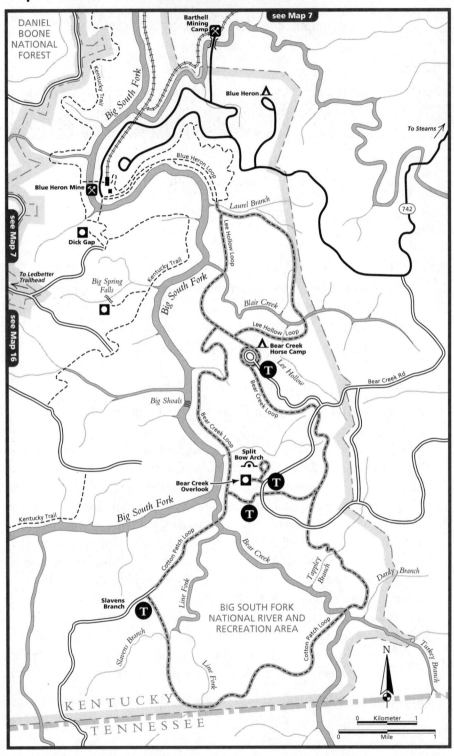

see Map 7

DANIEL
BOONE
NATIONAL
FOREST

Barthell
Mining
Camp

Big South Fork

Kentucky Trail

Blue Heron

To Stearns

Blue Heron Loop

Blue Heron Mine

Laurel Branch

742

see Map 7

Dick Gap

Lee Hollow Loop

To Ledbetter
Trailhead

Big Spring
Falls

Kentucky Trail

Big South Fork

Blair Creek

see Map 16

Lee Hollow Loop

Bear Creek
Horse Camp

T

Lee Hollow

Bear Creek Rd

Big Shoals

Bear Creek Loop

Bear Creek Loop

Split
Bow Arch

Bear Creek
Overlook

T

T

Kentucky Trail

Big South Fork

Cotton Patch Loop

Line Fork

Bear Creek

Tapley
Branch

Dardy Branch

Slavens
Branch

T

Slavens Branch

Line Fork

BIG SOUTH FORK
NATIONAL RIVER AND
RECREATION AREA

Cotton Patch Loop

Turkey Branch

K E N T U C K Y

T E N N E S S E E

N

0   Kilometer   1

0   Mile   1

head and see Map 8. Although the Bear Creek Equestrian Campground and Trailheads are nearby, you should walk, bike, or drive over from the campground to hike these trails, since horseback riding is not allowed on Bear Creek Road, and there are no hitches in or around the trailhead.

Trail Description

These two trails start from the same gravel parking area across the road from the Indian Kettle Holes and the old Newtie King home site. Clear signs point you to both trails.

Bear Creek Overlook Trail: Head west from the gravel parking area and continue past the trailhead sign and portable toilets on a gravel road flanked by an incredibly dense stand of young sumac. In about 0.2 mile the road narrows and turns to dirt, passes a sign stopping motorized vehicles from proceeding farther, punches into a mixed forest of Virginia pine and young maple and oak, and emerges from the woods at the overlook in another 0.1 mile.

The overlook is a wood platform with a low fence and interpretive display highlighting a panoramic westward view (from about 190 to 360 degrees) into the most remote section of the river gorge. If you are spending any time exploring the area, you have a great view of where you may have been and/or where you might be going. If you have done (or are going to do) the canoe trip between Leatherwood Ford and Blue Heron (Trail 50), this is one of the two stretches where the river gorge is oriented directly east-west. If you have done (or will be doing) the Kentucky Trail (Trail 23), it lies along the right (north) bank of the river and disappears into Troublesome Creek Gorge, way off to the west at the "end" of the gorge. The steep drop into the gorge on Bear Creek Loop (part of Trail 8) and Cotton Patch Loop (Trail 9) lies below and left (south) of you. You can also pick out the Line Fork ravine, up which Cotton Patch Loop climbs to the Slavens Branch Trailhead. To the north, the river passes through Big Shoals and on to the Blue Heron area but unfortunately has been hit hard by the degraded waters of Bear Creek, which is still suffering effects of acid mine drainage.

Split Bow Arch Loop: Punch into the woods on the north side of the gravel parking area and descend steps carved into a sandstone bluff, then switchback to a spot under the bluff. After 0.2 mile the trail splits into a loop. Go left (west) and descend more steps into a ravine covered in hemlock and rhododendron; cross a tiny creek, and ascend more stairs. At Split Bow Arch, more stairs climb up into the arch opening. The railing of Split Bow Arch Overlook, just off Bear Creek Road, can be seen above and on the left (north) side of the arch's deck. This arch is thought to have been formed from the weathering of a narrow ridge that split away from the plateau edge (hence the name), rather than from head-cut erosion. However, head-cut erosion clearly caused the narrow finger of sandstone to split away from the main ridge in the first place. In any event, water—and its freeze-thaw cycle—was the erosive force, causing large slabs to fall from beneath the more resistant strata forming the deck of the arch, eating into the narrow ridge from both sides, and eventually meeting in the middle, forming the arch. To continue on the trail, pass through a crack and emerge at the end of the main ridgeline; returns to the trailhead in a few tenths of a mile.

8 Bear Creek–Lee Hollow Loop

TYPE OF TRAIL: Horseback riding, mountain biking, and hiking.

TYPE OF ADVENTURE: Double loop from river to rim, with side trip to Blue Heron Mine.

TOTAL DISTANCE: 10.2 miles.

DIFFICULTY: Moderate.

TIME REQUIRED: Half to full day.

SPECIAL CONCERNS: Steep slopes, creek crossings, road crossings.

WATER AVAILABILITY: Good on trail, abundant at trailhead.

SCENIC VALUE: Excellent: wide range of habitats but some mining impacts.

USGS MAP: Barthell.

BEST STARTING POINTS: Bear Creek Horse Camp.

Overview: These two short loop trails are great by themselves but make the perfect ride when combined into one horseback riding or mountain-biking loop. Bear Creek Loop is about 6 miles long; Lee Hollow Loop is about 4 miles long. Less enthusiastic riders (or horses) can split the mileage into two easy days. Better yet, do one loop in the morning, take a siesta at

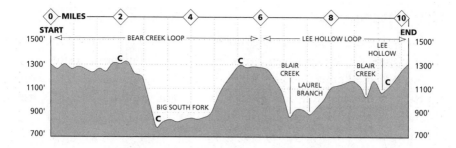

your campsite, then do the other loop in the evening. We start the trail description from Bear Creek Horse Camp, the most popular starting point for each loop.

From Lee Hollow Loop, Laurel Branch Trail provides a great side trip to the Blue Heron Mine, a historical site with interpretive displays, a mine entrance, a huge coal tipple, rest rooms, drinking fountains, soda machines, and a snack bar that is open when the Big South Fork Scenic Railway has a train parked at the mine. (See the History of Charit Creek Lodge and Area Towns chapter for details on this interesting historical site.) The river crossing at Blue Heron is beautiful and allows you to go swimming and water your horse. Beyond the mine, a climb to Dick Gap Overlook (Trail 6) gives you a great view of the river gorge and the Blue Heron Mining Community (see Laurel Branch Trail at end of this chapter). All of this adds only about 5 miles to whatever else you are doing. For a really long day (20-plus miles) or backcountry adventure with pack horses, combine some or all of these trails with Cotton Patch Loop (Trail 9).

Finding the trailheads: Follow directions to Bear Creek Horse Camp (Map 8). If you use Bear Creek Equestrian Trailhead, enter the trail description at mile 2.4. To enter from Cotton Patch Loop (Trail 9), use Slavens Branch Trailhead and enter the trail description at either mile 2 or 3, depending on which way you travel. Mountain bikers can start at Blue Heron Mine, but deep, tire-coating coal dust mud will force even experienced riders to carry their bikes for the first mile. Horseback riders cannot start this trail from the mine and cannot even trailer horses into the gorge. Dick Gap Trailhead is suitable for starting near the mine area but includes a long, bumpy drive from anywhere, and vehicle security is questionable. If you start at Blue Heron Mine or Dick Gap, flip to mile 7.3 and follow the description of the spur trail backward.

Trail Description

We cover these two loops as one, doing both clockwise from Bear Creek Horse Camp, starting with Bear Creek Loop. Mileages in the opposite direction are provided in parentheses. If you want to do only Lee Hollow Loop, flip to the note after mile 5.4 below. Whether you are staying at the horse camp or simply parking at the trailhead there, follow the perimeter trail around to its southern end, near the campground kiosk and entrance road. We do not account for any extra mileage around the short perimeter trail.

0.0 (10.2) On the south end of the perimeter trail, look for a sign for Bear Creek Loop, which heads southeast, parallel to the campground entrance road. The trail drops away from the road and rolls across two dry ravines, then runs along the south side of the road right-of-way only about 20 feet from the pavement before turning away from the road again.

0.8 (9.4) Cross Bear Creek Road. The trail runs generally parallel to the gravel road for a while, crossing two small, dry ravines covered in hemlock forest, then ascends gently.

1.5 (8.7) Cross an unnamed gravel road that leads west out to Bear Creek Road.

2.0 (8.2) Turn right (west) at the signed intersection with Cotton Patch Loop (Trail 9), which is shared with Bear Creek Loop for another mile. Descend into a storm-damaged area around the old Newtie King homesite.

2.4 (7.8) Cross Bear Creek Road, where you will notice the grassy parking area for the Bear Creek Equestrian Trailhead across the road. The trailhead has eight hitching posts that will be shaded in the afternoon, but there were no other facilities as of August 2001. Look in the south end of the parking area for signs pointing you down to the gaging station at the confluence of Bear Creek and the Big South Fork River. Turn right (west) on the gravel road and plunge steeply into the gorge. Horseback riders should tighten their girth and check their tack, and bikers should check their brakes twice. This descent is long and fast enough to make your ears pop on the way down and will be a strain on even the best equipment. Going the other way, this climb can be cleared on a bike without stopping, but just barely, and requires fifteen minutes of slow grinding in granny gears.

3.0 (7.2) Near the bottom of the hill, you will reach an important fork. Cotton Patch Loop turns left (south), passes an old river gage, and crosses

Bear Creek, which has been severely affected by acid mine drainage. You can go swimming at the river just below the gage. A nice flat rock is waiting for you at the confluence if the water is not too high, and the river is beautiful in the afternoon sun. While this is easy on foot, it is probably unsafe to bring horses to the river at this spot; cross-tie your horses near the gaging station and walk down to the river.

Bear Creek Loop turns right (north) and skirts the river on its east bank. From this point it is about 3 miles back to Bear Creek Horse Camp in either direction. Pass through a gate restricting vehicles from the trail along the river and climb away from the river. The brown building elevated above the river on your left at mile 3.2 is a U.S. Geological Survey gaging station and relay tower. Look for the water elevation measuring sticks, which come all the way up the hill to this spot—giving you an idea of how high the water really gets during flood stage. Continue north along the wide gravel trail and head up into the valley of Salt Branch.

3.4 (6.8) Cross Salt Branch and begin a steep ascent to a point above a steep slope on an inside bend in the river. Drop back down to the river near Big Shoals, a great stretch of river with big boulders pinching the river into a shallow runway where you can swim and fish near a nice campsite.

4.4 (5.8) Start ascending the east slope of the gorge, heading gradually away from the river. Make a right (east) turn into the narrow valley of a small creek, now ascending along the southern slope of the ravine—a dark, north-facing slope with lots of gigantic beech and hemlock. Some of the beech trees are very large, possibly virgin, avoided by loggers because its wood has little commercial value. You may also notice some large hemlocks riddled with sap wells made by yellow-bellied sapsuckers, a kind of woodpecker.

4.8 (5.4) Descend briefly and cross the small creek, then make a leftward turn, now heading north and climbing steeply in a ravine. The trail curves around the upper edge of the ravine below a rock wall and reaches the tip of a narrow spine, makes a hairpin turn, and climbs northward along the spine to the top of the ridgeline where Bear Creek Horse Camp lies.

5.4 (4.8) At the top of the climb lies a critical intersection. To return to Bear Creek Horse Camp, turn right (southeast) onto the wide, level trail. This is the 0.3-mile section of trail shared by the two loops. The campground is 0.5 mile away, making Bear Creek Loop just under 6 miles, not counting any mileage on the perimeter trail.

To continue on the double loop, turn left (northwest) on the level, nearly singletrack trail. You are now on Lee Hollow Loop. Follow the wide ridgeline, climbing knobs and dipping into saddles for nearly a mile on a fast, fun trail that eventually drops to the base of a bluffline.

Note: Enter the trail description here if you want to do Lee Hollow Loop first. From Bear Creek Horse Camp, find the trail past the metal gate at the very northeast end of the perimeter trail, and head northwest. In about 0.2 mile, turn left at the intersection where the trail is shared between the two loops and continue 0.3 mile to the intersection where the two loops split apart. Read on, subtracting 5 miles from the rest of the mileages.

6.2 (4.0) The trail drops very steeply into Blair Creek Gorge. The descent is smooth gravel at first, but the last bit is rocky and dangerous, littered with baseball- to football-sized boulders, described by mountain bikers as "baby heads" because of their size and the need to avoid running over them at all cost. You will begin to notice the Big South Fork River Gorge through the trees.

6.8 (3.4) Cross Blair Creek, the bottom of which is nearly banana-yellow from residual acid mine drainage. The yellow slime is "yellow-boy," a precipitate colonized by a type of anaerobic bacteria. The water is safe for your (and your horse's) skin to come into contact with for brief periods, but *do not* splash your face, *do not* water your horse, and *do not* filter creek water for your own use. Climb steeply out of Blair Creek Gorge on a good treadway; skirt the eastern slope of the river gorge for a few tenths, then descend steeply into the ravine of Laurel Branch.

7.3 (2.9) The trail forks, with the left fork leading northwest to Laurel Branch just around the corner and another 1.8 miles (one-way) to the Blue Heron Mine. Because the trail lies entirely on an old mining tram, the elevation change is negligible, so this is an easy 3.6-mile addition to your loop. To visit the mine, flip to the description of the trail between Lee Hollow Loop and Blue Heron Mine (and Dick Gap Overlook) at the end of this chapter. After visiting the mine area or watering your horse at Laurel Branch, come back to this intersection and take the other fork.

Back on Lee Hollow Loop just south of Laurel Branch, turn east up the south slope of the Laurel Branch drainage, climb gently among large beech, tulip poplar, hemlock, oak, maple, and white pine, and pass a rock shelter. The gravel trail is wide and bikeable, with little mud.

8.0 (2.2) Reach the top of the climb; in another 0.2 mile, pass a gated intersection with a gravel road leading east out to Mine 18 Road. From here the trail lies on the west edge of a ridge with a nice hemlock forest on the slope of Blair Creek Ravine below. A tiny rock house with a trickle of water is not a reliable source for horses, in addition to the damage your horses' hooves will cause to this sensitive area. The north end of this ridge has suffered some of the worst devastation from the 1998 winter storm we have seen. After that, descend rapidly along the headwaters of Blair Creek.

9.0 (1.2) Reach Blair Creek, a beautiful, flat-bottomed creek cutting through thin soil and flowing over the sandstone caprock. Confused? This is the upper headwaters of the same creek you crossed a few miles before, where it was severely damaged by acid mine drainage from a mine below you. Climb steeply out of the ravine up to a rock overhang on the northern tip of a ridge, then descend into Lee Hollow, namesake of this trail.

9.3 (0.9) Cross the small creek at the bottom of Lee Hollow in a dark, cool forest of mostly hemlock. After the creek, curve right and climb hard, reaching more rock walls and two cool (literally) shelters on either side of the trail in a sort of box canyon. Many critters inhabit crack-filled rock walls at about 1,200 feet in elevation throughout the NRRA, including small mammals; slimy, longtail, zigzag, and green salamanders; and the spiders and crickets they eat. Head north from the rock wall; curve around the next ridge to the north, eventually turning southwest again, and reach the top of the plateau at about 9.5 miles.

9.9 (0.3) Reach a T intersection on the edge of the Bear Creek Horse Camp safety zone. The right fork is the 0.3-mile section of trail shared by both loops. Turn left to return to camp.

10.2 (0.0) After reaching the metal gate at the perimeter trail on the northeast end of Bear Creek Campground, head back to camp or back to the nearby equestrian trailhead. If you started on Lee Hollow Loop and want to do Bear Creek Loop next, go back to camp and start the description from the very beginning.

Laurel Branch Trail (a spur trail between Lee Hollow Loop, Blue Heron Mine, and Dick Gap Overlook)

0.0 (1.8) Reach Laurel Branch, a narrow creek cascading over beautiful rock terraces and a small waterfall, and go downstream in the creekbed for about 50 feet. Immediately north of here you come out into the river gorge and reach a four-way intersection with Blue Heron Loop (Trail 5), a hiking trail that turns up wood stairs on the left and goes down to the river on the right. The horse trail stays elevated above the river on a wide, flat pathway, the old Blue Heron coal tram. You will be high above the river but can see it through the trees.

0.9 (0.9) The hiking trail veers off and heads down toward the river.

1.1 (0.7) A staircase leads down to a reclaimed mine area. After this the trail changes in character from a hard-packed railroad grade to an extremely muddy, perpetually wet trail that is not fun on a bike because the sticky mud will coat your tires. Although most of the mud comes in fairly short sections, it is unavoidable due to steep drop-offs or thick briers.

1.8 (0.0) Reach a series of hitching posts, allowing you to tie your steed and visit the Blue Heron Mine (and snack bar). Directly below the hitching posts, the trail switches back downward, crosses the hiking trail, and heads down to the river. You can water your horses and go swimming in the river, but watch for people fishing, swimming, and boating—sure to spook a wary horse.

You can also cross the river and make the climb to Dick Gap Overlook (Trail 6), which affords a spectacular overlook of the Blue Heron Mining Community. However, this requires crossing the river and making a steep, 400-foot ascent to the gorge rim and back, from an elevation of 730 feet at the river to more than 1,100 feet at the overlook parking area. This is the same type of gorge climb found elsewhere in the NRRA, but the trail can be wet, muddy, and rocky and may even be closed to horse access or rerouted. Cross the river and ascend steeply up the gorge slope on the wide, rocky trail to the overlook parking area. Horses are prohibited from the overlook, so you must cross-tie or picket-line your horse and continue 0.3 mile to the overlook on foot. The view is worth the trip, if your horse is not too tired from the rest of the day's travels. Return to Lee Hollow Loop the way you came.

Slavens Branch Area

9 Cotton Patch Loop

TYPE OF TRAIL: Horseback riding, mountain biking, and hiking.

TYPE OF ADVENTURE: Plunge in and out of river and tributary gorges on a wide, gravel trail.

TOTAL DISTANCE: 9.2 miles.

DIFFICULTY: Moderate.

TIME REQUIRED: Half day.

SPECIAL CONCERNS: Two gravel road crossings, numerous creek fords, steep grades.

WATER AVAILABILITY: Adequate on trail; none at trailhead.

SCENIC VALUE: Good: beautiful gorges and creeks, but mining and other impacts.

USGS MAPS: Oneida North and Barthell.

BEST STARTING POINT: Slavens Branch Trailhead.

Overview: This loop is like a roller coaster, crossing Bear Creek twice and dipping into narrow gorges of three of its tributaries. The numerous short climbs are tiring, but riders will find plenty of places to water and sponge their horses along the way. A short side trip to a swimming hole at the confluence of Bear Creek and the Big South Fork River cools you off near the end of the trip. There are no hitching posts at the swimming hole, so bring a picket line or rope to cross-tie your horses. This loop is plenty long for most riders and their horses, but it can be combined with part or all of Bear

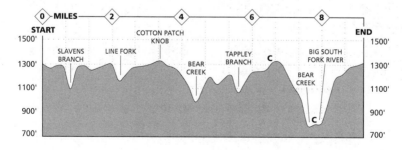

Creek–Lee Hollow Loop (Trail 8) for an epic, all-day ride. A connection with a trail leading to the river near Huling Branch, to Cub Branch Trail, and supposedly on to Station Camp area is not included for the reasons discussed in "How to Use This Book".

This is one of the few horse trails in the NRRA that is also a good mountain bike trail. The trail surface is mostly gravel and hardpack, rather than the deep sand and mud often found on horse trails in the NRRA. There is no singletrack, but the trail is challenging and fun—and you get to splash through all the creek crossings. This loop is rarely used, but you are likely to encounter horses on the popular Bear Creek Loop at the overlook and the swimming hole on the river, a must-do for bikers. Stay alert on the fast downhill sections, and always be prepared to stop and give horses the right-of-way.

Finding the trailhead: Follow directions to the Slavens Branch Trailhead and see Map 8. If you start at Bear Creek Trailhead, enter the description at mile 7. From Bear Creek Horse Camp, use Bear Creek Loop (part of Trail 8) to access this loop, and enter description at mile 6.6 if you join it on the plateau or mile 8.5 if you join it near the river.

Trail Description

Whether horseback riding or biking, we recommend traveling counterclockwise from Slavens Branch Trailhead so that you can swim and enjoy the river before making the final climb out of the gorge. Clockwise mileage is provided in parentheses.

0.0 (9.2) From the Slavens Branch Trailhead parking area, head back out to the road, turn right, and proceed northeast down the road.

0.3 (8.9) Turn right at the signs onto Cotton Patch Loop and head southeast into the woods, following a wide ridge in a mixed forest. In a few tenths, pass around a metal gate and descend steeply to Slavens Branch. The forest on the way down suffered severe damage from the 1998 winter storm but is recovering.

0.8 (8.4) Cross Slavens Branch, a permanent water source flanked by rhododendron and a low rock wall. The climb out of the ravine is steep and loose at first but flattens out at about a mile, then traverses knobs and saddles on a wide ridge between Slavens Branch and Line Fork.

2.3 (6.9) After a steep, fast descent to Line Fork, cross the creek near a nice overhang. Line Fork exemplifies most headwater creeks on the plateau, flat-bottomed creeks cutting through thin topsoil and cascading over flat sandstone shelves. This creek may be low during the fall in most years but is likely a permanent water source, as tiny fish have made their way upstream to this point. The eastward climb out of this ravine is steep but bikable because the trail is well groomed. At the top of the climb, you may notice extensive damage to pine trees. This was caused by a severe outbreak of southern pine beetles, a native species discussed in the ecology section.

2.7 (6.5) Reach the well-signed intersection with Willie Boyt Road and turn left (northeast). The NRRA boundary is not far south of this spot.

3.4 (5.8) The hill above you is Cotton Patch Knob. At 1,320 feet, it is the highest point on this trail, but you will follow along its northwest flank. Unfortunately, southern pine beetles have devastated the forest in this area, just a part of the natural scheme of things. The trail gets wide and winding, and the next half mile of the descent is really fast and fun on horse or bike.

4.1 (5.1) The descent becomes steep, rocky, and dangerous, obvious from a sign saying STEEP, ROCKY, LEAD YOUR HORSE. At that point there is a nice view of Bear Creek Gorge, and you will hear water below. The descent is not too bad and passes lots of interesting rock walls.

4.4 (4.8) Reach Bear Creek, which runs in a narrow gorge along the base of a large rock wall. There are some flat spots to camp along here, but the ravine has suffered tree damage from the 1998 storm. If the creek seems to have a sandier bottom, more sandbars, or milky-white water after rains, this is caused by erosion and runoff from the City of Oneida and developed areas outside the park that drain into this watershed. This creek has been severely damaged by acid mine drainage; we recommend not camping along this creek—or at least not drinking the water. Continue upstream and cross the creek near Turkey Branch on rocks that are slimy from acid mine drainage. We always see a few minnows here, a sign that mining impacts may not have eliminated all signs of life. The climb out of the gorge is very steep for the first 100 feet, the grade probably 25 percent or steeper. The rest of the climb is nearly as steep, so think carefully about the condition of your horse before doing this one in the saddle. Most bikers will have to push their rigs on this climb.

4.7 (4.5) Reach the top of the climb; shortly after, descend partway into the ravine of Dardy Branch. The trail stays on the ravine slope rather than descending to the creek. At a sign, go left and climb to the top of the ridge between Dardy Branch and Tappley Branch.

5.4 (3.8) Begin a very fun, very fast descent to Tappley Branch, a tributary of Bear Creek. A few tenths later, cross Tappley Branch, a narrow waterway that is probably permanent but may be nothing more than a trickle in the fall. The beautiful stand of rhododendron along the creek makes the extensive storm damage in the surrounding forest tolerable, and there are some nice hemlocks along the trail. Climb steeply out of the ravine on a few wide switchbacks.

6.1 (3.1) Top out on a wide ridge covered by a young forest damaged by the 1998 storm. Soon afterward, enter the southeast corner of a brambly old field and follow an old road north along the east edge of the field. Soon after, cross Bear Creek Road (gravel) and enter the woods on another wide gravel trail, ascending a hill through some young pines also damaged by the 1998 storm.

6.6 (2.6) At the three-way intersection, turn left (west). Cotton Patch Loop and Bear Creek Loop share a common trail until you reach the gaging station down at the river. The right fork (north) is Bear Creek Loop (part of Trail 8), which leads to Bear Creek Horse Camp.

7.0 (2.2) Cross Bear Creek Road again and enter the grassy parking area for the Bear Creek Trailhead. As of August 2001, the trailhead had eight nice hitching posts in a grassy area that should be shaded in the afternoon, but there were no other facilities. Turn left (south), and look in the south end of the parking area for signs pointing you down to the gaging station at the confluence of Bear Creek and the Big South Fork River. Turn right (west) on the gravel road and plunge steeply into the gorge. Horseback riders should tighten their saddle and check their tack first. Bikers should check their brakes before making this descent, which is long and fast enough to make your ears pop on the way down and will be a strain on even the best equipment. Going the other way, this climb can be biked without stopping but requires fifteen minutes of slow grinding in granny gears.

7.5 (1.7) Near the bottom of the gorge slope, stay left (south) at a fork and follow the Bear Creek drainage upstream to continue on Cotton Patch Loop. The right fork takes you north along the Big South Fork River on Bear Creek Loop (part of Trail 8), and on to Bear Creek Horse Camp, 3 miles from this point. If you want to stop for a swim, continue on the trail and look to your right (west) for the gaging station tower. You can get down to the river here. A nice flat rock is waiting for you at the confluence if the water is not too high, and the river is beautiful in the afternoon sun. While this is easy on foot, it is probably unsafe to bring horses to the river at this spot; cross-tie your horses in the large, flat area near the gaging station and walk down to the river. To continue on the loop from the gaging station, turn south along the east bank of Bear Creek, descending slightly (but heading upstream). Shortly thereafter, cross Bear Creek just downstream of its confluence with Line Fork. The rocks in the creek may be covered with whitish or bright yellow precipitate ("yellow-boy") from acid mine drainage. We do not recommend watering your horses here. There may be some deep mud just after the crossing. After the mud, ascend the north slope of Line Fork watershed on a wide gravel trail in a hemlock forest. This climb can be cleared on a mountain bike without stopping, given a little patient grinding.

8.7 (0.5) Pass around the metal gate and continue uphill; pass the intersection with the rest of Cotton Patch Loop where you turned into the woods some hours before.

9.2 (0.0) Arrive at Slavens Branch Trailhead. (If doing this trail clockwise, head east on the gravel road.)

Station Camp Area

10 Pilot-Wines Loop

TYPE OF TRAIL: Horseback riding, mountain biking, and hiking.

TYPE OF ADVENTURE: Roller-coaster ride on the plateau, with a dip into the river gorge.

TOTAL DISTANCE: 11.5 miles.

DIFFICULTY: Moderate.

TIME REQUIRED: Full day.

SPECIAL CONCERNS: One gravel road crossing, some creeks may be dry, steep slopes, dangerous overlook, confusing section near river, construction near trail.

WATER AVAILABILITY: Adequate on trail; abundant at (or near) trailheads.

SCENIC VALUE: Good: beautiful river and tributary gorge scenery and rock shelter; storm damage and some construction activities near boundary.

USGS MAPS: Oneida North and Barthell SW.

BEST STARTING POINT: Station Camp Horse Camp or Equestrian Trailhead.

Overview: This fun loop traverses a bunch of shallow headwater ravines, climbs small knobs, and dips into shallow saddles high on the plateau—a roller-coaster ride for the first 5 and the last 4 miles. A side trip leads to Bronco Overlook, a shelf overlooking the river gorge. At Pilot Rock, a huge boulder at the tip of a narrow ridge, the trail dumps you quickly into the gorge of Williams Creek where it joins the gorge of the Big South Fork River. A short side trip brings you down to the river at its confluence with Williams Creek. There's a really nice swimming hole and place to water your horses here and a great opportunity to see a very remote stretch of the river. Another side trip leads to Indian Dome Rock House, a humongous rock shelter with a domed roof, hence the name. The "Wines" part is named for Little Wines Creek, a tributary of Grassy Fork. The treadway is generally wide and groomed and only muddy in a few places, so horseback riders and moun-

Map 9—Station Camp Area

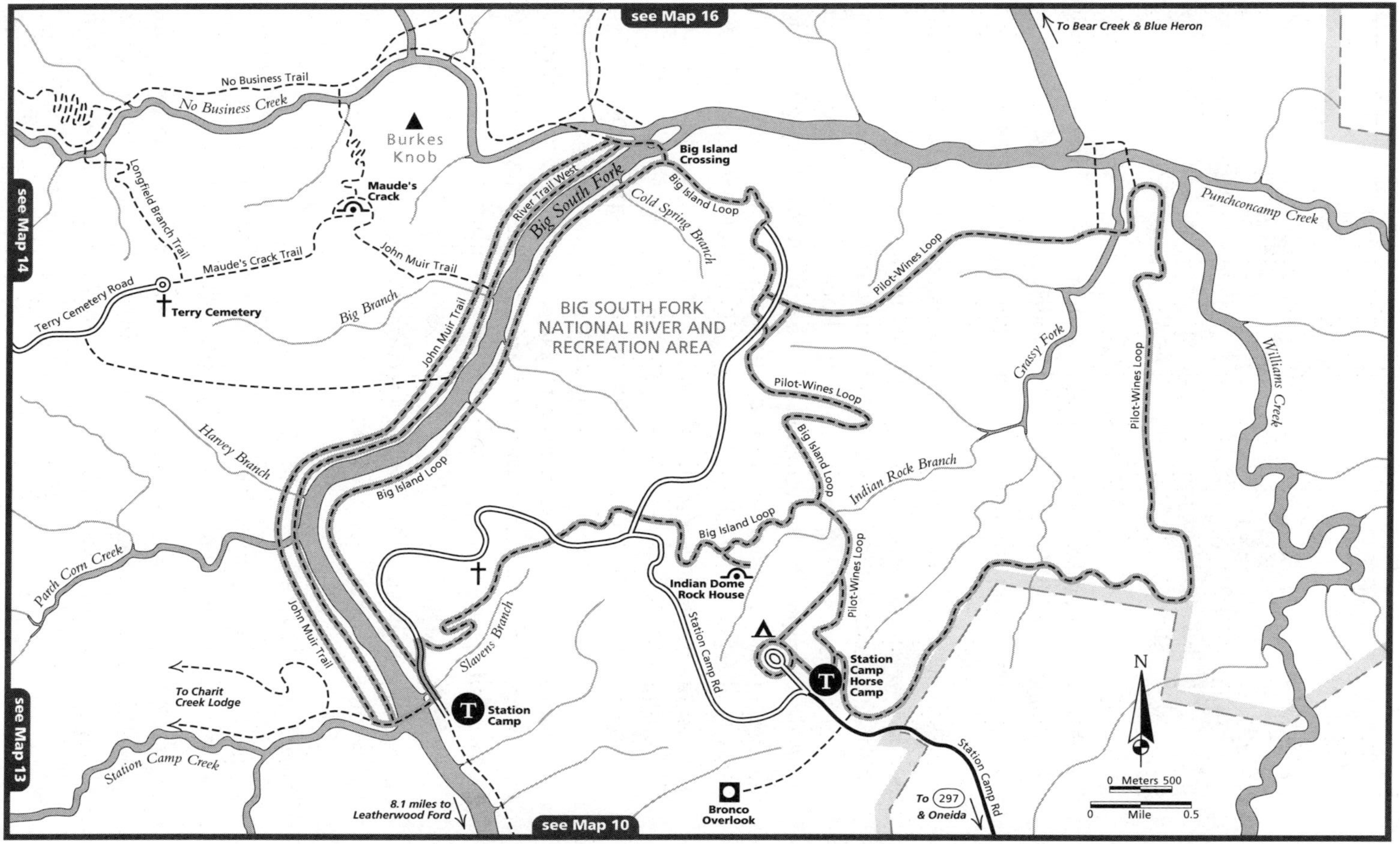

Punchoncamp Creek

Williams Creek

To Bear Creek & Blue Heron

Pilot-Wines Loop

Grassy Fork

Pilot-Wines Loop

Indian Rock Branch

Big Island Loop

Pilot-Wines Loop

Big Island Loop

Station Camp Horse Camp

Big Island Loop

Indian Dome Rock House

Station Camp Rd

Station Camp Rd

To (297) & Oneida

Bronco Overlook

see Map 16

Big Island Crossing

Big Island Loop

Cold Spring Branch

Big South Fork

River Trail West

BIG SOUTH FORK NATIONAL RIVER AND RECREATION AREA

Sitvens Branch

Station Camp

see Map 10

Burkes Knob

Maude's Crack

John Muir Trail

John Muir Trail

Big Branch

Big Island Loop

8.1 miles to Leatherwood Ford

John Muir Trail

No Business Trail

No Business Creek

Maude's Crack Trail

Harvey Branch

To Charit Creek Lodge

Station Camp Creek

Longfield Branch Trail

Terry Cemetery Road

Terry Cemetery

Purch Corn Creek

see Map 14

see Map 13

N

0 Meters 500

0 Mile 0.5

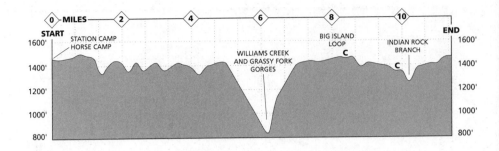

tain bikers will find it fast and fun. Water is adequate for horses, but barely so in summer and fall. Creek crossings are widely spaced and some may be dry, so let your horses guzzle at each source you encounter, especially in late summer and fall.

NPS signs and other trail guides indicate that this loop is 14.8 miles long, but we are not sure what this mileage includes. We obtained 11.5 miles for this loop without including the 3-mile side trip to Bronco Overlook, the 1.2-mile side trip to Indian Dome Rock House, or the short side trip to the swimming hole on the river. For a really difficult, long day ride, endurance training route, or overnight pack trip, combine this trail with the 13.7-mile Big Island Loop (Trail 11). These trails are shared for 1.7 miles, so the whole trip is really about 23.5 miles. Because we described each of these loops counterclockwise, the descriptions can be combined easily. For athletes in training, this combination is a great "epic ride" on horse or bike and adds two more beautiful river access points, making the otherwise strenuous trip safe and enjoyable. Finally, the Cub Branch Trail—a supposed link to the Bear Creek area appearing on some maps and in other trail guides—is impassable in the very few places the trail was ever cut, so we steer you away from that trail.

Finding the trailheads: Follow the directions to the Station Camp Horse Camp and Equestrian Trailhead and see Map 9.

Trail Description

We cover this loop counterclockwise from Station Camp Horse Camp but also provide clockwise mileages (in parentheses).

0.0 (11.5) From Station Camp Horse Camp, take the perimeter trail to the southeast end of the campground near the fee kiosk, then continue southeast on the short trail paralleling Station Camp Road on its east flank. In

0.1 mile you will emerge at the Station Camp Equestrian Trailhead parking area, a large gravel lot rimmed with hitching posts. Pilot-Wines Loop begins on the east end of the parking area. Punch into the woods and turn right (south) to go counterclockwise.

0.2 (11.3) At this intersection, the left fork continues the loop; the right fork leads southwest across Station Camp Road to Bronco Overlook, an unprotected sandstone shelf perched above the river gorge about 1.5 miles away. We do not add this 3-mile side trip to the loop mileage, but as the only overlook on this trail, it is worth the trip. The road leading to the overlook is passable by vehicles, so watch carefully. Tie your horse at one of the many available hitching posts while you walk out to the overlook. It faces generally southeast, giving you a great view down the river gorge.

Back on the loop, continue generally southeast within earshot of Station Camp Road. The trail turns gradually leftward, eventually heading northeast along the NRRA boundary. The smooth trail lies along a wide ridge with saddles and knobs. Sandy spots only briefly interrupt the groomed gravel trail. The forest is young because it is recovering from recent logging practices. Small maple, red and white oak, tulip poplar, white pine, and chestnut oak are pioneers of what will hopefully be an impressive mixed forest in years to come.

Wilderness Resorts shares the boundary with the NRRA for the next few miles, and you may hear or see construction of cabins or roads and will intersect a number of side trails that lead out to this new resort. To keep impact to a minimum in this area and other areas of the NRRA surrounded by new residential and resort developments, only one trail will be allowed to be built as an official access for each development.

1.2 (10.3) Begin a fun descent on switchbacks past some small rock overhangs and reach a sandstone-bottomed creek at 1.4 (10.1) miles. Cutting through the thin soil to the sandstone caprock on the plateau surface, this narrow waterway is typical of most headwater creeks on the plateau, which flow peacefully for miles, then plunge steeply into the river gorge.

1.8 (9.7) Pass another trail on the right from outside the NRRA and start a gradual descent on a wide, singletrack path with fun turns. Reach a tiny creek at 2.2 (9.3) miles, and ascend again. The roller coaster continues for another 3 miles, so enjoy! Some of the side trails have signs with mileages, but when we did this loop in summer 2001, the numbers were off by more than a mile on the high side.

4.5 (7.0) Perched on a narrow ridgeline, you can see out through the very young forest to east and west, occasionally passing through areas damaged by southern pine beetles.

5.0 (6.5) Reach a fork with a sign indicating that the horse camp is 6.4 miles away. The unnamed trail to the left was not clear in summer 2001 due to storm damage and may not be cleared by the NPS in the future. Continue straight ahead on the loop and begin a long, steep, very rocky descent. Inexperienced bikers should exercise caution, and horses with tender feet should be allowed to make the descent without you on their back. The trail heads down in a space between two rock walls. Going clockwise, this will be a tough climb on bike or horse.

5.4 (6.1) Reach a saddle on the narrow ridge leading north to Pilot Rock, a huge boulder at the north end of the ridge perched over Williams Creek Gorge. Williams Creek is audible to the east. There is a good campsite at the end of a big rock, but no water lies nearby. Turn right and drop off the saddle; descend steeply into a beautiful, dark, primeval beech-hemlock forest on very steep slopes lined by a few small rock walls. Listen for the metallic song of the wood thrush. Bikers will find this a really fun descent on a wide trail with a singletrack feel and should be able to clear it going the other direction. The path turns gently toward the west as it skirts the very north tip of the ridge below Pilot Rock, which you will see towering above your left shoulder as you descend into the gorge of Grassy Fork.

6.2 (5.3) Reach an important intersection at Grassy Fork; there may be a sign pointing you in the right direction, but the mileage may be off. The loop continues straight ahead; the right turn is a side trail that leads down to a fantastic swimming hole on the river. We suggest turning right (north) and visiting the river before continuing on the loop, even if you don't plan to swim. The swimming hole is only about 0.2 mile from this intersection, so we did not add this mileage to the loop. Head downstream along the lush, but often muddy east bank of Grassy Fork to its confluence with Williams Creek. Cross Williams Creek, then turn left, heading downstream along the north bank. The trail leads down to a point just downstream of where Williams Creek flows into the river. Unless spring floods have changed things, you should find a nice gravel bar in the shade under some river birch and sycamore. Please picket-line or cross-tie your horses so that they do not damage riverside trees. To get back on the loop, go back the opposite way to the intersection, heading upstream along Williams Creek and Grassy Fork.

Back on the loop, cross Grassy Fork, a gorgeous tributary. The creek is lined with hemlock, magnolia, beech, sycamore, and river birch, although lots of trees lie in the creek, damaged from the 1998 storm. Grassy Fork has very good water quality and is worth filtering for a good guzzle. If you have not made the side trip to the river, let your horses have a guzzle, too, as they are in for a big climb. The trail climbs the tip of a narrow draw at the end of a ridgetop, becomes roadlike, and the forest opens up a bit at about 6.4 miles—but you are not done climbing.

6.5 (5.0) Intersect a trail running along a small creek, with signs clearly pointing you straight ahead. Cross the creek, which may be nearly dry in summer and fall, and continue climbing. First you follow a ridgeline, then make a sharp right (west) turn and do a brutal climb, which lasts about 0.4 mile.

7.2 (4.3) Pass through a metal gate at the top of the climb, passing a sign excluding motorized vehicles from proceeding into the gorge the way you came. Another sign may have inaccurate mileages and indicate that you are on the LITTLE WINES LOOP, an older name for this trail. From here back to camp, the trail is fast and fun.

8.3 (3.2) Reach the gravel surface of Big Island Road at a sign pointing the way but without mileages. Cross the road, and immediately afterward, reach an important intersection with Big Island Loop. If you are combining Big Island Loop and Pilot-Wines Loop, or simply want to head down to Big Island, turn right (north) and flip to mile 3 of the Big Island Loop description (see next trail). To continue on Pilot-Wines Loop, turn left (south), riding parallel to Big Island Road. The two trails are shared for the next 1.7 miles. Soon after the intersection, you will cross Big Island Road again and continue on its east flank. The trail veers eastward along a narrow, dry ridge for a while, then veers back westward toward the road again.

9.5 (2.0) Cross a small, ephemeral creek lined with hemlock, pawpaw, and magnolia.

10.0 (1.5) Reach an important three-way intersection with lots of signs. The right fork is where Big Island Loop leaves the Pilot-Wines Loop and heads west to Indian Dome Rock House, a worthwhile 1.2-mile (round-trip) side trip to a humongous rock house that is domed like an outdoor bandshell. We do not include this trip in the mileage here, but thanks to NPS signs, the trail to the rock house is fairly obvious. For detailed description, flip to mile 11.6 in the description of Big Island Loop (Trail 11). To head back to camp on the Pilot-Wines Loop, take the left fork, which turns straight east and descends into the ravine of Indian Rock Branch. In about 0.2 mile, the trail crosses the creek on a wood bridge in an area devastated by the 1998 storm, with massive piles of pine tree boles. Please do not water your horses here; there is a low-water crossing just 50 feet away—a nice, wide creek with good water. Climb steeply out of the ravine and start on a long stretch of soft sand, which is easy on a horse's hooves, but mountain bikers will find cruel punishment this close to the end of the loop.

10.9 (0.6) Reach a fork in the trail. The right fork leads directly back to the horse camp in about 0.5 mile; the left fork leads directly back to the equestrian trailhead in about 0.6 mile.

11.5 (0.0) Station Camp Horse Camp or Equestrian Trailhead. If you are going to go clockwise on the loop, head northeast on one of the wide, sandy horse trails.

11 Big Island Loop

TYPE OF TRAIL: Horseback riding, mountain biking, and hiking.

TYPE OF ADVENTURE: Loop in the river gorge, with a spur to a spectacular rock house.

TOTAL DISTANCE: 13.7 miles.

DIFFICULTY: Strenuous.

TIME REQUIRED: Half to full day.

SPECIAL CONCERNS: Gravel road crossings; steep descent; long muddy climb; river crossing.

WATER AVAILABILITY: Good on trail; abundant at or near trailheads.

SCENIC VALUE: Excellent: The river gorge is beautiful, and Indian Dome Rock House is spectacular, but no overlooks.

USGS MAP: Barthell SW.

BEST STARTING POINT: Station Camp Horse Camp or Equestrian Trailhead.

Overview: This loop traverses the gorge slope from the plateau surface to river level and back and is simply great for horseback riding and mountain

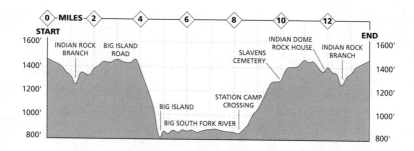

biking. The pathway on the plateau is smooth rolling gravel and sand. The pathway along the east bank of the river is flat and can be muddy—but not nearly as muddy as River Trail West, on the west bank of the river. The steep section leading to Big Island is groomed gravel with few rocky sections and is no problem either way on horse or bike. However, the steep section leading to Station Camp is nearly all slick mud, exposed sandstone, and deep, narrow ruts; we suggest doing that section in an uphill direction regardless of your mode of travel.

The loop itself is only about 10.9 miles long, but horses can access the loop only from Station Camp Horse Camp if they use a 1.4-mile spur trail, hence the 13.7 total miles. We include three logical side trips in the mileage: a 0.1-mile trip to the Big South Fork River at Big Island, a 0.1-mile trip to the river at Station Camp Crossing, and a 0.4-mile trip to Indian Dome Rock House. These are the main attractions of this loop, but there are at least four longer add-on trails leading to additional natural, geological, and/or historical attractions.

First, you can cross the river at Big Island and visit the historical No Business Community and Terry Cemetery via Longfield Branch–No Business Trails (Trail 19) and go on to Maude's Crack (Trail 18), adding about 8 miles (round-trip) to the loop, which includes a steep climb. Or cross the river at Station Camp Crossing and go west to the Charit Creek Lodge via Station Camp Creek Trail, described in Trail 21. This adds an easy 8 miles (round-trip) to the loop with lots of creek crossings. Before planning to cross at either of these locations, check to be sure that horses are still allowed to cross the river and, if so, that the river is running low enough to cross, or you may be disappointed. From Station Camp Crossing, River Trail East (Trail 12) takes you along the same side of the river to Angel Falls and back, adding 12 easy miles (round-trip) to the loop. Best of all, Big Island Loop is shared with the Pilot-Wines Loop (Trail 10) for 1.7 miles. Athletes looking for a long training session can combine the loops—going

The downstream side of Big Island

counterclockwise on both—making a 23.5-mile epic journey, not counting the wonderful side trips.

Finding the trailhead: Follow the directions to the Station Camp Equestrian Trailhead (and see Map 9). Horse trailers are not allowed in the gorge below Chimney Rocks, but bikers and hikers can start at Station Camp Crossing and River Access.

Trail Description

We cover this loop counterclockwise because the steep, muddy, and eroded section above Station Camp Crossing is safer to climb than descend. Bikers starting at Station Camp Crossing will miss the sandy access trails from the horse camp so should subtract three miles and enter the description at mile 8.2.

From the horse camp, take the perimeter trail around to where it meets the camp entrance road and fee kiosk; head northeast on the wide trail leading to Indian Dome Rock House and Big Island Loop, merging with Pilot-Wines Loop in about 0.5 mile. From the equestrian trailhead, punch into the woods and turn left (north) on the Pilot-Wines Loop, which will merge with the horse camp access trail in about 0.6 mile. After the two access trails merge, everyone is heading north on the Pilot-Wines Loop—a wide, sandy trail that descends steeply into the ravine of Indian Rock Branch.

1.2 Ford a tributary of Indian Rock Branch, a nice, wide creek with good water. Soon after the ford, the trail crosses Indian Rock Branch on a wood bridge in an area devastated by the 1998 storm, with massive piles of pine tree boles.

1.4 Intersect Big Island Loop and turn right to go counterclockwise on the portion of trail shared between Big Island Loop and Pilot-Wines Loop. Signs point you in the right direction, but the mileages along this route were slightly off in 2000.

1.9 Cross a minor headwater flanked with hemlock, pawpaw, and magnolia, then climb and crest a ridge at about 2.4 miles. The trail veers eastward along a narrow, dry ridge for a while, then veers back westward along the ridge, climbing knobs and dipping into saddles. Big Island Road comes into view at about 2.8 miles.

3.0 Reach a clearly marked intersection where Pilot-Wines Loop splits off Big Island Loop. The trail crosses Big Island Road, staying parallel to and within sight of the road. In about 0.2 mile, the trail curves around the upper reaches of a headwater ravine in a beautiful forest with an open understory. The trail is a hard-packed surface with really fast and fun turns on horseback or bike.

3.8 Intersect Big Island Road again at its very northern tip and enter the narrow, eroded parking and turnaround area. Go around the metal gate and begin the steep 0.9-mile plunge into the river gorge. Horseback riders should check their tack and tighten their girth, and bikers should make sure their brakes are in good order. The trail is well groomed and the descent is not so rocky or steep to be dangerous, but loose gravel can fell a mountain bike or trip a horse without warning. Entering the gorge below sandstone walls, you will enter a rhododendron and hemlock forest. The lower portion of the descent is a bit rockier than the upper.

4.8 At the bottom of the gorge slope, you will reach a tiny creek and a trail intersection with signs delineating loop mileages and Big Island Crossing to the right. We recommend visiting the river crossing to water your horse, splash your face, go swimming, and check out Big Island—a place where the river splits into two shallow riffles. Turn right (northwest) and walk your horse or bike a short distance to the river on the extremely rocky, wet trail through an old road cut.

If you plan to swim or wade in the river with your horses, be aware that several species of endangered mussels occur in the shallow shoal at Big Island Crossing. To accommodate all types of users without compromising the mussels, the NPS has flagged a narrow lane for horses. You can swim and play anywhere on the river, but please use only this cleared lane when watering or wading with your horses. The crossing could eventually be closed to horse traffic (or bridged) if a direct causal link between horse traffic and negative impact on mussels is made.

Big Island is nothing more than a massive pile of silt, sand, gravel, boulders, and logs deposited in the river by No Business Creek, which enters from the northwest. Like all other creeks on the Cumberland Plateau, this creek naturally carries huge loads of suspended particles—the product of erosive processes that eat into the gorge, knocking massive boulders off its rim. Although Big Island was probably a natural feature, past logging practices and activities in the No Business Community clearly influenced erosional processes and, in turn, the size and shape of the island. Note the small, twisted sycamores on the upstream side of the island, pummeled by water and floating debris with every flood. You may find a 20-foot-high pile of logs and debris on the west side of the island, blocking the old trail.

This intersection is also the connection for the No Business Trail (part of Trail 19), which continues west from Big Island for about 3 miles up into the No Business Creek watershed then climbs out of the creek gorge to a trailhead and parking area at Terry Cemetery and on to Maude's Crack (Trail 18). If you are accessing Big Island Loop from Terry Cemetery, enter the trail description here. After watering your horses or making a side trip, return to the intersection.

You can also cross the river here and take River Trail West all the way south to Station Camp Crossing and cross back over the river again. However, River Trail West is the muddiest trail in the NRRA (maybe the muddiest trail we have ever been on)—bad enough to suck the shoes off your horse. At no time of the year is this trail good for horseback riding, and it is nearly impossible to ride on a mountain bike because the sticky mud will coat your tires so badly they will lock up. Big Island Loop is much nicer, so stay on the east side of the river.

4.9 Back on Big Island Loop, turn right (southwest). For the next 3 miles you will be on a wide, level pathway perched slightly above river level on its east bank and will cross a number of tiny tributaries. Huge sycamore and river birch line the trail, their roots and branches adapted to the spring floods that scour their root systems and hang debris in their branches high above your head.

5.2 Cross Cold Spring Branch and soon pass a water-filled secondary river channel formed by a sandbar between it and the river channel. These are important breeding sites for amphibians. Soon you will notice hitching posts and a trail on the left leading up to Burke Cabin, perched above the river at 5.4 miles. The wood structure has a wide wraparound porch, a sandstone fireplace, several rooms, and usually some leftover items, including canned goods, gas, ketchup, garbage bags, a mirror, a broom, and a dustpan. The metal roof makes a great sound in a rainstorm!

Back on the trail, continue southwest along the river, crossing small tributaries at 5.5, 6.1, and 6.4 miles. The trail becomes a bit muddy in places and has been stabilized in places with coarse railroad gravel, making the trail bumpy for bikers and increasing the chance of horse hoof damage. Please do not leave the established pathway to go around puddles; the trail is firm even underwater.

8.2 After passing some big campsites, you will reach the parking area at the Station Camp River Access. You will want to water your horses well before making the difficult ascent to the gorge rim, so look for Station Camp Crossing—a wide gravel path leading down to the river just south of an interpretive sign and self-pay station at the north end of the parking area. This is only a 0.1-mile sidetrip. At the river, horses are confined to a narrow lane marked with flagging like the one at Big Island Crossing, also because of endangered mussels.

If you want to see more of the river corridor and add more mileage to this loop, continue south on River Trail East (Trail 12) for up to 6 miles (one-way) to a point just north of Angel Falls. Most of the trail is very similar to the section you just completed but ends in a complicated climb along a steep gorge slope. A gate prevents horses and bikes from continuing south to Leatherwood Ford on the Angel Falls Trail (Trail 37), but you can easily get to Angel Falls on foot. You can also cross the river to reach the Charit Creek Lodge on Station Camp Creek Trail, part of Trail 21. The trail is nearly flat but crosses the hemlock-lined creek six times near deep pools, and the lodge is a wonderful historical diversion with sodas, candy bars, and some great conversation. If you do either of these side trips, be certain to water your horses one more time before the brutal climb.

From Station Camp Crossing turn left (north), heading uphill on Station Camp Road. The trail shares the road for a short distance, so watch carefully for vehicles.

8.5 At a sign indicating that no horses are allowed on the road past that point, the trail leaves the road on the right (east) and climbs steeply on a muddy, eroded trail. After passing some nice sandstone walls, look for some large beech and tulip poplar. You are climbing the steep south-facing slope on the north side of Slavens Branch, a small creek like the others you crossed near the river. In less than a 0.5-mile you will reach switchbacks that alternate between level and steep.

9.4 High on the slope after a really muddy section, you will reach a rocky portion of the trail with exposed sandstone surfaces that could be dangerous even when dry. We describe this trail counterclockwise so that you are climbing rather than descending at this potentially dangerous spot. A flat section along a dry ridge with small trees and lots of storm damage may give the impression that you are done climbing, but you are far from done!

9.9 At a sandy intersection on your left, look for Slavens Cemetery near the road, a large site with lots of tombstones. Those of you making this brutal climb on a mountain bike may find this spot appropriate—but we assure you, the worst is over!

10.2 Cross Station Camp Road where a sign correctly indicates that you have been climbing for nearly 2 miles. The trail is very sandy on the north side of the road—great for horses, but it may be quite difficult on a mountain bike, especially after the climb. Pass a huge rock house with dripping or possibly flowing water and damp sand and mud underneath. Avoid watering your horses in these sensitive areas; horse traffic disturbs the soft soil, rendering it unsuitable for the rare plants that normally grow in these environments.

10.5 Cross another tiny headwater on a wood bridge among a carpet of ferns, big white oaks, hickories, and white pines. Please do not leave the trail to water your horses in this sensitive area.

11.1 Cross Big Island Road just north of its intersection with Station Camp Road. You may notice morning glories flowering in summertime. The next section is flat, groomed gravel.

11.6 Go right (south) at the fork leading to Indian Dome Rock House, one of the best rock shelters in the entire NRRA. You may hear lots of hooded warblers along this trail, small yellow birds flitting around nervously in understory trees.

11.8 Hitching posts indicate that horses (and bikes) should not go any farther. Continue to the rock house on foot; the trail is narrow and lies in a sensitive plant community, and horses and bikes will badly disturb the soil under the rock house. Inconsiderate riders who take horses and bikes into restricted areas will almost certainly be the cause of trail closures; please don't be part of the problem.

This large rock house is called a "dome" because the roof is higher on the inside than at the opening. Water percolates through the sandstone roof, causing thin slabs to slough off the roof, making the inside gradually taller and the overlying strata thinner. If all the physical forces are just right, in a geological wink of an eye, water will eat through the roof and give rise to a spectacular arch with a smaller rock house behind (like Needle Arch).

12.0 Back at the loop trail, turn right (east). The trail takes you along the plateau above Indian Dome Rock House, the top of which is a few hundred feet into the woods south of the trail.

12.3 This intersection closes Big Island Loop. Turn right on Pilot-Wines Loop, the access spur leading back to camp, and cross Indian Rock Branch at 12.5 miles.

13.2 At the fork go right to head back to camp in 0.5 mile, or go left to return to the equestrian trailhead in 0.6 mile. Your cumulative mileage is just under 14 miles, including the short side trips to Big Island Crossing, Station Camp Crossing, and Indian Dome Rock House.

12 River Trail East

TYPE OF TRAIL: Horseback riding, mountain biking, and hiking.

TYPE OF ADVENTURE: Ride an old tram road deep in the river gorge to Angel Falls.

TOTAL DISTANCE: 12 miles (round-trip).

DIFFICULTY: Moderate.

TIME REQUIRED: 2 to 4 hours.

SPECIAL CONCERNS: Short section along a steep slope; hiking-only trail south of Angel Falls.

WATER AVAILABILITY: Abundant on trail and near trailhead.

SCENIC VALUE: Excellent: dense riparian forest, clean river and creeks, but no overlooks.

USGS MAPS: Barthell SW and Honey Creek.

BEST STARTING POINT: Station Camp Crossing or Equestrian Trailhead.

Overview: This level trail immerses you in the beautiful riparian forest on the eastern bank of the Big South Fork River. For the most part, the trail is perched above the river, giving you a birds'-eye view of birds flitting around in sycamore, river birch, sweetgum, and other magnificent trees rooted along the bank of the river. A bird list for this trail would include any of the riparian species: pileated woodpeckers, wood thrushes, yellow-billed cuckoos, blue herons, kingfishers, and wood ducks, as well as many species of warblers. You will turn away from the river into ravines of small tributary streams, crossing them at fords or on wood bridges among rhododendron and hemlock. The pathway is mostly a wide logging and mining tram with a smooth dirt and gravel surface, but the tram is rutted and muddy in some spots. Near the south end, a precarious singletrack section makes you scramble along the steep gorge slope in deep, sticky mud.

Although the tram road physically extends south all the way to Leatherwood Ford as Angel Falls Trail (Trail 37), the multiuse designation ends just north of Angel Falls, a churning Class IV rapids surrounded by a splendid boulder garden. Leave your steeds and continue another 0.1 mile on foot to reach Angel Falls, a must-see area where you can swim, bask in the sun, or take a nap on a boulder beneath a twisted sycamore. A number of

Map 10—River Trail East, Grand Gap Loop, John Muir Trail

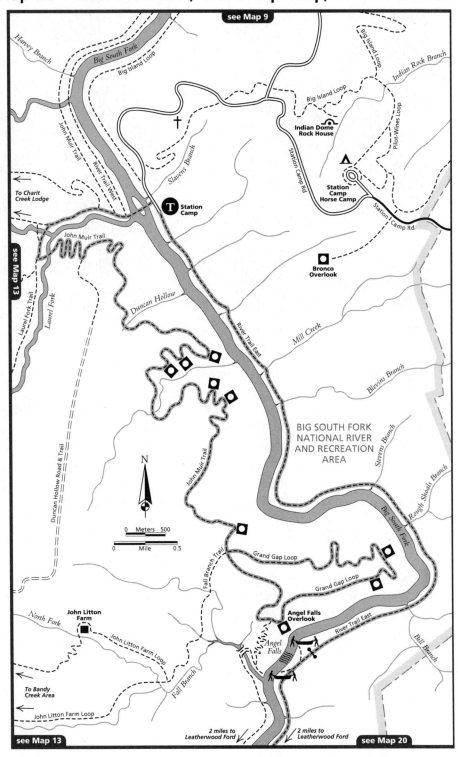

see Map 9

Harvey Branch

Big South Fork

Big Island Loop

Big Island Loop

Big Island Loop

Indian Rock Branch

Pilot-Wines Loop

Indian Dome
Rock House

Station Camp Rd

Station
Camp
Horse Camp

Station Camp Rd

John Muir Trail

River Trail West

Slavens Branch

To Charit
Creek Lodge

Station
Camp

John Muir Trail

see Map 13

Laurel Fork Trail

Laurel Fork

Duncan Hollow

River Trail East

Bronco
Overlook

Mill Creek

Blevins Branch

BIG SOUTH FORK
NATIONAL RIVER
AND RECREATION
AREA

Stevens Branch

N

Duncan Hollow Road & Trail

John Muir Trail

0   Meters   500
0   Mile   0.5

Fall Branch Trail

Grand Gap Loop

Big South Fork

Rough Shoals Branch

Grand Gap Loop

North Fork

John Litton
Farm

John Litton Farm Loop

Angel Falls
Overlook

River Trail East

Bill Branch

Angel
Falls

To Bandy
Creek Area

John Litton Farm Loop

Fall Branch

see Map 13

2 miles to
Leatherwood Ford

2 miles to
Leatherwood Ford

see Map 20

Kids enjoying the Angel Falls boulder garden

campsites lie along the river near Angel Falls, enabling an overnight stay in a remote stretch of the river gorge.

This trail is a good add-on to other hiking and multiuse trails. Hikers can start from either end of this trail. From the south, start on Angel Falls Trail (Trail 37) and just keep going. From the north, hikers and mountain bikers can start at Station Camp Crossing or the equestrian trailhead. Because horse trailers are not allowed in the gorge below Chimney Rocks on Station Camp Road, horseback riders can only reach this trail via other trails. The closest equestrian access from the east is Station Camp Equestrian Campground and Trailhead using Big Island Loop (Trail 11). From the west, horseback riders and mountain bikers can access this trail from Bandy Creek Equestrian Trailhead via Duncan Hollow Trail (in Trail 29) or from Charit Creek Lodge via Station Camp Creek Trail or Hatfield Ridge Trail (both in Trail 21).

Finding the trailhead: Follow directions to the Station Camp Area and see Map 10.

Trail Description

We start from the south end of the long gravel parking area at Station Camp Crossing. Mileages in the opposite direction are provided in parentheses.

0.0 (6.0) From the south end of the Station Camp parking area, head south past the metal gate that blocks vehicles from the trail. Here the groomed gravel trail is level. You will cross small, unnamed, intermittent tributary creeks at miles 0.4 (5.6) and 0.6 (5.4). Near a noticeably wider, permanent creek at mile 1.1 (4.9), the river has cut its way down to limestone—one of the few areas of the NRRA where limestone is exposed. Species of plants that are limited by lack of calcium in the rest of the NRRA are present in areas with limestone exposures. Mill Creek lies at mile 1.7 (4.3), followed quickly by Blevins Branch. All these small tributaries drain the east slope of the gorge, starting as surface runoff and groundwater bubbling from springs at the base of the sandstone bluffs lining the gorge, then picking up steam and cutting steep, narrow ravines into the gorge slope, eroding the gorge ever eastward in a process called head-cut erosion.

2.0 (4.0) The trail starts on a gentle, right-handed (westward) turn and at about mile 2.5 (3.5) reaches the westward tip of the wide ridge that diverted the river in this direction. Notice how the floodplain widens out on the inside bend of the river; the forces of deposition having taken over. The trail then curves back to the east and proceeds east-west.

3.0 (3.0) The physical character of the riparian zone changes from this point southward, littered with more huge boulders and rimmed by sandstone walls. Cross Stevens Branch, Rough Shoals Branch, and Bill Branch—all with larger watersheds than the previous creeks. The tram road starts getting soft in some spots but not as soft as many of the other river trails. You will pass a few backwater areas impounded by the tram road, mimicking nicely the natural process where water becomes ponded behind high sandbars deposited near the river channel. These ephemeral habitats are essential, fishless breeding sites for amphibians, including spotted salamanders, spring peepers, Fowlers toads, pickerel frogs, and wood frogs.

3.6 (2.4) After passing a small spring run originating from a rock shelter, you may see a faint suggestion of a road that climbs the gorge slope and over a culvert. This is the old John Smith Road, an access road to a mine site. Look for some really large tulip poplars between the trail and the river. In this area the top of the west side of the gorge is at a fairly low angle, so a late afternoon sun washes the gorge in beautiful light.

4.1 (1.9) In July 2001 the trail was washed out by flooding for more than 100 feet. If it has not been fixed, you may have to ride directly in the "new" streambed among large cobblestones.

4.4 (1.6) Cross a tiny creek with iron ore deposits on the rocks, an indication of low-level acid mine drainage resulting from past mining practices in the river gorge (see ecology chapter). Soon after that, pass through the John Smith Place, the remains of his old homesite and mine, now just an old field bisected by a tiny creek. Just beyond, the trail ascends steeply to an intersection with a gravel road on your left (east). This is an access trail from Angel Falls Village, a subdivision on the plateau outside the NRRA boundary. Descend to the river again.

4.8 (1.2) Cross another beautiful creek, then climb away from the river on a narrow singletrack path perched precariously along the gorge slope. The trail is slippery and dangerous in spots, so dismount to ensure that you or your horse don't lose your balance and slide down to the river. There are a few good campsites in this area, but most are a bit far from the river.

5.4 (0.6) Begin a very steep, muddy climb. The trail has been stabilized with water bars to prevent erosion in an area that stays wet most of the year.

6.0 (0.0) Reach the end of the trail at a horse-proof wood fence blocking travel farther south and a sign saying HIKING ONLY. This sign is routinely destroyed by dissatisfied customers, despite the fact that the NRRA allows more freedom of access than most other federal areas. Please heed the trail designations established by the NPS; failure to do so will probably result in less freedom. Be an ambassador for other considerate users!

On the other hand, don't miss Angel Falls just because you can't get there with your horse or bike. It is only 0.1 mile from the gate. You can tie your horse or lock your bike on the fence or picket-line or cross-tie your horse to nearby trees and walk to the wood platform overlooking Angel Falls. Better yet, walk down to Angel Falls to go swimming (*never* swim upstream of Angel Falls!), or rock-hopping, or take a nap. (Flip to Trail 37 for more on this wondrous area.)

Divide Road Area

13 Rock Creek Loop

TYPE OF TRAIL: Hiking only.

TYPE OF ADVENTURE: Trek in the riparian zone of a large, clean tributary.

TOTAL DISTANCE: 7.1 miles.

DIFFICULTY: Moderate.

TIME REQUIRED: Half day.

SPECIAL CONCERNS: A few slippery wooden bridges over small streams.

WATER AVAILABILITY: Abundant on trail; none at trailhead.

SCENIC VALUE: Excellent: mature riparian forest, few geological features, no vistas.

USGS MAPS: Sharp Place and Barthell SW.

BEST STARTING POINT: Rock Creek Trailhead.

Overview: The highlight of this trail is its beautiful section along the bank of pristine Rock Creek, a significant tributary to the Big South Fork River. Veterans of this trail may shed a tear or two after seeing the extensive tree damage from a winter storm in 1998, but this loop is still a gem. Rock Creek flows over wide, flat sandstone shelves, shallow riffles, and huge boulders into deep, emerald pools. The gorge is deep and dark, lined with hemlock and beech, and in one ravine near Coffee Trail looms some of the largest timber in the area.

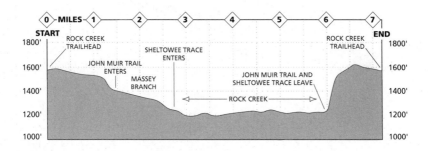

Map 11—Rock Creek Loop and John Muir Trail

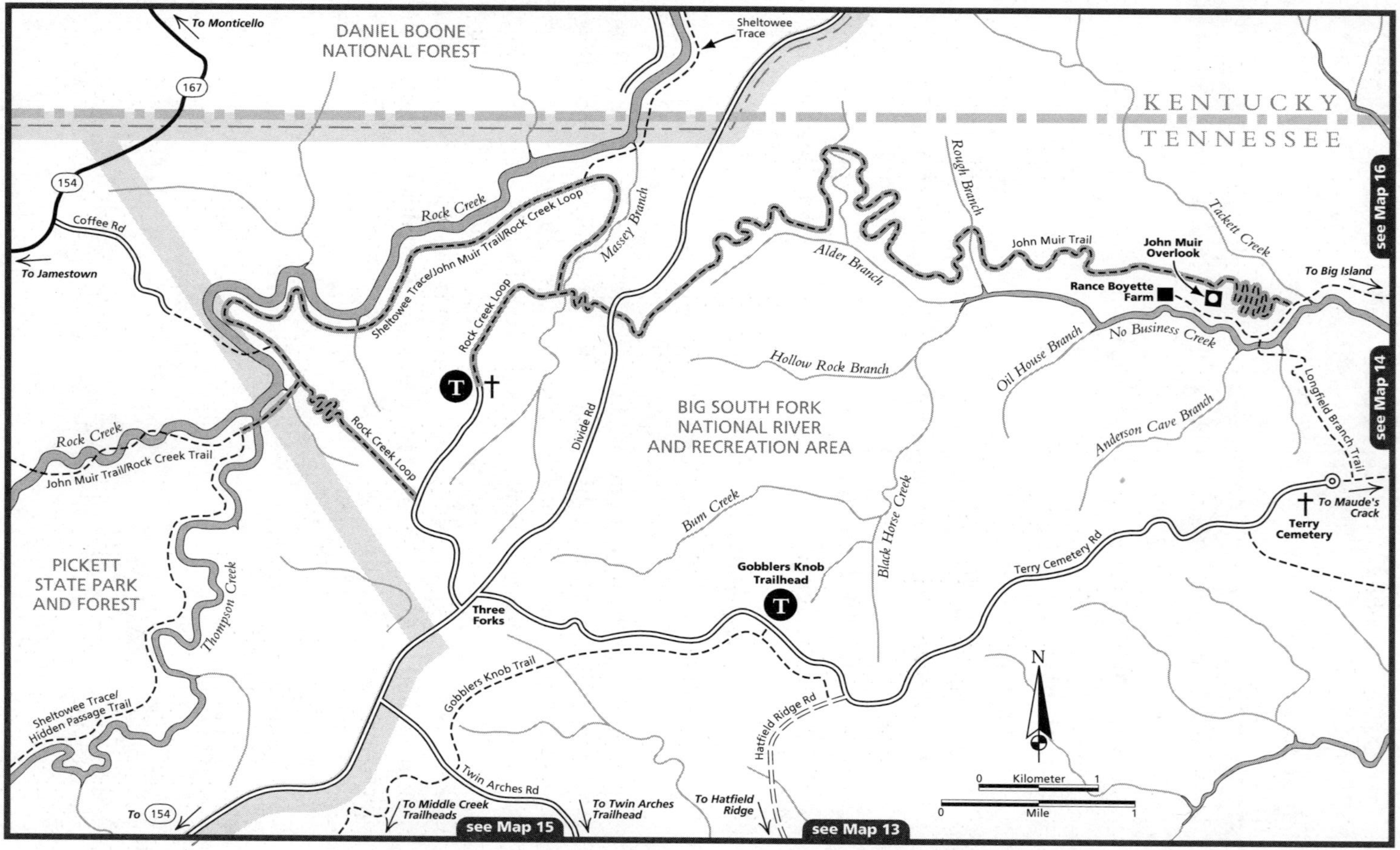

KENTUCKY

TENNESSEE

see Map 16

see Map 14

To Big Island

Longfield Branch Trail

To Maude's Crack

Terry Cemetery

Tackett Creek

John Muir Overlook

Rance Boyette Farm

No Business Creek

Anderson Cave Branch

John Muir Trail

Oil House Branch

Terry Cemetery Rd

Rough Branch

N

Kilometer

Mile

Alder Branch

Black Horse Creek

Hollow Rock Branch

BIG SOUTH FORK NATIONAL RIVER AND RECREATION AREA

see Map 13

Gobblers Knob Trailhead

Sheltowee Trace

Hatfield Ridge Rd

To Hatfield Ridge

Massey Branch

Bunn Creek

DANIEL BOONE NATIONAL FOREST

Divide Rd

Three Forks

To Twin Arches Trailhead

Rock Creek

Rock Creek Loop

Sheltowee Trace/John Muir Trail/Rock Creek Loop

Gobbler's Knob Trail

Twin Arches Rd

see Map 15

To Middle Creek Trailheads

To Monticello

Rock Creek Loop

To 154

Thompson Creek

To Jamestown

Coffee Rd

167

154

Rock Creek

John Muir Trail/Rock Creek Trail

PICKETT STATE PARK AND FOREST

Sheltowee Trace/Hidden Passage Trail

Rock Creek Loop intersects three other trails. The John Muir Trail (JMT), a 48-mile through-hike described in Trail 43, enters the loop at mile 1.4 and leaves it at 6 miles, then ends 2.1 miles to the west in Pickett State Park and Forest. The Sheltowee Trace, which is not described in our book because it may be relocated, enters the loop at mile 2.6 and leaves at mile 6 with the JMT. Coffee Trail, a spur trail at the end of a gravel road off TN 154 north of Pickett State Park and Forest, enters at mile 5.6.

Finding the trailhead: Follow directions to Rock Creek Trailhead and see Map 11.

Trail Description

Head north-northeast on the logging road past Blevins Cemetery, maintained by Connie Parsons, a Jamestown resident. Most of the graves mark workers of Stearns Coal and Lumber Company and their relatives. The trail flanks a knob, the highest point on the trail, then follows a wide ridgeline. In summer, wood frog tadpoles thrash about in the puddles along this road. Most road puddles are ephemeral, but some on this trail last long enough to support wetland and aquatic plants. Along with eastern spotted newts, these puddles support a whole community of predators that live off tadpoles, including diving beetles, dragonfly and damselfly naiads, water boatmen, water striders, back swimmers, and fishing spiders. A short stop with an aquarium net is sure to yield some critters that kids usually find interesting.

After a few tenths you will stay straight at a signed intersection; in a few more tenths stay right at another well-signed intersection in an oak forest. You will be going in and out of mixed and dry pine forests along the ridge and will see and hear a diverse array of birds, from pine warblers and blue jays on the plateau to wood thrushes and yellow-billed cuckoos in moist ravines.

1.4 Just after a nice grove of young magnolias, descend into the Massey Branch watershed on switchbacks and reach Massey Branch at a wood bridge for the JMT. Do not cross this bridge unless you are hiking east toward No Business Creek. Stay left on Rock Creek Loop, which is shared with the western portion of the JMT for the next 5 miles along the creek.

Massey Branch is beautiful, flowing along flat sandstone, but many downed trees make the creek hard to access. In a short while cross a footbridge over the creek and climb to a rock wall with a small rock shelter. The trail gets rocky, and you will be able to find old railroad ties and coal pebbles along the treadway, all that is left of a logging railroad that used to carry timber between sites in Tennessee and Bell Farm, Kentucky. The preservation of the railroad ties is remarkable, given that they were cut from the surrounding forest and not preserved with the usual creosote. The red color in the creek is a result of iron precipitating out of the water, but we found a huge number of crayfish and other aquatic insects, indicating that the creek has decent water quality. Watch your step on this trail, as the railroad ties can be slick.

With the creek on your right, a small waterfall plunges over the top of a rock shelter with walls of cross-bedded sandstone—caused by variations in the way the strata were deposited millions of years ago—reminiscent of the beautiful sandstones in Zion National Monument and other national parks in the western United States. After getting away from the rock overhangs, you may see the rock walls lining Rock Creek gorge way off in the distance.

2.4 The trail curves left around the very northeastern tip of the ridgeline above your left shoulder, emerges in Rock Creek Gorge, and descends gently along the northwestern slope of the gorge. Because this was a railroad grade, it is fairly open, and you will find blackberries in summer. In a short while, turn right off the railroad grade and descend on two switchbacks past an immense white oak with a double trunk.

2.6 Stay left at the fork in the trail, the point where the Sheltowee Trace—marked by turtle blazes—meets the loop. If you are backpacking there is a fantastic campsite just after you get down to the creek in a dark hemlock forest, with access to Rock Creek at a sandbar. For the next 3.4 miles the trail lies along the south bank of Rock Creek in a really nice forest of large beech, hickory, hemlock, tulip poplar, and white pine, with plenty of rhododendron along the way. Watch carefully for the blazes, as this trail can be confusing where it joins and leaves the old railroad bed. You will return to the old railroad bed after some time, then back to the creek, then back up, and so on. The trail crosses wide alluvial plains of tributary streams and climbs up and down the side slopes, often on rock stairs, welcome footholds that keep you from slipping on the muddy slopes. There will be more good campsites under the hemlocks along the trail, some with swimming holes.

This is a good example of the cooler, darker aspect of north-facing slopes, which harbor very different plant communities from drier, south-facing slopes. You may see lush areas blanketed with maidenhair fern, two kinds of trillium, and basswood among huge beech trees. Watch for red efts, the fluorescent-orange terrestrial stage of eastern spotted newts. At creek crossings, aquatic invertebrates dwell under every rock, and some ravines are so dark and moist that you may see salamanders sitting out on the rocks during the daytime! Drip-walls, seeps, and stagnant backwaters support liverworts and sphagnum moss and fields of humongous boulders. We could not even begin to list the birds we have seen on this trail. Although river birch often show signs of beavers, the big piles of damaged trees are a result of the winter storm of 1998. Where Rock Creek flows over shallow sandstone shelves, you can see smallmouth bass patrolling for dace and other small fish and redhorse suckers rasping algae off the surface of submerged logs.

5.6 Coffee Trail is on your right, a short trail that crosses Rock Creek and ascends steeply to a gravel road off TN 154 among some of the largest beech, hemlock, and poplar in the region. A short side trip part way up the slope is worthwhile, but the trail is very steep.

6.0 The JMT and Sheltowee Trace leave Rock Creek Loop and enter Pickett State Park and Forest. Stay left to finish the loop, but gather your strength for the brutal climb just ahead. A campsite here lies in a low pocket that will flood if it rains, but it has nice access to the creek. The steep trail is well marked, passing moss-covered rocks, a beautiful rock house, and lots of rock outcrops. You will see at least three species of magnolia along this short climb.

6.2 Reach the top of the ridge, and continue southeast for another half mile. There are a few splits in the trail where a dirt logging road intersects it, but the trail is well blazed.

6.7 Turn left (north) on the gravel access road and head toward the trailhead at Blevins Cemetery, at 7.1 miles.

TYPE OF TRAIL: Hiking only.

TYPE OF ADVENTURE: Walk along the base of massive rock walls, overhangs, and rock houses.

TOTAL DISTANCE: 3.5 miles.

DIFFICULTY: Easy.

TIME REQUIRED: 2 to 4 hours.

SPECIAL CONCERNS: Some dangerous bluffs and possible falling rocks.

WATER AVAILABILITY: Adequate on trail; none at trailhead.

SCENIC VALUE: Excellent: very interesting geological area, but no overlooks.

USGS MAP: Sharp Place.

BEST STARTING POINT: Middle Creek Trailhead.

Overview: The geological wonderland along this great trail will be a surprise, as topographic maps barely suggest the massive Pennsylvanian Era sandstone walls you will be walking beneath. The trail is a wide, groomed path and is very easy to follow—worth your time if you really want to see lots of big walls on a fairly short trail. Many interesting fungi, mosses, liverworts, vascular plants, and animals can be found in the cool, moist habitats near the base of these walls. Springs emerge from the base of some walls, around which you will find wetlands supporting marsh vegetation. These are the headwaters of Ben Creek, a tributary of Laurel Fork of Station Camp Creek, which flows into the Big South Fork River.

For day hikers this short trail is best when combined with Slave Falls Loop (Trail 15), which leads to a spectacular waterfall, a narrow sandstone arch, and a humongous rock house. This 8.5-mile day hike makes the drive over more worthwhile. We describe the 0.8-mile trail connecting these loops in each individual trail chapter. Backpackers can add Twin Arches Loop (Trail 16) to that—a triple loop of about 19 miles—and include an overnight stay at Charit Creek Lodge, which allows you to make the entire trip with only a light day pack! This is truly the best two-day trip in the NRRA.

Map 12—Middle Creek, Slave Falls, Twin Arches, and Charit Creek Areas

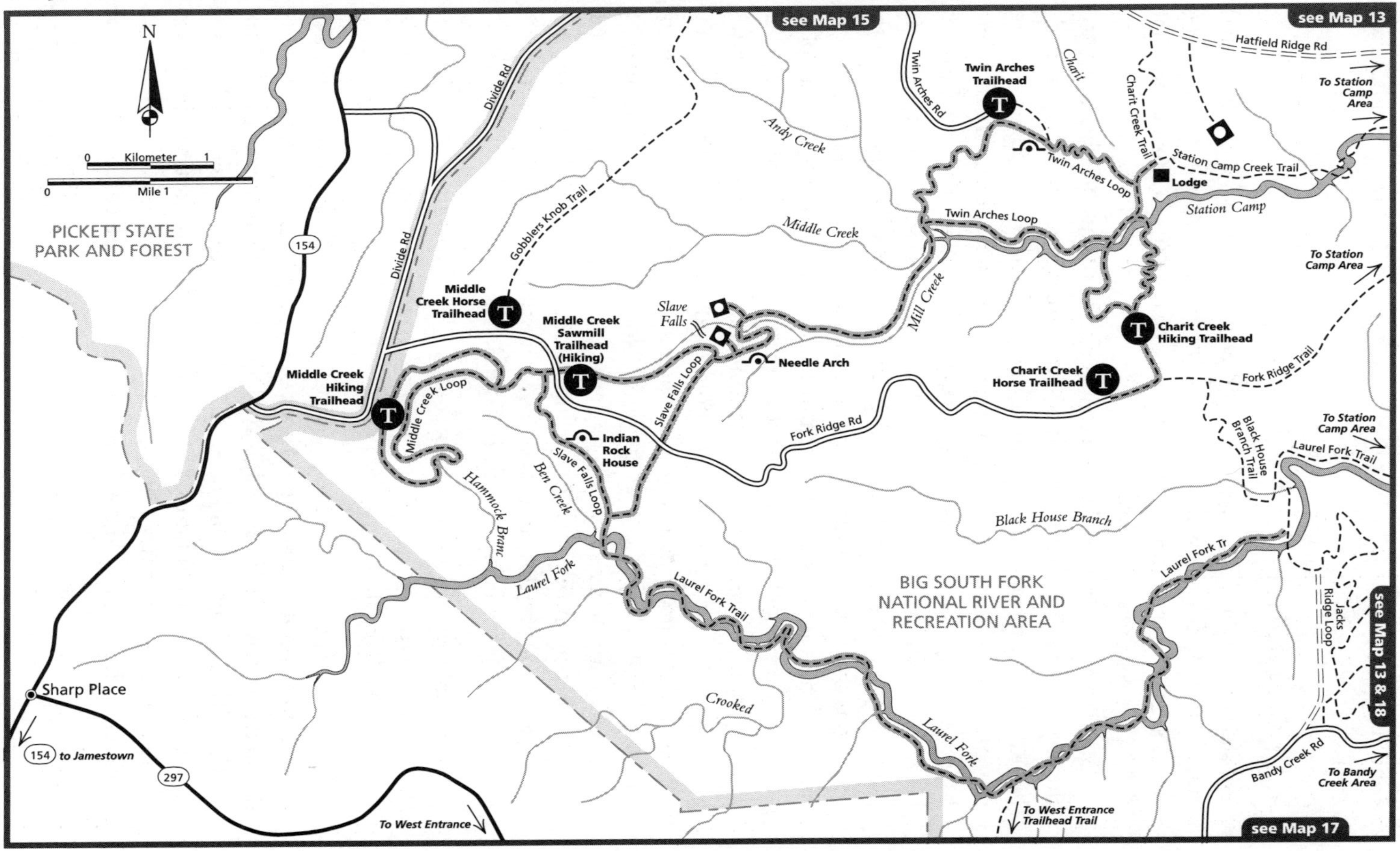

see Map 13

Hatfield Ridge Rd

To Station Camp Area

To Station Camp Area

Station Camp Creek Trail

Station Camp

Lodge

Charit Creek Trail

Charit

Twin Arches Loop

Twin Arches Trailhead

Twin Arches Rd

Twin Arches Loop

Mill Creek

Middle Creek

Andy Creek

Gobblers Knob Trail

Divide Rd

Middle Creek Horse Trailhead

Middle Creek Sawmill Trailhead (Hiking)

Slave Falls

Slave Falls Loop

Needle Arch

Middle Creek Hiking Trailhead

Divide Rd

154

PICKETT STATE PARK AND FOREST

N

Kilometer 1
0
Mile 1
0

To Station Camp Area

Charit Creek Hiking Trailhead

Charit Creek Horse Trailhead

Fork Ridge Trail

To Station Camp Area

Laurel Fork Trail

Black House Branch Trail

Black House Branch

Fork Ridge Rd

Indian Rock House

Slave Falls Loop

Ben Creek

Hammock Branc

Zunzal Fork

BIG SOUTH FORK NATIONAL RIVER AND RECREATION AREA

Laurel Fork Tr

Laurel Fork

Laurel Fork Trail

Crooked

see Map 13 & 18

Jacks Ridge Loop

To Bandy Creek Area

Bandy Creek Rd

see Map 17

To West Entrance Trailhead Trail

To West Entrance

Sharp Place

154 to Jamestown

297

see Map 15

Finding the trailhead: Follow directions to Middle Creek Trailhead and see Map 12.

Trail Description

We start at Middle Creek Trailhead and take you clockwise on the loop. If you are starting from Sawmill Trailhead, Slave Falls Loop, or other trails to the east, add 0.8 mile for the Middle Creek–Slave Falls Connector and start the trail description at mile 1.0.

Starting at the trailhead sign, go left (northeast) just inside the edge of the woods. At 1,705 feet in elevation, you are at the highest spot in the NRRA. In spring and early summer, listen for the cricketlike songs of mountain chorus frogs calling from road puddles near the trailhead. These frogs once helped us get back to our vehicle in the dark after our flashlight burned out! The trail parallels Divide Road in a dry, mixed forest with a few pines, then swings right (east) and parallels Fork Ridge Road. Note the numerous tree boles on the ground in various stages of decomposition by fungi and tiny animals that perform the important task of recycling plant biomass. The older the log, the better the habitat for worms, millipedes, centipedes, and insects and the salamanders, skinks, snakes, forest birds, and mammals that consume them. Red-eyed vireos, wood thrushes, and yellow warblers are regulars in this area, but you will hear a lot of upland and edge birds using the road corridor. Notice the transition to upland-plateau pine forest, a relatively young association identified by the presence of Virginia and shortleaf pine, lowbush blueberries, mountain laurel, and greenbrier. You are close to the edge of some tall bluffs, so don't wander in the woods without being extremely careful.

0.8 Veer right (south) and start descending. Water bars have been placed in the trail to prevent erosion. The trail takes you to the base of the bluffs that you were walking above only minutes before.

1.0 Reach a signed intersection with the Middle Creek–Slave Falls Connector, an 0.8-mile upland trail that takes backpackers and long-distance day hikers to Sawmill Trailhead, Slave Falls Loop, Twin Arches Loop, Laurel Fork Trail (Trail 17), and beyond. This connector is easy to follow and relatively flat (from 1,560 to 1,570 feet in elevation). It skirts the upper rim of the headwater streams of Ben Creek in a mixed upland forest, passing a sandstone bluff in an old field area, and meeting Slave Falls Loop near

Sawmill Trailhead (flip to mile 4.0 in that trail description). To continue on Middle Creek Loop, stay right at the intersection.

1.1 Cross a small creek on a footbridge, and prepare yourself for some spectacular geological scenery. For the next 2 miles, this trail goes back and forth along the convoluted southeastern slope of a ridgeline, intercepting one rock wall after another. We stopped counting after reaching ten massive walls, which actually form one continuous bluffline.

If you brought a flashlight, walls with numerous pencil-thin, horizontal cracks are very good for spotting slimy, zigzag, and even green salamanders. The wider cracks harbor huge crickets, millipedes, many different kinds of orb-weaving spiders, and even small mice and ground squirrels, which cache nuts and make nests in spots that seem impossible to reach without flying. High above, cliff swallows make nests on the rock walls.

Groundwater flows from the base of many of these walls, creating a cool, moist environment perfect for mosses, liverworts, and Lucy Braun's snakeroot, an endangered plant. Stay on the trail in moist areas, because even foot traffic can seriously damage the fragile vegetation growing on soft wet soil. Unfortunately, big piles of dirt at the second and third walls indicate that someone pilfered them of their historical and archaeological treasures. Northern dusky and four-toed salamanders love the sphagnum moss lining spring areas; larval spring, red, mud, and longtail salamanders can be seen where water collects into pools.

3.0 At the southern end of the series of rock walls, cross a few spring-fed creeks and climb up and down some rock stairs; after intercepting the wall about the tenth time, you will veer right (west) and ascend to the top of the bluffline.

3.2 Turn right on a nearly level logging road, which leads 0.3 mile back to the trailhead. We have seen hundreds of mountain chorus frogs, American toads, and gray tree frogs calling in the puddles along this road, which are apparently long-lived enough to harbor bullfrogs, eastern spotted newts, hellgrammites, and even aquatic beetles. In the evening you are likely to hear barred owls hooting.

15 Slave Falls Loop

TYPE OF TRAIL: Hiking only.

TYPE OF ADVENTURE: Hike to a high waterfall, sandstone arch, and massive rock house.

TOTAL DISTANCE: 4.2 miles.

DIFFICULTY: Easy.

TIME REQUIRED: 2 to 3 hours.

SPECIAL CONCERNS: Some slippery rocks, dangerous bluffs.

WATER AVAILABILITY: Abundant on trail; none at trailhead.

SCENIC VALUE: Excellent: interesting geological features, but no vistas.

USGS MAP: Sharp Place.

BEST STARTING POINT: Sawmill Trailhead.

Overview: Slave Falls, a high, free-falling column of water; Needle Arch, a narrow, 30-foot sandstone arch; and Indian Rock House, a humongous domed room, are the attractions that brighten this already wonderful loop. Although this trail is great for everyone, it provides a few special challenges for novice and even expert photographers interested in capturing great images of geological features. A few hints will save you some time, but you will have to rely on your knowledge of lenses (bring a 28mm or wider), exposure time (bring a tripod), and film latitude to get the great shots. Slave Falls faces directly east and Needle Arch is a southeastern exposure, so morning is the best time to photograph them. Bring a sturdy tripod so that you can blur the water with at least a one-second exposure. Indian Rock House is a southwest-facing room that is nicely lit anytime after noon.

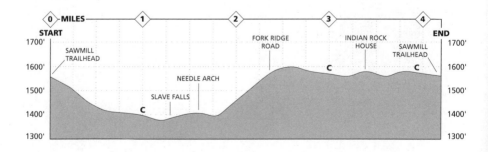

Slave Falls

However, this dark feature is somewhat difficult to photograph (bring a graduated neutral-density filter), so build your photography plans mainly around Slave Falls.

Day hikers should connect this trail with Middle Creek Loop (Trail 14), a 3.5-mile loop in a wonderland of high sandstone walls. Using the 0.8-mile connector trail, this makes a moderate day hike of 8.5 miles in fairly level terrain. Backpackers can connect this trail with Twin Arches Loop (Trail 16), one of the best trails in the NRRA. Including the 2-mile connector trail, this makes the entire trip about 14 miles long. Or combine all three of these loops for a 19-mile backpacking and geological extravaganza. A stay at Charit Creek Lodge means you can complete any combination of these loops with a light day pack. Slave Falls Loop is also the main entry point for Laurel Fork Trail (Trail 17), a long hiking trail generally used for backpacking and through-hiking to the Station Camp Area and beyond. Combine this with part of Trail 21 and a stay at the Charit Creek Lodge for an unforgettable backpacking trip.

Finding the trailhead: Follow directions to Sawmill Trailhead and see Map 12.

Trail Description

We describe this trail clockwise but also provide mileages in reverse (in parentheses) to make connections easier.

0.0 (4.2) From the grassy parking area at the trailhead, punch into the woods and head generally north, paralleling Fork Ridge Road on a wide trail in a young mixed pine, maple, and oak forest; then pass through a ravine with hemlock and sassafras (a bright green, three-lobed leaf).

0.1 (4.1) Turn right (east) onto the Slave Falls Loop at a sign with reassuring or frightening mileages, depending on your point of view. Once away from the road, the forest is a bit older, with nice hemlock, maple, poplar, white oak, chestnut oak, white pine, and hickory. Crows, chickadees, tufted titmice, red-eyed vireos, and black-throated green warblers can be heard along the trail.

0.6 (3.6) Cross a headwater stream that meanders across a wide floodplain covered in ferns. If you look carefully, you may notice a few American chestnut saplings—once the dominant forest tree in eastern North America until falling prey to a fungus introduced from Europe (see ecology section). Their leaf edges are saw-toothed, like that of a chestnut oak leaf if it had pointy instead of rounded teeth, and the saplings will succumb to the fungus before reaching maturity. After crossing a few more tiny tributary streams, the trail enters a dry forest dominated by Virginia pine, mountain laurel, and blueberry at the edge of the steep-walled ravine of Mill Creek on your left (north). Faint side trails lead to narrow, unprotected rock ledges from which you can see a rock wall and cavernous shelter, but be extremely careful, especially with children.

1.0 (3.2) At this signed intersection, instead of turning right (south) on Slave Falls Loop, forge ahead to Slave Falls and Needle Arch. In a few hundred feet you will reach yet another intersection. Here you can either turn left to go directly to Slave Falls in 0.2 mile or go straight to reach Needle Arch in 0.2 mile; we take you to the falls first. Turning left to Slave Falls, the trail descends quickly into the Mill Creek ravine and follows along the base of the bluffline that you may have seen from above. Different-sized cracks with different light and moisture regimes provide a wide range of microhabitats along the bluffline, resulting in a diverse array of plants, salamanders, and arthropods on the bluff walls. Look for the narrow vein of coal near ground level, formed over millions of years as ancient leaves were covered by sediments and became compressed beneath the immense weight of the sandstone strata above.

1.2 (3.0) Reach the protected overlook of Slave Falls, where Mill Creek plunges over a horseshoe-shaped bluff undercut by the erosive force of water. The falls face east and the sky opening ranges between 50 and 120 degrees, so photographs seem to be the best in the morning. In summer you can see fantastic reflections and rainbows in the morning mist when the sun shines directly on the falls.

The overlook platform is fenced for a good reason. The area under Slave Falls cannot be reached from the platform without climbing down a steep, muddy, eroded slope that has already suffered damage from unethical foot traffic. This is prohibited because it kills herbaceous vegetation and exposes the roots of trees lining the gorge, making the steep slope vulnerable to further erosion and other damage. The crumbling shale, soft mud, and fragile plants behind the falls are particularly vulnerable to damage from foot traffic.

During a salamander survey for the NPS, Todd hiked up Mill Creek to the base of Slave Falls (from below Needle Arch; see below) and found the aquatic larvae of northern dusky, spring, and two-line salamanders, along with a diverse array of aquatic invertebrates. These are all indicators of good water quality and indicate that at least the aquatic communities of Mill Creek have partially recovered from the extensive logging done in the area not long ago. From the falls overlook, return the way you came. You can visit the north side of the falls on the connector trail discussed below, so read on.

1.4 (2.8) Back at the intersection, turn left and go 0.2 mile to Needle Arch.

1.6 (2.6) Needle Arch, a narrow sandstone spine that looks like half of the eye of a sewing needle, is a classic example of a Cumberland Plateau sandstone arch. Once part of the rock shelter behind the arch, the composition of its sandstone roof and the erosive forces of water and ice had to be just right for such a thin spine to remain standing. There is a nice interpretive plaque at the arch. To continue Slave Falls Loop, return to the loop intersection at mile 1.0 above, and flip to mile 1.8 below.

Note: If you want to visit the north side of Slave Falls or are connecting with Twin Arches Loop (Trail 16), the 2-mile Slave Falls–Twin Arches Connector is described in the next few paragraphs. The trail descends nearly 400 feet in elevation, from 1,420 feet at Needle Arch to 1,040 feet at Jakes Place on Twin Arches Loop. From Needle Arch, continue walking east on the wide ridge covered in Virginia and shortleaf pine, mountain laurel, blueberry, and witch hazel. The trail starts descending and hugs the very eastern tip of the ridge upon which Needle Arch sits, curves back to the west, and enters the ravine of Mill Creek. The sandstone bluffs have odd iron deposits formed by differential erosion. The north-facing slope is covered with large hemlock, chestnut oak, beech, and magnolia, but you can see across the ravine to the south-facing slope due to tree-fall gaps from the 1998 storm. Continue descending toward Mill Creek, crossing numerous seeps, some supporting salamander populations and interesting bright-red slime mold.

Cross Mill Creek about 0.2 mile downstream of Slave Falls and veer back to the right (east). The 1998 storm felled many trees here, opening the previously rhododendron-lined creek zone to blackberries and even some marsh plants, which do well in sunny forest gaps. Shortly afterward, you will reach an intersection on your left with a trail that leads 0.2 mile upstream along the north side of Mill Creek to a wood overlook platform on the north side of Slave Falls. Please do not climb down to the plunge pool, because the trail is so wet, muddy, and slippery that you would do a lot of damage to the fragile plants in the area and would probably have to climb back down the creekbed to get back on the trail.

After revisiting Slave Falls, return to the intersection and hike east on the narrow path perched on the steep-sided slope of Mill Creek Gorge. The trees have been exposed to storm damage. There are many open areas choked with blackberries and other sun-loving herbaceous species, but you will also see some massive hemlock, white pine, white oak, and beech. Many types of fungi and invertebrates are attacking the boles of downed trees. Numerous small seepages flow across the trail for the next mile, and one of them has a nice waterfall that feels really good splashing on your face on a hot day. The trail stays fairly level, but the creek descends in its steep ravine as you proceed downstream, giving you great views into the canopy (great for bird-watching). There is a nice campsite between the trail and the creek. However, if you stay there, be careful on the steep, eroded trail leading down to the creek, and try not to cause any more damage to the creek bank. Much better campsites lie just ahead on Twin Arches Loop. Just after passing through a power line right-of-way inhabited by gnomelike cedars, you will cross Station Camp Creek on a wood bridge and intersect the Twin Arches Loop (Trail 16) near Jakes Place. This is the end of the connector, so flip to mile 2.7 in our description of Trail 16.

1.8 (2.4) Back at the intersection with Slave Falls Loop, turn left and ascend to a metal gate at the end of a two-rut logging road, blocking horses and motorized vehicles from proceeding down the trail. The forest is mostly white oak, maple, white pine, sassafras, blueberry, smilax, and mountain laurel. During summer you may startle large schools of silvery wood frog tadpoles in the puddles along the road. Adult wood frogs are identified by their overall bronze coloration and dark "mask" on their face. Continue hiking generally southwest on this logging road.

2.4 (1.8) Cross Fork Ridge Road and enter the headwater ravine of Thompson Branch, another tributary of Laurel Fork of Station Camp Creek. The berm of Fork Ridge Road has ponded some water that would have entered this watershed. Although it is artificial, it functions as a fish-less breeding site for amphibians and a valuable water source for forest mammals and birds, analogous to the many natural water-collecting depressions on the Cumberland Plateau. You will cross two footbridges and criss-cross Yellow Cliff Road, a logging and mining tram built by the Stearns Coal and Lumber Company. Follow the red arrowhead blazes across a wide ridgeline and enter the watershed of Ben Creek, another tributary of Laurel Fork.

3.0 (1.2) Reach the intersection with Laurel Fork Trail (Trail 17), which plunges into the dark, hemlock-covered gorge of Laurel Fork, a tributary of Station Camp Creek. There may be no signs at this intersection. If you are backpacking that trail, make a left turn (southwest) and begin the longest and most beautiful hike through a riparian zone in the NRRA (flip to the description of Trail 17, which starts on the Slave Falls Loop).

To continue on Slave Falls Loop, stay right (north) at this intersection. You will cross a wood bridge at a nice rock house with a spring and start descending into the very upper headwaters of Laurel Fork in a nice forest with lots of hemlock and magnolia.

3.4 (0.8) Look through the trees to the right for Indian Rock House, an immense overhang with a domed roof and sandy floor. The tiny cone-shaped pits in the sand are made by ant lions, the larval form of a flying insect that employs an ingenious method to capture ants and other insects. Their prey wander over the edge of the pit, tumble to the bottom of the cone, and are gobbled up by the ant lion.

After visiting Indian Rock House, continue north on the loop. The next rock wall on the trail looks something like a breaking wave. It has water-filled cracks that harbor red salamanders and a spring run flowing over solid sandstone. Thousands of cave crickets cling to the low roof in huddling masses—a serious gross-out even if they don't rain down on your head. After this wet rock house, you will zigzag along the side of the ridge and enter a pine zone where we have seen box turtles, black rat snakes, bobcats, and many species of birds, despite (or as a result of) the extensive damage caused by a winter storm in 1998. Stay straight on the loop trail at a confusing signed intersection. Another interesting wet rock wall has a sand "boil" where water comes out of the ground and flows under some nicely placed wood boardwalks that keep you from damaging the fragile wetland zone around the spring.

4.0 (0.2) Reach the intersection with the Middle Creek–Slave Falls Connector, which heads west to Middle Creek Loop (Trail 14) in about 0.8 mile. If you are combining these loops, turn left. The connector is easy to follow and relatively flat (from 1,560 to 1,570 feet in elevation), skirting the upper rim of the headwater streams of Ben Creek in a mixed upland forest and passing a sandstone bluff in an old-field area. This spur trail enters Middle Creek Loop at mile 1.0. To finish Slave Falls Loop turn right (east) and cross Fork Ridge Road, then make an immediate right (south) turn on the spur trail leading to Sawmill Trailhead.

4.2 (0.0) Sawmill Trailhead. If you are following the loop counterclockwise, go north on the spur trail, turn right (west), and cross Fork Ridge Road.

16 Twin Arches Loop

TYPE OF TRAIL: Hiking only.

TYPE OF ADVENTURE: Walk in a geological and biological wonderland.

TOTAL DISTANCE: 5.5 miles.

DIFFICULTY: Moderate.

TIME REQUIRED: Half day.

SPECIAL CONCERNS: Steep, ladderlike stairways, very dangerous ledges, falling rocks.

WATER AVAILABILITY: Adequate on trail; none at trailhead.

SCENIC VALUE: Spectacular: simply one of the best day hikes in the NRRA.

USGS MAP: Barthell SW.

BEST STARTING POINT: Twin Arches Trailhead.

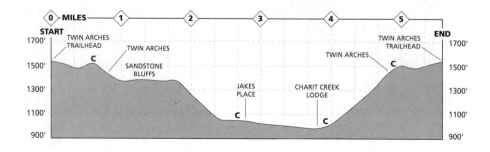

North Arch of Twin Arches

South Arch of Twin Arches

Overview: This trail has some of the best geological scenery in the NRRA, and Twin Arches are arguably the most impressive rock arches in the eastern United States. North Arch has a clearance of 51 feet and a span of 93 feet, and its deck is 62 feet high; South Arch has a clearance of 70 feet and a span of 135 feet, and its deck is 103 feet high. These features are beyond describing with words and are impossible to capture with photographs, although we try both. Equally impressive are the high sandstone bluffs of different colors and textures that tower above the trail. Deep in the gorge of Station Camp Creek and its tributaries, you will find Charit Creek Lodge nestled along the waterways that formed the arches through head-cut and lateral erosion. The buildings and surrounding fields, bordered by steep gorge slopes and high sandstone bluffs, will immerse you in a time when life was simpler yet more challenging and day-to-day activities were centered around survival.

This is a great way to access Charit Creek Lodge. If you hiked to the lodge from one of its other trailheads, we highly recommend that you at least make an out-and-back trip to Twin Arches, just over a mile from the lodge on a steep trail. You have other options for hiking or backpacking this loop, which is only 4.1 miles long without the 0.7-mile access trail. For a geological extravaganza, include Slave Falls Loop (Trail 15), which passes Slave Falls, Needle Arch, and Indian Rock House—all spectacular features. This trip includes the 2-mile Slave Falls–Twin Arches Connector, described briefly below, making the two-loop trip about 14 miles long. Adding Middle Creek Loop (Trail 14), a 3.5-mile hike in a wonderland of high sandstone walls (plus its 0.8-mile connector trail), makes the three-loop trip about 19 miles long. Starting at Middle Creek Trailhead and staying overnight at the lodge could be the best two-day "backpacking" trip on the Cumberland Plateau, requiring only day packs! That trip starts with Middle Creek Loop.

Finding the trailhead: Follow directions to the Twin Arches Trailhead and see Map 12.

Trail Description

We describe this trail counterclockwise, but also provide clockwise mileages (in parentheses) to make connections easier.

0.0 (5.5) The trail starts at the east end of the parking area on a wide trail with lots of water breaks. Descend slowly as you walk northeast in a young forest of oak, hickory, maple, and pine with a ground cover of dense mountain laurel, eventually grading into drier sites with lichen-moss communities near the plateau edge. The NPS has gone out of its way to make a special footpath in this area to keep people off these fragile plant communities, so please keep your group on the trail. You will probably hear the loud, long, bubbling trills of pine warblers.

0.3 (5.2) Although a sign points you left at this fork, both trails reach the same place eventually, so it does not matter which way you go. The left fork leads down stairs to the base of North Arch, but we prefer to start this wonderful hike with a magnificent view from the top of the arches, so take the right fork and climb a short flight of stairs. Take the short spur leading to a view of the massive rock walls lining Hatfield Ridge to the northeast, then get back on the trail.

0.7 (4.8) Descend a long, steep flight of stairs to the bare sandstone "deck" of the arches. Do not approach the rounded edge of the deck; it is deceptively dangerous, especially in areas with loose pine needles and thin soil. This was once a great example of the extremely fragile lichen-moss community on shallow tabletop soil; unfortunately, foot traffic has eliminated these plants from all but the edges of the deck. Lots of eastern fence lizards will be seen perched on the deck's scraggly Virginia pines, with shallow root systems exposed and damaged by foot traffic. Try to walk on already-bare rock surfaces to keep the problem from getting worse. Bird-watchers will enjoy the canopy-level view and might have some close encounters with warblers and other species normally heard rather than seen. Lots of butterflies, beetles, and other interesting insects await the avid bug-watcher.

At the end of the deck, a faint trail climbs up a steep rock face to a spectacular panoramic view of Station Camp Creek Gorge. However, if you are not nimble enough to climb it without using the fragile vegetation as a handhold, please do not make the climb. We mention this secret spot with trepidation, in the hopes that our words will impress upon you the fragility of the vegetation communities that grow on these types of sandstone exposures. The weathered sandstone surface has shallow pits that make great napping spots. Please stay on the already-exposed areas of sandstone, and never approach the deceptively rounded edge. The pine trees are small and gnarled because of the high winds, harsh conditions, and thin soil on the deck. You will be lulled to sleep by mourning doves, cedar wax-wings, and the wind in the pines on this lofty perch. Wood thrushes and yellow-billed cuckoos beckon you from below.

When you are done on the deck, head down the stairs on the east side of the deck to a point between the twins: the beginning of the loop trail. We start the loop from North Arch, so turn right (south) and visit the larger South Arch first. The underlying cause of rock shelter and arch formation and the honeycombed surface of the rocks is small variations in the rate of erosion in rock strata of different age and chemical composition. A narrow crack in the rock in the southwest corner of the South Arch brings you through the ridge to the very tip of the ridgeline. Now head to North Arch.

To go counterclockwise on the loop, walk west beneath North Arch and look for a trail on your right that heads northwest along the base of the bluffline. To go clockwise and visit Charit Creek Lodge first, head east from the staircase and follow our description backward from mile 4.8 below. Heading northwest from North Arch, the next mile of trail lies at the base of some of the largest and most interesting sandstone bluffs in the region.

Although the bluff appears to be one massive wall skirting the southwestern edge of a ridge, topographic maps clearly show blufflines punctuated by steep, forested ridges, or "draws." The trail takes you out around these forested slopes and back to the bluffs many times in the next mile. In a number of overhanging areas, the erosive action of water and ice has caused big flakes to fall from under the dense capstone. These are the early stages in the formation of rock shelters, which eat their way into the side of the ridge from both sides, narrowing it and eventually meet in the middle to form an arch. Different walls appear to be in different stages of arch formation; one wall even has a place where you can see through a window under a newly forming small arch. However, tiny arches like this one are simply flakes falling off the bluff wall and last only an instant in geological time. It will be millions of years before this wide ridge becomes narrow enough to form more arches like the twins.

The bluffs have lots of interesting honeycomb or curtainlike formations, most caused by the action of water eroding strata of different hardness, grain size, and composition. In some spots, a bituminous coal vein gives you an eye-level view of what happened when the immense weight of sediments accumulating over millions of years slowly compressed layers of Pennsylvanian Era vegetation. Cliff swallows construct their nests high on the bluffs, their way of avoiding predators.

At the base of the bluffs, you will find ferns, mosses, liverworts, Lucy Braun's snakeroot, pawpaw, and other fragile plants that prefer cool, dark microclimates. A flashlight will expose the spiders, millipedes, cave crickets, and many other arthropods that live in the bluff cracks. The tiny cone-shaped pits in the sand were excavated by ant lions, ingenious larval insects described in the ecology section. The powdery sand below some of the bluffs is saltpeter, an ingredient of gunpowder, which was mined in the past. Water from drip-walls and springs collects in sand-bottomed spring runs with wetland plants growing along their edge—great habitat for many species of amphibians. These are the headwaters of Andy Creek, which flows into Laurel Fork of Station Camp Creek, a primary tributary of the river.

The southwest-facing slopes and ravines below the bluffs are blanketed by many species of plants, and this trail is a wildflower enthusiast's dream. Hemlock, poplar, beech, rhododendron, pawpaw, and ferns dominate the slopes, and you may notice a very large chestnut oak and the largest umbrella magnolia we have seen in the NRRA. Along with the constant scoldings of gray and ground squirrels, we generally hear chickadees, red-eyed vireos, tufted titmice, eastern phoebes, indigo buntings, nuthatches, pileated woodpeckers, and hooded, yellow, pine, black-throated green, and black-and-white warblers along this trail.

1.8 (3.7) Pass through a gap in the bluff and start the descent into the gorge of Andy Creek along a draw dominated by tulip poplar, chestnut oak, and white pine, some fairly large. At the tip of the draw you can hear Andy Creek off to the south. Descend the west slope of a steep-sided valley with a small waterfall free-falling over an undercut ledge. The ravine is shaded by large beech and hemlock and the understory layer is open, so the ground is covered in Boston fern, chain fern, Solomon's seal, and many other herbs. Five-lined skinks share downed trees with fungi and arthropods, decomposers of huge amounts of forest biomass.

2.5 (3.0) Enter the grassy old field of Jakes Place—an old homestead that is being invaded by gnomelike eastern red cedars and other forest species that will eventually render the field a forest unless the area is managed as a cultural landscape. This should be a great place to go birding early in the morning after a stay at Charit Creek Lodge, and serious birders should do this trail in the morning and evening. Prairie warblers are abundant, identified by their yellow color and ascending song, like a cicada or a reward in a hand-held video game.

When Jacob Blevins, Jr. (Jake), and his wife, Viannah, moved here in 1884, the house was already old. Many families lived at Jakes Place, which was built around 1816, but the Blevinses, who lived here until the 1930s, were the last. The gravesites of two of Jake and Viannah's children are located nearby. All that remains of Jakes Place is the firebox of the sandstone chimney. Joe Simpson bought Jakes Place and used the logs from the house to build the far bunkhouse cabin at Charit Creek Lodge.

Along with white-tailed deer, you may notice feral hog tracks along the trail. Hogs damage vast areas of ground cover and wetland vegetation with their rooting and wallowing. Approaching a wide floodplain, an open zone is carpeted with honeysuckle, an exotic vine from Asia that invades disturbed sites and eventually covers everything in sweet-smelling yellow flowers. Cross the marshy wetland on a boardwalk, and enter another old field with a fantastic campsite on the southeast edge.

2.7 (2.8) At the southeast end of the field, east of the campsite, lies an intersection with the Slave Falls–Twin Arches Connector, the 2-mile trail leading west to Slave Falls Loop (Trail 15) and beyond. If you are going to Slave Falls Loop or Sawmill Trailhead, turn right (south) here, cross the creek, and follow Mill Creek upstream for 2 miles. The trail climbs nearly 400 feet in elevation, from 1,040 feet at Jakes Place to 1,420 feet at Needle Arch. You will know you are on the connector if you pass through a power line right-of-way within a few minutes; the power line never crosses Twin Arches Loop. (For a detailed description of the connector trail that can be easily followed in reverse, flip to the "note" after mile 1.6 in the description of Trail 15.)

To continue on Twin Arches Loop, head east from the campsite on the southeast edge of the field, cross the small footbridge over Mill Creek, and pass a great swimming hole a few hundred yards east of the campsite. The beech and sycamore-dominated floodplain forest is fabulous, but the invasions of cedars and honeysuckle indicate that people have lived and worked in this area for some time. There is a phenomenal campsite under a dense canopy of hemlock. The trail winds its way along the north bank of the creek for about a mile.

3.6 (1.9) The trail descends and joins the Charit Creek Lodge Horse Trail (Trail 22) at an oblique angle near a humongous white oak tree, then passes the fallen chimney of the Tackett family cabin and graves from 1863. Soon after, you will pass the beautiful wood suspension bridge for the Charit Creek Hiking Trail (Trail 22) on your right.

3.9 (1.6) Charit Creek Lodge lies in the open area on your right (east) after you pass some horse hitching posts and cross Charit Creek on a culvert bridge. An overnight stay in this wonderful historical structure or one of the separate cabins is some of the best medicine money can buy. If you are day hiking, stop in for a soda, candy bar, and a chat with the folks running the lodge. (See the appendix for reservation information.)

After visiting the lodge, cross back over the bridge, turn right (north), and punch into the woods. The trail takes you upstream along the west bank of Charit Creek, a wide, flat floodplain in a dark forest of hemlock, beech, tulip poplar, and chestnut oaks shading mayapples, tiger lilies, and many other photogenic wildflowers. Soon you will veer left and start the very steep climb on switchbacks and long wood stairways. The forest changes to white pine, sugar maple, basswood, dogwood, white oak, pin oak, witch hazel, smilax, and many types of fern.

4.8 (0.7) Reach the base of Twin Arches, completing the loop. Photographers will want to check out the arches again, because the light surely has changed. Pictures of North Arch will be better in the afternoon, but South Arch is blocked on its west side by some large trees. Leaving the arches, you can go up and over the deck the way you came, or turn right (northeast) from the east side of North Arch and climb another set of stairs, reaching the spur trail about 0.3 mile from the trailhead.

5.5 (0.0) Arrive back at Twin Arches Trailhead.

TYPE OF TRAIL: Hiking only.

TYPE OF ADVENTURE: A long day hike, one-way through-hike, or part of a backpacking loop in a beautiful riparian zone.

TOTAL DISTANCE: 10.3 miles (one way).

DIFFICULTY: Easy.

TIME REQUIRED: Full day.

SPECIAL CONCERNS: All thirty creek fords are dangerous or impassible during floods.

WATER AVAILABILITY: Abundant on trail; none at west trailhead; abundant at east trailhead.

SCENIC VALUE: Excellent: healthy riparian forest and creek, but no big vistas.

USGS MAPS: Sharp Place, Stockton (optional), Honey Creek, and Barthell SW.

BEST START/END: Sawmill Trailhead (west) and Station Camp Crossing (east).

Overview: Laurel Fork is a tributary of Station Camp Creek, a slightly larger creek that flows into the Big South Fork River at Station Camp. This extraordinarily beautiful flat-bottomed creek is lined with huge boulders and primeval hemlock forests. A little creek rock flipping will reveal crayfish, mayflies, stoneflies, hellgrammites, water pennies (larval beetles), and many other kinds of invertebrates. These critters are all indicators of good water quality and are essential food for larval salamanders and fish. Fingerling smallmouth bass and bluegill may be found in pools, and northern hog

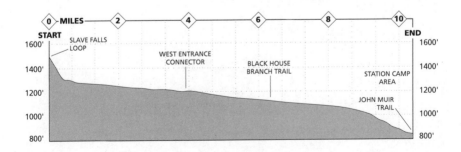

Map 13—North Bandy Creek Area

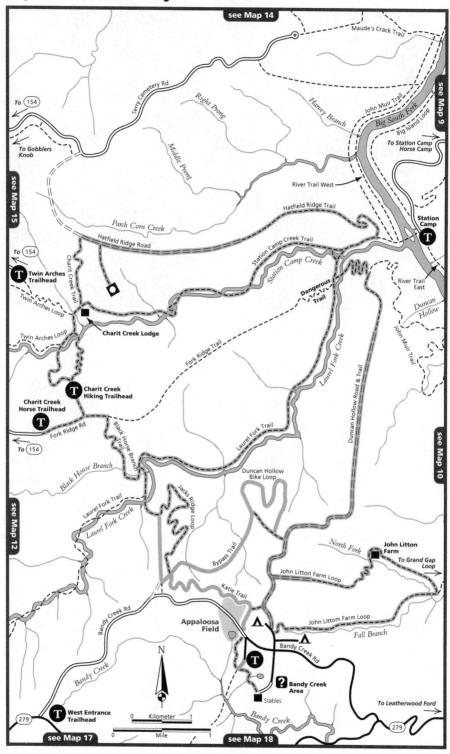

see Map 14
see Map 9
see Map 15
see Map 10
see Map 12
see Map 17
see Map 18

Maude's Crack Trail

To (154)

To Gobblers Knob

Terry Cemetery Rd

Right Prong

Middle Prong

Harvey Branch

John Muir Trail

Big South Fork

Big Island Loop

To Station Camp Horse Camp

River Trail West

Hatfield Ridge Trail

Station Camp

Parch Corn Creek

Hatfield Ridge Road

To (154)

Twin Arches Trailhead

Charit Creek Trail

Twin Arches Loop

Twin Arches Loop

Charit Creek Lodge

Station Camp Creek Trail

Station Camp Creek

Dangerous Trail

River Trail East

Duncan Hollow

John Muir Trail

Fork Ridge Trail

Laurel Fork Creek

Charit Creek Hiking Trailhead

Charit Creek Horse Trailhead

Fork Ridge Rd

To (154)

Black House Branch Trail

Black House Branch

Laurel Fork Trail

Laurel Fork Creek

Laurel Fork Trail

Jacks Ridge Loop

Bypass Trail

Duncan Hollow Bike Loop

Duncan Hollow Road & Trail

North Fork

John Litton Farm

To Grand Gap Loop

John Litton Farm Loop

John Littom Farm Loop

Fall Branch

Katie Trail

Bandy Creek Rd

Appaloosa Field

Bandy Creek Rd

Bandy Creek Area

Stables

To Leatherwood Ford

N

West Entrance Trailhead

279

Bandy Creek

Bandy Creek

279

0   Kilometer   1

0   Mile   1

Laurel Fork, with rhododendron in bloom

suckers, stone rollers, dace, creek chubs, and many other kinds of minnows are visible in the clear water. We see red efts, eastern box turtles, five-lined skinks, garter snakes, black rat snakes, and copperheads nearly every time we hike this trail. Riparian birds are abundant; unfortunately you are walking along the creek nearly the entire way, so birds will be high above your head and are best identified by their songs, so leave your binoculars behind. Kingfishers, wood thrushes, yellow-billed cuckoos, red-eyed vireos, pileated woodpeckers, hooded warblers, chickadees, and Carolina wrens will be the most common voices you will hear. Gray squirrels are abundant and deer and hog tracks cross the trail frequently, but the chance of seeing a reintroduced black bear should get your blood flowing.

This is one of the most popular trails for backpackers because of its staggering beauty, cool temperatures, great water access, and connections with lots of other great trails. This makes it easy to organize backpacking loops of nearly any length. However, do not hike this trail in or after bad rain storms, because it is subject to severe and rapid flooding. Because some portions of the floodplain lie outside the NRRA boundary and have been deforested, creek waters can rise to dangerous levels in hours. Also, we suggest hiking in river sandals in the section with frequent creek crossings, rather than changing footwear frequently.

Finding the trailhead: There are five main access points but no trailhead devoted exclusively to this trail; it can only be reached via other routes. Directions to each are provided in the "Local Directions" section. The best access, Sawmill Trailhead, takes you to the very upstream (west) end of this trail via an easy 1.2-mile walk on Slave Falls Loop (Trail 15—see Map 12). This is the route described below. Farther downstream, a 1.8-mile trail leads into Laurel Fork Gorge from the West Entrance Trailhead, described as the last section of the West Entrance Trails (Trail 27). Jacks Ridge Loop (in Trail 28) and Black House Branch Trail (in Trail 29) get you farther into the gorge from the Bandy Creek area, but these busy horse trails are soft sand and tough walking. Black House Branch Trail gets you to the same spot from Charit Creek Lodge in 2.8 miles. The downstream (eastern) terminus of this trail connects with no fewer than five other trails in the Station Camp area (Map 13), including the John Muir Trail (JMT) (Trail 43). This terminus can be reached with a 0.8-mile hike across the Big South Fork River from the Station Camp parking area. However, before planning to cross the river, consult a park ranger about river water levels.

Trail Description

We describe this trail downstream (west to east) from its western terminus at Slave Falls Loop (Trail 15) to its eastern terminus at the JMT at Station Camp. For folks going against the grain, we also provide upstream mileages (in parentheses). We describe only the trail itself but give mileposts and chapter numbers for connecting trails.

To access this trail from the grassy parking area at Sawmill Trailhead, enter the woods and stay left (north), paralleling Fork Ridge Road for 0.1 mile. Turn left (west) at the T intersection with Slave Falls Loop, and immediately cross Fork Ridge Road. Make an immediate left (south) turn on the Slave Falls Loop, and hike toward Indian Rock House, which you will pass at 1 mile. In another 0.2 mile you will reach the Laurel Fork Trail intersection, a right (southwest) turn. For a more detailed description of this section of Slave Falls Loop and its wonderful rock house, follow the description backward between mile 4.2 and 3.0, then return to this point. You have gone 1.2 miles.

0.0 (10.3) At an intersection at the very southern tip of Slave Falls Loop, turn right (south) onto Laurel Fork Trail and immediately start descending into the dark hemlock forest of Laurel Fork Gorge on four switchbacks. Can you find the rock arch on the other side of Ben Creek?

0.4 (9.9) Cross Ben Creek, a tributary of Laurel Fork. Put on some river sandals or footwear that can get wet, because you will cross Laurel Fork thirty more times over the next 6 miles. We do not describe this trail in great detail, because the nature of a creek is to change with every flood season. The trail may be blocked by logjams or covered by deposited sand and cobble—or even flowing on the other side of an island. Pay attention to your surroundings, and keep track of the number of times you cross Laurel Fork (don't count tributaries). The trail crosses a number of old roadbeds that follow the creek and ascend its side slopes, but the hiking trail stays within earshot of the creek for nearly its entire length and is well marked with red arrowhead blazes. Even if you make a bad turn on an old road, the trail will likely cross your path again.

The first few crossings come quick. At the fourth crossing, note the evidence of an ancient sea floor in some of the flat rocks laying in the creek bed—the concreted remains of sands deposited millions of years ago. In a twist of irony, these rock layers that were formed by water are now being eroded and crushed into sand by water, are resuspended and carried downstream by water, and will fall out of the water column and be reconstituted into layers as water slows in pools in the river. After the fourth crossing there is a big sandstone bluff and a flat campsite under a dark hemlock forest. Narrow depressions, called oxbows, are historical creek channels, showing how creeks wander back and forth in their valleys. Some are filled with water and sphagnum moss, providing breeding sites for many kinds of amphibians. At some crossings the channel is braided and you end up on an island in the middle of the creek. A number of fantastic campsites can be found under hemlocks all along this creek.

3.5 (6.8) After the fourteenth crossing you will skirt the ravine slope and pass Salt Pine Road on your left (north), which leads out of the gorge to Fork Ridge Road, explaining the horse tracks you often see in this area. Horses are not supposed to be on this trail, so if you see horseback riders, let them know, but be courteous—they may simply be lost.

3.8 (6.5) After crossing the creek the eighteenth time, a wide trail on your right leads 1.8 miles up the gorge slope to West Entrance Trailhead. In the next 2.5 miles you will ford the creek twelve more times. The creek gets larger as you go downstream, but the crossings do not get any more difficult in this flat-bottomed waterway.

6.3 (4.0) Join Black House Branch Trail, a horse trail on your right that crosses Laurel Fork and climbs up to Jacks Ridge Loop and back to the Bandy Creek area (all described in Trail 29). Veer left (north) on the shared trail and continue downstream along Laurel Fork for another 0.2 mile. Cross Black House Branch just upstream of its confluence with Laurel Fork immediately reaching an intersection where Laurel Fork Trail turns right (northeast) off Black House Branch Trail and turns east, following Laurel Fork all the way to Station Camp. From this point on, you will be elevated well above creek level on its north bank on a wide, flat path that is easy to follow.

8.5 (1.8) Just after passing a particularly large boulder, you will notice a campsite downslope on your right, perched above a clear pool in the creek. A group of boulders in the creek has created a spillway, and there is a rock ledge overlooking a narrow chute of water and the pool below.

9.8 (0.5) Enter the old fields of Station Camp, undergoing secondary succession. You may notice areas that look as though they were rototilled—damage caused by feral hogs.

10.1 (0.2) Fork Ridge Trail, a horse trail that makes a treacherous climb to Fork Ridge and continues west to the Charit Creek Lodge trailheads, enters at an angle to your left. Continue straight ahead.

10.3 (0.0) The elevated wood bridge on your right that crosses Laurel Fork is part of the JMT (Trail 43), a 48-mile-long trail that will eventually span the NRRA and beyond. If you are taking the JMT south to Leatherwood Ford, turn here and cross the bridge, and flip to mile 20.4 in the description of that trail. If you are heading back to the Bandy Creek area on Duncan Hollow Road (part of Trail 29), cross the hiking bridge and start the steep climb on the wide horse trail, flip to mile 5.8 of that description, and follow it backward to the campground.

If you are connecting with any other trails in the Station Camp area, continue on the horse trail past the bridge. To reach Charit Creek Lodge via Station Camp Creek Trail, continue east past the bridge on the wide horse trail and look left for a bridge crossing Station Camp Creek. Cross the bridge and turn left (west) on Station Camp Creek Trail, and flip to mile 7.0 of Trail 21. To connect with the northern section of the JMT or go swimming at the Big South Fork River at Station Camp Crossing, turn right (east) on Station Camp Creek Trail and head toward the river. At the intersection with Hatfield Ridge Trail and nearby JMT, which head north along the west bank of the river, turn right and go another 0.2 mile to reach

Station Camp Crossing. Please cross the river in the narrow, flagged lane constructed by the NPS to keep traffic localized in one spot to protect the endangered freshwater mussels found in the river. Although the crossing was constructed mainly for animals more than five times as heavy as yourself, it is simply a lot easier to walk in the lane, which has been cleared of big boulders. You will reach the parking area on the east side of the river at the end of Station Camp Road, a total of 12.5 miles from Sawmill Trailhead.

18 Maude's Crack Trail

TYPE OF TRAIL: Multiuse.

TYPE OF ADVENTURE: Short visit or connection to a great geological feature and overlook.

TOTAL DISTANCE: 1.2 miles (one-way).

DIFFICULTY: Easy.

TIME REQUIRED: 1 to 2 hours.

SPECIAL CONCERNS: Dangerous, unprotected overlook and dangerous crack climb.

WATER AVAILABILITY: None on trail or at trailhead.

SCENIC VALUE: Excellent: remote overlook, interesting geological feature.

USGS MAP: Barthell SW.

BEST STARTING POINT: Terry Cemetery Trailhead.

Overview: This is a great short trip to a large crack in a sandstone bluff that gives you firsthand knowledge of the erosive forces that shaped the river gorge. As a bonus, you get to visit a north-facing overlook with a grand view of the sandstone caprock looming above No Business Creek Gorge. South-facing bluff walls across the gorge turn orange at dawn and again at dusk, giving the impression of a miniature, forested version of the Grand Canyon.

By itself, this is a great trip on a horse or bike, or on foot, but because of the long drive to Terry Cemetery, this trail is probably best done in combination with some other activity or trail in the area. Regardless of your

Map 14—Maude's Crack and No Business Creek Area

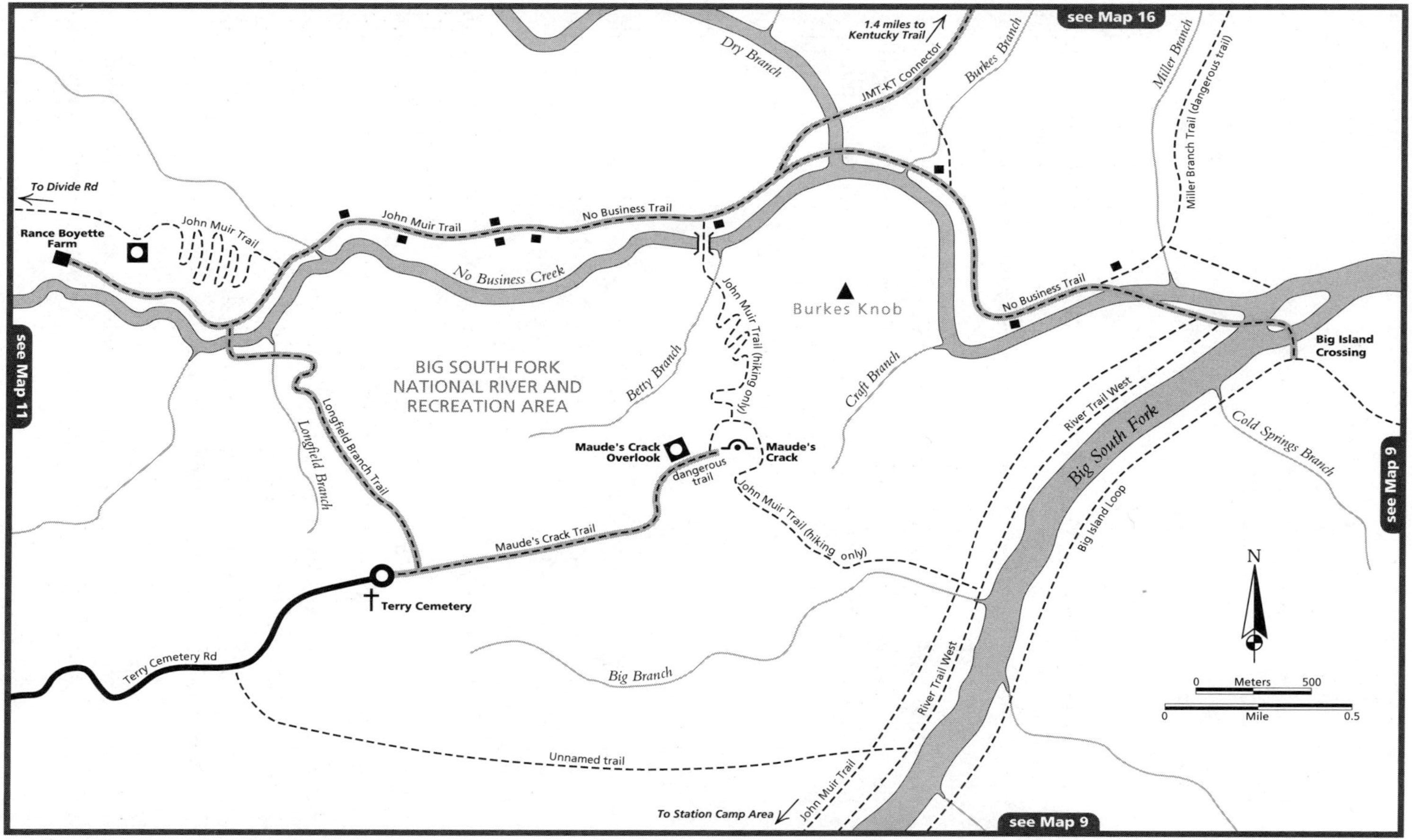

see Map 9
see Map 16
see Map 9
see Map 11

Big Island Crossing

Cold Springs Branch

Miller Branch Trail (dangerous trail)

Miller Branch

Burkes Branch

No Business Trail

River Trail West

Big South Fork

Big Island Loop

River Trail West

John Muir Trail

1.4 miles to Kentucky Trail

JMT-KT Connector

Dry Branch

Craft Branch

Burkes Knob

John Muir Trail (hiking only)

Maude's Crack

John Muir Trail (hiking only)

To Station Camp Area

No Business Trail

Berry Branch

Maude's Crack Overlook

Dangerous trail

Big Branch

No Business Creek

John Muir Trail

BIG SOUTH FORK NATIONAL RIVER AND RECREATION AREA

Maude's Crack Trail

Unnamed trail

John Muir Trail

Longfield Branch Trail

Longfield Branch

Terry Cemetery

To Divide Rd

Rance Boyette Farm

Terry Cemetery Rd

N

0   Meters   500
0   Mile   0.5

mode of transportation, you can easily spend an entire day exploring No Business Creek and/or Big South Fork River gorges from the Terry Cemetery Trailhead. If you are on horseback or bike, this makes a great out-and-back trip before or after a trip into the gorge on Longfield Branch–No Business Creek Trails (Trail 19).

If you are day hiking, you can make a great loop by connecting this trail with the JMT (Trail 43), below the crack. Hike southeast down to the Big South Fork River on the JMT, turn northeast along the river to Big Island, then west up No Business Creek Trail (in Trail 19). Make the steep climb up to John Muir Overlook and back, and return to Terry Cemetery via Longfield Branch Trail (in Trail 19). If you are through-hiking the JMT or the Kentucky Trail (Trail 23), this is the best connecting trail to or from Terry Cemetery.

Warning: Direct access to Maude's Crack Overlook, Maude's Crack, and the trails below Maude's Crack is by hiking only. Mountain-bike riders must leave or carry their bikes and horseback riders must tie their horses to the hitching posts and walk to the overlook.

Finding the trailhead: Follow directions to Terry Cemetery Trailhead and see Map 14.

Trail Description

Head directly east from the trailhead parking area. Immediately after entering the woods, you will pass on your left (north) the intersection with Longfield Branch Trail (in Trail 19), which descends to No Business Creek. Continue straight ahead (east) on the usually muddy jeep trail on a wide ridge covered in Virginia and shortleaf pine, maple, mountain laurel, and blueberry (three kinds, all tasty). The trail has a few minor ascents and descents but basically drops from 1,420 feet at Terry Cemetery to about 1,300 feet at Maude's Crack Overlook.

0.9 Pass a gate blocking an abandoned trail that used to drop off the ridge on your right and descend into the ravine of Big Branch.

1.0 The jeep trail narrows, turns left (north), drops through a narrow saddle on a ridge, then turns gradually back to the right (east) as it ascends to the top of a knob.

1.2 At the top of the knob, the jeep trail ends at a spot barely wide enough to turn around. The trail is hiking only past this point. Horses must be tied to hitching posts if available, or properly cross-tied if no hitches are available, and bikes must be left here. From here, look on the north side of the jeep trail for an opening in the blueberry and laurel thicket near the rim of the gorge. The trail descends gradually on the north side of the knob along a series of dangerous, unprotected ledges at the top of very high, sheer bluffs, so be extremely cautious. This is Maude's Crack Overlook.

From here, you are looking directly north into No Business Creek Gorge. Notice all the exposures of sandstone caprock that define the Cumberland Plateau. The exposure is north, between about 240 and 70 degrees. Burkes Knob is in the foreground to the northeast at about 40 degrees. The long line of tall bluffs off in the distance to the north-northwest (between about 310 and 5 degrees) are at the very end of Stoopin Oak Road, which lies on the ridge just north of Chestnut Ridge. John Muir Overlook is way off to the west-northwest (at about 295 degrees) atop of a pointy knob at the end of Chestnut Ridge but is not actually visible from your location.

Maude's Crack—a long, near-vertical crack between 5 and 10 feet wide and over 50 feet from top to bottom—is directly behind you. It splits nearly in two an immense, office building–sized boulder. This is a dramatic example of the erosive forces of water; eventually, half the boulder will break free and roll down the slope to rest in Betty Branch below. The crack is difficult to photograph, but a few things might help. When looking down through the crack from above, you are looking east-northeast at about 60 degrees, so midday in midsummer is the only time you have a chance of photographing a shaft of light shining partly into the crack. *Hint:* Kick up some dust to make the shaft of light visible! Afternoon is probably the best time to shoot the sandstone rock wall and the impressive opening of Maude's Crack from below, since the rock wall faces generally north-northwest.

This natural crack in the bluff was named after Minnie Maude Roysdon, who lived near No Business with her husband, the Reverend Isham Roysdon. She used this crevice to get to a large rock shelter that the couple lived under after their house burned down. When her husband and coworkers were cutting timber in the gorge, she used this shortcut to bring them lunch.

TYPE OF TRAIL: Horseback riding and mountain biking.

TYPE OF ADVENTURE: Short trip to a historical area and/or connection to other trails.

TOTAL DISTANCE: 4.2 miles (one-way).

DIFFICULTY: Moderate.

TIME REQUIRED: 1 to 2 hours.

SPECIAL CONCERNS: Steep climb, creek crossing, deep mud.

WATER AVAILABILITY: Abundant on trail; none at trailhead.

SCENIC VALUE: Excellent: lush wetlands and river gorge, historical area.

USGS MAP: Barthell SW.

BEST STARTING POINT: Terry Cemetery Trailhead.

Overview: These two trails are a logical combination, so we describe them as one. Longfield Branch Trail is a direct route between Terry Cemetery Trailhead and the west end of No Business Creek Trail and leads into the historical No Business Community. It provides the only access for horseback riders and mountain bikers into the gorge from this trailhead.

The No Business Trail lies along the north bank of No Business Creek between Longfield Branch Trail and Big Island on the Big South Fork River. It takes you directly through the No Business Community, a historical area. Some stone foundations, chimneys, and a few old barns are all that remain of a community that in the 1930s was home to more than 125 people. There were two general stores, a gristmill, a blacksmith shop, a school,

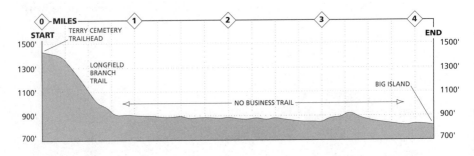

two churches, a post office, and many farms. Dewey Slaven, who left in 1960, was the last resident of No Business, and the last remaining house was removed by the NPS in 1992.

These trails connect you with any trails leading to Big Island. River Trail West, a very muddy trail not described in this book, takes you to the Station Camp area after about 4 miles. However, if possible, we suggest crossing the river at Big Island and riding the riverside portion of Big Island Loop to Station Camp area and back, a round-trip of about 16 miles. For a whopping 22-mile ride, add Big Island Loop to these trails, if it is possible to cross the river. These trails are essential connections to the south terminus of the Kentucky Trail (KT) (Trail 23), a hiking-only trail that goes north to Blue Heron Mining Community and beyond. This is also a good access point for the John Muir Trail (JMT) (Trail 43), a hiking-only trail running from one end of the NRRA to the other.

Finding the trailhead: Follow directions to Terry Cemetery Trailhead in the "Local Directions" section.

Trail Description

We describe these trails from Terry Cemetery Trailhead to Big Island. Mileages in the opposite direction are provided in parentheses.

0.0 (4.2) From the loop parking area east of Terry Cemetery, head directly east on Maude's Crack Trail (Trail 18), a wide, potholed 4WD trail.

0.1 (4.1) Immediately after entering the woods, look for a metal gate blocking vehicles from a gravel road leading obviously downhill on your left (north). This is Longfield Branch Trail, which descends steeply along the east slope of Longfield Branch, a tributary of No Business Creek. Horseback riders should double-check their tack and tighten their girth, and mountain bikers should double-check their brakes. Soon you will pass beneath a sandstone wall composed of the strata that caps the plateau. These strata form the massive bluffs that line the river gorge. The pathway makes a few turns near the bottom of the gorge, turning west and crossing Longfield Branch then briefly following No Business Creek upstream.

0.8 (3.4) Just after fording No Business Creek at an upstream angle, reach No Business Trail, which is shaded by a dense canopy of hemlock. This wide, well-trodden pathway runs east-west along the north side of No Business Creek all the way to Big Island on the Big South Fork River. About 0.7 mile to the west lies the Rance Boyette Farm. Turn right (east).

1.0 (3.4) Pass an intersection with the JMT (Trail 43) on the north. This leads up to the John Muir Overlook but is a hiking-only trail and is extremely steep, with stairs. The JMT shares the No Business Trail for the next 1.2 miles.

1.2 (3.0) Ford Tackett Creek and continue east, entering the No Business Community, where you will see only remnants of homes, rock walls, and fences among old fields. A jeep trail to the north leads up to Stoopin' Oak Road, high atop the plateau. Note how the vegetation is reclaiming this area. Beavers have constructed a number of dams in the creek, impounding water and creating swampy areas with willow, cattail, river cane, and many other kinds of wetland plants. Unfortunately, feral hogs have caused extensive damage in this area.

2.2 (2.0) Pass an intersection with the JMT on the right (south), which crosses a wood suspension bridge over a beaver dam. This hiking-only trail leads up the gorge slope to the low side of Maude's Crack, then back down to the west bank of the river all the way to the Station Camp area. If you are connecting with the south portion of the JMT, flip to mile 26.0 in the Trail 43 description.

2.5 (1.7) Reach an intersection on the north with the John Muir–Kentucky Trail Connector, which forms a small triangle with the other trail near Burkes Branch (mile 3.1 below). Continue straight ahead and cross Dry Branch at 2.8 (1.6) miles. If you are connecting with the KT, flip to mile 25.0 in the Trail 43 description.

3.1 (1.1) Just east of fording Burkes Branch, reach another intersection on the north with the John Muir–Kentucky Trail Connector, which forms a small triangle with the other trail near Dry Branch (mile 2.5 above). Continue along the wide, bumpy, gravel path.

3.8 (0.4) Reach a fork in the trail. Straight ahead, No Business Trail officially continues a few hundred feet along the north side of No Business Creek, then intersects Miller Branch Trail. However, you should probably avoid this portion of the trail. First, because of recent changes in the floodplain, the trail reaches Big Island Crossing only with considerable effort. Also, Miller Branch Trail is another trail we strongly recommend avoiding and do not cover in this book. In short, it is extremely steep, eroded, and badly placed. It leads out to Laurel Hill Road, then on to Divide Road and Peters Mountain Trailhead, a rarely used area of the NRRA.

Turn right (south) at the fork and descend to the wide, flat-bottomed No Business Creek; cross it at an angle, walking downstream at an angle for about 50 feet. Continue downstream along the south side of No Business Creek on an extremely muddy trail leading down to Big Island. If you are on a bike, we suggest carrying it to Big Island Crossing.

4.2 (0.0) Reach Big Island Crossing, at the confluence of No Business Creek and the Big South Fork River. Crossing the river here connects you with Big Island Loop (Trail 11, mile 4.8). In 2001 this area had been dramatically changed by recent floods, and a 25-foot pile of trees and debris had been dumped on Big Island directly over the trail. Consult a ranger to find out about the best route to cross the river and the status of this crossing. As of this writing, it was under review due to critically endangered mussels in the area. If you can cross here, please cross within the marked corridor, and be sure to do so only when the water is low and you can see the bottom.

20 Gobblers Knob Trail

TYPE OF TRAIL: Horseback riding, mountain biking, and wagon train.

TYPE OF ADVENTURE: Out-and-back trip or connection on a rolling, gravel trail.

TOTAL DISTANCE: 5.6 miles (one-way).

DIFFICULTY: Easy.

TIME REQUIRED: 1 to 2 hours.

SPECIAL CONCERNS: Entire trail is sunny, hot, and dry in summer.

WATER AVAILABILITY: Poor on trail; none at either trailhead.

SCENIC VALUE: Good: within earshot of road in young forest, but leads to great spots.

USGS MAPS: Sharp Place and Barthell SW.

BEST STARTING POINT: Middle Creek Equestrian Trailhead.

Overview: If you need a smooth, gravel pathway for galloping your horses or pulling a wagon, this is a great trail. It lies entirely on the plateau surface

Map 15—Gobblers Knob Trail

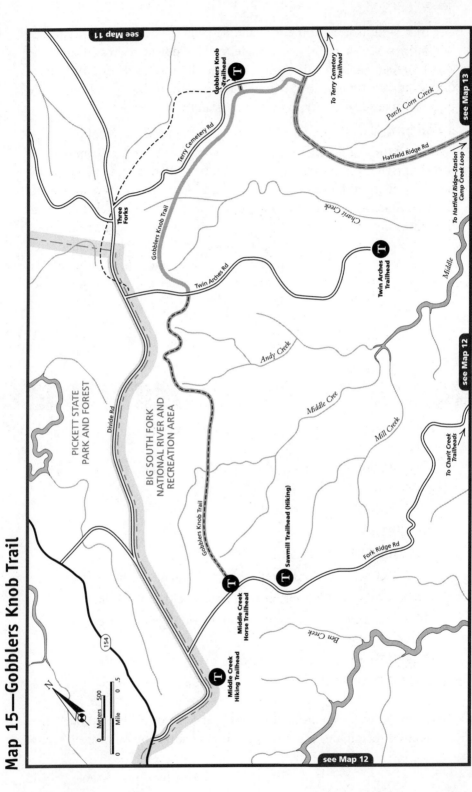

see Map 11

Gobblers Knob Trailhead

To Terry Cemetery Trailhead

Parch Corn Creek

see Map 13

Terry Cemetery Rd

Hatfield Ridge Rd

To Hatfield Ridge–Station Camp Creek Loop

Three Forks

Gobblers Knob Trail

Charit Creek

Twin Arches Rd

Twin Arches Trailhead

Middle

PICKETT STATE PARK AND FOREST

Divide Rd

BIG SOUTH FORK NATIONAL RIVER AND RECREATION AREA

Andy Creek

Middle Cree

Middle Cree

Mill Creek

see Map 12

To Charit Creek Trailheads

Gobblers Knob Trail

Sawmill Trailhead (Hiking)

Fork Ridge Rd

Middle Creek Horse Trailhead

Middle Creek Hiking Trailhead

Ben Creek

154

N

Meters 500

0

Mile .5

0

see Map 12

but makes frequent short ascents to ridgetops and knobs and descents into saddles and headwater ravines of Middle Creek, Andy Creek, and Charit Creek—all tributaries of Station Camp Creek, which empties into the Big South Fork River at Station Camp. The trail ranges only between 1,440 and 1,600 feet in elevation, but numerous short climbs and descents in and out of these headwater ravines add up to more than 600 feet of climbing in 12.2 miles. This trail is hot and dry, with few creek crossings; headwaters barely flow, if at all, in late summer and fall. This trail is not very scenic, but short side trips lead to some very scenic spots. Mountain bikers may find this trail a bit too mushy after heavy horse traffic, but most of the time it is a fun trail.

As of August 2001 mileages on most of the NPS trail signs along this trail suggested that the distance between Middle Creek Equestrian Trailhead and Gobblers Knob Trailhead was 6.4 miles. We measured the route twice with a meticulously calibrated bike computer, and both times got slightly less than 5 miles for the same distance. In fact, the distance from Middle Creek Equestrian Trailhead all the way to Hatfield Ridge Trail (in Trail 21) is only about 6.8 miles. If you are looking for a full-day ride, combine this trail with the Hatfield Ridge–Station Camp Creek Loop (Trail 21) by taking Hatfield Ridge Road to its intersection with Charit Creek Trail, and pick up the description of that trail at mile 1.0. Or you can add this as an out-and-back spur off Trail 21 from Charit Creek Lodge. If this is too much, simply take this trail to the Charit Creek Overlook and back, or to the lodge and back (about 15.6 miles round-trip for either trip). Gobblers Knob Trailhead is another starting point, but unless your horses are pulling wagons, we see no reason to use that remote trailhead.

Finding the trailhead: Follow directions to Middle Creek Equestrian Trailhead and see Map 15.

Trail Description

We describe this trail from Middle Creek Equestrian Trailhead to Gobblers Knob Trailhead (west to east) and include the short section on Hatfield Ridge Road that connects this trail to the Hatfield Ridge Loop and beyond. Mileages are also provided in the opposite direction in parentheses. We do not provide a trail profile; simply assume that you will make a number of climbs and descents of 20 to 60 vertical feet in each small tributary ravine shown on Map 15—and then some.

0.0 (5.6) As of August 2001 Middle Creek Equestrian Trailhead was a grassy field with six hitching posts and a trash can, but no picnic tables. The surrounding forest is young, so shade is sparse in the middle of the day. The trail starts on the north end of the grassy area and heads north on a wide, gravel pathway. Signs are plentiful, but mileages may be inaccurate.

0.3 (5.3) Drop into a ravine and cross a headwater tributary of Middle Creek. It is difficult to water a horse in this small, steep-sided creek without trampling lots of vegetation; please wait for the next tributary, a more reliable source with better access. After climbing out of the ravine, the trail appears to be following an old coal tram and/or logging road.

1.2 (4.4) Drop into a ravine lined with hemlock and rhododendron and cross a narrow, sandy-bottomed stream, another headwater tributary of Middle Creek. This is the most reliable source of water on the entire trail but may dry up by late summer or fall in dry years. After this, the trail climbs out of the Middle Creek watershed.

1.4 (4.2) Cross Middle Creek Road. Signs may be plentiful, but mileages may be inaccurate. The trail drops into the Andy Creek watershed, but you may not encounter flowing water.

1.8 (3.8) Drop into a deep, dark ravine with hemlock and white pine, and pass some nice sandstone bluffs. This is the edge of the sandstone caprock that lies at the surface of the Cumberland Plateau. This type of sandstone is more resistant to erosion than the underlying strata, so it forms the steep walls of the river gorge, breaking off in large chunks only after water washes away the underlying layers (see geology section).

2.7 (2.9) Pass through a cleared power line right-of-way. There should be lots of prairie warblers singing in low bushes and on the forest edge, identified by a raspy, ascending song that sounds something like a reward in a hand-held electronic game. You may hear nuthatches and hairy woodpeckers and are likely to scare up some turkeys in the young white oak, maple, and white pine forest that follows. The trail climbs gradually out of the Andy Creek watershed.

3.1 (2.5) Cross Twin Arches Road, again passing signs that may have inaccurate mileages. Just after this, pass a few sandstone overhangs that you will appreciate if it is raining. One of these is likely to become an arch one day. The trail descends gradually into the upper reaches of the Charit Creek watershed, but, again, there will be little or no water.

4.0 (1.6) Continue straight through this intersection with an unmarked trail.

4.4 (1.2) The trail comes within sight of Terry Cemetery Road and continues along the southern edge of its right-of-way.

5.0 (0.6) Reach the access trail to Gobblers Knob Trailhead, a wide gravel parking area rimmed with metal hitches on the other (north) side of Terry Cemetery Road. Again, signs may give incorrect mileages to Hatfield Ridge Road and Middle Creek Equestrian Trailhead. To continue on this trail to Hatfield Ridge Road and beyond, continue east, staying parallel to the road, and begin a gentle right-handed (southward) turn.

5.6 (0.0) The eastern terminus of the trail at Hatfield Ridge Road, just west of the intersection of Hatfield Ridge Road and Terry Cemetery Road. Officially, this is the end of the trail, but we tack on some mileage to a few very scenic places rather than turn you back to the trailhead, which would give you a trip with few scenic amenities and almost no water for horses.

Turn right (west) to start down Hatfield Ridge Road, which will take you to Charit Creek Overlook and/or Charit Creek Lodge. In another 1.2 miles (6.8 miles from Middle Creek Equestrian Trailhead), you will reach the T junction with a trail on your right (south) leading steeply downhill to Charit Creek Lodge, where you will find water for your horses and sodas and candy bars for you. The lodge lies another mile from this intersection.

This is also your entry point to the Hatfield Ridge–Station Camp Creek Loop (Trail 21). For a detailed description, enter the loop at mile 1.0 of the Trail 21 description. If not the loop, we recommend that you at least go to Charit Creek Overlook, which lies about a mile from the T junction. To do this, stay straight on Hatfield Ridge Road, climbing steadily uphill on a gentle right-hand turn. In 0.4 mile, turn right on the spur trail leading another 0.7 mile to Charit Creek Overlook. You might want to go to Charit Creek Lodge for a soda and a dip in Station Camp Creek, where you can also water your horses, before making the trip back. Remember, you will have to add twice the mileage for these extra side trips, which will give you a full day of riding.

21 Hatfield Ridge–Station Camp Creek Loop

TYPE OF TRAIL: Horseback riding, mountain biking, and hiking.

TYPE OF ADVENTURE: Visit a great overlook, then drop into the gorge and swim in the river.

TOTAL DISTANCE: 11 miles (with trip to overlook).

DIFFICULTY: Moderate.

TIME REQUIRED: Half day.

SPECIAL CONCERNS: Steep grades, portion shared with vehicles, six creek fords.

WATER AVAILABILITY: Abundant on trail and at trailhead.

SCENIC VALUE: Spectacular: lofty overlook, remote gorges, significant historical site.

USGS MAP: Barthell SW.

BEST STARTING POINT: Charit Creek Lodge or Trailhead.

Overview: This loop is fantastic on horseback or mountain bike, and it is so remote that it makes a great hike as well. It starts with a steep climb to a fast, flat section on a wide ridge leading to a short spur to a spectacular overlook. It brings you to the Big South Fork River for a midday swim. The final stretch lies along Station Camp Creek, a clean, midsized creek flowing over shallow riffles and deep emerald pools among humongous boulders and dense stands of hemlock. You must ford Station Camp Creek six times on this loop, so be certain to consult a ranger about water levels before you hit the trail.

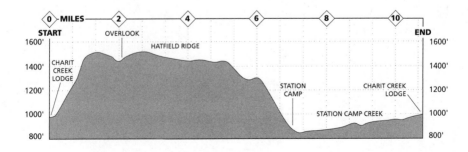

To fully experience Big South Fork Country, we recommend an overnight stay at Charit Creek Lodge, a quaint historical lodge in the valley of Station Camp Creek. In fact, the best way to see this area of the NRRA is to pack your stuff down to the Charit Creek Lodge one day, spend the night at the lodge, do this loop the next day, spend another night at the lodge, do another trail the next day, and so on. The lodge hosts will make you a nice bag lunch for a nominal fee (lunch is included for multi-night stays). If you are doing this trail after lunch, you should ask the lodge hosts when you should return so that you do not miss dinner.

We start this loop from the lodge, but you can start from many other locations. We usually ride to the lodge from the Bandy Creek Equestrian Trailhead, using the first 2.3 miles of the Katie–Jacks Ridge–Bypass–Duncan Loop (Trail 28), then taking Black House Branch Trail (described in Trail 29) to the lodge trailhead. For a really strenuous day, combine the north part of this loop (on Hatfield Ridge) with Duncan Hollow–Station Camp–Black House Branch (Trail 29). Or start from Station Camp Equestrian Trailhead, descend into the gorge on Big Island Loop (Trail 11), and cross the river at Station Camp Crossing. For a 22-mile adventure, combine this loop with either Gobblers Knob Trail (Trail 20) or River Trail East (Trail 12).

Finding the trailhead: Follow directions to the Charit Creek Lodge trailheads (and see Map 13) and head down to the lodge on one of the Charit Creek Lodge trails (Trail 22).

Trail Description

Because there is no water on Hatfield Ridge, clockwise is the smartest way to do this loop from Charit Creek Lodge, regardless of your start time or mode of travel. Going clockwise, you will finish the brutal climb and dry section on Hatfield Ridge first. Then you can water your horses, go swimming, or clean the mud off your bike in the Big South Fork River, after which Station Camp Creek will cool you off six times in the last 4 miles.

0.0 (11.0) From the lodge or the horse hitching posts near the lodge, find Station Camp Creek Trail—a steep, rocky gravel road on the north side of the lodge. Head east, climbing steeply, and look left (north) for an intersection with a gravel trail that ascends steeply. If you are staying at Charit Creek Lodge with horses, you must walk to the new horse barn, which is about 0.2 mile east of the lodge, and start there. From the barn, go left (west, toward the lodge) on Station Camp Creek Trail and look for the gravel trail on your right (north) that ascends steeply up to Hatfield Ridge. We start our mileage at the lodge.

0.1 (10.9) Turn north up the wide, rocky trail that ascends steeply to Hatfield Ridge along the east slope of the ravine of Charit Creek, which is lined with beautiful hemlock and beech and plunges over a number of tiny waterfalls. This 540-foot climb can be cleared without stopping on a mountain bike, but takes at least fifteen minutes of slow grinding in granny gears. Ouch!

1.0 (10.0) Turn right (east) at the intersection with Hatfield Ridge Trail. Watch for vehicles, because the trail along Hatfield Ridge is multiuse from this point to a metal gate to the east at mile 3.7; most of the year, even 2WD vehicles can handle this road. (This may change, pending the outcome of the GMP process.) Make a gentle right turn as you climb on loose gravel and sandstone outcrops.

1.4 (9.6) Turn right (south) onto the 0.7-mile spur trail leading to Charit Creek Overlook, which lies at the very southern tip of a wide ridge covered on its north end by a mixed upland forest of maple and oak. The forest grades into drier habitats dominated by Virginia pine, mountain laurel, and blueberry as you proceed southward to the gorge rim.

2.1 (8.9) About 100 yards from the overlook, horseback riders and mountain bikers must dismount and proceed on foot. The NPS built a nice set of hitching posts that will keep your horse within earshot. The overlook is protected by a wood rail fence but provides a fantastic view of Charit Creek Lodge, the cabins, and surrounding grassy fields. Dangerous rock outcrops are accessible to the east of the overlook; if you have kids with you, do not let them venture from the protected area. You can see bluffs to the west and may be able to pick out the top of Twin Arches, but the view to the east is mostly blocked by trees. Photographers will want to get up early and climb to this overlook to capture the fog blanketing the gorge. The lodge buildings gradually appear as the fog lifts, and the sun lights up the east-facing bluffs, slopes, and ridges to the west. You should see rufous-sided towhees and fence lizards at the overlook and might hear the calls of American toads and gray tree frogs echoing in the gorge.

2.8 (8.2) Back at the intersection with Hatfield Ridge Road, turn right (east). The road stays between 1,300 and 1,400 feet in elevation for the next

3 miles but ascends and descends often along the spine of Hatfield Ridge, which is a series of knobs and saddles. You can really get some wind in your hair on this level section of soft sand and dirt or, more often, mud. You will pass a number of pullouts that serve as great backcountry campsites for hunters. The ridgetop vegetation is entirely young, secondary-growth maple and oak, but the forest is recovering nicely from past logging efforts.

3.4 (7.6) On your right (south), a faint, grass-covered jeep trail leads about 0.5 mile to Breakaway Point, an extremely dangerous series of high vertical and overhanging bluffs at the southern tip of a narrow ridge jutting southward off Hatfield Ridge. This ridge lies roughly parallel to and east of the one leading to Charit Creek Overlook. The view is absolutely fabulous, but the point is unprotected and almost beyond dangerous. We would not even mention this spot if it were not an established rock-climbing area. Do not go anywhere near the edge of these bluffs without being tied to something or someone, and do not venture out on the point in windy conditions.

The jeep trail ends long before reaching the point; blocked by downed trees, thick mountain laurel and blueberry, and tangles of greenbrier. We strongly recommend avoiding this trail on horseback; cross-tie your horse or use a picket line between two solid trees and walk instead. There is a large campsite along the access trail that should give you plenty of room for horses, but the point is a long way from this spot. You cannot get a mountain bike to the point without carrying it or puncturing your tires on greenbrier, so leave it behind.

3.7 (7.3) Go around a metal gate at a wide turnaround and parking area, the eastern end of vehicle access on Hatfield Ridge Road. Past the gate, the next few miles of the trail are better for lack of vehicles and will be great fun on horse or bike!

5.6 (5.4) On your left note the natural water-filled depression lined with sweetgum trees. The water may appear stagnant and is stained dark with tannins (pigments released by fallen leaves), but it supports lots of frog tadpoles and aquatic insects so should be OK for horses, too. This is a great example of a wood frog breeding site, but you might also find American toads, spadefoot toads, mountain chorus frogs, gray tree frogs, and their tadpoles in this ephemeral puddle. This is a valuable ridgetop resource for forest mammals and birds, including turkey, deer, and raccoon. In another 0.2 mile, you will pass through the final saddle and ascend to the last knob at the very eastern tip of Hatfield Ridge, which looms over Big South Fork

River Gorge. There are no unobstructed overlooks of the river, but you will be swimming in it soon.

6.0 (5.0) Begin the fast, eastward descent into the river gorge on gentle switchbacks. This fast downhill section lies on a wide singletrack trail among large beech, hemlock, and maple. After turning west and descending the north slope of the valley of a small unnamed creek, you will skirt and then cross the creek and turn back to the east, with Hatfield Ridge above your right shoulder. This beautiful gorge-slope forest is as good as it gets. Soon after, you emerge in the river gorge, turn gradually south, and descend gradually, staying well above the river until the very last few tenths, which descend steeply to Station Camp.

7.0 (4.0) Reach Station Camp Creek Trail, a rocky trail wide enough for a vehicle. To return directly to Charit Creek Lodge along Station Camp Creek, turn right (west) at this intersection. First you should go swimming, or at least visit the Big South Fork River, so turn left (east) and head to the river at Station Camp Crossing, only about 0.1 mile from this intersection. At the river, you can cross-tie or picket-line your horses within sight of the swimming hole. But remember, this is a busy river crossing where horses, bikers, and hikers may show up at any time; to keep the trail safe for yourself, your horses, and other users do not cross-tie your horses so that they block the trail. Afterward, retrace your steps.

If you plan to swim or wade in the river with your horses, be aware that several species of endangered mussels occur in the shallow shoal at Station Camp Crossing. To accommodate all types of users without compromising the mussels, the NPS cleared most of the large rocks out of a narrow lane at the crossing. You can swim and play anywhere on the river, but please use only this cleared lane when watering or wading with your horses. This crossing could eventually be closed to horse traffic (or bridged) if a direct causal link between horse traffic and negative impact on mussels is made.

After your swim you can explore the network of trails in the Station Camp area but you must return to Station Camp Creek Trail eventually to finish the loop. At its intersection with Hatfield Ridge Loop, continue west. Very soon you will reach another intersection with signs indicating mileages to numerous locations. If some of the mileages seem off, remember that we included the 1.4-mile round-trip to Charit Creek Overlook in our running total. You will ford Station Camp Creek the first of six times near here.

Horseback riders crossing the river at Station Camp Crossing

7.8 (3.2) Continue straight ahead (west) at the intersection with a trail leading south to the Bandy Creek area via Duncan Hollow Road. A sign gives fairly accurate mileages to Bandy Creek Campground (6.3), Station Camp Horse Camp (6.1), and Station Camp Crossing (0.9). If you entered the loop via Duncan Hollow Road, this is where you started; if you want to return the same way you came, this is your turn.

After this intersection the trail is wide but rocky, with lots of ups and downs, and usually remains wet from numerous seeps that drain groundwater from deep inside Hatfield Ridge. Massive boulders line the trail. These broke away from the bluff walls on the south edge of Hatfield Ridge and tumbled down to your position, imparting a rugged appearance to the gorge of Station Camp Creek.

9.3 (1.7) The grassy field being reclaimed by succession on the right (north) side of the trail was probably the home of Johnathan Blevins, who lived in the lodge building. The grave of Jonathan Blevins lies in Hatfield Cemetery, a small opening in the woods at the end of a faint pathway on the east end of the homestead about 100 feet north of the main trail. It is probably easiest to cross-tie or picket-line your horses and hike to the cemetery, which is often overgrown with briers and blackberries.

9.5 (1.5) After entering a dark, primeval hemlock forest along Station Camp Creek, cross the creek once, again at 9.6 miles near a beautiful flowering magnolia tree on the waters edge, a third time at 9.7 miles, and a fourth and fifth time at about 9.8 miles—both times near a massive rock leaning over the creek. Water pennies, the pancake-shaped larvae of tiny aquatic beetles, can be found adhering to the underside of many rocks in this creek. These insects are intolerant of pollution so are valuable natural indicators of water quality, which is very good in this creek. For the next mile you will make short ascents and descents along the base of the boulder-littered south slope of Hatfield Ridge.

10.8 (0.2) The horse stables are on your left. If you are staying at the lodge on horseback, stall your horse and head back to the lodge area on foot and wait for the dinner bell. If you are returning to Charit Creek Equestrian Trailhead, continue west for another 0.2 mile, passing the lodge, crossing Charit Creek on a culverted bridge, and turning left (south) on Charit Creek Trail, which leads back to the trailhead in 1.5 miles. There is another creek crossing where you can water your horse once more before the brutal climb back to the trailhead.

22 Charit Creek Lodge Access Trails

TYPE OF TRAIL: One hiking-only trail, one multiuse trail.

TYPE OF ADVENTURE: Short trip to a rustic lodge in a beautiful valley.

TOTAL DISTANCE: 0.8 mile hiking one-way; 1.5 miles on horseback or bike one-way.

DIFFICULTY: Easy in, moderate out.

TIME REQUIRED: 15 to 45 minutes.

SPECIAL CONCERNS: Steep descent in, steep ascent out.

WATER AVAILABILITY: Adequate on trails; none at trailheads.

SCENIC VALUE: Excellent: dense slope forest, clear creek, picturesque lodge.

USGS MAP: Barthell SW.

BEST STARTING POINT: Charit Creek Hiking or Equestrian Trailhead.

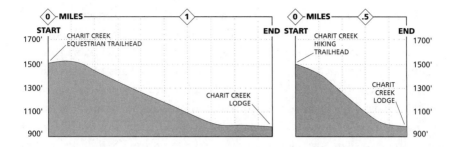

Overview: These two short trails provide the shortest, easiest access to Charit Creek Lodge, a rustic hostel deep in the gorge of Station Camp Creek where you can spend the night and eat like a king (see History of Charit Creek Lodge chapter). Walk-ins are welcome, but spring and fall can be busy and space is available on a first-come, first-served basis, so call ahead and make a reservation (see listing in appendix).

Which trail you take to the lodge will depend on your mode of transportation. Hikers will prefer the shorter, scenic route on the hiking trail, which descends near some rock walls and crosses Station Camp Creek on a beautiful wood suspension bridge. Anyone visiting the lodge should walk over and enjoy the rushing water of the creek from this bridge.

Horseback riders and mountain bikers must take the gravel road down to the lodge or come in from another trailhead. The horse/bike trail lies on the steep groomed gravel access road that brings vehicles to the lodge. It provides a great view of the Station Camp Creek gorge, passes by some rock walls and a historical site, then lies along the creek for a ways.

You can also reach the lodge on a number of other hiking and multiuse trails, affording many different options for distance, trail type, and scenic value. We usually ride to the lodge from the Bandy Creek Equestrian Trailhead, using the first 2.3 miles of Katie–Jacks Ridge–Bypass–Duncan Loop (Trail 28), then taking Black House Branch Trail (described in Trail 29) to the lodge trailhead.

Hikers and mountain bikers can start from the Big South Fork River at Station Camp Crossing (see Map 13) and head west for about 4 miles on Station Camp Creek Trail (in Trail 21). In addition to crossing the river, you must ford the creek six times; make sure you ask about river levels before you make the trip, and wear a pair of river-worthy shoes or sandals. Horseback riders can make the same trip but must start from the plateau at Station Camp Equestrian Trailhead and head into the gorge on Big Island Loop (Trail 11).

From the north, hikers can reach the lodge via Twin Arches Loop (Trail 16), starting from Twin Arches Trailhead. This 1.6-mile route takes you past Twin Arches, a truly spectacular geological formation. Hikers can also start from the west at Sawmill Trailhead and use Slave Falls Loop (Trail 15) or, even farther west, from Middle Creek Loop (Trail 14). These trails take you past Slave Falls and Needle Arch, two more great geological features.

From the lodge you have easy access to some great trails! Hikers will want to go to Twin Arches and back or do the entire 5.5-mile loop. The Hatfield Ridge–Station Camp Loop (Trail 21) is a great trail for every type of user and leads to a spectacular ledge overlooking the beautiful valley surrounding the lodge. We recommend Duncan Hollow–Station Camp–Black House Branch Loop (Trail 29), a strenuous 15.5-mile journey with lots of gorge ascents and descents.

Finding the trailheads: Follow directions to the Charit Creek Trailheads (also see Maps 12 and 13). Horseback riders must park at the Charit Creek Equestrian Trailhead. Mountain bikers can park at the hiking trailhead, but cannot use the hiking trail.

Hiking Trail Description

Punch into the woods at the trailhead and begin the descent. Soon after, descend a series of switchbacks and rock staircases down into the gorge of Station Camp Creek. On the way down you will pass some nice rock walls flanked by dark hemlock forests. At the bottom, Station Camp Creek will meet you on your left. Continue downstream (north) for a short distance along its east bank, then turn left (west) and cross the new suspension bridge over the creek. Before this beautiful bridge was built, hikers had to continue along the creek aways, then ford the creek near the pole barn. Immediately after crossing the bridge, turn right (north) on the gravel road leading to the lodge. This is the access road for lodge staff but also serves as the horse/mountain bike trail described below. After a short distance you will reach hitching posts at the intersection with Twin Arches Loop and Station Camp Creek Trail. The lodge is on your right (east), so cross the bridge over Charit Creek.

Horse/Mountain Bike Trail Description

From the equestrian trailhead, steer your horses east on Fork Ridge Road. If you are a mountain biker and parked at the hiking trailhead, read on.

0.2 At the end of the road, turn left (north) toward the gravel parking area for Charit Creek Hiking Trailhead. Look for a gated gravel road on your left (west). Go around the gate, pass some spectacular outcrops of the sandstone caprock that forms the surface of the Cumberland Plateau, and plunge into Station Camp Creek Gorge. The view of the forest is great as you traverse a gentle horseshoe turn at the southwestern tip of a rocky knob. After that the gravel road descends very steeply to Station Camp Creek along the slope of a small ravine. Be careful!

1.2 Reach Station Camp Creek on your left (north), and veer right (east); continue along its southern bank for a short distance, then cross over to the northern bank at a ford.

1.3 Pass the chimney of Tackett Cabin, which belonged to the Tackett family. The chimney fall of the cabin is located near a big rock on the north side of the gravel road. A group of Confederate sympathizers came to the cabin in 1863, and the old woman who lived there was afraid they would take and/or kill her two teenage boys. She hid the boys under a feather mattress, got on top of it, and pretended to be too sick to move. The men left without incident, but sadly, the boys suffocated under the mattress, and they were buried near the big square boulder adjacent to the cabin.

1.4 Pass a suspension bridge hanging over Station Camp Creek. This bridge is *not* for horses! Continue north on the gravel road, eventually walking on the west bank of Charit Creek, a tributary of Station Camp Creek that drains the northern slope of Hatfield Ridge.

Note: Just after the bridge, you will reach a trail on your right that crosses Charit Creek near the old pole barn. Do *not* turn here! Continue north on the gravel road.

1.5 Reach some hitching posts near the intersection with Twin Arches Loop and Station Camp Creek Trail. The lodge is on your right (east), just across the bridge over Charit Creek.

Note: Whether you are just stopping for a soda or staying for a week, tie your horses at these hitching posts and walk to the lodge. If you are staying overnight at the lodge and have a barn stall reserved, get your stall assignments and stall key (they have locks!) before proceeding to the barn.

After getting squared away, continue over the bridge and proceed straight east on Station Camp Creek Trail, climbing over a short hill. At the top you will notice on your left (north) the trail leading up to Hatfield Ridge and eventually the Charit Creek Overlook. Continue directly east on Station Camp Creek Trail. The horse barn is on your right less than 0.2 mile from the hill. Have a great time!

23 The Kentucky Trail ("KT")

TYPE OF TRAIL: Mostly hiking-only, with some short sections on horse trails.

TYPE OF ADVENTURE: Epic through-hike in the Big South Fork River Gorge.

TOTAL DISTANCE: 20 miles (one-way).

DIFFICULTY: Easy to strenuous, depending on section traveled.

TIME REQUIRED: 2 to 4 days.

SPECIAL CONCERNS: Long vehicle shuttle trips, numerous creek crossings and unprotected overlooks, some remote and rarely maintained sections requiring bushwhacking, requires backcountry permits for each overnight stay.

WATER AVAILABILITY: Good to Abundant (see introduction to each section).

SCENIC VALUE: Spectacular: clean tributary creeks, remote river gorge habitat, immense rock walls, two fantastic gorge overlooks, interesting historical areas.

USGS MAPS: Barthell SW, Oneida North, and Barthell.

START/END POINTS: From south to north, Terry Cemetery, Peters Mountain, Ledbetter, Dick Gap Overlook, and Blue Heron Mine.

Overview: Going south to north, we start you on a 2.5-mile section that takes you to Maude's Crack and Overlook, then drops you into the No Business Creek Gorge, where you will pass through the remnants of a community of subsistence farmers. The next 10.3 miles climbs and drops into the deep gorges of Difficulty and Troublesome Creeks, two important historical areas. This section takes you along the Big South Fork River in the

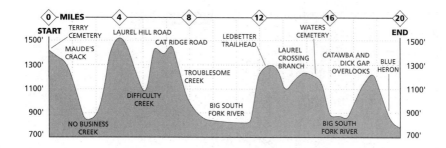

most remote part of its gorge, then returns you to the plateau at Ledbetter Trailhead. Backpackers should stay overnight along the river and bring some fishing tackle and bait for smallmouth bass.

The section from Ledbetter Trailhead to Blue Heron Mine (7.2 miles) takes you into the river gorge along a historical tram road used by the mining company. Here you will encounter Big Spring Falls, a 100-foot free-falling waterfall in a primeval hemlock forest, then visit Catawba and Dick Gap Overlooks, both spectacular northward views of the river gorge and the Blue Heron Mine. After the overlooks you get to cross the tipple bridge, suspended high over the river, and visit the mine itself. On this section, you will become intimate with many of the activities associated with the Blue Heron Mine, both positive and negative, and will witness the dramatic recovery of the forest after such a short time.

Although the Kentucky Trail (KT) continues north to Yamacraw Bridge and connects with the Sheltowee Trace, we end our description at the Blue Heron Mine because some sections are poorly maintained and tough to find, others lie in rural-residential areas, and much of it may soon be rerouted. If you want to do a longer through-hike, tack the KT onto either the southern or western half of the 48-mile John Muir Trail (JMT) (Trail 43). Combined, these two trails make probably the best through-hike on the Cumberland Plateau. Our descriptions of both trails include ways to link them near Maude's Crack, using the JMT–KT Connector.

For those preferring to do this trail piecemeal, the 12.8-mile stretch between Terry Cemetery and Ledbetter Trailhead is a great day hike if you can get someone to drop you off, or if you don't mind a long shuttle drive after a long hike. The 7.2-mile section between Ledbetter and Blue Heron Mine is also a great day hike, and the vehicle shuttle is relatively painless.

Finding the trailheads: See directions to each trailhead in the "Local Directions" section, and refer to Map 16, which covers all the parts of the

Map 16—The Kentucky Trail

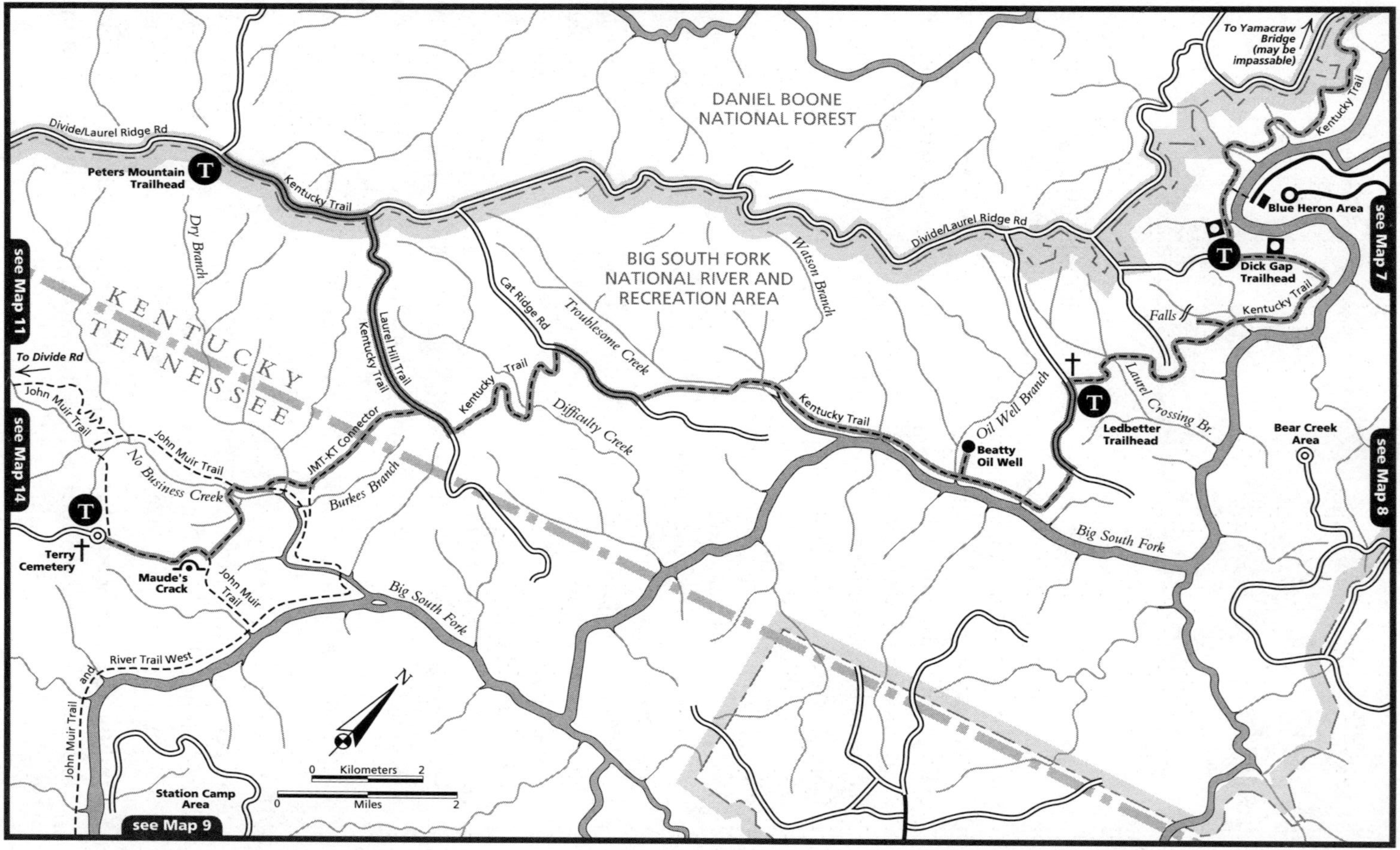

see Map 7
see Map 8

Blue Heron Area

To Yamacraw Bridge (may be impassable)

Kentucky Trail

Bear Creek Area

Dick Gap Trailhead

Kentucky Trail

Falls

Laurel Crossing Br.

Ledbetter Trailhead

Big South Fork

Divide/Laurel Ridge Rd

Beatty Oil Well

Oil Well Branch

Kentucky Trail

DANIEL BOONE NATIONAL FOREST

Watson Branch

BIG SOUTH FORK NATIONAL RIVER AND RECREATION AREA

Troublesome Creek

Difficulty Creek

Cat Ridge Rd

Kentucky Trail

Laurel Hill Trail

Kentucky Trail

Burkes Branch

Big South Fork

Kentucky Trail

Divide/Laurel Ridge Rd

Peters Mountain Trailhead

Dry Branch

KENTUCKY
TENNESSEE

JMRT-KT Connector

John Muir Trail

No Business Creek

Maude's Crack

John Muir Trail

River Trail West

Station Camp Area

see Map 9

John Muir Trail (?)

To Divide Rd

Terry Cemetery

John Muir Trail

N

Kilometers

Miles

see Map 11
see Map 14

KT we describe. Peters Mountain Trailhead, the official southern terminus of the KT, requires that you walk Divide Road for 1.6 miles and Laurel Hill Road for 1.9 miles and tolerate substandard scenery. You can also reach the KT via Laurel Hill and Cat Ridge Roads, spurs off Divide Road a few miles east of Peters Mountain Trailhead, but these rough roads will surely snare a 2WD vehicle. Terry Cemetery Trailhead makes the best starting point, and is worth driving the extra mileage from Blue Heron area.

Shuttle times vary considerably depending on the through-hike you choose but will usually be more than one hour (one-way), including a stretch on Divide Road, a bumpy gravel road that may slow you down substantially during certain times of the year. Ask a ranger about road conditions and about leaving your vehicle at trailheads for long periods of time. If you are worried about crossing the Big South Fork River at Blue Heron Mine, don't fret—you can cross the tipple bridge high above the river.

Trail Description

We describe this trail from south to north, starting at Terry Cemetery and ending at Blue Heron Mine.

Terry Cemetery Trailhead to JMT-KT Connector (2.5 miles): From Terry Cemetery Trailhead, you have two options for reaching the JMT-KT Connector (Map 13), both about 2.5 miles long. We prefer hiking the much more scenic Maude's Crack Trail (Trail 18), a muddy, potholed jeep trail leading to a spectacular overlook and ending with a challenging descent through Maude's Crack, a long, narrow crack in a sandstone bluff. (As of this writing, the trail through Maude's Crack was not an "official" NPS trail, but hiking through the crack was not prohibited, either.) From Terry Cemetery, walk east on the muddy jeep trail for 1.1 miles, following the Maude's Crack trail description, then return to this chapter.

At Maude's Crack the only way to reach the trails below is through the crack on a very steep trail, which will be loose dirt in the best conditions and slippery mud after rains. Be ready to spend part of the 0.1-mile trip on your hindquarters. At the bottom, look below you (north) for signposts indicating the JMT (Trail 43; see mile 25.0–26.0 for details). Get on the trail and turn left (west), descending the switchbacks on the west face of Burkes Knob for 1 mile to the wood bridge over Betty Branch. Cross the wood suspension bridge over No Business Creek a few hundred feet later, and reach No Business Trail (Trail 19; mile 2.2) soon thereafter. Turn right (east) and continue 0.3 mile to the intersection with the JMT–KT Connector, passing through part of the historical No Business Community. You have gone 2.5 miles.

If you are less adventurous—or this is your first backpacking trip—do miles 0.0–2.5 of the Longfield Branch–No Business Trails (Trail 19). Turn left (north) off Maude's Crack Trail about 0.1 mile east of Terry Cemetery onto Longfield Branch Trail—a wide gravel horse trail that plunges steeply into No Business Creek Gorge. Cross the creek at 0.8 mile, and turn right (east) on No Business Trail; hike another 1.7 miles through the historical No Business Community, and look left for the well-signed intersection for the JMT–KT Connector. You have gone 2.5 miles.

Note: If you are making a connection from the John Muir Trail, enter the description here.

JMT–KT Connector to Ledbetter Trailhead (10.3 miles): The JMT–KT Connector, a 1.4-mile section between No Business Trail and the plateau surface, connects you with the KT at Laurel Hill Road. From there the KT continues another 8.9 miles to Ledbetter Trailhead.

2.5 Head north at the well-signed intersection with the JMT-KT Connector near Burkes Branch. There is another signed intersection about 0.3 mile east near Dry Branch if you missed this turn. The beginning of the JMT–KT Connector is actually two short trails, forming the triangle shown on Map 14. The west trail crosses Dry Branch and the east trail crosses Burkes Branch, both very soon after leaving No Business Trail.

2.9 The two trails intersect near the bottom of the ridgeline between the two creeks, after which the trail climbs steeply up to the plateau surface along a narrow, rocky ravine. Soon you will encounter south-facing bluffs that tower over the No Business Community.

3.4 At the top, continue northeast along a wide, dry ridge bounded on both sides by sheer bluffs. The trail becomes a wide logging road and is gated at the KY–TN state line.

3.9 Reach Laurel Hill Trail, a wide multiuse trail, and turn right (east). You are now on the "official" KT. Continue on this road for a short distance and look for an opening in the woods on your left (north) where the KT leaves Laurel Hill Road.

4.2 Turn left (north) and punch into the woods on the KT; follow a wide, dry ridge covered with Virginia pine and mountain laurel for a short stretch. Descend into Difficulty Creek Gorge on a narrow ridge with oaks and hemlock on switchbacks and drop to the base of a sandstone bluff. You can visit a small waterfall via a short side trail. Back on the trail, cross an unnamed creek on a wood bridge in a moist hemlock, beech, and rhododendron forest. Difficulty Creek should be audible below.

5.4 Cross Difficulty Creek on a new wood bridge. Student Conservation Association volunteers camped near this spot for two months in the summer of 2000 and built this beautiful bridge with their bare hands. The trail climbs steeply out of the gorge on switchbacks.

6.1 Reach Cat Ridge Road, another wide multiuse trail on a wide ridge at plateau level. A sign at this intersection indicates (accurately) that you will cross Troublesome Creek in 2 miles and reach Ledbetter Trailhead in 6.8 miles. Turn right (east) and continue on this curvy road for about a half mile; look left for the place where the KT leaves the road.

6.7 The KT leaves Cat Ridge Road on your left (north). A sign accurately says you will cross Troublesome Creek in 1.3 miles and reach Ledbetter Trailhead in 6.1 miles. Punch into the woods and immediately descend switchbacks into Troublesome Creek Gorge among huge boulders and sandstone walls. Some of the switchbacks are faint, so watch for blazes. The hemlock, poplar, white oak, maple, beech, and magnolia are a bit larger in this drainage, and you will pass some beech trees growing precariously from cracks in a sandstone wall. Stop and take a look at the plant community on this north-facing slope so that you can compare it with the plant communities on the long stretch of south-facing slopes coming up (see ecology section).

8.1 Cross Troublesome Creek on a large wood bridge, veer right (east), and continue on the north bank of the creek. The trail rises and falls along the south-facing gorge slope of this beautiful tributary gorge. Do you notice a difference in the plant community?

8.5 Ford Lone Cliff Branch just upstream of its confluence with Troublesome Creek, and veer left (north), heading upstream along Lone Cliff Branch for a short stretch. Stay right at the trail intersection just afterward; the left (north) fork leads steeply up to private property near Kidd

Cemetery. Stay right at another similar intersection, following Watson Branch up to Stepping Rock, and ford Watson Branch. All of these crossings and intersections are within 0.2 mile of one another. For the next half mile the trail ascends and descends along the north bank of Troublesome Creek, crossing some minor, rocky streams.

9.5 Reach the Big South Fork River at a point where it turns and flows directly east for about 4 miles among humongous boulders—our favorite section of the river. The light along this trail is phenomenal, as the sun shines directly down the gorge in the morning and evening. There are some fantastic campsites here and periodically for the next few miles; if you plan on camping, you should stop here. The KT along the river is wide, like a tram road, and easy walking, so you should be able to bag some trail miles. However, this remote section of the river is where you should be walking slowly, taking in the great scenery, smelling the flowers, and taking pictures. River access pathways are intermittent, but you should be able to find plenty of fishing spots.

10.5 Ford Oil Well Branch, which used to be spanned by a wood bridge. The creek was named for the Beatty Oil Well, the first commercial oil well in the United States, located at the end of a short spur trail on the east side of the creek. The well was originally slated for extracting salt brine, a necessary staple, but struck crude oil instead. Since crude oil was nearly useless back then, the gusher was left to flow into the Big South Fork River—the first oil spill in the United States. The original well casing was made from a hollow tree, which disintegrated; all that remains is a black pipe from an unsuccessful attempt at reaching the oil again in the 1940s.

Continue along the river for another mile, passing an impassable road that leads north out to Ledbetter Trailhead and fording a few small streams in a bouldery zone.

11.5 At a small unnamed creek, turn left (north) away from the river and begin the tough but necessary climb out of the river gorge to Ledbetter Trailhead, which lies on the plateau about 450 feet higher than the trail along the river.

12.2 Reach the gravel road that leads to Ledbetter Trailhead, and turn left (west). The impassable road that leads to the river near Beatty Oil Well joins this road at Hill Cemetery.

12.8 Reach Ledbetter Trailhead—a hot grass-and-gravel parking area on the east side of the road.

Ledbetter Trailhead to Blue Heron Mine (7.2 miles): From Ledbetter Trailhead head north on the gravel road and look for a sign directing you off the road at King Cemetery.

12.9 Turn right (east) at King Cemetery. Some of the folks buried here were Mine 18 workers who walked to the mine every day, others were timber cutters, and some were subsistence farmers who stayed in the area for as long as they could after Mine 18 was closed.

Just after the cemetery, pass through a gate with a sign that says NO VEHICLES BEYOND THIS POINT and start descending gradually along a dry pine ridge with very young white pines, maples, and dogwood—a forest in the early stages of succession. Descend a bit and round a curve to the left; arrive at the edge of a deep ravine, then descend some switchbacks on a singletrack trail into a north-facing slope forest with lots of hemlocks, beeches, and many different oaks.

13.7 Reach Laurel Crossing Branch, a creek that cuts through a thin layer of soil and flows across the sandstone caprock of the plateau surface, and cross it on a wood bridge. Turn abruptly right and follow the creekbed downstream for a few hundred feet with the creek on your right. Cross North Fork of Laurel Crossing Branch on a wood bridge, after which the trail becomes like a tunnel beneath dense rhododendron and hemlock.

The trail soon turns away from the creek and climbs a few switchbacks into a young mixed forest of Virginia pine, blueberry, greenbrier, sassafras, pawpaw, and lots of mountain laurel, then descends into a hemlock forest and crosses a small foot bridge. You will pass through an open zone with lichens and mosses growing on exposed sandstone. This is a unique and fragile habitat, so please stay on the already barren surfaces.

14.7 The trail approaches Waters Cemetery but abruptly turns right (south) away from it. You will sweep gradually left on a horseshoe-shaped curve, circling all the way around to the north side of the cemetery. The trail emerges in an old field. Look straight ahead (bearing about 20 degrees) and walk into the very north corner of the field, then look left for trail blazes. The trail turns left (northwest) and follows the north edge of the old field on a dirt road in a mixed forest of young pine and hickory. In a few more tenths you will enter a larger old field covering a knoll with a great view. The planted pines are being overtaken by young winged sumac, poplar, oak, and maple. Head northeast (bearing about 50 degrees) through the field and punch into the young woods again at a trail blaze. You will soon notice the river gorge on your right (east).

15.8 Begin the descent into the river gorge on rock stairs, then a series of switchbacks. The trail leads down below the bluff line, climbs over a beautiful saddle on a ridge, then descends a dark, north-facing slope to the base of some smaller bluffs.

16.3 Reach the intersection with a short spur leading to Big Spring Falls; a worthwhile side trip. The falls drop from a sandstone shelf more than 100 feet high, starting with a cascade and ending with a free-falling column of water that lands in a beautiful plunge pool surrounded by rhododendron. The habitat beneath the falls is very fragile, so please view the falls from within the fenced overlook area.

Back at the intersection, continue descending into the gorge and cross the bridge over the creek that drains Big Spring Hollow. The trail follows the creek downstream a bit on switchbacks and passes a few good campsites. Soon after, reach the level of the electric tram that once brought tons of coal from the mines to the Mine 18 tipple for sorting. The trail generally follows the tram route all the way to Mine 18.

17.2 The trail crosses a small creek near Dick Gap Falls, turns left (west), and follows the creek upstream on the northern slope of its ravine. A set of stairs puts you on top of a flat rock.

18.1 Catawba Overlook, named for the catawba rhododendron in the area, lies on the right (north) side of the trail. It provides an unobstructed, panoramic northward view of the Blue Heron Mining Community and the river gorge at Devil's Jump Rapids. To the west you can see the tip of the bluff on which Dick Gap Overlook (Trail 6) is perched. We take you to this must-see overlook next.

18.6 A horse trail joins the KT and leaves it shortly thereafter. This trail connects the Dick Gap Trailhead with the river and on to Lee Hollow Loop and Bear Creek Loop (both in Trail 8). We recommend turning left onto this trail and following it uphill to the ridgeline above you and on to Dick Gap Overlook, which provides an even better view of the Mine 18 tipple. (Flip to our description of Trail 6.)

After visiting Dick Gap Overlook, continue down into the gorge on wet, slippery steps and wood stairs, reaching the base of the massive sandstone bluffs on which Dick Gap Overlook is perched. There are some big trees in this area—one massive shagbark hickory in particular.

19.4 Pass through the ravine of Three West Hollow, named after the third mine shaft on the west side of the river, and cross it on a wood bridge just upstream of its confluence with the river. You will pass a few damaged tram cars with the coal still in them.

19.7 Reach the Mine 18 tipple bridge and cross the river beneath a canopy of large sycamore, river birch, sweetgum, and other trees lining the banks of the river. Flip to the section on the history of the Blue Heron Mining Community. Better yet, find out about the people in this area by visiting the interesting interpretive displays, which have old pictures and oral histories recorded by mine workers and their descendants. Visit the main mine shaft, then get a snack at the snack bar (if it is open). Your vehicle lies in the parking area below at about mile 20.0.

24 Bandy Creek Campground Loop

TYPE OF TRAIL: Hiking only.

TYPE OF ADVENTURE: Nicely groomed gravel trail—great for a family walk, bird-watching trip, short jog, or cross-country training session.

TOTAL DISTANCE: 1.3 miles.

DIFFICULTY: Easy.

TIME REQUIRED: 15 to 40 minutes.

SPECIAL CONCERNS: Crosses a busy horse trail, four footbridges, and two parking lots.

WATER AVAILABILITY: None on trail; fountains at trailheads.

SCENIC VALUE: Fair: lots of pond creatures, deer, and birds, but also many human and horse facilities and a wastewater treatment plant.

USGS MAP: Honey Creek.

BEST STARTING POINT: Bandy Creek Visitor Center parking lot.

Overview: This groomed, fine gravel treadway circumnavigates the large, open field southwest of Bandy Creek Visitor Center. It lies along the interface between the plateau and headwater ravines that drain into Bandy Creek. The forest consists of relatively young white pine, silver maple, red maple, white oak, and hickory, but some large trees can be found in the forest outside the southern edge of the loop. The trail stays just inside the tree line, which is nice for morning or evening bird-watching trips. Along with many other species of birds, you should see common flickers, great crested flycatchers, indigo buntings, and white-breasted nuthatches and hear red-eyed vireos, hooded warblers, and barred owls at night. The visitor center pond supports lots of critters (see ecology section). The grass around the pond is regularly mowed, so it is easy to reach for photographs of red-winged blackbirds, frogs, snakes, and dragonflies. For an additional treat, gather the kids and bring a flashlight to the pond after dark!

Map 17—Bandy Creek Area (Hiking and Biking)

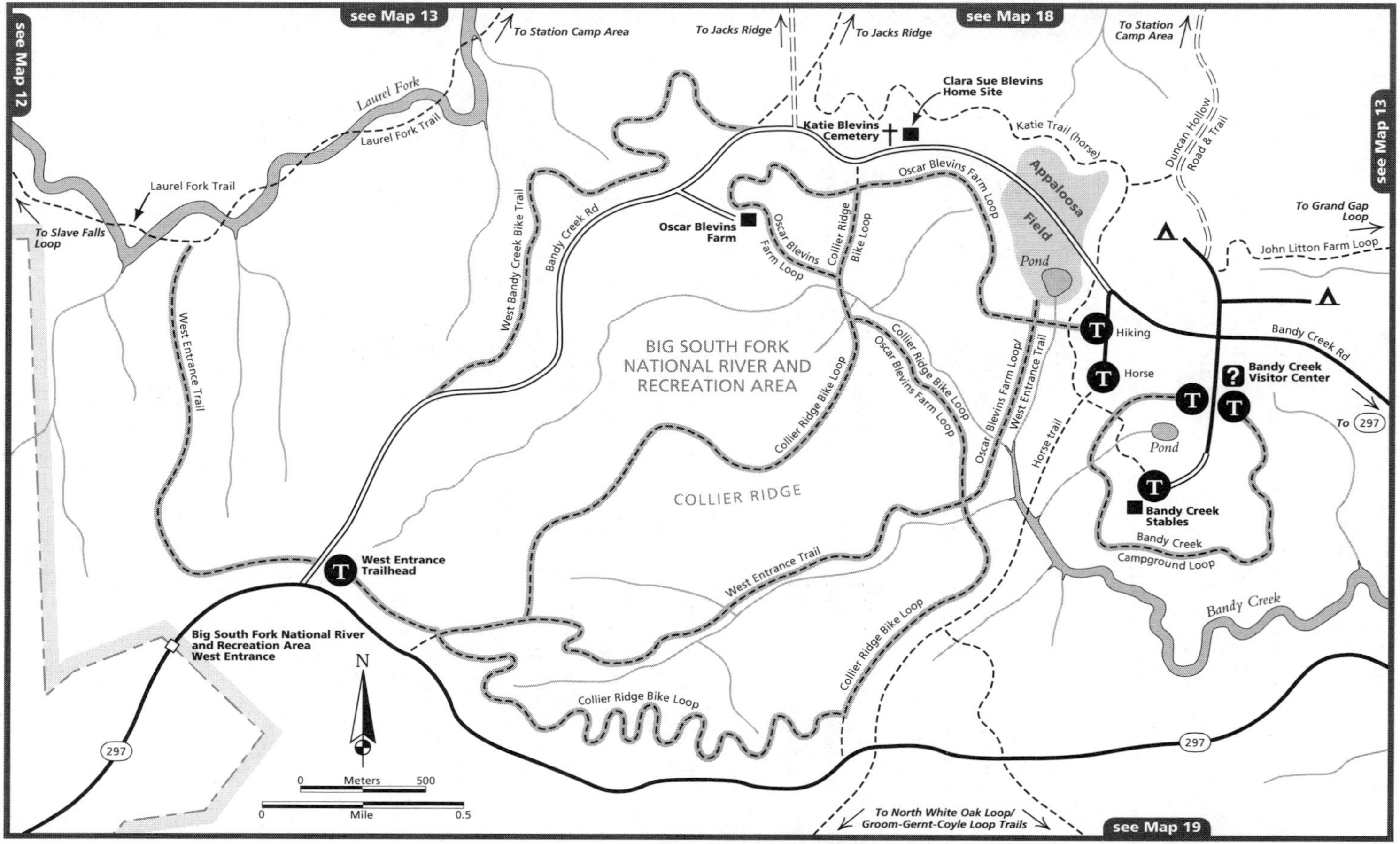

see Map 13

To Grand Gap Loop

John Litton Farm Loop

Bandy Creek Rd

To (297)

Bandy Creek Visitor Center

Bandy Creek Stables

Bandy Creek Campground Loop

Bandy Creek

(297)

see Map 19

To Station Camp Area

Duncan Hollow Road & Trail

Hiking

Horse

Pond

Horse Trail

West Entrance Trail

see Map 18

Appaloosa Field

Pond

Clara Sue Blevins Home Site

To Jacks Ridge

Katie Trail (horse)

Oscar Blevins Farm Loop

Oscar Blevins Farm Loop

Collier Ridge Bike Loop

Collier Ridge Bike Loop

To North White Oak Loop/ Groom-Gernt-Coyle Loop Trails

Collier Ridge Bike Loop

Katie Blevins Cemetery

To Jacks Ridge

Collier Ridge Bike Loop

Oscar Blevins Farm Loop

Collier Ridge Bike Loop

BIG SOUTH FORK NATIONAL RIVER AND RECREATION AREA

COLLIER RIDGE

Oscar Blevins Farm

West Entrance Trail

Collier Ridge Bike Loop

To Station Camp Area

Bandy Creek Rd

West Bandy Creek Bike Trail

Laurel Fork

see Map 13

Laurel Fork Trail

Laurel Fork Trail

West Entrance Trail

West Entrance Trailhead

N

Meters 500

0

Mile

0.5

Big South Fork National River and Recreation Area West Entrance

297

To Slave Falls Loop

see Map 12

Finding the trailhead: Follow directions to the Bandy Creek area and see Map 17. There are actually two trailheads, within sight of each other. One is directly behind the visitor center building; the other is west of the visitor center between the pond and the amphitheater. Both trailheads are marked with signs and a red arrowhead. We prefer to follow the trail clockwise, starting from the trailhead near the visitor center.

Trail Description

Enter the woods to the right of the visitor center. At 0.3, 0.4, 0.6, and 0.8 mile, you will cross small wooden footbridges. These can be slippery when wet. Note the steep headwater ravines of Bandy Creek to the east, the large trees in the forest to the south of the loop, the wonderful magnolia forest in many headwater ravines below the trail, and the southern pine beetle damage along the west part of the loop.

0.9 Cross the bridge over the covered concrete ditch that rises from the wastewater treatment plant for the Bandy Creek Campground. Because the Big South Fork NRRA lies so far from the closest municipalities, a separate treatment plant was constructed to deal with human waste generated in the Bandy Creek area. The treated effluent meets water quality standards upon discharge, as required by state and federal laws, is odor-free, and will not interfere with your outdoor experience.

1.2 Cross the horse trail that connects Bandy Creek Stables with the rest of the horse trails in the area. Be very careful here, and follow proper trail etiquette (horses always have the right-of-way). Horse traffic can be very heavy, especially on weekends, and you have a good chance of encountering novice riders on guided trips. If you are jogging at this point, slow down and be considerate of other users. Emerge from the woods southwest of the pond, cross the dam, and pass the amphitheater on your left. After crossing the dam, turn right along the paved footpath to finish the trail.

TYPE OF TRAIL: Hiking only.

TYPE OF ADVENTURE: Self-guided cultural and natural history tour.

TOTAL DISTANCE: 4 miles.

DIFFICULTY: Easy.

TIME REQUIRED: 2 to 3 hours.

SPECIAL CONCERNS: One road crossing and two bike crossings.

WATER AVAILABILITY: Adequate on trail; abundant at trailhead.

SCENIC VALUE: Good: important cultural areas, but busy trail in storm-damaged forest.

USGS MAP: Honey Creek.

BEST STARTING POINT: Bandy Creek Campground Trailhead.

Overview: This is an interesting trail for cultural and natural history buffs alike. The Oscar Blevins Farm, located along the trail above the headwaters of Bandy Creek, is a historic site representative of the region's late-nineteenth- to mid-twentieth-century farms. For photographers interested in historical structures, morning and evening have both good and bad aspects for shooting here, but evening light is probably the best. While you are in the mood for cultural history, we also take you to the Clara Sue Blevins homesite and Katie Blevins Cemetery, both located on the north side of Bandy Creek Road. Again, evening light is best for photographing these sites.

We describe the trail clockwise with the NPS trail brochure, in which detailed cultural and natural history notes correspond to numbered poles along the trail. It is worth your time to stop in at the Bandy Creek Visitor Center, visit with the helpful park rangers, and get the trail brochure before your hike. We do not attempt to describe the natural and cultural features along this trail in as much detail as does the NPS brochure, but we give you some basics.

Finding the trailhead: Follow directions to the Bandy Creek area, stop at the visitor center and get your trail brochure, then walk or drive to Bandy Creek Campground Trailhead. If you are walking from the visitor center, head west across the parking lot, get on the trail to the right (north) of the amphitheater, and walk 0.2 mile inside the edge of the woods to the trailhead.

Trail Description

From the trailhead, proceed northwest through a young forest with severe damage caused by a winter storm in 1998 that dumped wet, heavy snow that bent young Virginia pines into strange arches. The trees are young because this area was a farm field less than forty years ago. The storm was a minor setback in a process called secondary succession—the slow return of a forest or other habitat to the ecological conditions present before disturbance, which on the Cumberland Plateau would have been an eastern deciduous (hardwood) forest. Eastern fence lizards are abundant in this hot, dry habitat. After the field, cross a wide, well-trodden horse trail and a footbridge over a small headwater stream.

0.2 The trail splits into a loop. Go left to follow the loop clockwise with the trail brochure.

0.5 Descend into a headwater ravine on its north slope above a small waterfall, and climb down a set of wood stairs. The rock wall is the exposed edge of the sandstone caprock forming the top layer of the Cumberland Plateau (see geology section). The additional moisture provided by the waterfall and splash-pool creates conditions favorable for Lucy Braun's spiderwort, ferns, liverworts; mosses; and slimy, green, and northern dusky salamanders. The cool habitat below the ledge is very fragile, so stay on the trail. Continue on the trail with the creek on your left and soon reach a trail on your right leading up the slope to Muleshoe Rock Shelter; the name indicates that this shelter was used as an animal pen. Rock shelters like this have been used by native peoples for tens of thousands of years for protection from the elements. In the fall you may see the blooms of Lucy Braun's snakeroot, a threatened plant that occurs only in these types of environs. Yellow-billed cuckoo, red-eyed vireo, black-throated green warbler, pileated woodpecker, yellow-shafted flicker, and white-breasted nuthatch are just some of the birds you will see and hear in the moist ravines along this trail.

0.7 Cross Bandy Creek, which got its name from a nearby homestead in the early 1800s that was abandoned. Over time the word "abandoned" was shortened to "bandy." This creek flows south across TN 297 and enters the Big South Fork River just upstream of Leatherwood Ford.

1.0 Cross a headwater stream of Bandy Creek on a wood footbridge, and pass the trail leading to West Entrance Trailhead on your left (west). Soon after, the trail joins Collier Ridge Bike Loop (Trail 34), marked by blue bike blazes. Watch carefully for bikers, who will be going downhill really fast at this point; they all should be coming straight at you, not up from behind you, if they are doing the loop in the proper direction. On the bike loop you will enter the Billie Blevins farmstead, an old field in the early stages of secondary succession, evident by the winged sumac and forest tree saplings. Black rat snakes and garter snakes are often found in early successional habitats under tin roofing and other building debris. Towhees, prairie warblers, and great crested flycatchers are likely to be seen or heard. Hop over King Branch and step up some bare sandstone; Bandy Creek should appear in the gully on your right (east).

1.6 At the wide bike loop intersection, stay left, then hop across the creek. Only 30 yards later, turn left off the bike trail at the red arrowhead blazes; enter a young mixed forest and soon cross Bandy Creek on a wood bridge.

2.0 As you approach the Oscar Blevins Farmsite, you can see a beautiful split-rail fence on the edge of the forest and a root cellar or springhouse—a rock fridge where early settlers kept their perishable food cool. Turn left at the gravel access road for the farm, and take some time to visit the interesting historical structures. The field is not undergoing natural succession because the NPS leases this land to local farmers so that they can grow traditional crops like sorghum, used to make molasses and feed livestock. The horses grazing in the pastures are used by park rangers for Pioneer Day and for backcountry patrolling. Fifteen apple trees were planted at the farmsite in 2001. These are just a few of the National Park Service's efforts to maintain certain sites in their historical condition, an important part of the overall plan for the NRRA.

Oscar Blevins moved here with his new wife, Ermon, in 1940 after growing up on Station Camp Creek. They first lived in the cabin built by the Reverend John B. Blevins, a Baptist preacher and Oscar's great-uncle. The original cabin, constructed of hand-hewn oak, pine, and poplar logs, was built around 1879; a second room and a rear lean-to were added in the early 1900s. This cabin, located in front of the barn, is an example of the simple cabins constructed by pre-Revolutionary Kentucky settlers, which had a fireplace in the gable end, often with a small window near the chimney, a puncheon floor, a loft, and a shed attached to the rear. The corncrib was built around the same time as the log cabin. The cabin and corncrib are eligible for the National Register of Historic Places, and the farm area has been proposed for "cultural landscape" status.

Oscar and Ermon built a new frame house in a style that was typical of the region, called the "Cumberland House." Their new house was completed in 1950, a year before their son, Lawrence, was born. The large barn, which is used by the NPS to stable their horses, was added in 1963. Oscar and Ermon lived and worked on their farm until their property was bought in 1980 as part of the Big South Fork NRRA. Oscar died in 1989 and is buried in the Katie Blevins Cemetery, which you may visit during your hike.

After visiting the farmsite, head back to the intersection with the gravel access road; look north for where the hiking trail punches into the woods and heads uphill. You will cross a few footbridges over some brambly creeks in areas severely damaged by the 1998 storm.

2.6 Cross Collier Ridge Bike Loop again. As before, watch carefully—bikers may be going very fast on this steep downhill section of the course. They are supposed to yield to hikers but will be watching their own tires on this rocky trail, so don't assume they will even see you. Although there are lots of small pines along the trail, a few monstrous white pines stand out against the extensive storm damage.

2.9 The garbage pits you see before you are a reminder of how folks in this area once disposed of garbage. Notice how their version of "the dump" was located well away from the homesites and water sources. Unlike a municipal solid waste site, these pits are not lined with impervious clay, fitted with vent tubes to release methane gas, or covered with dirt to reduce the smell. But keep in mind that most of their soaps, dyes, and cleaning agents were natural, and they did not generate even a fraction of the amount of toxic substances, plastic, or cardboard that we do today. Most importantly, what they used, they used sparingly, a concept that we could stand to adopt these days.

3.1 A faint trail on the left (east) leads across Bandy Creek Road to Clara Sue Blevins Farm and Katie Blevins Cemetery. Although you could drive to this site, it is worth going there now if you have the time, since it adds only

0.2 mile to the loop. The Clara Sue Blevins house is a double-pen log structure without the central chimney. The double-pen house, also called a "tenant house," is a story-and-a-half house with two front rooms and a central chimney or stove flue. The downstairs rooms serve as a parlor and a guest room; upstairs are sleeping rooms. A lean-to rear addition, which is no longer standing, contained the kitchen and dining areas. The east end was built out of hewn yellow-pine logs in 1929. The chimney, which has recently been restored to its original sandstone construction, is in the east gable end. The west end was built after the family already occupied the east room. The log house, log barn, and corncrib are all eligible for the National Register of Historic Places, and the farm area has been proposed for "cultural landscape" status.

The double-crib log barn was constructed by George or Lora Blevins in 1929. The sheds were added later. A single-pen log corncrib was built around the same time. The barn was partially restored in 1996 with the addition of new logs.

Katie Blevins Cemetery, located adjacent to the Clara Sue Blevins homesite, is worth a short visit. You can ramble through the last resting places and read the tombstones of some of the early residents of the Big South Fork NRRA. The first person to be buried here was Jacob Blevins (1811–1869). The cemetery is named after Jacob's wife—Catherine, or Katie—who is also buried here. John and Elvira Litton also are buried here. You can visit their beautiful old farmstead on the John Litton Farm Loop (Trail 26). Now, back to the loop.

Head south and continue on the main loop trail, which swings gently toward the west in a pretty forest, reaching an abrupt transition to a young forest.

3.8 End of the loop. Turn left (south) and head back to the trailhead, at mile 4.0.

TYPE OF TRAIL: Hiking only.

TYPE OF ADVENTURE: Creekside hike to a historical area or connection to long loop.

TOTAL DISTANCE: 6.3 miles.

DIFFICULTY: Moderate.

TIME REQUIRED: 3 to 4 hours.

SPECIAL CONCERNS: Ladders, stairs, creek crossings, rock hopping, vehicles and horses.

WATER AVAILABILITY: Good on trail; abundant at trailhead.

SCENIC VALUE: Good: interesting historical area, young forest, no overlooks.

USGS MAPS: Honey Creek and Barthell SW.

BEST STARTING POINT: Bandy Creek Hiking Trailhead.

Overview: This popular loop is convenient for those camping at Bandy Creek Campground and is a great trail for observing most of the natural and cultural features on the plateau. It starts along the headwaters of Fall Branch, a beautiful watershed lined with lush forest and sandstone walls. You will visit the John Litton/General Slaven Farm, an interesting old homestead with a long split-rail fence, a pond, and some interesting structures in various stages of restoration. If you like photographing historical structures, both morning and evening light is superb in the valley of the Litton Farm. However, the old log barn gets the best light in the morning. The return trip currently lies on a gravel road but may eventually be

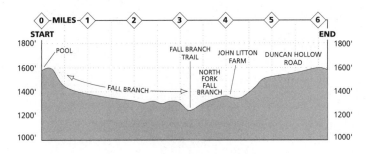

rerouted into the forest. For now, there are great bird-watching opportunities along the edges of fields and road corridors, and you will pass some important experimental vegetation plots in Scott State Forest.

For a fantastic 17-mile day hike, two-day backpacking trip, or practice for the Big South Fork Trail Race, combine the first part of the loop with Fall Branch Trail and Grand Gap Loop (Trail 39). Fall Branch Trail is short, has no trailhead per se, and serves only as a link between this trail and Grand Gap Loop (see the end of this chapter).

Finding the trailhead: Follow directions to the Bandy Creek Hiking Trailhead and see Map 13. If you are camping at Bandy Creek Campground, start near the pool (at mile 0.2 below).

Trail Description

From the Bandy Creek Hiking Trailhead, go northwest through young, storm-damaged pine woods. Cross Bandy Creek Road and reenter the woods; skirt the south edge of Loop A of Bandy Creek Campground, pass the pool, and look for the hiking trail that enters the woods just south of Duncan Hollow Road. This intersection is the beginning of the loop. If you need morning light for photographing the old barn, go clockwise, starting down Duncan Hollow Road. Counterclockwise corresponds with the route of the Big South Fork Trail Race and is the best direction for an afternoon hike. This puts you in a deep, cool ravine during the heat of the day, at the farm in pretty afternoon light, then on gravel roads that are good for bird-watching at dusk and guide you back to camp if you run late. We take you counterclockwise.

0.2 Punch into the woods near the pool, with white pine, maple, oak, and dogwood, and veer north along Duncan Hollow Road. Listen for songs of the red-eyed vireo, tufted titmouse, white-breasted nuthatch, brown creeper, and numerous warblers amongst the hubbub of the campground. The trail veers gradually back to the south and descends on switchbacks to the headwaters of Fall Branch, a flat sandstone-bottomed creek that cuts through the thin soil and flows directly on the plateau caprock beneath humongous white pines. Turn left and follow the trail directly eastward down the north bank of the creek.

0.6 Descend the moss-covered sandstone bluff on two wood ladders and rock-hop along a tiny creek emanating from a rock overhang. You will follow the creek downstream from high in its headwaters, as the hemlock and white pine forest gets older, darker, and more primeval and wood thrushes become more abundant. Continue for over a mile along rock walls and overhangs, winding in and out of the ravine slope, sometimes on switch-backs.

2.2 Just after passing some decent campsites on the right, reach Fall Branch Falls and its incredible campsite, which will surely be taken on busy week-ends if you do not plan ahead. You can swim in the pool under the falls, but the 1998 storm and recent pine beetle damage has cluttered the falls area and the pool with woody debris. Hopefully, the vast army of tiny decom-posers in this moist ravine will have done their job by the time you hike the trail.

After the falls, the creek loses elevation as you hike on a nearly level trail, skirting the ravine slope in a mixed forest damaged by storms and southern pine beetles. The thin soil around the root balls of toppled trees indicates their vulnerability. The damage has opened up the forest to inva-sion by sun-loving plants, including blackberries, which will be abundant and tasty in June and July. Chickadees will scold you constantly, and we have seen indigo buntings and nest-defending hooded warblers in this area. Standing dead-trees bring a diverse array of woodpeckers, including the pileated, flicker, hairy, and downy woodpeckers, and yellow-bellied sap-sucker.

3.1 Cross the North Fork of Fall Branch on a wood bridge and reach the intersection of Fall Branch Trail. A right turn leads to Grand Gap Loop in 1.9 miles. To hike Fall Branch Trail to Grand Gap Loop, see the end of this chapter. To continue on the loop trail to the farm, turn left and hike gen-erally northwest up the north slope of the ravine of North Fork of Fall Branch Creek, passing a rock wall stained red with iron deposits. Despite some tree damage in some spots, the hemlocks and beech trees are fairly large along this trail; rhododendron is dense, and the mountain laurel blooms are outstanding. Listen for black-throated green warblers and red-eyed vireos.

3.8 After some rock ledges, look through the trees on your left for the orig-inal split-rail fence at the edge of the John Litton/General Slaven farm-stead. At mile 4 turn into the farmsite at an old road, and cross the earthen dam and wood-plank bridge over the spillway of a small wooded pond with lots of stunted bluegill and huge tadpoles. Only certain kinds of tadpoles will be found in permanent ponds that contain fish. Among these, bullfrog and green frog tadpoles are the large yellow-green ones—living two years in this stage before they metamorphose! Like toad tadpoles, these also taste bad to fish.

Walk generally west on a gravel road, and turn left (south) at the intersection just past the old English-style barn built by John Litton. The vehicle access road leading up the hill goes straight west out to Duncan Hollow Road but is gated and used only by NPS vehicles and the crews doing the farm reconstruction. To exit the farm on foot, continue south and look for a footbridge over a creek on the southwestern edge of the farm.

4.2 Cross the footbridge mentioned above and start the steep ascent out of the North Fork Ravine on wood stairs and switchbacks, eventually reaching the plateau surface.

4.8 Emerge at the end of a U-shaped field, veer right and stay along the edge of the field; eventually you will veer west and enter a "tunnel" of vegetation just inside the edge of the woods. When you emerge from the tunnel, you may hear frogs calling from a pond on the very south edge of the field. Veer north and walk among the short trees invading the field from the forest. Listen for prairie warblers here; they are abundant in edges and old fields, and their voice is unmistakable: an ascending, repeated buzz that sounds like a cicada or a reward sound in a hand-held video game. Binoculars will not be needed—simply stand still and these tiny yellow birds will scold you from the trees right next to the trail. We also regularly see bluebirds, swallows, indigo buntings, and great crested flycatchers.

5.0 Turn left (west) onto the gravel road at the alternate trailhead. Before you head back to camp on the gravel road, you might want to look around for signs of a new trail. This portion of the trail may be relocated in the near future.

5.3 Join Duncan Hollow Road at the power line and stay left (west). Soon after, you will veer gently southward and pass two interesting research plots in Scott State Forest. The American chestnut research plot is an attempt to bring back the once-dominant forest species of eastern North America, which succumbed to an exotic fungus from Europe. Another plot is a breeding experiment for white pine.

6.1 Reach Bandy Creek Campground Loop A Road. Continue back to your vehicle at the trailhead in only 0.2 mile, head back to your campsite, or enjoy the pool!

Fall Branch Trail to Grand Gap Loop

This easy 1.9-mile trail connects John Litton Farm Loop and Grand Gap Loop (Trail 39) on a winding but simple-to-follow singletrack path (see Map 10). It starts at about 1,300 feet in elevation, makes a few short forays into and out of secondary tributary ravines, and ends at the northwestern tip of Grand Gap Loop at about 1,360 feet. The cumulative climb is less than 200 vertical feet, nowhere is the trail steep, and there are two spots to get water before reaching the very dry Grand Gap Loop. If you are continuing on either Grand Gap Loop or the JMT, you should filter some water at the creek crossing at mile 4.7 below. We continue the mileage from the intersection mentioned above.

3.1 Turn right off the John Litton Farm Loop, following the North Fork of Fall Branch downstream toward its confluence with Fall Branch. Shortly you will pass a great rock house then begin a sweeping counterclockwise turn at the end of a knob.

3.8 Pass on your left an old ramp used by loggers to roll logs down to the bottom of the ravine, where they would be loaded on trucks and hauled away for milling. Cross the logging road and watch for some very dangerous bluffs, indicated by a sign. After the bluffs, the ravine opens up and you may be able to pick out the sandstone walls below Angel Falls Overlook.

4.7 Cross a stream on a footbridge. This is the last water for a long while, so tank up!

5.0 Reach Grand Gap Loop and the JMT at a logging road. To continue on Grand Gap Loop, see mile 5.4 of the description for that trail. (We present the loop counterclockwise.)

TYPE OF TRAIL: Hiking only.

TYPE OF ADVENTURE: Route connecting Bandy Creek area with Laurel Fork Gorge.

TOTAL DISTANCE: 5.1 miles (one-way).

DIFFICULTY: Moderate.

TIME REQUIRED: 2 to 3 hours.

SPECIAL CONCERNS: One road crossing, multiple bike trail crossings, steep grade.

WATER AVAILABILITY: Adequate on trail; abundant at one trailhead, none at other trailhead.

SCENIC VALUE: Fair: young forest with extensive storm damage, not very remote.

USGS MAP: Honey Creek.

BEST STARTING POINT: Bandy Creek Campground or West Entrance Trailhead.

Overview: Because these two trails are a logical combination, we describe them in one chapter, going in one direction. These trails are mainly used for short out-and-back trips or as part of longer backpacking loops. The West Entrance to Bandy Creek Trail takes you along a headwater tributary of Bandy Creek to the West Entrance Trailhead, hence the name. It shares Oscar Blevins Farm Loop (Trail 25) for the first mile. The West Entrance to Laurel Fork Connector Trail brings you from the West Entrance Trailhead down into the beautiful gorge of Laurel Fork and intersects Laurel Fork Trail (Trail 17) at mile 3.8. Going the opposite way (returning to

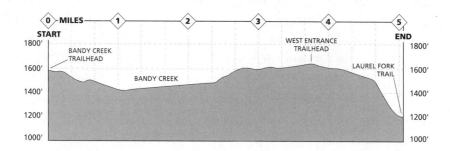

Bandy Creek area from a long backpacking loop from the north), you must climb out of Laurel Fork Gorge, making your cumulative climb 655 feet (see trail profile).

Finding the trailhead: Follow directions to the Bandy Creek Campground Trailhead or the West Entrance Trailhead in the "Local Directions" section (also see Map 17).

Trail Description

We describe these trails from east to west—from Bandy Creek Campground Trailhead to West Entrance Trailhead, then on to Laurel Fork Trail. Mileages in the opposite direction are provided in parentheses. We merely paraphrase the description of the Oscar Blevins Farm Loop (Trail 25) for the first mile, so flip to that chapter for details.

0.0 (5.1) From the Bandy Creek Campground Trailhead, proceed northwest through a young forest damaged by a winter storm in 1998 that dumped wet, heavy snow and bent young Virginia pines into strange arches. Just after crossing a horse trail, the trail splits. Go left (south) on the Oscar Blevins Farm Loop and West Entrance to Bandy Creek Trail, which are shared for another 0.8 mile.

0.5 (4.6) Descend into a headwater ravine on its north slope above a small waterfall and climb down a sandstone bluff on wood stairs. Continue on the trail with the creek on your left; soon you will reach a trail on your right leading up the slope to Muleshoe Rock Shelter, the name indicating this shelter was used as an animal pen. Shortly afterward, cross Bandy Creek.

1.0 (4.1) Cross a headwater stream of Bandy Creek on a wood footbridge, and come to a fork in the trail. Turn left (west) on the West Entrance to Bandy Creek Trail. The right (north) fork is the rest of Oscar Blevins Farm Loop.

1.2 (3.9) Watch carefully for mountain bikers as you cross Collier Ridge Bike Loop (Trail 34), and continue west into an area of relatively massive white pine trees along the creek. Shortly you will pass through an area damaged by an ice storm in 1998; leave Scott State Forest at about mile 1.7 (3.4).

1.9 (3.2) Cross a series of log bridges in a low area covered in hemlock, rhododendron, and ferns—the headwaters of Bandy Creek. West of this area you will ascend gradually on a few switchbacks to a dry, mixed-forest area.

2.5 (2.6) At the top of the plateau, the trail joins an old logging road.

2.7 (2.4) The hiking trail joins Collier Ridge Bike Loop (Trail 34). The paths are shared for the next 0.3 mile, so watch carefully for mountain bikers. They should be going fast here. After leaving the bike loop, the trail continues northwest, parallel to TN 297.

3.4 (1.7) Reach West Entrance Trailhead. To continue west down to Laurel Fork, go through the grass-and-gravel trailhead parking area and look for the trail where it crosses Bandy Creek Road (gravel) just north of its intersection with TN 297. Continue west, parallel to TN 297.

3.8 (1.3) Turn north away from TN 297, and follow another old logging road for a while through a young forest on a wide ridgeline, descending gradually toward the edge of Laurel Fork Gorge.

4.7 (0.4) After passing an exposure of sandstone capped with lichen, moss, and Virginia pines (please do not trample this fragile community growing directly on the sandstone), begin a steep descent into Laurel Fork Gorge. In a few tenths, the trail splits to make a single switchback, which is not as steep as the main trail. We suggest taking the switchbacks.

5.1 (0.0) Meet Laurel Fork Trail (Trail 17) on the south bank of the creek. To continue east or west along Laurel Fork Trail, flip to mile 3.8 of the Trail 17 description. If you are just starting this trail and heading all the way back to the Bandy Creek area, filter and guzzle some tasty Laurel Fork water before making the climb out of the gorge; you will not encounter a reliable water source for another 3 miles.

28 Katie–Jacks Ridge–Bypass–Duncan Loop

TYPE OF TRAIL: Horseback riding and mountain biking.

TYPE OF ADVENTURE: Fun loop on well-trodden, smooth, sandy paths.

TOTAL DISTANCE: 9.6 miles.

DIFFICULTY: Easy.

TIME REQUIRED: 2 to 3 hours.

SPECIAL CONCERNS: Busy sections shared with all types of users, deep sand.

WATER AVAILABILITY: Poor on trail; abundant at trailhead.

SCENIC VALUE: Fair: young upland plateau forest with tree damage.

USGS MAPS: Honey Creek and Barthell SW.

BEST STARTING POINT: Bandy Creek Equestrian Trailhead.

Overview: We combined North Bandy Creek Trail, Katie Trail, Jacks Ridge Loop, Bypass Trail, and part of Duncan Hollow Trail (in Trail 29) for a nice horseback riding loop north of the Bandy Creek Area. Having these trails in one chapter with mileages in both directions should help you plan outings or special equestrian events that require connections with other areas and trails to the north. Connections include the challenging Duncan Hollow–Station Camp–Black House Branch Loop (Trail 29), which takes you to Charit Creek Lodge and Station Camp Crossing, the Hatfield Ridge–Station Camp Creek Loop (Trail 21), and beyond.

We strongly urge against doing these trails on a mountain bike. All are busy horse trails, ensuring frequent courtesy stops. The deep yellow sand

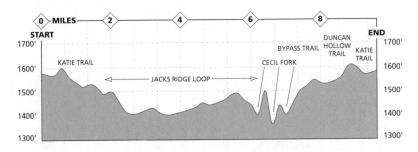

Map 18—North Bandy Creek Area

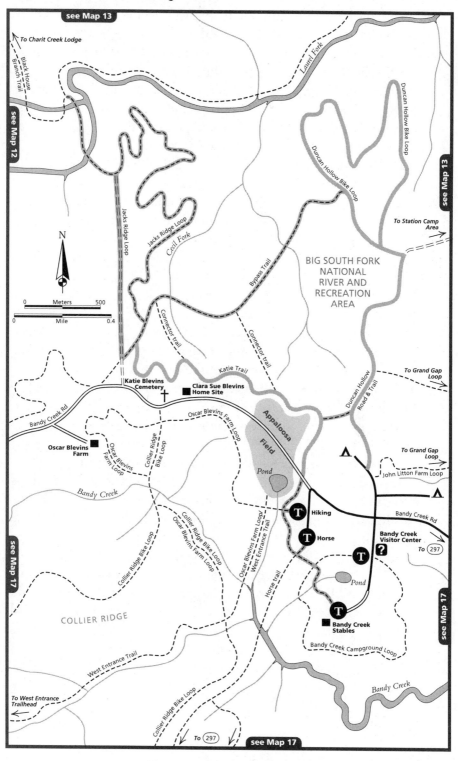

see Map 13

To Charit Creek Lodge

Black House Branch Trail

see Map 12

Laurel Fork

Duncan Hollow Bike Loop

see Map 13

Duncan Hollow Bike Loop

N

Jacks Ridge Loop

Jacks Ridge Loop

Cecil Fork

Bypass Trail

BIG SOUTH FORK NATIONAL RIVER AND RECREATION AREA

To Station Camp Area

0 Meters 500
0 Mile 0.4

Connector trail

Connector trail

Katie Trail

To Grand Gap Loop

Katie Blevins Cemetery

Clara Sue Blevins Home Site

Appaloosa Field

Duncan Hollow Road & Trail

Bandy Creek Rd

Oscar Blevins Farm Loop

Oscar Blevins Farm Loop

Collier Ridge Bike Loop

Oscar Blevins Farm

To Grand Gap Loop

John Litton Farm Loop

Pond

Bandy Creek

Collier Ridge Bike Loop

Oscar Blevins Farm Loop

Oscar Blevins Farm Loop

West Entrance Trail

Horse trail

T Hiking

T Horse

T

Bandy Creek Rd

Bandy Creek Visitor Center

?

To (297)

Pond

Collier Ridge Bike Loop

COLLIER RIDGE

T
Bandy Creek Stables

see Map 17

West Entrance Trail

Bandy Creek Campground Loop

To West Entrance Trailhead

Bandy Creek

Collier Ridge Bike Loop

see Map 17

To (297)

see Map 17

on both trails is often so loose and fluffy that even the fattest tires will bog down miserably, especially in dry months. The NRRA boasts three bike-only trails within a few miles of the Bandy Creek area and a number of lesser-used horse trails that are great for biking.

North Bandy Creek Trail (0.6 mile) is one of the most important and heavily used trails in the NRRA. Stretching between the Bandy Creek Equestrian Trailhead and Katie Trail, it provides the only link between equestrian trails south and north of the Bandy Creek area.

Katie Trail, named for Katie Blevins, links the North Bandy Creek Trail to Duncan Hollow Trail, Jacks Ridge Loop, and beyond. Its soft yellow-sand surface is like that of a sandbox, and the route is curvy, making it a fun trail. This 1.4-mile trail is easily accessed on foot and lies along the north edge of Appaloosa Field, so it is one of the best trails for watching or photographing special equestrian events. The Clara Sue Blevins Farm and Katie Blevins Cemetery, significant historical sites discussed in the Oscar Blevins Farm Loop (Trail 25), lie along the trail.

Jacks Ridge Loop is a popular trail that skirts the edge of a wide ridge perched above the gorge of Laurel Fork of Station Camp Creek. Vehicles were still allowed on a portion of the loop as of this writing, but the pathway is soft yellow sand, so may be impassable for those without 4WD capabilities. The well-trodden path is close to camp, easy to follow, and easy on horse hooves. Part of this loop is used by Bandy Creek Stables for their short ride, and part or all of it is routinely included in special equestrian events. The loop itself is only 4.2 miles long, but done from the equestrian trailhead (an easy 7.4-mile trip), it is a fabulous moonlight ride!

The 2.2-mile Bypass Trail provides another link between Jacks Ridge Loop and Duncan Hollow Trail. Originally known as the Duncan Hollow Bypass Road, its wide gravel surface is well groomed and appears driveable, but vehicles are not supposed to be on this trail. Twice it dips into Cecil Fork, a tributary of Laurel Fork of Station Camp Creek. We also included two well-trodden singletrack connector trails between the Bypass Trail and Katie Trail used by Bandy Creek Stables for their guided one-hour rides. Our loop is closed by a 0.6-mile ride on Duncan Hollow Trail, then Katie Trail returns you to North Bandy Creek Trail. The east part of the Bypass Trail and much of the Duncan Hollow Trail (1.2 miles total) shares the Duncan Hollow Bike Loop (Trail 33), so watch carefully—and be ready for surprises.

Finding the trailhead: Follow directions to the Bandy Creek area in the "Local Directions" section. We start the description from Bandy Creek Equestrian Trailhead. If your horses are stalled at Bandy Creek Stables, mount up at the stables, enter the woods just southwest of the pond, and proceed 0.3 mile to the equestrian trailhead.

Trail Description

We describe this entire loop clockwise but also provide mileages in the opposite direction (in parentheses).

0.0 (9.6) Bandy Creek Equestrian Trailhead. Go right (north) on North Bandy Creek Trail.

0.4 (9.2) Just after crossing Oscar Blevins Farm Loop (Trail 25, a hiking trail), the trail crosses Bandy Creek Road at an angle. Watch for vehicles and bikes, which are usually going fast at this point! Punch into the woods, continue north, and reach the east end of Appaloosa Field.

0.6 (9.0) Meet the Katie Trail at a T intersection, the beginning of our loop. A right (east) turn takes you counterclockwise on the loop to Duncan Hollow Road in 0.4 mile; a left (west) turn leads to Jacks Ridge Loop in 1 mile. Go left (clockwise) and skirt the north edge of Appaloosa Field.

0.7 (8.9) A singletrack trail on your right (north) connects with the Bypass Trail in 0.5 mile (at mile 6.4 below). (Bandy Creek Stables usually turns here on their one-hour guided horseback trip.) The trail enters the woods immediately after passing that trail. Just before a short downhill section, a faint trail on your left (south) leads 50 feet to the Clara Sue Blevins Farm and Katie Blevins Cemetery. Both sites are worth a quick visit, but horses are not allowed around the historical structures or cemetery, so cross-tie them in a good spot and walk over. Back on the trail, descend slightly, curve around to the west, and enter another field, skirting its edge.

1.3 (8.3) Just after entering the field with Katie Blevins Cemetery on its south end, pass a faint trail on your right (north). This is another shortcut that intercepts the Bypass Trail in about 0.3 mile (at mile 6.1 below), also used by Bandy Creek Stables on their one-hour guided horseback rides. Towhees, prairie warblers, and great crested flycatchers should be singing in the field.

1.6 (8.0) A T intersection with the Bypass Trail marks the western terminus of Katie Trail. A right turn takes you northeast for 2.2 miles to Duncan Hollow Trail; doing that allows you to skip Jacks Ridge Loop, limiting your trip to about 5.4 miles. To continue clockwise on our loop, turn left (southwest) and proceed a few hundred feet to the intersection at the west half of Jacks Ridge Loop, a wide, sandy road going straight north-south. This road connects with Bandy Creek Road about 0.1 mile south of this spot. As of this writing, vehicles were allowed on this road. Turn right (north) to go clockwise on the 4.2-mile-long Jacks Ridge Loop.

1.9 (7.7) Pass a jeep trail going off to the right (east).

2.3 (7.3) Reach a fork in the trail at a wide spot sometimes used as a secondary trailhead. The left fork is Black House Branch Trail, part of the challenging Duncan Hollow–Station Camp–Black House Branch Loop (Trail 29). That trail drops steeply into Laurel Fork Gorge, crosses it and Black House Branch, climbs steeply out of the gorge, and reaches the Charit Creek Lodge Trailheads (Trail 22) in about 2 miles. If you are going to the lodge or connecting with trails beyond, flip to the Trail 29 description, enter the description at mile 13.1, and follow it backward.

The right fork is the rest of Jacks Ridge Loop. For the next few miles you will be winding along the edge of Jacks Ridge, with views into Laurel Fork and Cecil Fork Gorges.

2.9 (6.7) Cross a power line right-of-way, where you will likely hear prairie warblers singing. Cross the same right-of-way again, and make a hairpin turn, taking you southeast. Laurel Fork Gorge is visible to the northeast. Black bears have been sighted in this area and in Laurel Fork Gorge, so watch carefully. They were reintroduced into the NRRA a few years ago and are holding their own.

3.6 (6.0) Cross the power line right-of-way again.

4.1 (5.5) Cross a wood bridge and then another at mile 4.5 (5.1).

4.8 (4.8) A faint trail off to your left (east) and another one nearby lead to the Bypass Trail. We suggest avoiding these unofficial shortcuts and continuing on Jacks Ridge Loop.

5.7 (3.9) Reach a T intersection with the Bypass Trail. The intersection where you started Jacks Ridge Loop at mile 1.6 (8.0) is just down the trail on your right (southwest). If you only want to ride Jacks Ridge Loop (making a 7.3-mile trip), return to that intersection and go back to the trailhead the way you came. To continue clockwise on our suggested loop, turn left (northeast) on the Bypass Trail.

6.1 (3.5) Pass the intersection with a trail on the right (south) that leads to Katie Trail in 0.3 mile (see mile 1.3 above). Soon after, cross a low spot in the Cecil Fork headwater ravine, then ascend to a wide ridge.

6.4 (3.2) At the top of the ridge, pass the shortcut on your right (south) that leads in 0.5 mile to the Katie Trail (mentioned at mile 0.7 above). Soon after, descend into a larger tributary of Cecil Fork.

6.7 (2.9) Cross a tributary of Cecil Fork on a wide wood bridge constructed for vehicle traffic. Stop here to water your horse, since this is the only reliable water source on the trail, using the already established paths. The trail climbs steeply out of the ravine and passes through a power line right-of-way. Continue ascending and veer right (east); descend briefly to a tiny wet crossing, then veer northeast and continue climbing.

7.2 (2.4) Intersect Duncan Hollow Bike Loop (Trail 33) on your left at a right-hand turn, now heading southeast. Watch closely for mountain bikers, which should be coming toward you if they are doing the loop in the proper direction. You will be sharing the loop with bikers for the next 1.2 miles. Although you have the right-of-way, never assume that mountain bikers know the rules of engagement—or will even see you if they are racing their buddies.

7.8 (1.8) The intersection of the Bypass Trail and Duncan Hollow Road. Turn right (south). You may be sharing the trail with vehicles coming from Bandy Creek Campground.

8.0 (1.6) Another part of the Duncan Hollow Bike Loop joins the trail from the west. Be ready, because bikers could spook your horses as they emerge from the woods.

8.1 (1.5) Pass through a wide power line right-of-way.

8.4 (1.2) The fields on both sides of the road are part of Scott State Forest Experimental Station. Here experiments are being conducted on white pine, an important commercial species, and the American chestnut, once the dominant tree species in the eastern deciduous forest, now reduced to pathetic "stump shoots" by the introduction of an exotic fungus from Asia.

8.6 (1.0) Turn on Katie Trail, which joins Duncan Hollow Road at an angle on your right (west) on the western edge of the Scott State Forest experimental field. Those of you going counterclockwise on this loop should watch carefully for bikers and vehicles on Duncan Hollow Road, a multi-use road.

9.0 (0.6) Reach the T intersection with North Bandy Creek Trail, closing the loop. Turn south to go back to the trailhead.

9.2 (0.4) Cross Bandy Creek Road, then Oscar Blevins Farm Loop (Trail 25) shortly thereafter.

9.6 (0.0) Arrive back at Bandy Creek Equestrian Trailhead. Add another 0.3 mile for the trip back to Bandy Creek Stables.

29 Duncan Hollow–Station Camp–Black House Branch Loop

TYPE OF TRAIL: Horseback riding, mountain biking, and hiking.

TYPE OF ADVENTURE: Long, tough ride with dips into and out of two deep gorges.

TOTAL DISTANCE: 15.5 miles.

DIFFICULTY: Strenuous.

TIME REQUIRED: Full day.

SPECIAL CONCERNS: Two very steep descents and climbs on loose gravel, six creek crossings.

WATER AVAILABILITY: Good: Middle section lies along a creek.

SCENIC VALUE: Excellent: diverse historical and natural scenery, but no overlooks.

USGS MAPS: Honey Creek and Barthell SW.

BEST STARTING POINT: Bandy Creek Campground or Equestrian Trailhead.

Overview: If Kym had only one day to horseback ride in the NRRA, she would pick this set of trails, for many reasons. It warms you up on flat trails in pretty morning light, dumps you deep in the gorge in the heat of the day,

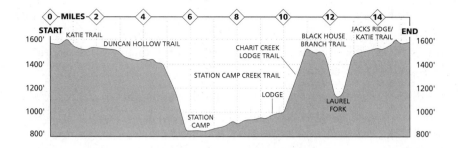

takes you to the river for a swim, and treats your horses to lots of great watering holes. It stops you at Charit Creek Lodge for a snack and some lively conversation, then challenges you and your horse with two tough gorge climbs.

Todd loves this trail for a fun but tough mountain bike ride. The sections of deep sand are worse torture than any of the gorge climbs, but they are a small part of the ride. All the gorge climbs can be cleared without stopping—with granny gears and a little luck. The grade at the end of Duncan Hollow Trail is the steepest, and if you can clear it without stopping, you should be proud. The creek crossings are superfun but can be slick, so either walk across, be prepared for a fall, or just fall on purpose and go swimming.

We start you on Duncan Hollow Trail, a wide, gravel road. It runs between Bandy Creek Campground and Station Camp, an historical area deep in the gorge of Laurel Fork of Station Camp Creek about 0.8 mile west of the Big South Fork River. The road is nearly level for the first 4 miles, and its scenic value is relatively low until it drops into the gorge, so this trail is usually used to connect with other trails or make loops. Some older trail maps suggest that this trail is 10 miles long, more than twice its actual length.

Once in the gorge, you connect with Station Camp Creek Trail, a 3-mile section of Trail 21. If you really want to test your mettle as a biker, or the stamina of your horse or yourself as a rider, do the north half of Hatfield Ridge–Station Camp Creek Loop instead of the south half along Station Camp Creek. It takes you up to Hatfield Ridge, then back down to Charit Creek Lodge. This allows you to add Charit Creek Overlook, a spectacular overlook of the entire lodge area, but adds another very steep gorge climb and descent for a total of three gorge climbs and descents!

After lounging at the lodge for a while, climb to the top of Fork Ridge and join Black House Branch Trail. This 1.8-mile connector trail dumps you into Laurel Fork Creek Gorge, one of the prettiest riparian zones in the NRRA, then makes a final climb to Jacks Ridge Loop (in Trail 28). From there you can get back to camp myriad ways, all of them on flat, dry ridgelines on the plateau, but we take you back on the Katie Trail (in Trail 28).

Finding the trailhead: Follow directions to the Bandy Creek area. Other good starting points for this trail include Charit Creek Lodge Trailhead (Trail 22), Station Camp Equestrian Trailhead (horses), or Station Camp Crossing (bikers) (see Map 13 and Map 18).

Trail Description

The logical starting point for horses is the Bandy Creek Equestrian Trailhead, and the best direction is counterclockwise, but we also provide clockwise mileages in parentheses. This is a complicated loop with lots of connections, so we include a lot of details to keep you from getting lost. The trail starts and ends on Trail 28 and the middle section lies on Trail 21, but we also describe those sections here for clarity. Horseback riders starting from Bandy Creek Stables should punch into the woods west of the stables and ride 0.3 mile to Bandy Creek Equestrian Trailhead.

For mountain bikers the first 1.2 miles is part of Duncan Hollow Bike Loop (Trail 33). Starting at the visitor center, head north across Bandy Creek Road; enter the campground area on the gravel path west of the fee kiosk, and head toward "Loop A." Continue past the pool and look for Duncan Hollow Road, a gravel road on your right immediately north of the pool parking area. The road is marked with a wood road sign, a small sign with a blue bike symbol, and one with a 4x4 symbol. This intersection is about 0.2 mile from the visitor center parking area. Ride north on the gravel road for 0.5 mile and enter our description at mile 1.0 below.

0.0 (15.5) From the equestrian trailhead, head right (north) on North Bandy Creek Trail (in Trail 28) and cross Oscar Blevins Farm Loop (Trail 25, a hiking trail) after 0.3 mile.

0.4 (15.1) Cross Bandy Creek Road and continue north for 0.2 mile to a T intersection with Katie Trail (in Trail 28). Turn right (east), punch into the woods on a singletrack trail, and continue another 0.4 mile under a dense canopy of young maple and oak north of the campground.

1.0 (14.5) Join Duncan Hollow Road and veer left (north). You may encounter vehicles and bikers on this stretch of the road, so be careful;

don't assume others will follow proper trail etiquette. Bikers entering the trail at this point should give horseback riders the right-of-way. The fields on both sides of the road are part of Scott State Forest Experimental Station. Here experiments are being conducted on white pine and the American chestnut.

Now that all users are finally at the same spot, the mileages from the other starting points are as follows: 1.3 mile from Bandy Creek Stables, and 0.5 mile from the visitor center (bikers).

1.5 (14.0) Pass through a power line right-of-way and continue north. This multiple intersection has the southern portion of Duncan Hollow Bike Loop (Trail 33) on your left and a secondary access road for the John Litton Farm Loop (Trail 26) on your right. Duncan Hollow Road heads generally north through a young pine forest, so you will likely hear lots of pine warblers. Soon after, mountain bikers may be entering the road from a bike trail on the left, so watch carefully.

1.9 (13.6) Reach the intersection with the Bypass Trail (in Trail 28), a multiple-use trail that connects to Jacks Ridge Loop (also in Trail 28) and Duncan Hollow Bike Loop (Trail 33). Stay right to continue on Duncan Hollow Road. You should now be heading directly east.

2.7 (12.8) At a sharp leftward (northward) bend, pass an intersection with a gravel road on your right; continue north. Soon after, a gravel road leading to the Grand Gap Loop (Trail 39) is on your right (east). Continue north.

3.4 (12.1) Enter Mitchell Field, Mitchell Burke's old farm- and homesite. The structures have been removed, and the pasture is being reclaimed by blackberries, sumac, and forest trees. Birders should look for prairie warblers and great crested flycatchers scouting for insects and red-shouldered hawks hunting for small mammals. There is a great campsite for backcountry horseback riders under some trees at the old homesite on the south end of the field. Remember, you need a permit to stay overnight in the backcountry.

Continue through Mitchell Field and reenter the woods at its north end. A bit farther north, a trail going off to the left (west) is simply an old logging road, so continue north. North of here, the road becomes much sandier and may pose problems for bikers in dry months.

4.9 (10.6) Just after passing another old logging road on the right (east), pass through a gate keeping motorized vehicles from proceeding into the gorge. The descent into the gorge is nearly a mile long, with some very steep sections on loose gravel and small boulders. Horseback riders should stop at the hitching posts to check their tack and tighten their girth; mountain bikers should double-check their brakes.

Soon after the gate you will drop steeply between two sandstone bluffs and enter a headwater ravine draining the east slope of Laurel Fork Gorge. The forest changes dramatically from a dry, upland plateau forest to a mesic slope forest with hemlock, beech, tulip poplar, red oak, chestnut oak, shagbark hickory, magnolia, and rhododendron. You are likely to hear, and possibly see, red-eyed vireos, hooded warblers, black-throated green warblers, wood thrushes, pileated woodpeckers, and other "gorge birds." On the right is a large sandstone wall with interesting iron deposits, where differential erosion rates in different types of rock have left swirly patterns. We have found salamanders in this area, a sign of recovery in the short period since this region was completely denuded of trees. The trail follows the wall for a bit, then gets very steep, descending the west-facing gorge slope. Watch your speed in the loose gravel.

5.8 (9.7) At the bottom of the gorge slope, you will find some hitching posts, which are good for checking your tack or getting off for a dip in the creek before you. The horse trail fords Laurel Fork just west of an elevated hiking bridge and on the north bank, comes to a **T** intersection with Fork Ridge Trail—a ridiculously steep horse trail that we intentionally left out of this book. You have entered the Station Camp area, a historical encampment. The Big South Fork River is only 0.8 mile east of this intersection. Turn right (east) and follow the wide, sandy path to the river. On the way to the river, you will pass the signed intersections with Station Camp Creek Trail and Hatfield Ridge Loop, but we describe the trail as if you were going to the river.

We have seen a lot of cool critters among the river cane in this area. You can tell the creek is in good condition by the mayflies and stoneflies that scurry along the undersides of flat rocks in Laurel Fork. Darters, dace, and sunfish are visible in its superclear waters. Map turtles and eastern box turtles may be found nesting on the bank; queen snakes mate in piles of woody debris at waters edge. With the large amount of edge habitat, birds are diverse, and white-tailed deer and feral hogs are abundant.

6.6 (8.9) Just after passing the trail leading up to Hatfield Ridge, reach the Big South Fork River at its confluence with Station Camp Creek. This is

Station Camp Crossing. At the river you can cross-tie or picket-line your horses within sight of the swimming hole. But remember, this is a busy river crossing; horses, bikers, and hikers may show up at any time, so to keep the trail safe for yourself, your horses, and other users, please do not cross-tie your horses so that they block the trail. Afterward, retrace your steps to Hatfield Ridge Loop.

Several species of endangered mussels occur in the shallow shoal at Station Camp Crossing. To accommodate all types of users without compromising the mussels, the NPS cleared most of the large rocks out of a narrow lane at Station Camp Crossing. You can swim and play anywhere on the river, but please use only this cleared lane when watering or wading with your horses. The crossing could eventually be closed to horse traffic if a direct link between horse traffic and significant impacts to mussels is made.

6.8 (8.7) At the intersection with Hatfield Ridge Loop, continue west. Very soon you will reach another intersection with signs indicating mileages to numerous locations. Turn right (west) on Station Camp Creek Trail (part of Trail 21) to go directly to Charit Creek Lodge in 3.1 miles, without any climbing. We describe the trail briefly below, but flip to mile 7.8 of the Trail 21 description for details. If you want to add another big gorge climb, a wonderful overlook, and another gorge descent (a 7-mile trip), turn right (north) on Hatfield Ridge Loop and flip to mile 7.0 of the Trail 21 description. That trip adds about 4 miles to your ride, 2 of them on steep slopes.

Continue straight ahead (west) at the intersection with a trail leading south to the Bandy Creek area via Duncan Hollow Road. If you want to return to camp the same way you came, this is your turn. A sign gives fairly accurate mileages to Bandy Creek Campground (6.3), Station Camp Horse Camp (6.1), and Station Camp Crossing (0.9).

After this intersection, ford Station Camp Creek. The trail is wide but rocky, with lots of ups and downs, and usually remains wet from numerous seeps that drain groundwater from deep inside Hatfield Ridge. Massive boulders line the trail. These broke away from the bluff walls on the south edge of Hatfield Ridge and tumbled down to your position, imparting a rugged appearance to the gorge of Station Camp Creek.

8.3 (7.2) The old field on the right (north) side of the trail was probably the home of Johnathan Blevins. His grave lies in Hatfield Cemetery, a small opening in the woods at the end of a faint pathway on the east end of the homestead about 100 feet north of the main trail. It is probably easiest to cross-tie your horses and hike to the cemetery, which is often overgrown with briers and blackberries.

8.5 (7.0) After entering a dark hemlock forest along Station Camp Creek, cross the creek once, again at 8.6 miles near a beautiful flowering magnolia tree on the water's edge, a third time at 8.7 miles, and a fourth and fifth time at about 8.8 miles—the last two times near a massive rock leaning over the creek. For the next mile you will make short ascents and descents along the base of the boulder-littered south slope of Hatfield Ridge.

9.7 (5.8) The lodge's horse stable is on your left. If you are a preregistered guest staying at the lodge on horseback but find the stalls are locked, tie your horses to a hitching post and walk across the field to the lodge to get everything squared away. If you are just passing through or are not preregistered at the lodge, continue west for another 0.2 mile, pass the lodge, and cross Charit Creek on a culverted bridge. Leave your horses at the hitching posts just across the creek while you visit the lodge, eat lunch, or register for a horse stall.

To continue on this loop, head south on Charit Creek Lodge Trail (Trail 22), which leads 1.5 miles up to Charit Creek Trailhead and Black House Branch Trail. It is easy to find your way out of the valley—simply follow the well-traveled gravel road past the chimney of Tackett Cabin, cross Station Camp Creek, and start the climb to Charit Creek Trailhead. Flip to the description of that trail for details. Water your horses once more before the brutal climb to the trailhead.

11.0 (4.5) After going around a metal gate, emerge adjacent to the gravel parking area of the Charit Creek Hiking Trailhead. Veer right (south) and go by the parking area to a T intersection. To reach Charit Creek Equestrian Trailhead, turn right (west) and go 0.2 mile down Fork Ridge Road. To ride back to Bandy Creek Area, turn left (east) on a dirt road that enters the woods; this is Fork Ridge Trail. After 3 miles Fork Ridge Trail makes an extremely dangerous descent into the gorge at Station Camp; follow this trail for only about 0.1 mile, then turn right (south) onto Black House Branch Trail, another dirt road.

11.7 (3.8) Just after passing through a power line right-of-way, stop at the hitching posts and adjust your tack for the gorge descent ahead. Go around the metal gate restricting vehicle access into Laurel Fork gorge, and again pass through the power line right-of-way. Descend steeply.

12.3 (3.2) At the bottom of the gorge slope, join the Laurel Fork Trail (Trail 17, a hiking trail), cross Black House Branch, turn east, and continue downstream along its south bank. Shortly thereafter, cross it again just upstream of its confluence with Laurel Fork. Shortly after, cross it again and stay left (south) as the Laurel Fork Trail splits off to your right (west) and continues upstream along the north bank of Laurel Fork.

12.6 (2.9) Cross Laurel Fork and continue along its south bank. Prepare yourself and your horse for a steep ascent, the final gorge climb of this loop. The steep gorge slope is covered with good-sized hemlock, beech, tulip poplar, and oak, and you will pass under some impressive rock walls.

13.1 (2.4) Immediately after going around a metal gate, emerge from the woods at a wide fork at the north end of Jacks Ridge Road, about 0.8 mile north of Bandy Creek Road. This is sometimes used as a secondary trailhead for Jacks Ridge Loop, and vehicles might be parked or turning around there, so watch carefully. The left (northeast) fork is Jacks Ridge Loop but adds 3.5 miles to your trip, probably an unwelcome idea at this point. Take the right (south) fork to return to the trailhead using the shortest possible route. You can flip to the trail description for the Katie–Jacks Ridge–Bypass–Duncan Loop (Trail 28) and follow that loop backward from the north end of Jacks Ridge Loop (mile 2.3) to Bandy Creek Equestrian Trailhead (mile 0.0), but we describe the main points in the correct direction below.

The soft sandy trail leads directly south through some dry, mixed woods. Horses love the soft yellow sand, but mountain bikers may find this section cruel punishment. Most bikers end up bogged down and walking. Do *not* leave the trail and ride in the woods on horse or bike—it is not only bad etiquette but you are putting your horse at risk for injury. Besides, the sharp spines on greenbrier vines will tear up your horse's legs and flat a bike tire in an instant.

13.9 (1.6) A complicated intersection with the Bypass Trail (in Trail 28) marks your turn onto Katie Trail. Bandy Creek Road is about 0.1 mile south of this spot, and bikers should ride the road 1.4 miles back to where they started, as the sand on Katie Trail is legendary. The wide gravel road going left (northeast) is the Bypass Trail, which connects with Duncan Hollow Bike Loop and, finally, Duncan Hollow Road at mile 1.9 in the description above. Horseback riders should head south on Katie Trail, the well-trodden sandy trail that quickly curves around to the left (east) and enters the field with Katie Blevins Cemetery on its south end. Towhees, prairie warblers, and great crested flycatchers should be singing on the edge. Continue through another field with the cemetery visible to the south, then skirt the north end of Appaloosa Field.

14.9 (0.6) Meet the North Bandy Creek Trail at the T intersection where you were hours ago, closing the loop. Turn right (south), cross Bandy Creek Road in 0.2 mile, and continue another 0.4 mile to Bandy Creek Equestrian Trailhead. Bikers still on the trail should turn left (east) on Bandy Creek Road to head back to the visitor center, reaching it in another 0.4 mile.

15.5 (0.0) Bandy Creek Equestrian Trailhead. You did it! Add another 0.3 mile for the trip to the stables.

30 North White Oak Loop and Overlook

TYPE OF TRAIL: Horseback riding or mountain biking.

TYPE OF ADVENTURE: A long, roller coaster ride on a nicely groomed trail.

TOTAL DISTANCE: 15.2 miles.

DIFFICULTY: Moderate.

TIME REQUIRED: Full day.

WATER AVAILABILITY: Poor on trail; abundant at trailhead.

SPECIAL CONCERNS: Two paved road crossings; gravel portions shared with vehicles; deep sand; many sunny, hot, and dry sections.

SCENIC VALUE: Good: nice creeks and overlook, but young forest with tree damage.

USGS MAP: Honey Creek.

BEST STARTING POINT: Bandy Creek Equestrian Trailhead.

Overview: This loop is easily reached from the Bandy Creek area and is probably the most popular horseback riding trail in the NRRA. The sandy, well-trodden pathway is easy to follow and is gentle on horse hooves. It

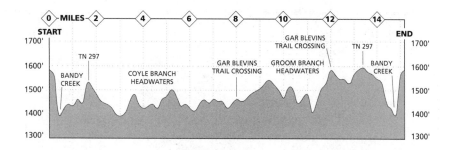

MILES

START

END

0   2   4   6   8   10   12   14

1700'

1600'

1500'

1400'

1300'

1700'

1600'

1500'

1400'

1300'

TN 297

BANDY
CREEK

COYLE BRANCH
HEADWATERS

GAR BLEVINS
TRAIL CROSSING

GROOM BRANCH
HEADWATERS

GAR BLEVINS
TRAIL CROSSING

TN 297

BANDY
CREEK

lacks the brutal, 500-foot gorge climbs that punish even the most athletic steeds on other trails in the NRRA. This is simply a great trail for riding your horse in the woods, especially if you like to trot, rack, or canter on fun, curvy trails.

This fun trail is far from the most scenic in the NRRA. Most of the trail is exposed or covered by young forest trees that have been damaged by the 1998 storm or southern pine beetles; it also lacks the beautiful sandstone bluffs and rock houses for which the NRRA is known. As a result, most of this loop is hot and dry, so start as early as possible in the summer months. Water for horses is sparse in summer and fall, so let them get plenty before you start, and let them drink whenever possible. Make sure you have plenty of water for yourself, too.

To spice up the scenery, we add a short visit to North White Oak Overlook. We also give directions for adding a trip to Leatherwood Overlook (Trail 32) and trails leading down to the O&W Railroad Grade, a wide path deep in the gorge of North White Oak Creek, one of the prettiest waterways in the NRRA. If you or your horse runs into problems during the ride, you can cut the trip to 7.8 miles by taking the shortcut shown on Map 19.

A great add-on to this trail is the Groom-Gernt-Coyle Loop (Trail 31), a 15.8-mile trail that includes a section on the O&W Railroad Grade. Portions of these two loops are shared, so the combined trip is actually only 25.2 miles long. This is a great combination if you are thinking about entering an equestrian competition for the first time, want to better your 25-mile ride time, or are just looking for a really long ride on soft, well-trodden paths. To combine the two loops, follow the description below to mile 12.3, turn onto Groom Branch Trail (some call it West Entrance Trail), and flip to mile 2.9 in the description for Trail 31.

We strongly urge you to against doing this loop on a mountain bike, especially on weekends. You are guaranteed to pass horseback riders on this trail, and the rules of trail etiquette will require frequent stops and/or

Map 19—South Bandy Creek Area

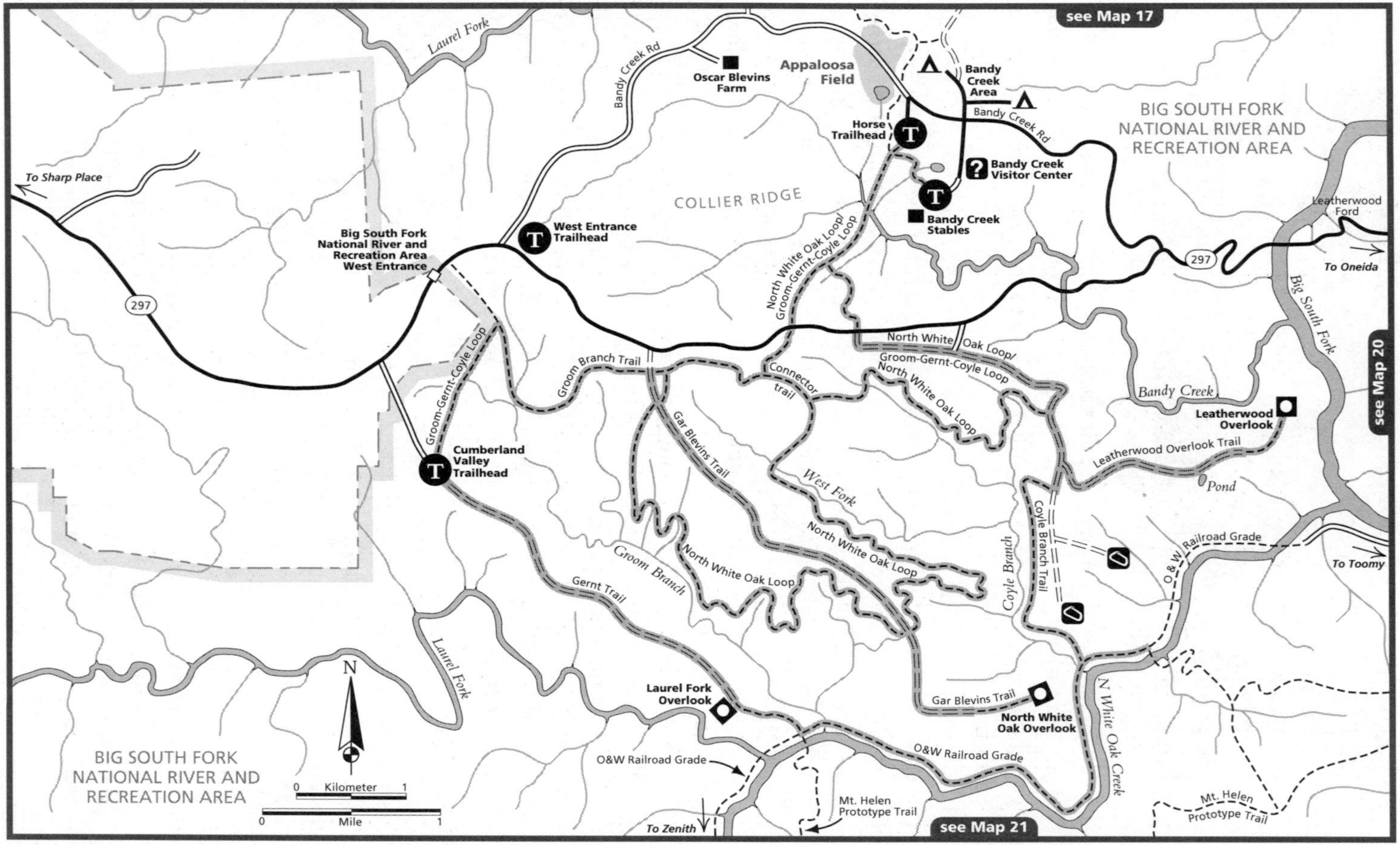

see Map 17
see Map 20
see Map 21

BIG SOUTH FORK
NATIONAL RIVER AND
RECREATION AREA

Leatherwood Ford

To Oneida

Big South Fork

To Toomy

Bandy Creek Rd

297

Leatherwood Overlook

Leatherwood Overlook Trail

Bandy Creek

Pond

O&W Railroad Grade

N White Oak Creek

Mt. Helen
Prototype Trail

Bandy Creek
Visitor Center

Bandy
Creek
Area

Coyle Branch Trail

North White
Oak Overlook

Bandy Creek
Stables

North White Oak Loop

Groom-Gernt-Coyle Loop

North White Oak Loop

Coyle Branch

Gar Blevins Trail

Horse
Trailhead

Appaloosa
Field

North White Oak Loop/
Groom-Gernt-Coyle Loop

Connector
trail

West Fork

North White Oak Loop

O&W Railroad Grade

Mt. Helen
Prototype Trail

Oscar Blevins
Farm

COLLIER RIDGE

Gar Blevins Trail

North White Oak Loop

Laurel Fork
Overlook

To Zenith

Bandy Creek Rd

West Entrance
Trailhead

Groom
Branch Trail

Groom Branch

Gernt Trail

O&W Railroad Grade

Laurel Fork

Cumberland
Valley
Trailhead

Groom-Gernt-Coyle Loop

Big South Fork
National River and
Recreation Area
West Entrance

Laurel Fork

297

To Sharp Place

BIG SOUTH FORK
NATIONAL RIVER AND
RECREATION AREA

N

0   Kilometer   1
0   Mile   1

dismounts on your part. Moreover, the deep yellow sand makes it torturous for even experienced riders, especially in dry months. The NRRA boasts three bike-only trails (Trails 33–35) and a number of lesser-used horse trails that are great for biking.

Finding the trailhead: Follow directions to Bandy Creek Equestrian Trailhead. If you are keeping your horses at Bandy Creek Stables, mount up at the stables, enter the woods just southwest of the pond, and proceed about 0.3 mile to the equestrian trailhead. If you are doing a special equestrian event that starts from Appaloosa Field, add 0.3 mile to each milepost, then tack 0.3 mile on at the end. All users can also start this loop at the gravel parking area off TN 297, about 1.5 miles west of its intersection with Bandy Creek Road, and enter the trail description at mile 1.8. Because you enter the loop directly and eliminate South Bandy Creek Trail, the loop is only 13.6 miles long (not counting the overlook) using this unofficial trailhead. Bikes are *not allowed* on the trail between the stables and equestrian trailhead so park at the equestrian trailhead or ride over from the campground or visitor center on Bandy Creek Road. Better yet, start at the gravel road on TN 297 mentioned above, and avoid the sandy section north of TN 297.

Trail Description

We describe this trail clockwise—the typical direction for special equestrian events and guided trail rides from the stables and the direction preferred by most riders we know; counterclockwise mileages are provided in parentheses.

0.0 (15.2) From the equestrian trailhead, travel south on South Bandy Creek Trail through the remnants of an old campground, and descend steeply through a hemlock forest into the hemlock- and rhododendron-lined ravine of Bandy Creek.

0.5 (14.7) Cross Bandy Creek; this sandy crossing is a great place to water your horse, especially on the way back. After crossing the creek, climb briefly into a dry, sandy stretch in a young forest with lots of damage from the 1998 winter storm.

0.8 (14.4) Reach an important fork in the trail, where the loop portion of North White Oak Loop begins. To do the loop clockwise, turn left (southeast) at this intersection. To go counterclockwise, turn right (southwest), flip to mile 14.4, and follow the description backward. Going clockwise, the next section is fast, curvy, and fun, turning slalomlike among pines on a trail of yellow sand. An NPS sign suggests that this loop is 20.3 miles long WITH OVERLOOKS, but we logged 23 miles for this loop, with both overlooks included.

1.4 (13.8) Cross a small tributary of Bandy Creek on a wood bridge among hemlock, ferns, and pawpaw, then ascend to another part of the trail that is full of fun curves and soft sand.

1.7 (13.5) Cross TN 297, the main road through the NRRA. Although the speed limit is 35 mph, most drivers seem to go considerably faster. The safest way to cross a paved road in a group is to wait for everyone in your party to arrive at the crossing, then cross together. On the other side the trail reenters the woods but turns sharply left (east) and continues parallel with TN 297, just inside the edge of the woods.

1.8 (13.4) Enter a large grassy field and continue southeast on White Pine Road, a gravel, multiuse trail. Watch for vehicles and bikes. The road bisects a number of old farm fields, some still in use, others being allowed to recover naturally.

2.0 (13.2) At a gravel intersection, look for the farm pond on your right (south). Water your horses here, because water may be hard to come by for many miles. Continue east on the gravel road, soon passing on your left (north) a rutted gravel road that leads out to TN 297. Then pass farm fields on your left and right, where you are sure to be scolded by chickadees, prairie warblers, and other edge-loving birds.

2.6 (12.6) The road turns sharply right (south) and follows the east edge of the field.

2.7 (12.5) Reach a critical junction for this loop. In 2001, the NPS sign pointed right (west) to North White Oak Overlook and Cumberland Valley Trailhead. To continue on the loop, turn right (west) and follow a narrow ridgeline, then descend into a creek valley. Exposed sandstone on this trail could be slippery for horses, whether wet or dry. Jump to mile 3.1 below.

Note: If you have time to make a side trip to Leatherwood Overlook or a side trip to North White Oak Creek, this is your intersection.

The trip to the overlook adds 5.4 miles (round-trip) to your day. It is a great ride, and we often go there and back from the Bandy Creek area, which we described as a separate adventure, the Leatherwood Overlook

Trail (Trail 32). A condensed version follows, without adding any mileage to subsequent mileposts. To reach the overlook, keep going straight south on White Pine Road. In about 0.5 mile you reach a fork in the road. Take the left fork (still a gravel road), veer left, and enter a beautiful field along a wide ridgeline, heading east along its northern edge. This field is a really fun place to let your horse go, but there may be holes and obstacles in the field; stay on the road if the grass is long. The pond on your right is a good place to water your horses. About 1.5 miles from the previous intersection—at the east end of the field at a sign under a lone red maple—enter the woods and proceed east for another 0.5 mile. Once in the woods, the trail turns gradually northward and descends to six hitching posts near the overlook. Horses are not allowed past this point, so tie your horses and proceed the remaining 0.1 mile to the overlook. Watch very carefully for sheer drop-offs along the left side of the trail as you approach the overlook, a good reason horses are not allowed on this narrow trail. The protected overlook gives you a grand view of the Leatherwood Ford area of the Big South Fork River Gorge. Return the way you came and turn west on the North White Oak Loop, adding 5.4 miles to subsequent mileposts.

From here you can also go down to the O&W Railroad Grade (Trail 44), a beautiful trail deep in North White Oak Creek Gorge with access to water. Keep going straight south on White Pine Road. In about 0.5 mile you reach a fork in the road. Go straight through the intersection; shortly, turn right (west) on Coyle Branch Trail. It descends 1.6 miles steeply into the gorge and reaches Coyle Branch near its confluence with North White Oak Creek, where hitching posts and soft sitting spots await your arrival. Return the way you came, adding about 4.2 miles to subsequent mileposts.

3.1 (12.1) After descending a bit, cross a tributary of Coyle Branch on a wood bridge. This tributary was dammed in its upper headwaters to form the pond you visited at mile 2.0.

3.5 (11.7) Enter Scott State Forest, a State of Tennessee inholding devoted to important silvicultural research, including selective breeding of white pine and restoration of the once-dominant American chestnut. You will cross the Scott State Forest boundary many times on this loop, but we do not mention it again.

4.1 (11.1) Cross a tributary of Coyle Branch in a wide floodplain covered in ferns followed by many more similar crossings in the next mile, some with large hemlocks and white pines.

5.3 (9.9) Reach the intersection for the 0.5 mile shortcut leading to Groom Branch Trail and the Cumberland Valley Trailhead. If you (or your horse) have bitten off more than you can chew, use this trail to shorten your outing to 7.8 miles. To take the shortcut, turn right (west), climb a dry ridge to the other side of the loop, and flip to mile 13.2 in this trail description. Otherwise, continue southwest on the loop. For the next 2.5 miles the trail dips into countless shallow headwater ravines flanking nearly dry creeks. In one section the trail parallels West Fork of Coyle Branch on its southwest bank; the trail is curvy and fun.

7.9 (7.3) Cross Gar Blevins Trail, a sandy multiuse trail not described in this book. This is an opportunity to visit North White Oak Overlook, a worthwhile side trip of only 2.4 miles (round-trip). To visit the overlook, turn left (south) and follow the short description below, then return to this intersection. Otherwise, cross the road and continue straight ahead (west) on North White Oak Loop. (We do not add the mileage for this side trip to subsequent mileposts.)

Gar Blevins Trail is a wide, sandy path that heads straight south for about 0.5 mile, curves gradually leftward (eastward), and reaches a group of hitching posts about 1.1 miles from North White Oak Loop. Horses are not allowed farther on this trail, so tie them firmly to the hitching posts and proceed 0.1 mile to the overlook on foot. Steep metal stairs lead to the top of a flat rock covered by Virginia pine, lowbush blueberry, and mountain laurel. The protected overlook faces generally east into the gorge of North White Oak Creek. This peaceful, remote overlook is guarded by eastern fence lizards, five-lined skinks, chickadees, and pine warblers. After a quick snack, or a peaceful afternoon nap, return to the intersection and go left (west) on North White Oak Loop. You are entering the Groom Branch watershed and will follow it upstream, crossing many of its tributaries.

9.2 (6.0) Continue straight at an unmarked trail leading up to Gar Blevins Road.

10.0 (5.2) Cross a footbridge over a low spot blanketed by ferns, hemlock, and white pine.

10.7 (4.5) Cross a creek likely to have flowing water, after which the trail narrows to a beautiful wide singletrack pathway, crossing a few smaller creeks. At mile 11 (4.2) you will begin the steady ascent to the wide ridgeline upon which Gar Blevins Road is perched.

12.1 (3.1) Cross Gar Blevins Road less than a mile from TN 297 and veer left (north), riding parallel to and on the east side of the road.

12.3 (2.9) Reach a T intersection. The left (west) fork is Groom Branch Trail, which continues west, connecting to the Gernt Trail at Cumberland Valley Trailhead. If you want to tackle the Groom-Gernt-Coyle Loop (Trail 31), turn left and flip to mile 2.9 in the description. To continue on North White Oak Loop, turn right (east), and ride parallel to TN 297.

13.2 (2.0) Reenter Scott State Forest; 0.1 mile east of the boundary, pass on your right the connector trail mentioned at mile 5.3, which heads southeast to shortcut the loop. Stay left, still paralleling TN 297, which gets gradually closer as you proceed northeast.

13.7 (1.5) Cross TN 297, remembering our safety suggestions from before, and continue north.

14.4 (0.8) Reach the intersection that closes the loop, the same spot as mile 0.8 above. Return to the trailhead the opposite way you came, and let your horse drink awhile at Bandy Creek before the final ascent to the trailhead. Riders starting at trailheads other than Bandy Creek should turn right at this intersection and flip to mile 0.8 above.

15.2 (0.0) Reach Bandy Creek Equestrian Trailhead. If you went to both overlooks (7.8 more miles), your total mileage is about 23 miles. Bandy Creek Stables is another 0.3 mile away.

TYPE OF TRAIL: Horseback riding or mountain biking.

TYPE OF ADVENTURE: Long ride with a stop at a nice overlook and a drop into a creek gorge.

TOTAL DISTANCE: 15.8 miles.

DIFFICULTY: Moderate.

TIME REQUIRED: Full day.

WATER AVAILABILITY: Adequate on trail; abundant at trailhead.

SPECIAL CONCERNS: Two paved road crossings; gravel portions shared with vehicles; deep sand; many sunny, hot, and dry sections; unprotected overlook.

SCENIC VALUE: Spectacular: great overlook, picturesque fields, dense riparian forests, and one of the most beautiful creeks in the area.

USGS MAPS: Honey Creek and Stockton (optional).

BEST STARTING POINT: Bandy Creek Equestrian Trailhead.

Overview: The trails making up this loop are used for endurance rides and other special equestrian events. After a long, flat, sandy section and a visit to a nice overlook, the Gernt Trail plunges into the gorge of North White Oak Creek, a spectacular waterway meandering around humongous boulders and stalling in deep pools along the O&W Railroad Grade (Trail 44). In the gorge you will ford two beautiful tributaries, Groom Branch and Coyle Branch, at their confluence with North White Oak Creek. The trail along Coyle Branch is one of the prettiest in the NRRA, lined with hemlock, beech, and tulip poplar.

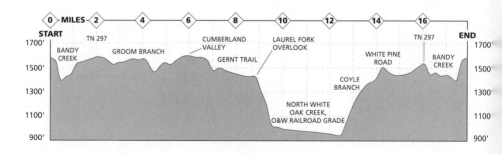

This is a tough loop on a mountain bike due to deep sand on the Gernt and South Bandy Creek Trails, but other portions make it worth doing on a bike. Bikers should start at Cumberland Valley Trailhead. This is a fairly popular loop, so watch carefully for horseback riders, and follow the rules of etiquette. As of 2001, four-wheelers were allowed on the Gernt Trail and the O&W Railroad Grade, but since they could not use any trails on steep slopes leading into or out of North White Oak Creek Gorge, they could not connect these trails.

The trail to Leatherwood Overlook (Trail 32) is a great add-on, if you and your horse can handle the extra 4.2 miles. This loop is often combined with North White Oak Loop (Trail 30) to make a 25-mile endurance ride. If you are thinking about entering an equestrian competition for the first time, want to better your 25-mile ride time, or are just looking for a really long ride on soft, well-trodden paths, this is a great combination. To combine the two loops into a 25.2-mile journey, follow the description for North White Oak Loop clockwise to mile 12.3, then turn onto Groom Branch Trail (some call it West Entrance Trail) and flip to mile 2.9 in the description below.

Finding the trailhead: Follow directions to Bandy Creek Equestrian Trailhead and see Map 19. If you are keeping your horses at Bandy Creek Stables, mount up at the stables, enter the woods just southwest of the pond, and proceed about 0.3 mile to the equestrian trailhead. If you are doing a special equestrian event that starts from Appaloosa Field, add 0.3 mile to each milepost, then tack 0.3 mile on at the end. All users can also start this loop at the gravel parking area off TN 297 about 1.5 miles west of its intersection with Bandy Creek Road and enter the trail description at mile 14.0. Bikes are *not allowed* on the trail between the stables and equestrian trailhead so should park at the equestrian trailhead or ride over from the campground or visitor center on Bandy Creek Road. Better yet, start at the gravel road on TN 297 mentioned above and avoid the sandy section north of TN 297. All users can also start from Cumberland Valley Trailhead at the north end of the Gernt Trail and enter the trail description at mile 5.2. Because you enter the loop directly and eliminate South Bandy Creek Trail, the loop is only 14.2 miles long using either of these trailheads.

Trail Description

We describe this trail counterclockwise because it is easier to negotiate the deep sand and steep portion of the Gernt Trail in a downhill direction, and we prefer climbing rather than descending Coyle Branch Trail. Clockwise mileages are provided in parentheses.

0.0 (15.8) From the equestrian trailhead, travel south on South Bandy Creek Trail through the remnants of an old campground; descend steeply through a nice hemlock forest into the hemlock- and rhododendron-lined ravine of Bandy Creek.

0.5 (15.3) Cross Bandy Creek; this sandy crossing is a great place to water your horse, especially on the way back. After crossing the creek, climb briefly into a dry, sandy stretch in a young forest with lots of damage from the 1998 winter storm.

0.8 (15.0) Reach an important fork in the trail, the loop portion of North White Oak Loop. Take the right (west) fork and head uphill through a pine forest. You will be going counterclockwise on that loop until it reaches the intersection with Groom Branch Trail at mile 2.9 below.

To combine this trail with North White Oak Loop, it is best to turn left (southeast) at this intersection and flip to mile 0.8 in that trail description. Ride the first 12.3 miles of that loop, then come back to this loop at mile 2.9 in the trail description below.

1.5 (14.3) Cross TN 297, the main road through the NRRA. Although the speed limit is 35 mph, most drivers seem to go considerably faster. The safest way to cross a paved road in a group is to wait for everyone in your party to arrive at the crossing, then cross together. On the other side, the trail reenters the woods and continues southwest, parallel with TN 297 on your right for a short distance, then veers away from the road and heads south.

2.0 (13.8) The trail on your left is the 0.5-mile connector trail that heads southeast to shortcut North White Oak Loop. Stay right and proceed west, leaving Scott State Forest in about 0.1 mile, and eventually return to within earshot of TN 297.

2.9 (12.9) Reach a T intersection where Groom Branch Trail splits off the North White Oak Loop and continues west, connecting to the Gernt Trail at Cumberland Valley Trailhead. Proceed straight through the intersection, going directly west in a mixed forest of silver maple, white and red oak, and white and Virginia pine. Soon after, you will cross Gar Blevins Trail, a yellow sand road that leads north out to TN 297.

Note: The left (south) fork of the above intersection is the rest of North White Oak Loop. If you are combining these trails and want to enter this loop at this intersection, turn south and enter the North White Oak Loop at mile 12.3 and go backward.

4.0 (11.8) Cross a creek, the upper headwaters of Groom Branch. The trail ascends and descends in a number of headwater ravines for the next mile.

4.5 (11.3) Reach intersection with a trail leading north out to TN 297 just inside the NRRA boundary. Turn left and begin a southwestern descent along the NRRA boundary into a tributary gorge, then ascend again to the Cumberland Valley Trailhead.

5.2 (10.6) Reach Cumberland Valley Trailhead, a wide, gravel parking area just south of TN 297 on the very west end of the NRRA. The Gernt Trail leaves the parking area on its south end (on your left) and heads generally southeast along a wide, sandy ridge for about 2.5 miles. The yellow-sand path follows the old road that descends to the O&W Railroad Grade at the site of the former community of Gernt, a stop along the O&W Railroad.

7.6 (8.2) Reach an intersection with a metal gate blocking vehicle access just before the Gernt Trail drops steeply into the gorge. First, turn right (south) on the short spur trail leading to Laurel Fork Overlook. This short side trip will be very worth your time.

7.7 (8.1) Tie your horses to the hitching posts and walk the short distance to Laurel Fork Overlook, an unprotected sandstone ledge with a vast western exposure (from about 170 to 350 degrees). You are looking up into the gorge of Laurel Fork, a major tributary of North White Oak Creek (yes, there are two Laurel Forks in the NRRA; the other drains into Station Camp Creek). The tall bluffs to the north glow orange-red at sunset. These are exposures of the Pennsylvanian sandstone caprock that form the surface of the Cumberland Plateau (see the geology section).

7.8 (8.0) Back at the Gernt Trail, go around the gate and plunge steeply into the gorge. Horseback riders should check their tack and tighten their girth; bikers should double-check their brakes. Dipping below some large sandstone walls at about mile 8.0 (7.8), this dangerous section becomes steep, wet, muddy, slippery, and rocky all at the same time, so be careful.

View from Laurel Fork Overlook

8.4 (7.4) At the bottom of the descent, reach the O&W Railroad Grade, an old railroad bed still black with coal soot. This intersection is all that remains of Gernt, a mining and lumber camp where coal and lumber were loaded on trains and taken to Oneida for transfer to the Southern Railway. The riparian forest trees are reclaiming this area nicely.

An unbelievably beautiful crossing of Laurel Fork lies only 0.3 mile west of this location and is worth a quick visit—especially since you just had a glimpse of its vast watershed from the overlook. The flat, cobbled creek bottom is a great place to just wade around.

Back at Gernt, continue on the O&W Railroad Grade along North White Oak Creek in a downstream direction. This is one of the main tributaries of the Big South Fork River. You may encounter some really large, deep puddles in the trail. There is *no* need to leave the railroad grade to go around these puddles; the hard railroad tram surface makes the bottom of the puddles firm, not at all muddy. Many of the side trails that other users have made to get around these puddles are actually muddier and much more dangerous than the main trail! Also, leaving the trail causes you to trample plants and increases your risk of snakebite.

8.6 (7.2) Briefly leave the railroad berm to cross Groom Branch, a bouldery tributary that drains the watershed between Gernt and Gar Blevins Trails. Water your horses, then continue on the railroad bed, gradually turning south, passing some incredible campsites at about mile 10 (5.8), then turn sharply north at a bend in North White Oak Creek. You may see the beautiful flowers of multiflora rose, an exotic from Asia, along the trail. Unfortunately, this species has become firmly established in North America and represents a severe threat to native plant communities.

11.1 (4.7) Leave the railroad berm to cross Coyle Branch, a beautiful, clear tributary in the bottom of a steep ravine, up which you will soon be riding. A group of hitching posts makes this a logical place to stop and take it all in. Be sure to water your horses here, because they face a long, steep climb, and the nearest water source lies more than 2 miles from this spot. Also be sure to check your tack and tighten your girth. Head north from the hitching posts on the trail that takes you up the eastern slope of Coyle Branch Gorge. This climb can be done without stopping on a mountain bike but may require some tedious grinding in the smallest of granny gears.

12.6 (3.2) Reach a T intersection with White Pine Road, a wide gravel road on the plateau that connects with TN 297 in a few miles. This gravel road is a multiuse trail, so watch for vehicles and bikes for the next few miles. Turn left (north) to continue on the loop. A right (south) turn takes you into a long, beautiful ridgetop pasture with two ponds on its edge—a great place to run your horses or get them some water if they need it badly.

12.7 (3.1) Reach the intersection with the trail leading east to Leatherwood Overlook. If you and your horse have the energy, we highly recommend taking the 2.1-mile side trip, which adds 4.2 miles (round-trip) to your day. The trip is so nice that we often go there and back from the Bandy Creek area and described it as the Leatherwood Overlook Trail (Trail 32). We briefly describe the route in the paragraph below, but do not add the mileage onto subsequent mileposts.

Turn right (east), veer gradually left, and enter a beautiful field along a wide ridgeline, heading east along its northern edge. This field is a really fun place to let your horse go, but there may be holes and obstacles in the field so stay on the gravel road if the grass is long. A pond on the south side of the field is a good place to water your horses. About 1.5 miles from the previous intersection—at the east end of the field at a sign under a lone red maple—enter the woods, and proceed east for another 0.5 mile. In the woods the trail turns gradually northward and descends to six hitching posts near the overlook. Horses are not allowed past this point, so tie your horses and walk the final 0.1 mile to the overlook. Watch very carefully for sheer drop-offs along the left side of the trail as you approach the overlook, a good reason horses are not allowed on this narrow trail. The protected overlook gives you a grand view of the Leatherwood Ford area of the Big South Fork River Gorge. Return the way you came and turn right (north) on White Pine Road, adding 4.2 miles to subsequent mileposts.

13.2 (2.6) Reach a T intersection where North White Oak Loop meets White Pine Road on your left (west). In 2001 the NPS sign mentioned only that North White Oak Overlook and Cumberland Valley Trailhead were down the trail to the west. Continue straight north on White Pine Road along the east edge of a field. The road turns sharply left (west) and bisects a number of old farm fields, some still in use, others being allowed to go fallow and return to forest.

13.7 (2.1) Continue past the rutted gravel road on your right (north) that leads out to TN 297. Soon after, at another gravel intersection, look for the farm pond on your left (south), probably a welcome sight to your horses at this point. After your horses drink their fill, continue northwest on the gravel road, entering a large field off TN 297. This is an alternate, albeit unofficial, trailhead for this loop.

14.0 (1.8) Enter the woods on the very northwest edge of the field near TN 297 and ride parallel to the road for a few hundred feet. After a sharp right turn, cross TN 297, remembering our safety suggestions from before, and continue north.

15.0 (0.8) Reach the intersection which closes the loop, the same spot as mile 0.8 above. Return to the trailhead the opposite way you came, and let your horse drink awhile at Bandy Creek before the final ascent to the trailhead. Riders starting at trailheads other than Bandy Creek (e.g., Cumberland Valley Trailhead) should turn left at this intersection and flip to mile 0.8 above.

15.8 (0.0) Reach Bandy Creek Equestrian Trailhead. If you went to Leatherwood Overlook (4.2 more miles), your trip was about 20 miles long. If you started with North White Oak Loop, your total mileage is about 25.2 miles. If you added both overlooks to that (7.8 more miles), you have gone an impressive 33 miles! Bandy Creek Stables is another 0.3 mile away.

If you started at Appaloosa Field, veer left (northwest) on the horse trail, turn left (north) on Bandy Creek Road, and add another 0.3 mile to your journey.

32 Leatherwood Overlook Trail

TYPE OF TRAIL: Horseback riding or mountain biking.

TYPE OF ADVENTURE: Fun, fast ride through picturesque fields to a great overlook.

TOTAL DISTANCE: 10.8 miles (round-trip).

DIFFICULTY: Easy.

TIME REQUIRED: 2 to 4 hours.

SPECIAL CONCERNS: Two paved road crossings; gravel portions shared with vehicles; deep sand; sunny, hot, and dry sections.

WATER AVAILABILITY: Adequate on trail; abundant at trailhead.

SCENIC VALUE: Good: scenic overlook, young forest with damage, trail not remote.

USGS MAP: Honey Creek.

BEST STARTING POINT: Bandy Creek Equestrian Trailhead.

Overview: This wonderful overlook provides a grand view of the river gorge around Leatherwood Ford, hence the name. The nice thing about this overlook is that it feels fairly remote when you are there. However, it is very accessible; a 2WD vehicle can usually get to within 0.6 mile of the overlook. This is great for squeezing in one last ride or watching the sun set over the gorge without traveling a long distance back in the dark. The

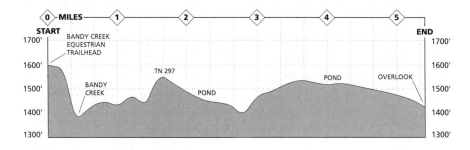

View from Leatherwood Overlook

soft, winding, sandy treadway is great fun on horseback but may be a significant challenge on a mountain bike, despite being mostly a level gravel road (295 feet of climbing one way, 350 feet the other).

There are a number of interesting things to see along the trail. Bandy Creek is a beautiful, sand-bottomed waterway flanked by sandstone bluffs, hemlocks, and rhododendron. The fields you encounter along the way give you a real sense for the isolated farming lifestyles people once experienced within the boundaries of the Big South Fork NRRA. A morning or afternoon canter through the particularly beautiful field nearest the overlook, with the wind in your hair and deer and turkey all around you, is truly an unforgettable experience. The two ponds along the way are alive with spring peepers, green frogs, bullfrogs, and their tadpoles, as well as the shorebirds, eastern spotted newts, and larval and adult dragonflies that eat them. The forest edges and fence lines along this trail are great for seeing black racers, prairie warblers, great crested flycatchers, hawks, turkey, and white-tailed deer; the woods near the overlook are alive with red-eyed vireos, hooded warblers, and pileated woodpeckers. At the overlook, it is a treat to see turkey vultures and red-tailed hawks catching updrafts in the gorge.

Bandy Creek Stables offers four-hour guided horseback rides to this overlook and back, using the route we describe. This trail lies on the first 2.7 miles of North White Oak Loop (Trail 30), and the last 2.7 miles of the Groom-Gernt-Coyle Loop (Trail 31), parts or all of which are logical add-ons to this great trail. For a more complete Big South Fork adventure, take the 1.6-mile Coyle Branch Trail down to the O&W Railroad Grade, a wide path deep in the gorge of North White Oak Creek, one of the prettiest waterways in the NRRA. This 3.2-mile addition gives you a relatively easy 14-mile day with a guaranteed watering hole halfway through.

Finding the trailhead: Follow directions to Bandy Creek Equestrian Trailhead. If you are keeping your horses at Bandy Creek Stables, mount up at the stables, enter the woods just southwest of the pond, and proceed about 0.3 mile to the equestrian trailhead. All users can also start this loop at the gravel parking area off TN 297 about 1.5 miles west of its intersection with Bandy Creek Road and enter the trail description at mile 1.8, knocking 3.6 miles off the trip. Bikes are *not allowed* on the trail between the stables and equestrian trailhead so park at the equestrian trailhead or ride over from the campground or visitor center on Bandy Creek Road. Better yet, start at the gravel road on TN 297 mentioned above and avoid the sandy section north of TN 297. If you are short on time or energy, you can drive to within 0.6 mile of the overlook on White Pine Road; however, be advised that sandy areas may render this road impassable to 2WD vehicles in dry times!

Trail Description

Starting at Bandy Creek Equestrian Trailhead, travel south on South Bandy Creek Trail through the remnants of an old equestrian camp, and descend steeply through a nice hemlock forest.

0.5 Cross Bandy Creek, a beautiful sand-bottomed creek. This is a great place to water your horse, especially on the way back. After crossing the creek, climb briefly into a dry, sandy stretch in a young forest with lots of damage from the 1998 winter storm.

0.8 Reach a Y intersection, where the North White Oak Loop begins. Go left (southeast) on the loop, and descend into the ravine of a small tributary of Bandy Creek. You will be following the North White Oak Loop until mile 2.7 below.

1.4 Cross the tributary on a narrow wood bridge (water is not available for horses), then continue climbing into a dry pine zone where the trail becomes soft and sandy. This is a really fun place to trot your horse through some tight turns. Storm damage was extensive in February 1998; in some areas many trees have been lost, but the forest is recovering nicely. Mountain bikers may have to walk through some of the softer sandy areas.

1.7 Cross TN 297, the main road through the NRRA. The crossing has a good view down the road in both directions, two horse-crossing signs, and a painted crosswalk, but always be wary of vehicles, which are usually going faster than the posted 35 mph speed limit. If you are traveling in a group, always venture across the road together. On the other side, the trail reenters the woods but turns sharply left (east) and continues parallel with TN 297, just inside the edge of the woods.

1.8 Enter a large grassy field and join White Pine Road, a gravel multiuse trail. This open area serves as another trailhead for any of the trails south of TN 297, and there is plenty of parking for horse trailers. Continue southeast on the gravel trail. The road bisects a number of old farm fields, some still in use, others being allowed to recover naturally. This is a good place to let your horse run, but remember that this is a multiple-use trail; be ready for vehicles and bikes to appear around any corner at any time.

2.0 At a gravel intersection, look for a farm pond on your right (south). This is another great spot for watering your horse or taking a break, but the mud can be fairly deep at the edge of the pond. This artificial pond was created to provide water for livestock by damming a headwater tributary of Coyle Branch. This type of pond is regularly used by white-tailed deer and other forest mammals and birds.

From the pond, continue east, passing on your left (north) a rutted gravel road that leads out to TN 297. Enter some farm fields, where you are sure to be scolded by chickadees, prairie warblers, and other edge-loving birds.

2.6 Make a sharp right turn at a fenceline along the edge of a field. Shortly after that (mile 2.7), leave the fields for the forest and pass the T intersection where North White Oak Loop leaves White Pine Road on your right (west). Proceed straight on White Pine Road.

3.2 Reach a fork in the road. White Pine Road continues straight ahead (south), leading to Coyle Branch Trail and the O&W Railroad Grade and also to "The Bowl," a climbing area at the end of a beautiful ridgetop field. Turn left for the Leatherwood Overlook Trail (still a gravel road), veer gradually eastward, and enter a beautiful field along a wide ridgeline, heading east along its northern edge.

4.2 Pass a pond on the south edge of the field. A quick stop at the pond in spring or summer might give you a glimpse of toad and frog tadpoles and adults, eastern spotted newts, patrolling dragonflies, and possibly some garter snakes or wading birds looking for a meal. You can also stop here to water your horse.

4.8 Reach the east end of the field at an intersection and a sign under a big lone red maple. A 2WD vehicle can make it to this point, but only horseback riders, mountain bikers, and hikers are allowed to proceed into the woods. To get to the overlook, proceed 0.5 mile straight ahead (east) directly into the woods. Once in the woods, the trail narrows, turns gradually northward, and descends to the overlook. Do not continue on the gravel road, which soon becomes unsafe due to extensive storm damage.

5.3 Reach a ring of six hitching posts; horses are not allowed past this point. Please tie your horses to the hitching posts, rather than vegetation, and proceed on foot for 0.1 mile on the narrow trail leading north to the overlook. Watch carefully for sheer drop-offs along the left side of the trail as you approach the overlook. Stay awhile and enjoy the view!

The overlook is a flat sandstone outcrop at the northern tip of a point high above the confluence of Bandy Creek and the Big South Fork River. The unobstructed view looks generally north and ranges from about 270 to nearly 90 degrees, so you get spectacular vistas in both morning and evening. The bridge at Leatherwood Ford is visible to the north, more than 500 feet below your elevation. The overlook makes a great halfway point to sit down, eat lunch, take a nap, and let the scenery of the gorge get under your skin. The rock platform is festooned with wood rails for safely looking out over its sheer cliff faces.

After a snack, or waking from being lulled to sleep by the wind in the pines, return to the trailhead the way you came, or add some other trails to your trip. You can finish North White Oak Loop (Trail 30) by entering our description of that trail at mile 2.7, making about a 20-mile journey. Add the Groom-Gernt-Coyle Loop (Trail 31) after that, and you will have completed 33 miles!

TYPE OF TRAIL: Mountain biking.

TYPE OF ADVENTURE: A fun but safe bike trail for beginner riders.

TOTAL DISTANCE: 4.9 miles.

DIFFICULTY: Easy.

TIME REQUIRED: 20 to 50 minutes.

SPECIAL CONCERNS: Vehicles and horses on gravel road, one creek crossing.

WATER AVAILABILITY: Fair on trail; abundant at trailhead.

SCENIC VALUE: Fair: young forest with storm damage, trail not very remote.

USGS MAPS: Honey Creek and Barthell SW.

BEST STARTING POINT: Bandy Creek Visitor Center or Campground.

Overview: This is the perfect trail for novices wanting to get a taste of off-road riding on dirt singletrack without getting hammered by tough climbs and frequent obstacles. If you are a beginner, try this trail before attempting Collier Ridge Bike Loop (Trail 34) or West Bandy Creek Bike Trail (Trail 35). First you get a nice warm-up on a smooth, gravel and sand road. The 2.1-mile loop section is wide singletrack with some fun downhill sections that are not dangerous, one fairly easy creek crossing, and a reasonable climb at the end. Experienced riders should be able to do this entire trail once in under twenty-five minutes so will probably want to do multiple laps.

You will be sharing Duncan Hollow Road with horseback riders, hikers, and vehicles of all types. You are likely to encounter one or all of these types

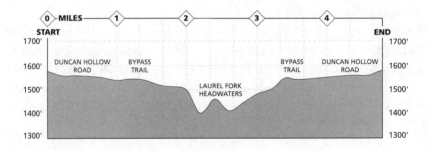

of users, especially on weekends, so always look ahead and follow proper trail etiquette.

Finding the trailhead: Follow directions to the Bandy Creek area (also see Map 18).

Trail Description

We provide more details in this description than usual, mostly to help you memorize the details of the course. The trail is actually well blazed and easy to follow.

0.0 Starting from the parking area across from the visitor center, go north across Bandy Creek Road, enter the Bandy Creek Campground area on the gravel path west of the fee kiosk, and head toward Loop A. Continue past the pool and look for Duncan Hollow Road, a groomed gravel road on the right immediately north of the pool parking area. Those coming from a campsite should also head to the pool. The road is marked with a wood sign, a blue bike blaze, and a 4x4 symbol.

0.2 Head north on Duncan Hollow Road. Watch for loose gravel on the initial descent, curving around below the campsites on Loop A. The road turns northeast away from the campground, levels off, and changes to more sand and dirt and less gravel.

0.5 Katie Trail, a horse trail, connects with Duncan Hollow Road from the left (west). Watch carefully for horses and please follow proper trail etiquette. Here you enter a field where Scott State Forest is conducting important experiments on white pine and American chestnut.

1.0 Cross the power line right-of-way and look left for a blue bike blaze showing where the bike trail leaves Duncan Hollow Road and punches into the woods. This fun singletrack section returns you to Duncan Hollow Road, so it does not matter if you miss this turn and ride the road. The mileage is about the same, either way. We prefer the singletrack route, as it allows you to ride a short distance without worrying about horses or vehicles. However, other bikers may be traveling the opposite way on this trail, so be extra careful!

1.1 The singletrack trail emerges onto Duncan Hollow Road. Turn left (north) on the road, and watch for horses and vehicles.

1.4 Reach the intersection with the Bypass Trail, a multiple-use trail described in Trail 28. Turn left (west), and keep watching for horses and vehicles.

1.5 A blue bike blaze on your right (north) shows where the bike loop turns off the Bypass Trail, but go straight to preserve the clockwise direction of the loop. This is safer for everyone. You are now on the loop portion of the trail. The wide pathway starts gently downhill.

2.1 Reach a Y intersection with the Bypass Trail veering left and a blue bike blaze pointing right for the bike trail. Go right, and start the bike-only portion of the loop. The loop starts as a fairly level singletrack trail along a wide ridge, but at 2 miles, get ready for a fast downhill section leading to some creek crossings. The real fun starts here! The trail descends sharply into a headwater ravine draining the north slope of Laurel Fork Gorge.

2.4 Cross a creek and turn right, following its east bank for 20 feet, then ascend steeply out of the ravine on its east slope, reaching the top at about 2.6 miles. Descend shortly after that.

2.9 Cross a headwater creek ravine and make a 0.1-mile ascent to a ridge-line. Turn right (south), then ascend gradually along the spine of that ridge to the Bypass Trail.

3.5 Reach the T intersection with the Bypass Trail that you passed at mile 1.4. Watch carefully as you emerge from the woods at this blind intersection because you could be hit by bikers and will surely spook any horses on the Bypass Trail in this area. You have finished the loop portion. To do another lap (2.1 miles), turn right (west). To return, turn left (east) and head east on the Bypass Trail, back the way you came.

3.7 At Duncan Hollow Road, turn right (south) toward camp. Or turn left (north) to do some flat miles on Duncan Hollow Trail (part of Trail 29) and flip to mile 1.9 of the description. Again, watch for horses and vehicles from here to camp.

3.9 Reenter the brief singletrack section on your right, marked by a blue bike blaze. Other bikers may be traveling the opposite way on this trail, so be extra careful! Continue through the power line right-of-way.

4.6 The horse trail leaves Duncan Hollow Road and heads west. Now free of horse traffic, you have only 0.3 mile to "dust" your buddies. Go for it (but watch for vehicles)!

4.9 Emerge from the woods, victorious and ready for a swim in the pool.

TYPE OF TRAIL: Mountain biking.

TYPE OF ADVENTURE: A lap (or two) on a wonderful mountain bike racecourse.

TOTAL DISTANCE: 8.4 miles.

DIFFICULTY: Moderate.

TIME REQUIRED: 40 to 90 minutes.

SPECIAL CONCERNS: Slippery creek crossings, eroded sections with exposed roots.

WATER AVAILABILITY: Fair on trail; abundant at trailhead.

SCENIC VALUE: Fair: young forest with storm damage, no overlooks.

USGS MAP: Honey Creek.

BEST STARTING POINT: Bandy Creek Visitor Center.

Overview: This trail, Todd's favorite, offers the best of two mountain biking worlds. For the novice, this trail will expose you to nearly all the technical aspects of mountain biking without breaking your will. For experienced riders and racers, this is a fantastic trail for honing some important skills. The course has everything: creek crossings, jumps, log crossings, sandstone climbs and drops, off-camber turns, exposed roots, short slalom sections through trees, and fast downhill sections. The "fair" scenery rating is based mostly on the young forest, tree damage, and lack of remoteness and should not turn you away. It is a pretty trail, within the narrow window of perception you will have while trying not to crash. The young forest is very dense in some spots, so clear or light-colored sport glasses work best.

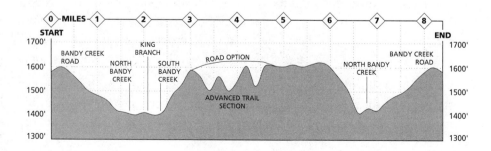

If you are interested in trying mountain bike racing, this is a great opportunity to test your mettle. As a racecourse this loop is relatively easy even by eastern standards (most courses have more than twice as much elevation change over a similar distance), but one lap is a good approximation of a beginner-class race; two laps, a fair approximation of a sport-class race; and three laps, a reasonable expert/pro-class race. (Respectable split times are provided in the trail description.) Novice bikers and those who find they have bitten off more than they can chew can avoid the "advanced" section of the trail by riding TN 297 then reentering the trail on a fun downhill.

The advanced section is much like the nearby West Bandy Creek Bike Trail (Trail 35), and together these trails make a really fantastic ride and are easy to connect. This trail is shared with three short sections of hiking trails and crosses a horse trail. Although the hiking trails are rarely used, please look ahead and follow proper trail etiquette. You will cross the horse trail while on a busy road, so horseback riders will probably be stopped and looking for vehicles. Remember, horseback riders always have the right-of-way, so be ready to slow down or stop.

Finding the trailhead: Parking is minimal at the point where the trail enters the woods, so we recommend starting from the Bandy Creek area (see the "Local Directions" section and see Map 17). This will give you about a mile to warm up and check the integrity of your rig before hitting the trail.

Trail Description

We provide more details in this description than usual, mostly to help you memorize the details of the course. The trail is actually well blazed and easy to follow.

0.0 Starting from Bandy Creek Campground or near the visitor center, turn west on Bandy Creek Road (paved). This is the warm-up.

0.3 The pavement ends and the road descends on loose gravel, so be careful. Loose, coarse roadway gravel is one of the most deceptively dangerous surfaces to ride even the best bike on. You will cross a horse trail at the bottom of the hill, so watch carefully for horseback riders and be ready to stop.

0.5 Climb a short hill and pass through Appaloosa Field. This has been the starting line for the Big South Fork Triathlon (which uses this loop for the mountain biking leg) and many equestrian events. At the northwest end of the field, begin a fast descent. This downhill section is very dangerous if the gravel is loose.

0.9 Pass the Clara Sue Blevins Farm and the Katie Blevins Cemetery on your right. You might want to visit these sites on your way back, when you are climbing the hill. Start looking to the left for a SCOTT STATE FOREST sign. Your warm-up is almost over.

1.1 Punch into the woods on the left just past the SCOTT STATE FOREST sign, and immediately begin a fast descent on a sandy, rocky stretch of singletrack that is often wet and slippery.

1.2 Oscar Blevins Farm Loop (Trail 25) crosses the bike trail, so watch for hikers.

1.3 Cross North Bandy Creek, a fun, wet crossing. Clear the mud off your glasses and be alert; the other end of Oscar Blevins Farm Loop joins the bike trail soon afterward (clearly marked as hiking only).

1.4 The bike trail splits here to form the Collier Ridge Loop. Please go left and ride the trail clockwise. This is important for everyone's safety, including your own. Besides, the course was designed for clockwise travel, especially the final downhill portion.

1.8 Cross King Branch—another fun, wet crossing (often dry in summer and fall)—and ride through the old Billie Blevins Farm, an open, fast, slightly downhill singletrack zone with some sandstone ledges that make great jumps. The trail descends more rapidly after you leave the farm area.

2.0 Stay to the right as the Oscar Blevins Farm Loop (Trail 25) splits off to the left. Climb to the top of a ridge, then descend and cross a wet area soon after that.

2.2 Cross the West Entrance to Bandy Creek Trail (Trail 27), a hiking trail. Watch for hikers!

2.3 Immediately after a sharp left turn, cross the flat (but slick) sandstone bottom of the beautiful, rhododendron-lined South Bandy Creek. Immediately after crossing the creek, climb steadily along an old road that would be reclaimed by the forest if not for the narrow singletrack bike trail. At two places, you get a chance to play on some sandstone slabs.

3.0 Within earshot of the highway, you will see a blue bike blaze on the right and a sign saying ADVANCED. This technical singletrack section has numerous short but steep climbs, some difficult log crossings, off-camber turns, narrow slalom runs between trees, and numerous exposed roots that can give your tires "pinch-flats" and chatter your teeth out of their sockets. Experienced riders can generally reach this point in fifteen to twenty minutes (or less).

Note: If you are a novice, if you ride a heavy clunker with few working gears and no shocks, if you were even the least bit intimidated by the trail so far (which has been easy), if it took you longer than thirty minutes to reach this point, or if you are simply exhausted, you should probably avoid the advanced section (for now). Simply continue on the wide path out to TN 297 and turn right (west); ride on the road until your odometer reads about 4.0 miles, and return to the trail when you see a blue bike blaze at the northeast end of a small clearing. Turn right, proceed through the clearing, and head northeast on the jeep trail at the northeast end of the clearing. At this point, skip ahead to mile 4.6 of the trail description and subtract 0.6 mile from the rest of our mileages.

3.1 On the advanced section you will immediately reach a sandstone ledge. This drop might be treacherous for beginners, but with time and additional wear and tear, it appears to be getting easier. Advanced riders can just go for it—the landing is good, but be ready for the creek crossing immediately afterward.

3.3 Reach the first steep, short, "little-ring" climb. *Hint:* Drop into your granny gears and sit back on the seat for traction. There is another climb like this after you drop into the next ravine.

3.6 Pass a faint trail at the top of a ridge, where you can go left (south) and walk out to TN 297 if you regret trying the advanced section. After this point the trail has numerous ups and downs, like a roller coaster, with some sharp turns and log crossings. Whee!

4.6 Emerge in a clearing adjacent to TN 297; look right (northeast) for a blue bike blaze, and punch into the woods on the wide singletrack trail. Experienced riders generally reach this point in less than thirty minutes.

4.7 The West Entrance to Bandy Creek Trail (Trail 27) joins the bike trail at a reverse angle on your left—at a sign that clearly points bikers to the right. You will not even see the hiking trail if you are not looking carefully. For the next 0.3 mile the bike and hiking trails are shared; you will be going fast, so watch out for hikers.

5.0 Leave the shared trail at a sign clearly pointing you left, while the hiking trail continues straight ahead. Shortly thereafter, watch closely for a large dirt pile—it makes either a great jump or a dangerous obstacle, depending on your perspective. The trail stays relatively flat, but very fast, for about another mile.

5.8 After climbing gradually, reach the highest elevation on the loop. The trail stays fairly flat until about mile 6.0, then begins a long, fast descent. Get ready for a great downhill singletrack adventure, but be careful of the numerous exposed roots in this section, especially if your bike does not have suspension on at least the front fork. Many roots, and the trunks of some small trees and shrubs that were cut near ground level, have become exposed due to compaction of the surrounding soil. These hard-to-see obstacles stick up just enough to cause a "pinch flat" or "snakebite," where your tire gets smashed between the object and the rim, making two small slits in the tube. Keep your weight off your seat just enough to keep this from happening to your especially vulnerable rear tire. These obstacles might also catch a pedal, so always keep your pedals up (at three and nine o'clock). The downhill section gets very fast and dangerous, especially in a deeply incised, eroded section.

6.5 Reach the Y intersection that forms the bike loop. To do one lap, go left and climb back out to Bandy Creek Road. Go right if you want to do the loop a second (or third) time.

6.8 Turn right on Bandy Creek Road and climb the now cruel hill that put the wind in your hair earlier. Stop for a short visit to the Clara Sue Blevins homesite and Katie Blevins Cemetery, where ghosts of the settlers of this area might look upon your colorful garb and high-tech rig in amazement.

8.4 Reach the visitor center parking area. For the whole course (from Bandy Creek area), a fast ride time is less than forty minutes. The loop itself is about 5.6 miles long, so if you did the loop twice, you will have done a total of 13 miles including the round-trip from the parking area (three laps would be about 18 miles). If you are practicing for a race that starts and finishes at Appaloosa Field (a 7.4-mile course), the best time we know of is thirty-four minutes.

35 West Bandy Creek Bike Trail

TYPE OF TRAIL: Mountain biking.

TYPE OF ADVENTURE: Gravel road warm-up to a curvy, rolling singletrack trail in the woods.

TOTAL DISTANCE: 6.8 miles (round-trip).

DIFFICULTY: Moderate.

TIME REQUIRED: 30 to 90 minutes.

SPECIAL CONCERNS: Vehicles, exposed roots and sandstone, creek crossings.

WATER AVAILABILITY: Poor on trail; abundant at trailhead.

SCENIC VALUE: Good: creek crossings and forests, but part lies on gravel road.

USGS MAPS: Honey Creek and Barthell SW.

BEST STARTING POINT: Bandy Creek Visitor Center or Campground.

Overview: Although the roller-coaster singletrack portion of this trail is less than 2 miles long, it is suitable for beginners, experts, and pros alike— and is just plain fun to ride. You will climb only 415 feet in either direction, usually in short spurts in and out of the upper reaches of small headwater ravines draining the north slope of Laurel Fork Gorge. This trail used to consist of two short arcs off Bandy Creek Road, but the arcs were connected with a section of new singletrack constructed in summer 2001.

Although you can drive to this trail directly and park along Bandy Creek Road, this trail is so short that we suggest warming up with a ride from Bandy Creek Visitor Center or Campground or the West Entrance Trailhead. Bandy Creek Road is a wide, gravel surface with moderate vehicle traffic, making it fairly dusty, but its fast downhill sections will surely get the wind in your hair. The singletrack portion is much like the "advanced" section of the nearby Collier Ridge Bike Loop (Trail 34). Together these trails make a really fantastic ride and are easy to connect.

Finding the trailhead: Follow directions to the Bandy Creek area and see Map 17. If you start at West Entrance Trailhead, follow the description backward from the end (mile 3.4).

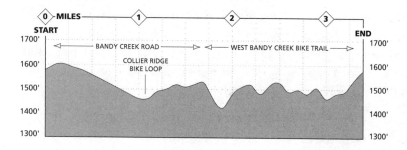

Trail Description

From Bandy Creek Campground or the visitor center parking lot, turn west on Bandy Creek Road (paved).

0.3 The pavement ends and the road descends on loose gravel, so be careful. Loose, coarse roadway gravel is one of the most deceptively dangerous surfaces to ride even the best bike on. Pass a horse trail at the bottom (watch out for horses getting ready to cross the road), climb a short hill to Appaloosa Field, then begin a fast descent. This downhill section is dangerous if the gravel is loose.

0.9 Pass the Clara Sue Blevins Farm and the Katie Blevins Cemetery on your right. You might want to visit these sites on your way back, when you are climbing the hill.

1.1 At the bottom of the hill, pass the SCOTT STATE FOREST sign and the entrance to Collier Ridge Bike Loop (Trail 34) on your left (south). Veer right (north), and climb again.

1.4 Pass the access road leading to Jacks Ridge Loop and Black House Branch Trail (both part of Trails 28 and 29) on your right (north).

1.6 The bike trail leaves Bandy Creek Road at a blue bike blaze on your right (north). The trail parallels the road for 50 feet, then turns right (north), punches into the woods, and climbs gently along an old road that would be reclaimed by the forest if not for the narrow singletrack bike trail. Shortly after, turn left (west) at another bike blaze, cross another old logging road, and begin a downhill section along the top of a narrow ridge.

1.9 Near the bottom, make a sharp left (south) turn and enter a dark hemlock-magnolia forest in the ravine of a small creek. Follow the creek upstream a short distance and cross it in a low, muddy area, still heading south. Climb the south creekbank, turn sharply west (right), and follow the creek upstream along the south slope of the ravine. Descend shortly afterward, cross another low area, and climb a few switchbacks until Bandy Creek Road becomes visible through the forest. The bike trail used to go out to the road here but now veers right (west) and stays in the woods. The next section is like a roller coaster.

2.5 At the top of a ridge, the trail joins another old logging road that climbs east out to Bandy Creek Road. However, a blue blaze quickly turns you right (west) onto a narrow, fun section of singletrack in dry Virginia pine woods. After a short, flat section, get ready for a short but steep and technical climb up an exposed sandstone ledge. This climb is no problem if you remain seated and apply all your weight to the rear tire, but it may be impossible or even dangerous when the sandstone is wet. Please stay on the already-exposed sandstone areas and avoid damaging the fragile lichen and moss communities that grow on a thin layer of soil or directly on the sandstone itself. The trail continues in a roller-coaster fashion from here and crosses another area of exposed sandstone, this time flat, at around mile 2.9.

3.2 Pass a nice rock house on your left and begin a short series of switchbacks. Be very careful on the small patches of exposed sandstone on these switchbacks. Moisture from the rock house and dense hemlocks has caused moss to grow on the rocks, and they are very slippery.

3.4 Emerge from the woods on Bandy Creek Road about 0.5 mile southwest of West Entrance Trailhead. You can turn around and go back the way you came or return on Bandy Creek Road, which shortens the return trip to 2.2 miles. Either way, the return trip is generally downhill all the way to the Collier Ridge Bike Loop—a great add-on trail as long as you are in the area (enter the description of that trail at mile 1.1). If you are coming from West Entrance Trailhead, after riding 0.5 mile turn left at the blue bike blaze—and get ready for some fun!

Leatherwood Ford and East Rim Areas

36 Leatherwood Ford Boardwalks

TYPE OF TRAIL: Hiking only, with good wheelchair access.

TYPE OF ADVENTURE: Lazy stroll to a walk-in picnic spot and great swimming hole on the river.

TOTAL DISTANCE: 0.5 mile.

DIFFICULTY: Very easy.

TIME REQUIRED: 30 to 60 minutes.

SPECIAL CONCERNS: Water covers trail during floods.

WATER AVAILABILITY: Abundant on trail and at trailhead.

SCENIC VALUE: Good: beautiful riparian area, but one of the busier spots in the NRRA.

USGS MAP: Honey Creek.

BEST STARTING POINT: Leatherwood Ford Parking Area.

Overview: Despite being a busy location (relative to the rest of the NRRA, where you rarely see anyone), we have probably spent more time at this wonderful spot than all other areas in the NRRA combined! The name comes from the small leatherwood shrub that grows along the river here. Native Americans and early settlers used the tough inner bark for shoestrings, baskets, and fish traps. The area is great for viewing wildflowers, bird-watching, picnicking, swimming, fishing, or just lying around on the old tram bridge in the sun with your family and friends. Photography opportunities are great all times of the day. The NPS, along with biology classes from Scott County High School in Oneida, made a wonderful self-guided nature trail and associated brochure for thirty species of trees along the Angel Falls Trail (Trail 37), but the brochure will help you identify trees here, too. This is a great way to start a day hike on Angel Falls Trail (Trail 37), Angel Falls Overlook Trail (Trail 38), or Leatherwood Ford Loop (Trail 40) or a backpacking trip on the John Muir Trail (Trail 43).

Finding the trailhead: Follow directions to Leatherwood Ford parking area and see Map 20.

Map 20—Leatherwood Ford Area

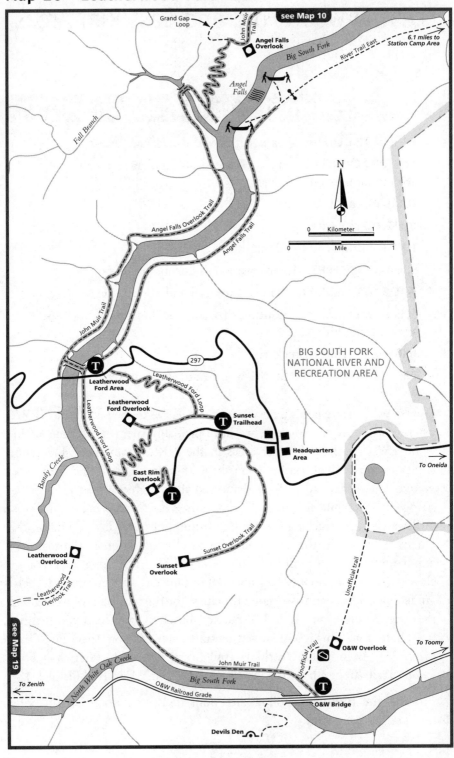

see Map 10

Grand Gap Loop

John Muir Trail

Angel Falls Overlook

Big South Fork

River Trail East

6.1 miles to Station Camp Area

Angel Falls

Fall Branch

Angel Falls Overlook Trail

Angel Falls Trail

John Muir Trail

N

0 Kilometer 1

0 Mile 1

297

BIG SOUTH FORK NATIONAL RIVER AND RECREATION AREA

Leatherwood Ford Area

Leatherwood Ford Loop

Leatherwood Ford Overlook

Sunset Trailhead

Leatherwood Ford Loop

Bandy Creek

East Rim Overlook

Headquarters Area

To Oneida

Leatherwood Overlook

Sunset Overlook Trail

Sunset Overlook

Leatherwood Overlook Trail

Unofficial trail

see Map 19

North White Oak Creek

John Muir Trail

Unofficial trail

O&W Overlook

To Toomy

To Zenith

Big South Fork

O&W Railroad Grade

O&W Bridge

Devils Den

Trail Description

Simply follow the short double-loop trail between the parking area and the river. You will notice a number of riverside benches on wide platforms where you can have a nice picnic or be lulled to sleep by the river.

Shoals of black, bituminous coal have been deposited by the river. Coal is much lighter than sandstone, so it sorts out of the water column differently, leaving shoals composed entirely of coal pebbles washed smooth by the action of water. This coal is often used for blacksmith's fires during Pioneer Day—but don't use it to cook burgers!

The river teems with life at Leatherwood Ford. Although this spot is a little busy to be a great fishing hole, smallmouth bass and bluegill are fairly easy for youngsters to catch. American toads of all sizes will hop across your path and often call proudly from rocks in the middle of the day. Northern water snakes are abundant and cruise along the shoreline in shallow water. These are *not* cottonmouths! Kingfishers cruise the river channel, great blue herons hunt in the shallows, and forest birds are surprisingly abundant for being so close to a parking area. River otters were released here, so you might catch a glimpse of a family of them cruising in a deep pool, but they are very rare sights at best.

Swallowtail butterfly at Leatherwood Ford

The surrounding riparian forest is diverse and recovering nicely from the effects of past logging practices. Large, twisted river birch and sycamore lining the riverbank are subjected to the brute force of spring floods and fight to maintain a foothold. The wads of leaves, sticks, and other debris perched high in shrubs and trees along the river indicate flood water levels! After spring floods, the ground will be stripped clean of its leaf litter and uppermost layer of soil up to the line of the highest flood. All of this material is carried downstream for about 30 miles to Lake Cumberland and will eventually fill this reservoir.

Wildflowers are abundant, and the wide trail makes photographing them relatively easy. Swallowtail butterflies hover over the mud banks. Five-lined skinks and fence lizards can be found basking on the root masses and driftwood below the boardwalk. Forest birds flit around in the forest and along the edge of the parking area, but bird-watching is better on Angel Falls Trail (Trail 37).

37 Angel Falls Trail

TYPE OF TRAIL: Hiking only.

TYPE OF ADVENTURE: Riverside hike to large rapids surrounded by massive boulders.

TOTAL DISTANCE: 4 miles (round-trip).

DIFFICULTY: Easy.

TIME REQUIRED: To fully enjoy Angel Falls, allow two hours or longer.

SPECIAL CONCERNS: Very dangerous rapids, slippery rocks, some rock-hopping.

WATER AVAILABILITY: Abundant on trail and at trailhead.

SCENIC VALUE: Excellent: deep in the river gorge, riparian forest, massive boulders, numerous wildflowers, abundant wildlife, but busy trail.

USGS MAP: Honey Creek.

BEST STARTING POINT: Angel Falls Trailhead at Leatherwood Ford.

Overview: This short, level trail takes you along the east bank of the Big South Fork directly to Angel Falls—not really a waterfall, but a narrow, dangerous chute and the second largest rapids on the Big South Fork River. Angel Falls used to be a waterfall but is now an impressive Class IV rapids with a dangerous undercut. The falls were dynamited by locals in the early 1950s in an attempt to improve boating on this part of the Big South Fork River. Instead of clearing the river, a dangerous technical rapid was created.

The rocks in the Angel Falls area are so interesting and fun to climb on that you will have a tough time dragging the kids, and maybe yourself, away. For the perfect hike, bring a good lunch, plenty of water (or a filter), sunglasses and sunscreen, a swimsuit, and a towel. The quiet, deep emerald-green pools below the falls are fantastic for swimming, and numerous ledges and cobble beaches make it easy to get into and out of the water. The fishing is great!

The NPS, along with biology students from Scott County High School in Oneida in the Partners-in-Education Program, made a wonderful self-guided nature trail with an informative brochure for thirty species of trees along this trail. Numbered wood posts associated with species accounts in the brochure will help you identify some of the common woody species in the NRRA. Brochures are available at either visitor center or at NPS headquarters.

Before or after your hike, check out the short Leatherwood Ford Boardwalks (Trail 36), the concrete-and-wood boardwalks between the parking area and the Big South Fork River. Picnic tables and barbeque grills line the parking area, and there are riverside benches on wide platforms along the boardwalk. The Leatherwood Ford area is a critter wonderland, and we have spent many unforgettable hours bird-watching from the boardwalk and parking lot, looking for water snakes hunting for fish in shallow riffles, stalking five-lined skinks basking on dead tree trunks and root masses, and chasing butterflies fluttering over muddy areas along the riverbank. This is also one of the best (and easiest) trails for photographing wildflowers in the NRRA.

For longer trips along the river, you can continue north past Angel Falls for 6 more miles (one-way) to Station Camp via River Trail East (Trail 12) and past Station Camp to Big Island via Big Island Loop (Trail 11). We recommend an 8-mile, one-way hike between Leatherwood Ford and Station Camp, which requires only a thirty-minute shuttle trip.

Finding the trailhead: Follow directions to Leatherwood Ford.

Trail Description

Starting from the gazebo, set out northward on the concrete path along the west side of the Leatherwood Ford parking area. Or, better yet, head down the stairs, turn right (north) before the old bridge, and walk along the river on the Leatherwood Ford Boardwalks (Trail 36), a wide concrete path between the parking lot and the river; flip to that chapter for more biological minutia. The path changes to a wood boardwalk, passes some riverside benches, and ends at a staircase leading back up to the parking lot near the Angel Falls Trailhead.

Bird-watching opportunities are great along the trail. Because it is an old tram road perched above the river, you can look into the trees downslope without having to crane your neck too badly. Kingfishers cruise up and down the river channel and dive into the water for fish. You should see at least one great blue heron perched on a rock or log or hunting for bluegills in a shoal with its stiletto bill. Carolina wrens sing a bubbly song ("tea kettle, tea kettle") but will scold you with a chatter as you pass by. Ovenbirds hunt on pinkish legs for leaf litter bugs. The metallic song of the wood thrush may be the most distinctive riparian song, besides maybe the loud, parrotlike call of the pileated woodpecker. Pileated woodpeckers are large birds that make loud drumming sounds on large standing-dead tree boles. Yellow, black-and-white, black-throated green, and hooded warblers are easy to spot from the elevated trail.

If there are few people on the boardwalks and on the trail, you'll probably see many lizards. If you see any large logs flecked by the sun, approach carefully and you might see a five-lined skink basking. You will probably also hear, but rarely see, ground skinks scurrying in the leaf litter right next to the trail. Garter snakes are abundant in the flood debris between the trail and the river—look closely and you will probably see one basking in a sunfleck. Although the eastern fence lizard is a denizen of drier habitats along the gorge rim, you also will likely see lots of them basking on the rocks at the edge of the forest at Angel Falls.

0.3 At the north end of the parking area, head north on the wide, flat trail—a railroad grade that once led to the Anderson Branch Mine. The trail lies on this old railroad grade the entire way and is easy to follow. The trail surface is black because it is composed largely of coal. Along the way you will rock-hop across three seepage areas and cross two creeks on wood bridges. With a little rock flipping, you may find crayfish, mayflies, and even a few northern dusky salamanders in any of these creeks (always put flipped rocks and logs back in their original position). This is good news, especially for Anderson Branch, which you cross on a bridge at 1.0 mile. Its headwaters were mined, evident in the reclaimed area on the gorge slope.

1.8 A narrow trail on the left leads down to the river above Angel Falls, the take-out point for the canoe portage. Continue ahead on the wide trail for the best access to Angel Falls.

2.0 The wood platform overlooking Angel Falls is worth a quick stop. Immediately north of the platform, the trail forks. The right fork ascends and continues along the river for about 0.2 mile to a gate preventing horses and 4WD vehicles from reaching the Angel Falls area from Station Camp, about 6 miles away. This point is the southern terminus of River Trail East (Trail 12).

The left fork is a narrow trail that leads down to the river below Angel Falls—the put-in for the canoe portage and the best way to get to the rocky river bank near Angel Falls. *Never* swim above the falls for any reason; this is a very dangerous chute with undercut ledges and logjams, and you could become trapped underwater even during times of low water flow.

The rocky area at Angel Falls is a great place to explore the tinier wonders of the Big South Fork River. We always see lots of swallowtails, skippers, purples, buckeyes, and other butterflies. Spiders sit and wait for prey above the water in rock cracks, and some are camouflaged to match the river rocks. Dragonflies patrol the river corridor and flotillas of whirligig beetles buzz spastically about the surface. Turn over a rock or two and watch tiny mayflies, caddis flies, and stoneflies scurry. These are a major component of aquatic food webs and are indicators of good water quality. Once we watched a huge stonefly emerge from the water, amble up onto a river rock, and make a long, bumbling flight across the river into a patch of emergent grass at water's edge.

TYPE OF TRAIL: Hiking only.

TYPE OF ADVENTURE: Explore the river gorge, then climb to a spectacular overlook.

TOTAL DISTANCE: 6 miles (round-trip).

DIFFICULTY: Moderate.

TIME REQUIRED: 3 to 4 hours.

SPECIAL CONCERNS: Brutal, hot climb including ladders and cables, unprotected overlook.

WATER AVAILABILITY: Abundant on trail and at trailhead; none at overlook.

SCENIC VALUE: Spectacular: healthy aquatic and riparian habitats, great overlook.

USGS MAP: Honey Creek.

BEST STARTING POINT: Leatherwood Ford Trailhead.

Overview: This is probably the most popular hiking trail in the Big South Fork NRRA—and for good reason. Still, you will probably not see many other people on any given day, especially weekdays. This trail takes you along the west bank of the Big South Fork River, crossing many tiny creeks and Fall Branch, one of the prettiest small tributaries of the river. The route includes a hot climb on switchbacks through a recently burned south-facing slope forest, so do not attempt this trail without bringing some extra water (better yet, bring a filter and get some tasty creek water at Fall Branch). Near the top, you must traverse a box canyon up to the gorge rim on some ladders, and one area has a cable-assisted climb, but most kids and

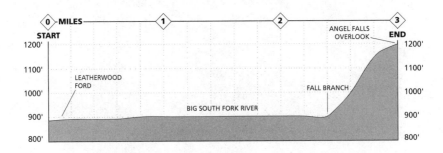

reasonably fit adults should find these obstacles only a minor setback. The climb is made worthwhile by the panoramic view at Angel Falls Overlook, arguably the best overlook in the NRRA.

Connecting this out-and-back trail with Grand Gap Loop (Trail 39) gives you a 12.4-mile day hike with many more spectacular views of the gorge. However, that loop is hot and dry; bring extra water, or carry a filter and use it often. This trail is just one short segment of the John Muir Trail, or JMT (Trail 43), a 48-mile through-hiking trail. This trail can easily be combined with any of the great trails starting from the Leatherwood Ford Trailhead (Trails 36, 37, and 39 through 42). We recommend browsing all those chapters as you plan your outing. For a perfect day, combine this trail with one of those trails after lunch and a swim in the river!

Finding the trailhead: Follow directions to the Leatherwood Ford Trailhead and see Map 20.

Trail Description

Starting near the gazebo, proceed down the stairs and across the river on the old wooden plank bridge built in 1938. Until the 1980s, this was the only means to get across the river without fording. This bridge will be underwater during high flow periods in spring. If it is, walk across the TN 297 bridge and climb down the rock stairs on the right (north) side of the bridge at the west end of the guard rail. Once on the west side of the river, go north on the wide footpath. You should see blue trail blazes that look like the silhouette of a man, John Muir.

Because it lies on the west bank of a river that flows generally northeast, this trail brings great photo opportunities in the morning, then completely different opportunities in the afternoon on your way out. However, because of the magnitude of spring floods, the trail is elevated above the river with few river access trails, most covered in poison ivy. The riparian forest is beautiful, and the ground cover plants are diverse. Trillium, mayapple, Solomon's seal, wild geranium, and fire pink grow among hundreds of other herbaceous and woody species, including abundant flowering dogwood trees. You are likely to see five-lined skinks basking in the sun on cut logs near the trail, water snakes hunting along the riverbank, and garter snakes just about anywhere. The birding is fabulous along this trail as well, as you traverse many habitat types. Carolina wrens, pileated woodpeckers, great blue herons, wood thrushes, chickadees, hooded and black-throated green warblers, indigo buntings, and the ubiquitous red-eyed vireos are reliable sightings; you might catch a glimpse of swallows "dipping" for a drink in the pools in the river.

0.2 Cross the first creek on a wood bridge. North of the creek, the trail follows along the base of high bluffs composed of Pennsylvanian sandstone. Bluffs with lots of cracks and drip-walls are particularly good habitat for woodland salamanders. Watch for tiny American toadlets crossing the path in summer.

0.6 Just before the second creek crossing, pass a nice campsite with good water access and a big pool for swimming. Cross the creek on a small bridge about 100 feet downstream of a beautiful cascading waterfall surrounded by drip-walls and moss. In Summer 2000 photographic opportunities were limited by lots of woody debris from storm and pine beetle damage. Look for both yellow and red trillium and maidenhair fern.

0.8 The third creek you will encounter is a bouldery stream with lots of plunge pools. Woody debris and garbage piled up on the upstream sides of tree trunks and hanging high in their branches are signs of high floodwaters (called "tides" by locals). Powerful spring floods are the reason the trail is elevated above the river—and the reason it may be difficult to get down to the river except at certain locations. The twisted sycamore and river birch you see lining the river are specially adapted to a life of regular disturbances.

1.2 On your right, near a boulder field, is a path leading to a nice campsite near the river with a great swimming hole. There is lots of pawpaw in this area. The lines of crumpled dirt you may see crossing the trail are signs of moles crossing under the trail. The mole leads an entirely subterranean existence, foraging for grubs with backhoelike arms and a highly sensitive nose. They have been honed by natural selection to the point they have nearly lost their sense of sight.

1.6 Cross another small stream on a footbridge. Look for musclewood, a small type of beech tree with a trunk that looks curiously like the musclebound limbs of a trained athlete or horse; appropriately, it's a very hard wood. River birch has peeling, golden bark saturated with oils and can be ignited even when wet—a great survival tip. The tulip poplar, buckeye, hemlock, and magnolia become noticeably larger as you proceed northward.

1.9 Turn away from the river and begin ascending the south slope of the ravine of Fall Branch, one of the prettiest tributaries in the NRRA. The

Eastern fence lizard

side slope is rendered muddy and slick by numerous seepage areas. Cross the large wood bridge among a wonderful boulder garden. These boulders are ridiculously slick, so be very careful if you go poking around in the creek. From the bridge turn right and follow Fall Branch downstream; look for a fork in the trail. Listen for hooded and black-throated green warblers in this area.

2.0 At an intersection, one trail leads straight south down to some fabulous campsites perched above the river on a humongous sandbar at the confluence of Fall Branch and the river. The other climbs steeply to Angel Falls Overlook. Turn left and begin the climb on switchbacks. The south-facing slope above you is covered with a lush layer of shrubs but very few large trees other than some hickory and chestnut oak. In April 1995 careless campers left a campfire burning near Fall Branch; it got away and raced all the way up to the bluffs below Angel Falls Overlook, consuming everything in its path.

Over the short term, we tend to view fire as a negative, destructive force and see only the local, short-term devastation that results. But fire is a natural disturbance that in certain situations increases forest diversity. This site is well on its way to a full recovery. In fact, bird-watching opportunities are grand on these switchbacks in the early morning and at dusk, with regular sightings of hooded warblers, tufted titmice, and at least three different woodpeckers. You should see numerous eastern fence lizards basking on logs, even in the hottest part of the day. April and October are the main fire seasons in this area, but practice good campfire etiquette all times of year, and in all locations. It is your duty and legal responsibility as a user of federal lands.

2.4 At the top of the burned area, you will reach a sandstone bluff; veer left, keep climbing along the base of the bluff, and reach a nice rock house. Turn and make a cable-assisted climb on a rock face carved with steps among a nice drip-wall and some dark crevices. Shortly after the cable-assisted climb, continue ascending through a long, wide box canyon. At the end, climb a ladder and some more short switchbacks.

2.8 At the top of the climb, you will reach the intersection with Grand Gap Loop (Trail 39). Go right to reach Angel Falls Overlook, only a few minutes' hike from this spot. You are now on top of the sandstone caprock of the plateau, which is covered in Virginia and shortleaf pine, maple, three different kinds of blueberry (all tasty), mountain laurel, American holly, greenbrier, sassafras, pawpaw, and witch hazel.

3.0 Reach Angel Falls Overlook. This unprotected overlook is extremely dangerous, so keep children within reach. This is the most deceptively dangerous type of overlook because the sandstone ledges slope gently downward, rather than having well-defined edges. A good rule to follow: Without ropes, stay at least one person-length from the edge of any ledge or beginning of any sloped rock face, especially when it's wet or covered with dry leaves, loose dirt, or pine needles.

Ironically, you will not be able to see Angel Falls through the trees below! However, you can see beautiful stretches of the river to the south and north. You are likely to see turkey vultures, red-tailed hawks, or red-shouldered hawks catching thermals in the gorge below. Listen for towhees, which are robin-sized, tricolored (black, white, and brown) birds that periodically say their name—"towHEE!" Towhees are abundant along the gorge rim at exposed rock outcrops adjacent to dry upland-plateau habitats supporting Virginia pine, mountain laurel, and blueberry. You should see at least a few eastern fence lizards basking on rocks or perched on Virginia pine trunks near the overlook.

39 Grand Gap Loop

TYPE OF TRAIL: Hiking only.

TYPE OF ADVENTURE: Hike along the rim of a narrow spine of the Cumberland Plateau.

TOTAL DISTANCE: 6.8 miles.

DIFFICULTY: Moderate.

TIME REQUIRED: 2.5 to 4 hours.

SPECIAL CONCERNS: Dangerous bluffs; blackberries cover trail by late summer.

WATER AVAILABILITY: Poor on trail; abundant at trailhead.

SCENIC VALUE: Spectacular: some of the best vistas in the NRRA.

USGS MAPS: Barthell SW and Honey Creek.

BEST STARTING POINT: Leatherwood Ford Trailhead or Bandy Creek Campground.

Overview: After enjoying the vista at Angel Falls Overlook, you will skirt the edge of the Cumberland Plateau, hiking way out to a number of points along a narrow spine of plateau caprock standing high above a squared-off horseshoe bend in the Big South Fork River. This trail lies entirely on the plateau in dry Virginia pine, mountain laurel, and blueberry. It is hot and dry, with few creek crossings—those being headwaters barely flow, if at all, in late summer and fall. The trail ranges only between 1,200 and 1,400 feet in elevation, but numerous short climbs and descents in and out of these headwater ravines add up to more than 500 feet of climbing in less than 7 miles. The wiggly trail profile would not add much information so was not included.

There is no official trailhead for this loop, so it is best done as a terminal loop from other trails. From Leatherwood Ford, hike the spectacular 2.8-mile Angel Falls Overlook Trail (Trail 38), making a day hike of 9.6 miles. You can also start at Bandy Creek Campground and hike a portion of the John Litton Farm Loop and Fall Branch Trail (both in Trail 26). This 17-mile trip is the course for the Big South Fork Trail Race. To connect these trails, simply follow the directions in each trail chapter. This trail is part of the John Muir Trail (Trail 43), an epic through-hike.

Finding the trailhead: The trailhead for Angel Falls Overlook Trail is at Leatherwood Ford; the trailhead for the John Litton Farm Loop is near the pool at Bandy Creek Campground. See directions to these trailheads in the "Local Directions" section.

Trail Description

This loop is shown in its entirety on Map 10. We prefer to hike this trail counterclockwise and see Angel Falls Overlook first (and do it again at the end!). Mileages in the opposite direction are provided in parentheses. You will make a number of climbs and descents of 20 to 40 vertical feet in each small tributary ravine along the trail.

0.0 (6.8) Starting at the **T** intersection with Angel Falls Overlook Trail, walk east.

0.2 (6.6) Reach Angel Falls Overlook. Stop and enjoy yourself; this is one of the best overlooks in the NRRA, and certainly the most popular. Unfortunately, it is extremely dangerous. Flip back to the description of Angel Falls Overlook Trail (Trail 38) for safety advice, photography hints, and biological and geological facts about the overlook area.

To continue counterclockwise on Grand Gap Loop, hike north from the overlook along the bluffline, following the blue JMT silhouettes. For the next few minutes, you will be walking along the top of sheer bluffs with numerous unprotected overlooks consisting of small platforms with thin or no soil and covered by pine needles. Take extreme care. This is obviously a very dangerous area; you could slip and fall easily—and it is hundreds of feet straight down.

0.4 (6.4) A sandstone arch is born: Notice the crack in the roof near the back of this rock house, formed by erosion from seasonal drainage and widened by winter freezing and thawing. Notice the distinct line between two vegetation types in this area: upland hardwoods (beech-maple-hickory) and drier Virginia pine forest on thin soil near the gorge rim. The trail goes back and forth between these two habitats often, so you get the feel for what limits their distribution. Listen for the song of the pine warbler, a long trill that remains flat in pitch. You may see hooded warblers—a tiny, bright yellow bird with a black nape and chin. Magnolias are abundant in moist ravines along this trail. After the arch, a large beech tree has fallen and left a gap in the forest canopy. This gap will be filled by the fastest growing, light-loving species—tulip poplar—followed by more shade-tolerant forms. Continue along the base of some small bluffs and overhangs.

1.0 (5.8) Reach an area that succumbed to fire in late October 1999 and was still recovering in 2001. You will descend on a few switchbacks to the lower side of the burn area and reach the bluffline again in about 0.2 mile, from which you can finally see the violent chute of Angel Falls to the southwest. For the next mile notice how the sandstone boulders in this area are in various stages of peeling away from the plateau surface. They tumble down to the river and block it, forming rapids. Shortly after, you will reach a rock shelter. Spending time under one of these in a storm gives you a feeling of how empowering these rock structures must have been to native peoples.

2.0 (4.8) As you approach the very eastern tip of the plateau spine, the trail joins an old road that drops steeply into the river gorge at the "Grand Gap," named for Grand Slaven, who ran livestock in this area. The hiking trail (JMT) turns left off this road immediately after joining it, so watch carefully, unless you want to end up in the gorge. Follow the sign pointing you toward Station Camp, which you will reach in about 13 miles if you are through-hiking the JMT. You should be walking generally north. After another 0.5 mile you will make a left turn across a narrow ridgeline and will eventually be on the north side of the large spine of the plateau, walking generally west but making numerous turns in and out of small ravines.

3.7 (3.1) The trail turns southwest away from the main river corridor and crosses a bridge over a small creek. Shortly afterward the trail skirts a bluffline with excellent views of the cliff faces on the other side of the river. You are walking along the edge of a similar bluffline at about the same elevation. Listen for pine warblers and rufous-sided towhees.

4.6 (2.2) Climb short switchbacks to a ridge top covered by young trees within sight of an old logging road splitting Grand Gap Loop in half, and continue northwest on the trail. Shortly afterward, you will veer north away from the road and drop into an open area being reclaimed by succession. This is the old farmsite of Alfred and Eva Smith, who lived and worked in the area until the demise of the Stearns Coal and Lumber Company in the 1940s.

5.4 (1.4) At this important intersection, signs should point you left to Leatherwood Ford in 4 miles (to finish Grand Gap Loop) or north to Station Camp Creek, which is 10.4 miles ahead on the JMT. If you are through-hiking the JMT northward, watch carefully, because JMT blazes were installed on the next part of the Grand Gap Loop as well; make sure you are going generally north. There are campsites in this area but no water.

If you are finishing Grand Gap Loop, cross the road and continue hiking generally southwest. Shortly after, you will reach Fall Branch Trail on your right, which leads to Bandy Creek Campground in 4.9 miles via John Litton Farm Loop. This is the turn for the 17-mile Big South Fork Trail Run. Continue straight ahead on the southwest part of the loop, which brings you through a dry forest with mostly Virginia pine, some with severe damage from southern pine beetles, which leave marks like bear claws.

6.1 (0.7) After a short climb, reach the grave of Archie Smith, one of nine children of Alfred and Eva Smith, who succumbed to pneumonia as a baby in 1932. After the grave site, descend to a nice campsite, which has no nearby water.

6.6 (0.2) Reach an unprotected overlook with a grand view of the Fall Branch watershed (northeast) and the point where Fall Branch flows into the Big South Fork River (directly south). Turn into the headwaters of another small drainage.

6.8 (0.0) At the familiar T intersection with Angel Falls Overlook Trail, think twice before hiking directly back to Leatherwood Ford. Everyone, especially photographers, should hike to the overlook again—as the light and character of the place will have changed dramatically since the last time you were there.

TYPE OF TRAIL: Hiking only.

TYPE OF ADVENTURE: Climb from river to rim and visit a protected overlook.

TOTAL DISTANCE: 3.3 miles.

DIFFICULTY: Moderate.

TIME REQUIRED: 2 to 3 hours.

SPECIAL CONCERNS: Unprotected cliffs, avoidable highway crossing.

WATER AVAILABILITY: Good on trail; abundant at trailhead.

SCENIC VALUE: Spectacular: beautiful forests, diverse habitats, broad overlook.

USGS MAP: Honey Creek.

BEST STARTING POINT: Leatherwood Ford Trailhead.

Overview: This beautiful loop is a great way to see the full range of habitat types in the gorge. The nicely groomed trail first passes through a dense riparian forest with massive sandstone boulders, then ascends a densely forested gorge slope. Switchbacks are well placed, so nowhere is the trail very steep. At the top you will enter the drier pine habitats on the plateau surface and visit a protected overlook with a view of the gorge at Leatherwood Ford. Leatherwood Ford got its name from the small leatherwood shrub that grows along the river here. Native Americans and early settlers used the tough inner bark for shoestrings, baskets, and fish traps.

On the plateau, you walk an edge between a farm field and mixed forest, pass over the earthen dam of a farm pond, then descend along a small creek in hemlock and rhododendron. Habitat diversity makes this trail very

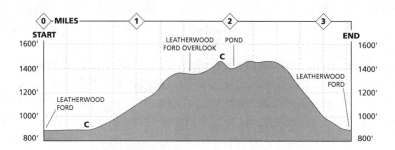

good for photographing and observing wildflowers and wildlife, and we spend a little extra time covering this subject. Because the trail lies on a west-facing slope of the gorge, a morning hike will be cool, dark, and damp, with the sun shining on the gorge slope across the river.

A few good trails can be combined with this loop to make a half- or whole-day adventure. Before or after doing this loop, you should at least check out the boardwalks and old bridge across the river at Leatherwood Ford (Trail 36). A hike to Sunset Overlook, a nice but unprotected rim platform at the end of Sunset Overlook Trail (Trail 42), adds 2.6 flat miles in the middle of the loop (mile 1.9 below). A trip to the O&W Railroad Bridge on the southernmost section of the John Muir Trail (Trail 43) adds about 4 miles, all along the river. For the perfect day, hike this loop in the morning while it is cool and the birds are out, then go for an afternoon swim below Angel Falls, adding a 4-mile round-trip on Angel Falls Trail (Trail 37). A picnic at Leatherwood Ford is a nice way to end any of these great adventures!

Finding the trailhead: Follow directions to Leatherwood Ford Trailhead, refer to Map 20 and park near the gazebo. If you only want to hike to the overlook, or prefer to start the loop from the plateau, use Sunset Trailhead. Hike westward on the 0.2-mile access trail, and enter the trail description at mile 1.9 below.

Trail Description

Starting from the gazebo and going counterclockwise (the ascent is not quite as steep this way), head south under the TN 297 bridge and continue on the wide, groomed gravel trail along the river. You may see mole burrows under the trail. Listen for the loud call of the pileated woodpecker, the metallic song of the wood thrush, and the conversational question-and-answer style of the red-eyed vireo, probably the most common forest bird in the gorge.

Soon after passing under the TN 297 bridge, you will cross wood bridges over two small creeks and pass a number of fabulous walk-in campsites and benches along the trail. You may notice a linear depression near the base of the gorge slope. This is merely a low area behind a huge sandbar deposited by the river during flood stage, upon which you have been walking. These natural low spots are important components of the floodplain, because they collect water and provide breeding sites for frogs that need temporary, fishless water sources for their tadpoles. Farther on, the trail enters a garden of humongous boulders; a side trail leads down wood stairs to a wood deck overlooking the river at Echo Rock Rapids. This is worth a quick visit, especially if rafts and kayaks are on the river. Echo Rock Rapids were created by rocks and gravel deposited by Bandy Creek, which flows into the river from the west, just south of your location.

0.5 Turn left at the intersection where Leatherwood Ford Loop leaves the old railroad grade and ascends the gorge slope on gradual switchbacks. We often see red efts crossing the trail in this area. Dry-skinned, vivid orange (nearly fluorescent) salamanders with red spots, efts are the terrestrial stage of the eastern spotted newt, the familiar green-and-yellow salamanders found in ponds on the plateau. Notice the many kinds of fungi and slime molds decomposing tree trunks lying on the forest slope and the gaps in the canopy resulting from fallen trees. Pawpaw and witch hazel are abundant, and you will notice river cane (bamboo) in wetter spots.

1.0 Cross a small creek in a steep ravine lined with rhododendron, which will be blooming in May and June; climb some rock stairs, switchback right (south), and approach some large rock faces. A little farther you will pass a large overhang and drip-wall and a deep dark cubbyhole framed by a boulder leaning against a bluff. Notice the ancient quartzite river cobble embedded in the sandstone and the coal deposits resulting from plants being compressed by the overlying strata for millions of years. If you brought a flashlight, you may spot a slimy salamander hiding in the cracks in these rocks. They are jet-black with tiny white starlike spots all over, reminding one of a clear, starry night! After walking south along the rock strata, the trail switches back left (north) and brings you to the top of the walls you were just walking beneath. Above the rock wall you will follow a tiny creek northward; on the north side of that creek, there are some nice rock faces covered with moss. Northern dusky salamanders reside in this creek. Continue climbing along the shelf of rocks into a drier forest with lots of white pine; listen for hooded warblers and tufted titmice.

1.5 Reach a signed intersection with the trail leading to Leatherwood Ford Overlook in 0.1 mile. To the right there is no sign—the loop trail just continues uphill. Go left to the overlook, passing through drier woods dominated by Virginia pine, white pine, maple, white oak, and mountain laurel. You may see ground pine, or club moss, an interesting plant that looks like miniature Norfolk pine trees. As you approach the gorge rim, the soil becomes thin and the forest opens up into Virginia pine, blueberry, and mountain laurel, then fragile lichen-moss habitat growing on bare sandstone. This habitat is easily damaged by foot traffic, so please stay on the trail.

1.6 At Leatherwood Ford Overlook a wood rail fence improves the safety factor; but remember, children love to climb on and through things, so be vigilant. You can see the TN 297 bridge and the Bandy Creek watershed across the gorge but will see only hints of the river through the treetops. The view is generally west, between 220 and 340 degrees, so photographers can capture fog in the gorge early in the morning, interesting shadows on the gorge slope in the afternoon, and a nice sunset. Along with the obligatory turkey vulture, you may see or hear crows, blue jays, rufous-sided towhees, chickadees, hooded warblers, pine warblers, eastern fence lizards, and many kinds of butterflies. Return the way you came to get back on the loop.

1.7 Back at the loop trail, turn left, ascend a short switchback or two into another dry lichen–moss–Virginia pine zone with witch hazel and American holly. After this you will enter a young maple and white pine forest, then descend into a small headwater tributary valley along the base of the East Rim Overlook Road berm, which may look like an earthen dam from your perspective. Notice the crayfish burrow turrets, which look like the tower of a hand-dripped sand castle (with a hole in it), and many buttressed tree trunks in this area; these indicate that you are in a wetland, albeit an artificial one created by water ponding behind the road berm. You are likely to find an eastern box turtle ambling along, or may even see one laying eggs in a sandy spot of the trail. If you encounter a black rat snake, it may rise up, expose its white belly, open its mouth, flatten its head, hiss, and may even vibrate its tail in the leaf litter. You might think it's a rattlesnake, but have no fear, it's harmless.

1.9 Stay left at the well-signed fork to continue the loop. The trail on the right leads about 0.2 mile to Sunset Trailhead, an alternate trailhead and the shortest route to the overlook. If you have just come from that trailhead, turn right at this intersection. The loop continues high above the west edge of a pond. In July 2001 there was a great example of a natural gap opened up in the forest canopy by a fallen hemlock. The trail descends to the pond and crosses the top of the dam.

2.0 This farm pond was constructed at the edge of the forest, making it extra good for all types of wildlife, insects to mammals. Amongst the crayfish turrets, the pond edge is covered in spike rush (the dark-green pointy plant with round, pencil-thin leaves), emergent grasses, sedges, and cattail; the open water area may be completely covered in pondweed. On moist summer days you will probably hear the territorial call of a gray tree frog: a short, birdlike trill broadcast intermittently from trees. This pond has a huge population of bullfrogs and similar-looking green frogs, which also call during the day. Bullfrogs emit the classic "jug-o-rum" call, while green frogs sound like a loose banjo string being plucked way too hard—"boink!" At night this pond comes alive with frogs!

After crossing the small footbridge over the dam spillway, turn left (north) and walk along the tailwater of the creek that was dammed to make the pond. Walk along the west edge of a large, domed field with milkweed, winged sumac, and blackberry, soon to be overtaken by the sapling sweetgum and tulip poplar that have taken hold. This is a good bird-watching and deer observation spot. You are likely to hear the chatter or staccato voice of a downy or hairy woodpecker, two small species that also have different drumming styles (when they bash their sharp-billed heads against

A farm pond in Appaloosa Field

the tree to get at beetle grubs). Great crested flycatchers are common along edges of fields near ponds.

At the north end of the field, notice the rock wall on the left. The creek runs along the wall and plunges over an overhang in a tiny waterfall. After that point you will reenter young, dry woods and continue hiking north, ascending slightly. Shortly after this, the trail swings left and joins an old road along a nice ridgeline—a pretty trail in afternoon light.

2.5 Plummeting into the gorge, leave the roadbed and head generally west on a series of singletrack switchbacks, long and gentle, like on other sections of this loop. You will probably hear every vehicle going in and out of the gorge from this point forward. The trail turns down under a bluffline on which you were previously walking, descends some rock stairs, passes a small overhang, and follows a small, rhododendron-lined creek. Listen for gorge birds, including the black-throated green warbler, hooded warbler, red-eyed vireo, Carolina wren, and wood thrush. There are some big rock walls on your right, and TN 297 will come into view. The steel manhole covers along the trail are access points for pressure relief valves for the pipe carrying the area's water supply, which is strung across the Leatherwood Ford Bridge below.

3.2 Either cross TN 297 and walk through the parking lot directly to your vehicle, or walk along the left side of TN 297 and climb down the rock stairs on the south side of the bridge abutment and turn right under the bridge to reach the trailhead in another 0.1 mile.

41 East Rim Overlook Trail

TYPE OF TRAIL: Hiking and wheelchair accessible.

TYPE OF ADVENTURE: Short visit to a spectacular but safe, protected overlook.

TOTAL DISTANCE: A few hundred feet.

DIFFICULTY: Very Easy.

TIME REQUIRED: 15 to 45 minutes.

SPECIAL CONCERNS: Side trails lead to some very dangerous cliffs, so watch children closely.

WATER AVAILABILITY: None available on the trail, at the overlook, or at the trailhead.

SCENIC VALUE: Spectacular.

USGS MAP: Honey Creek.

BEST STARTING POINT: East Rim Overlook Trailhead.

Overview: This paved trail, although one of the shortest trails in the NRRA, is a must-do—especially if this is your first time in the area. The view at the overlook is simply marvelous at any time but is especially good at sunset, as it ranges from about 180 to 350 degrees (generally west). After a rainstorm you can watch swirls of fog rise out of the gorge and brush your face with moisture from the forest (be sure the lightning has stopped!). You can visit this overlook often and never get bored, since the light on the valley differs by the hour.

The overlook is perched atop a sheer rock wall at about 1,400 feet of elevation. With its water level at about 880 feet, the Big South Fork lies more than 500 feet below. If there were no trees hiding the many layers of Mississippian and Pennsylvanian sandstone, the gorge might look something like a much smaller version of the Grand Canyon.

The overlook structure is a large, sturdy wood platform with plenty of bench space for sitting or napping. The platform is completely surrounded by a 4.5-foot-high wood fence; a chain-link fence was installed at the top of the cliff below the platform for extra safety. Camera lenses do not fit too well through the openings in the wood fence; if you use a tripod, bring one tall enough to get your camera above the top railing.

Finding the trailhead: Follow directions to the East Rim Overlook Trailhead and see Map 20.

Trail Description

Simply head west from your car on either the paved trail or the dirt trail that leads directly to the overlook. The paved trail is wheelchair-friendly and not very steep, but the overlook platform lies below the elevation of your car; be certain that you can make the return trip, or bring someone to push you back to your car. *Caution:* A number of dirt side trails lead to some very dangerous cliff walls, so be sure to keep young children in tow. Enjoy!

42 Sunset Overlook Trail

TYPE OF TRAIL: Hiking only.

TYPE OF ADVENTURE: Short out-and-back hike leading to a nice overlook.

TOTAL DISTANCE: 2.6 miles (round-trip).

DIFFICULTY: Very Easy.

TIME REQUIRED: 1 to 2 hours.

SPECIAL CONCERNS: Unprotected, potentially dangerous, fairly remote overlook.

WATER AVAILABILITY: Poor on trail; none at trailhead.

SCENIC VALUE: Good: overlook nice but with limited view, roads and buildings near trail.

USGS MAPS: Honey Creek.

BEST STARTING POINT: Sunset Trailhead.

Overview: This short but rarely used trail passes by two ponds and leads to a decent but not spectacular overlook, restricted by vegetation. It is a beautiful and remote place with a view of the river gorge and is especially worth a quick trip just before sunset, hence the name. The trail is nearly level, ranging between 1,400 and 1,440 feet in elevation. The walk back to the car at night will certainly be dark, so bring a flashlight and be ready to hear loud choruses of frogs in the three ponds along this trail.

Finding the trailhead: Follow directions to Sunset Trailhead and see Map 20.

Trail Description

Enter the woods on the south side of East Rim Overlook Road across from the Sunset Trailhead parking area, and walk parallel to the road east for a short distance along a ridgeline of mostly young maples and white pines. Shortly after, cross the gravel road by a firing range used by National Park Service Law Enforcement Rangers (not to worry), and pass a pond on your left. You should see hundreds of red-spotted newts and will probably startle some bullfrogs or green frogs, both of which squeak like a rubber duck as they jump into the water. A few tenths farther, the trail descends into a low area along a small creek with a wide floodplain supporting hemlocks and a number of different ferns. Slimy salamanders survive on arthropods under damp logs in the floodplain. Red-eyed vireos are abundant; if you are lucky you might hear a scarlet tanager. The trail passes by the back of the Resource Management facility, then over the berm for another pond, where many frogs can be heard at night. During the day you may hear the beautiful trill of a lone gray tree frog up in a tree, making you think he is a bird.

0.4 Reach another pond entirely covered by pondweed, rimmed by horsetails and sedges, and surrounded by forest. After passing the pond, look for a small spring on your right, about 50 feet off the trail; climb back up into a dry pine forest and start heading westward.

1.0 On your right you will notice a ravine that after a while seems to drop into nowhere. It is flowing directly over the edge of the gorge. Supporting maple, beech, hemlock, hickory, magnolia, and oaks, the forest in the ravine is noticeably more diverse than the dry pine forest on the ridgetop where you are walking. As you approach the edge of the gorge, the vegetation is dominated by mountain laurel, Virginia pine, and blueberry (tasty in July!). The interface, or ecotone, between the small ravine, upland plateau, and gorge edge is a good place to see interesting birds such as black and white warblers, magnolia warblers, and wood thrushes.

1.3 The trail descends to an unprotected overlook. The footing is poor on these sloped rocks, and the bluffs are high and sheer; never go near the edge, and watch children very carefully. To the north you will see the TN 297 bridge at Leatherwood Ford. You can also see the valley of North White Oak Creek drainage to the west through the trees. The overlook faces generally northwest, but the view is somewhat restricted by trees and shrubs. The walk back in the dark only takes about thirty minutes; the trail is easy to follow with a marginal flashlight—but watch carefully for copperheads and timber rattlesnakes, nocturnal hunters.

43 The John Muir Trail ("JMT")

TYPE OF TRAIL: Mostly hiking-only; some short sections on horse trails.

TYPE OF ADVENTURE: Epic through-hike with numerous river-to-rim ascents and descents.

TOTAL DISTANCE: 48 miles (one-way).

DIFFICULTY: Easy to strenuous, depending on section traveled.

TIME REQUIRED: 5 to 8 days.

SPECIAL CONCERNS: Long vehicle shuttle trips, numerous creek crossings and unprotected overlooks, some remote and rarely maintained sections requiring bushwhacking; requires backcountry permits for overnight trips.

WATER AVAILABILITY: Poor to abundant (see introduction to each section).

SCENIC VALUE: Spectacular: fabulous river gorge overlooks and immense rock walls, beautiful riparian forests, clean tributary creeks, interesting historical areas.

USGS MAPS: Honey Creek, Barthell SW, and Sharp Place.

START/END POINTS: From south to north: O&W Railroad Bridge, Leatherwood Ford, Station Camp Crossing, Terry Cemetery, Rock Creek Loop Trailhead, and Pickett State Park and Forest.

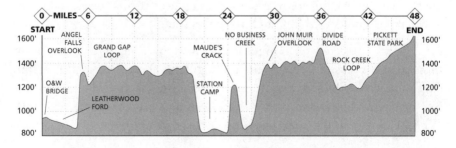

Overview: This trail has many spectacular vistas from the rim of the Cumberland Plateau, where you will be exposed to the erosive forces that formed the gorge and its geological oddities. You will be immersed in the most remote portions of the gorge and swallowed by the primeval forests blanketing four of its largest tributaries. After spending a few days on the trail, you will surely stand in awe of the settlers who lived in this beautiful but remote region.

Often called the father of our National Park system, John Muir was probably this country's most famous and influential naturalist and conservationist. (Along with a number of his supporters, he founded the Sierra Club.) During his thousand-mile journey from Indianapolis to the Gulf of Mexico, he crossed the Cumberland Plateau and Mountains just west of the Big South Fork region. He passed through Kentucky near the Wolf River Valley, entered Tennessee near Jamestown, and continued south past the Obed River.

When completed, this trail will provide the opportunity for an epic through-hike between the southwest and north ends of the NRRA and beyond! However, as of August 2001 a major reroute was proposed between Burnt Mill Bridge and Honey Creek Loop, and Honey Creek Loop was unsuitable for backpacking. Also, the NPS was planning the section between Honey Creek Loop and the O&W Railroad Bridge, but the route had not yet been approved. Thus, we start our description at the O&W Railroad Bridge.

The JMT may eventually be extended to the southwest from Burnt Mill Bridge to Joe Branch and Brewster Bridge and on to Peters Bridge and maybe the Obed National Wild and Scenic River. A western extension is proposed to connect Pickett State Park with Alvin C. York State Park (on U.S. 127 in Pall Mall, Tennessee), which would appropriately extend the trail into an area where John Muir actually walked. But as of this writing, your longest through-hike on the JMT will be between O&W Railroad Bridge and the west boundary of Pickett State Park, a total of about 48 miles. Call or stop by a visitor center or check the NPS Web site to find out if the southern and/or western sections have been completed and if maps are available.

The first 25 miles of the JMT can be combined with a 22-mile hike to Blue Heron and Yamacraw Bridge on the Kentucky Trail (Trail 23). This also provides a link with the Sheltowee Trace, which goes all the way to Yahoo Falls, into the Daniel Boone National Forest, and far beyond!

[However, many areas of the Sheltowee Trace are impassable or proposed for reroutes, so it is not described in this edition.]

Finding the trailheads: See directions to each trailhead in the "Local Directions" section, and refer to Maps 2 and 4. Shuttle times vary considerably depending on the through-hike you choose but will usually be more than one hour, one-way. You might want to put your vehicle in a safe spot at the end of your hike and pay someone to shuttle you to your start point. That way you won't have to shuttle vehicles after a long, final day of hiking.

Trail Description

We describe this trail from south to north, starting the JMT mileage at O&W Railroad Bridge and ending at the western boundary of Pickett State Park. Some segments are described in detail in other trail chapters. We refer you to the appropriate trail name and number, mileposts, and page numbers to help you follow the description seamlessly.

O&W Railroad Bridge to Leatherwood Ford (see Map 20): This easy, 2.3-mile section lies elevated above the Big South Fork River on its east bank. Head north on the wide trail just east of the guardrail of the O&W Railroad Bridge, passing left of a large campsite bounded by a massive, graffiti-painted boulder. Have your binoculars ready; you will be walking along a forested slope that puts the canopy of trees below you at your elevation. You have a good chance to see yellow, black-and-white, hooded, and black-throated green warblers and red-eyed vireos, which are usually high overhead at neck-craning angles.

0.2 Pass a steep creek that cascades down huge rocks to a plunge pool with sweetgum trees growing out of the water. Soon after, the trail becomes a singletrack path and climbs the hillside into a drier slope forest of beech, silver maple, red and white oak, dogwood, and witch hazel.

1.0 At an intersection, stay left on the narrow trail; at another creek crossing way above the river, look west through the woods for the V-shaped valley of North White Oak Creek, one of the largest tributaries of the river.

1.4 Turn left and descend into an area with a network of trails among boulders, river birch, rhododendron, and azaleas. Ground squirrels that live among the boulders will seem to be giving you directions out of their neighborhood. Five-lined skinks will be basking in the sunflecks that paint downed tree boles or rocks.

1.8 Reach the intersection with the Leatherwood Ford Loop (Trail 40), which goes right and ascends on switchbacks. Continue straight along the river. Shortly after, near some huge boulders, a side trail leads down some wood stairs to a wood deck overlooking the river at Echo Rock Rapids. This is worth a quick visit, especially if boaters are running the rapids. Back on the JMT, the trail is well-groomed gravel all the way to Leatherwood Ford; there are some nice walk-in campsites among spectacular boulders.

2.3 Pass under Leatherwood Ford Bridge and reach Leatherwood Ford Trailhead at a gazebo. This popular place has picnic tables, barbeque grills, a nice rest room, and outdoor shower stalls; the boat launch area is a great place to swim, wade, or relax.

Angel Falls Overlook Trail (see Map 20): This 2.8-mile section starts at Leatherwood Ford and follows the most popular trail in the NRRA up to Angel Falls Overlook (Trail 38). You will start on a flat, 1.9-mile section along the river but finish with a brutal climb from river-to-rim on switchbacks in a hot, sparsely forested zone—so be ready. Or make your first day light and camp near Fall Branch at one of the best campsites on the river. Near Angel Falls Overlook, the JMT continues on Grand Gap Loop (Trail 39). You are now at mile 5.1 in your journey.

Warning: the next two segments will be hot and dry in summer, so stock up on water at Fall Branch, the creek just before the brutal climb to the overlook.

Grand Gap Loop (Trail 39): The JMT lies on the eastern 5.4-mile portion of this 6.8-mile loop, from mile 0.0 to mile 5.4 in our trail description (see Map 10). There are many spectacular vistas and plenty of campsites from start to finish—but very little water. After completing this section, you will be at mile 10.5. However, you can knock 4 miles off this section by doing the 1.4-mile western part of the loop (follow that description backward from mile 6.8 to mile 5.4).

Grand Gap Loop to Station Camp (see Map 10): From the signed intersection at the west end of Grand Gap Loop (mile 5.4 of that description), this relatively flat, 11-mile section takes you along the rim of the river gorge past some campsites with truly spectacular vistas. The trail is hot and dry in summer, but there is usually enough water along the trail for backpackers. To be safe, make sure you have at least enough water for a full day of backpacking when you set out. If you want to camp at a vista away from a water source, plan ahead so that you can get plenty of water for your stay. We prefer to hike this section in one day and camp in the gorge. At the very end, this trail drops you into the gorge at Station Camp, an interesting historical area at the confluence of Station Camp Creek and Laurel Fork, less than a mile from the river. Station Camp Crossing is a great place to stop for a swim in the river if water levels are safe, but even if the water is too high for swimming, you should at least briefly visit this great spot.

Warning: If you start or end your trip at Station Camp Crossing, you must cross the Big South Fork River, which may be impossible or at least unsafe during certain times of the year. Always call ahead and ask a ranger about water levels if you are planning to begin or end your trip at Station Camp.

10.5 From the road splitting Grand Gap Loop, head north on the JMT.

10.9 Reach a spectacular, but very dangerous, unprotected overlook that faces southeast into the river gorge, with great views of the gorge and caprock along the rim on both sides. If you hiked the long portion of Grand Gap Loop, you walked along the very top of the blufflines to the east. Shortly after this overlook, the trail turns away from the gorge and continues through young pine woods for a few miles before reaching the gorge rim again. If you are hiking in July, grab some blueberries to brighten your meals—there are three kinds, all tasty.

11.4 Reach a rock shelter off to the southwest, then pass through a dry zone of lichen, moss, and Virginia pine growing directly on exposed sandstone.

12.4 Pass a series of nice rock walls and cross a wood bridge over a creek lined with rhododendron, sedges, and sphagnum. Soon after, cross an old logging road, drop down below another rock wall, and cross another small wood bridge over another headwater creek.

13.0 Climb down stairs near the edge of the gorge. You will be walking along the edge of the gorge or in nice creek valleys for the rest of this section of trail. The extensive tree damage is from a winter storm in 1998 and southern pine beetles.

13.3 A spur trail on your right leads to a narrow ridge covered by Virginia pine, mountain laurel, blueberry, lichen, and moss, and greenbrier to a point with a nice but unprotected overlook. If you go out to the overlook,

A fragile plant community growing on thin soil near the gorge rim

stay on the trail; trodding on the fragile lichen and moss will kill the plants and cause further erosion. The point offers an extensive view to the south and north. You can see another point at the end of the next spur trail and the JMT off to the north.

13.4 Enter a narrow box canyon. The opposing rock walls face east and west, forming a dark, narrow canyon with water flowing between. The canyon may be choked with downed vegetation, but the wet rock walls and cool, dark climate make prime woodland salamander habitat; we have seen green, longtail, zigzag, and slimy salamanders here.

13.5 A spur trail on your right leads to unprotected bluffs with a great view to the northeast. You cannot quite see the river from here, but there is a great view of the sandstone caprock lining the gorge. There is a nice campsite but no water, and it would be easy to lose control of a campfire here. For the next 3 miles you will skirt the upper rim of the large headwater ravine to the north, never climbing down into the valley. Rather, you will be hiking level around the upper reaches of its headwaters at the very front of head-cut erosion, where the creek cuts westward into the plateau. Back at the trail, veer south and enter a small hollow with a rock shelter on its west side. This is the last rock shelter and bluff you will see for a while; if you need protection from rain, take it here.

14.6 Cross a tiny creek on a footbridge. If you are looking for water and a campsite, continue hiking; a larger creek with campsites is not far away. You will cross a number of these flat-bottomed, rhododendron-lined minor headwaters for the next few miles.

14.8 After passing a really big, flat campsite with lots of logs, cross the largest creek along this 11-mile section of the JMT on a large wood bridge. The sign on the bridge had incorrect mileages in 2001. From here it is actually about 5.6 miles to Station Camp. This is the only place with reliable water, so camp nearby if you are spending the night on the plateau. The creek cuts through the thin soil and flows across the flat sandstone that caps the plateau. For the next few miles, the trail follows this creek downstream, curving around its many smaller headwater ravines and crossing two more tiny, ephemeral creeks.

16.7 After entering a Virginia pine, mountain laurel, and blueberry zone and reaching the edge of the bluffs lining the gorge, you can see the other side of the ravine where you were awhile ago but still cannot see the river itself. The trail bounces off the bluff three times at unprotected overlooks;

at each one you can see the other overlooks on this and the other side of the ravine you have been hiking around for the past 3 miles. (This feature is obvious on topographic maps as a dark line where all the contours run together.) At the last overlook, find yourself on the very eastern tip of a narrow spine towering over the river gorge, with the river visible below and spectacular bluffs on both sides of the gorge that will be glowing orange in early-morning or late-afternoon light. Continuing north from here, the trail skirts the very edge of the gorge for the next few miles, curving in and out of the upper end of steep headwater ravines that flow directly to the river. One, Duncan Hollow, is a bowl-shaped drainage covered with ferns and young trees. Grape vines infiltrate and blanket areas damaged by storms.

18.7 Pass an old logging road that leads to Duncan Hollow Trail (part of Trail 29) to the west.

19.2 Cross a bridge over a small creek emanating from a sandstone overhang. After crossing another small creek on a new bridge by another rock wall, you may notice some gigantic maple and beech trees along the trail along with white oak, black oak, dogwood, sassafras, pawpaw, and witch hazel. Gray squirrels and ground squirrels cache oak nuts in the cracks of rock walls lining the gorge.

19.4 Just after two big boulders, start the descent into the river gorge on a steep north-facing slope at the end of a tall ridge between the river gorge and Laurel Fork Gorge. Note the abrupt change from plateau forest to slope forest. The trail has eight switchbacks, so it is never very steep. On the forested slope with its large chestnut oaks, poplars, white oak, and beech, you will be able to see the canopy of the trees below you. Get out your binoculars; you will encounter different birds on the way down into the dense riparian forests below—wood thrushes, hooded warblers, nuthatches, pileated woodpeckers, and Carolina wrens being the most vocal. Pawpaw and magnolia are abundant. You will pass through some dark, primeval hemlock coves and cross small creeks with cascades and falls where northern dusky salamanders reside. At the bottom of the slope, you will reach a dense stand of river cane.

20.4 Cross the wood hiking bridge over Laurel Fork of Station Camp Creek and turn right (east) on the shared portion of Laurel Fork Trail (Trail 17) and Fork Ridge Trail (not described in this book), a wide trail on the north side of Laurel Fork. About 0.8 mile from the river, you are in Station

Camp, a historical settlement. This is a fantastic place for observing wildlife, so plan on removing your still-too-full backpack and looking around. We have seen numerous riparian-zone birds, deer, wild hogs, and box turtles—along with queen snakes mating in Laurel Fork and a female map turtle laying eggs near the hiking bridge!

The trails in this area are confusing because numerous trails criss-cross the historical Station Camp area, which is often overgrown with weeds (see Map 10). From the hiking bridge at Laurel Fork, go right and head east along the north bank of Laurel Fork on the wide horse trail. In less than 100 feet, look left for an intersection with a hiking trail that crosses Station Camp Creek on another elevated footbridge. Cross the bridge and reconnect with the horse trail. Continue east, first passing on your left an unnamed connector trail and then, again on your left, Hatfield Loop Trail (part of Trail 21), a horse trail that climbs out of the gorge to Hatfield Ridge.

21.2 The JMT leaves the horse trail as a hiking-only trail and heads uphill on your left (north). This intersection is only about 0.2 mile from the Big South Fork River at Station Camp Crossing, a potential starting or ending point for your trip. Before continuing on the JMT, head east on the horse trail down to the river at Station Camp Crossing and enjoy yourself. There is a great swimming spot where Station Camp Creek empties into the river, and the water is generally deep and moving slowly in summer. (For more about this crossing, see Trails 11 and 12.)

Station Camp to No Business Trail: This 4.8-mile section (Maps 9 and 14) includes a short trip to Maude's Crack, a spectacular sandstone wall with a huge crack and a nice overlook, if you have the energy for the climb. The connection with the Kentucky Trail (Trail 23) lies along this section.

Warning: If you start or end your trip at Station Camp Crossing, you must cross the Big South Fork River, which may be impossible or at least unsafe during certain times of the year. Always call ahead and ask a ranger about water levels if you are planning to begin or end your trip at Station Camp.

21.2 The JMT ascends briefly as it curves northward around the southeastern tip of a ridge and brings you back into the beautiful Big South Fork River Gorge. The hiking trail remains elevated far above the river all the way to Big Island. If you want to be closer to the river, use River Trail West (not described in this book), a horse trail routed along a historical wagon road between the JMT and the river. However, the trail is one long mud hole that is passable in only the driest of times.

22.0 After reaching the wide floodplain at the confluence of Parch Corn Creek and the river, veer west away from the river and head upstream along the creek, crossing it on a large wood bridge. There once was an interesting homesite and cabin a few hundred yards upstream from here, but the cabin was burned down by careless campers; all that remains is the chimney.

22.5 Cross Harvey Branch on a wood bridge. North of here, the JMT intersects the old wagon road a number of times, so get ready for some mud. Continue northeast along the river.

23.7 Just after crossing a footbridge over a small creek, pass a horse trail that heads steeply up the gorge slope, then follows a ridge line to Terry Cemetery Road. This unofficial trail is sometimes used for equestrian endurance rides and is just under 2 miles long.

23.9 Cross Big Branch. Shortly afterward, turn left (northwest) on the hiking-only trail (the JMT) that ascends the north slope of the steep-sided Big Branch Ravine, passing some rock walls in a great forest of beech, tulip poplar, and hemlock. We often see horse tracks on this trail, but do not be confused—this is a hiking-only trail. The folks on horseback are either lost, missed or ignored the trail signs that clearly say HIKING ONLY, or want to go to Maude's Crack so badly that they are not willing to obey NPS rules. If you see people on horseback on this trail, be polite, but ask them if they realize this trail is for hiking only. Help them find their way if they are lost.

Note: JMT through-hikers can avoid the climb to Maude's Crack by continuing northeast along the river for another mile to No Business Trail (part of Trail 19) at Big Island. After reaching Big Island, follow the No Business Trail description backward from mile 4.2 to mile 1.0 (see Map 14). Keep in mind you will be walking in lots of mud and will miss Maude's Crack.

Note: Through-hikers connecting with the Kentucky Trail, or KT (Trail 23), can make a connection from here in two ways: one easy; one not so easy. The easy way is nearly level but misses Maude's Crack. To go the easy way, continue northeast along the river for another mile to the No Business Trail at Big Island. After reaching Big Island, follow the No Business Trail description backward from mile 4.2 to mile 3.1 to its intersection with the JMT–KT Connector, then turn to the description of the KT (Trail 23; also see Maps 14 and 16). We prefer to connect with the KT using the more scenic way, which passes by Maude's Crack but includes a substantial climb. This route is described below.

24.7 After a harsh climb, begin switchbacks and look for two huge chimney rocks. You will then reach a tall sandstone bluff at the tip of the ridge split by Maude's Crack. Curve around the base of the bluff and pass by humongous boulders that have sloughed off its surface.

25.0 Reach Maude's Crack, a cool geological feature described in Trail 18. If you have the energy, hide your backpack in the woods and make the short climb up Maude's Crack to Maude's Crack Overlook, which gives you a nice overview of the No Business Creek Gorge, your next 5 miles of hiking. After visiting Maude's Crack, head north on the JMT, descending the west slope of Burkes Knob on switchbacks in a beech-hemlock forest. The gigantic beech trees are particularly beautiful in late-afternoon light.

Note: If you are starting or ending your JMT (or KT) through-hike at Terry Cemetery Trailhead, this is your connection, via Maude's Crack Trail (Trail 18). To begin from Terry Cemetery, hike east for 1.1 miles along a muddy jeep trail on a dry ridge to Maude's Crack Overlook; descend through Maude's Crack, and connect with the JMT just below. To end at Terry Cemetery, you must hike up into Maude's Crack and continue west past Maude's Crack Overlook for 1.1 level miles to the trailhead.

26.0 At the base of the western slope of Burkes Knob, cross Betty Branch on a small footbridge; immediately after, cross a beautiful wood bridge over No Business Creek. If the creek is not flowing here, it may be due to the industrial activities of beavers, which have had a dam site just below the bridge for many years. North of the bridge you may notice the remains of a two-story home built in the 1930s, which was removed by the NPS in 1992. Intersect No Business Trail immediately afterward, and turn left (west). Beavers have turned the valley into a wide wetland area.

Note: If you plan on leaving the JMT to through-hike the KT, this is your final chance at a connection. To reach the JMT–KT Connector, turn right (east) on No Business Trail (Trail 19, mile 2.2) and walk to the well-signed intersection near Dry Branch. Then flip to the description of the KT (Trail 23; also see Map 14).

No Business Trail: This easy-to-walk, easy-to-follow, 1.2-mile section lies mostly on a wide gravel road shared with horses (see Map 14). The trail is covered in detail in the description for Trail 19, going backward from mile

2.2 to mile 1.0. Head west on the trail, pass through the historical No Business Community, and rock-hop across Tackett Creek as you turn gradually southward. Just after crossing Tackett Creek, enter a primeval hemlock forest and look for the blue JMT blaze indicating the right turn (northwest) onto the hiking-only portion of the JMT. You are now at mile 27.2.

Warning: No Business Creek is your last source of water for a while, especially in late summer and fall. You are about to make a tough climb, and you have an opportunity to visit or camp near a great overlook with no water nearby. Water is very sparse after the overlook, so guzzle what you have, then filter a bunch more at No Business Creek.

No Business Trail to Rock Creek Loop: This 9.2-mile section brings you up to the spectacular John Muir Overlook. After the brutal climb, you will be walking for about 8 more miles on a hot, dry ridge with only a few creek crossings that have reliable water (Maps 11 and 14).

27.2 Just after fording Tackett Creek, turn right (northwest) at the signed intersection where the JMT splits off No Business Trail. On this trail, the creek is on your left and a rock wall is on your right. Shortly after the turn, begin a series of eleven long, gentle switchbacks on the south-facing slope of a round knob at the very southeastern tip of Chestnut Ridge. You will climb more than 500 feet in elevation over the next 1.4 miles, but the well-placed switchbacks are great for backpacking. The slope forest on the way up is mostly large hemlock and beech, but after the sixth switchback, you will enter an open, hot, dry zone. After the seventh switchback, climb a sandstone wall on a ladder. After the eleventh long switchback, scramble up an open sandstone area on some tight switchbacks. The plant community changes to that of the upland plateau: Virginia and shortleaf pine, white oak, and maple, with a low understory of mostly blueberry and mountain laurel.

28.5 Top out on the north side of the knob at the end of Chestnut Ridge. The view to the north through the trees is the Tackett Creek watershed. Walk counterclockwise around the top of the knob, cross over a saddle, and emerge on the south side of the ridge at a spectacular vista. The John Muir Overlook lies at the top of a bluff on the round knob at the very southeastern tip of Chestnut Ridge. A sandstone caprock perch, it is unprotected and very dangerous, with smooth, round edges that are often dusted with loose soil and pine needles. Stay well away from the ledge! Please do not set camp on the overlook; there are some great campsites in the saddle to the west for you to put your tent.

The overlook faces generally southwest (the exposure is about 150 to 350 degrees) into the upper reaches and headwater tributaries of No Business Creek. Terry Cemetery is directly above Longfield Branch at about 160 degrees from here, the far ridge at the eastern limit of your view. Anderson Cave Branch is directly south. The main bifurcation to the west separates Oil House Branch, at about 255 degrees, and the very upper portion of No Business Creek and Alder Branch, at about 275 degrees. You will be hiking up Alder Branch. The chimney of the old Boyette home may be visible in the valley below (at about 265 degrees) if not obscured by the dense canopy in summer. The Boyette family moved into this valley in the mid-1800s and remained there for three generations.

From the overlook, head northwest along the top of the bluffs, climb down a ladder, and straddle a narrow saddle between the knob and the main part of Chestnut Ridge. Shortly after climbing out of the saddle, stay left toward the southern edge of Chestnut Ridge as the trail joins an old two-rut logging road.

29.2 Pass through a post barricade across the road, and look left for the trail. Many old logging roads cross the trail in this area, so be sure to follow the blue JMT blazes. You will be walking on top of the plateau caprock for the next few miles in recently logged mixed upland forests supporting mostly young Virginia and shortleaf pine, maple, and oak.

30.2 This zone was just one of many areas devastated by tornados in April 1974. Shortly after, you will cross two footbridges and enter some nice hemlock woods.

32.0 Pass through another tornado-damaged area.

33.4 Stay on the trail as you pass through a zone of Virginia pine, lichen, and mosses growing on thin soil and exposed sandstone caprock. Soon after, cross a small creek on two footbridges, then cross it again and walk between the creek and a rock wall for a short stretch, then climb to the top of the sandstone bluff into another lichen-moss zone.

34.6 Climb down the bluff line on a ladder into a walled ravine; follow a wood boardwalk along the base of the wall, pass by a small waterfall, and cross another footbridge. You are now in the upper reaches of Alder Branch, a headwater stream that feeds No Business Creek.

36.0 After climbing out of Alder Branch Ravine, cross Divide Road and continue west in a mixed upland forest on a wide ridge. If you need to get back to a vehicle parked at Rock Creek Loop Trailhead, Divide Road is *not* the fastest way to get there, so stay on the trail. Soon after Divide Road, the JMT descends into the densely forested ravine of Massey Branch.

36.5 Cross Massey Branch on a wood bridge under hemlock and rhododendron and reach the intersection with Rock Creek Loop (Trail 13) on the west bank of the creek.

Rock Creek Loop (Trail 13): At the intersection, turn right (northeast) and follow the description of Rock Creek Loop counterclockwise from mile 1.4. If your trip ends at Rock Creek Loop Trailhead, proceed to mile 7.1, where your vehicle has been patiently waiting. If you are hurt or just plain pooped, you can turn left (southwest) and head back to the warmth and safety of your trusty vehicle—a paltry 1.3 miles from the intersection at Massey Branch. But you will be missing a final night at a great campsite on one of the better hiking trails in the NRRA—and a ridiculously steep climb near the end of your trip. Congratulations will be in order whichever way you go!! If you do Rock Creek Loop counterclockwise to the Rock Creek Loop Trailhead (another 5.8 miles), your cumulative mileage will be 42.3 miles! If you are going to finish the last bit of the JMT in Pickett State Park, read on.

Rock Creek Trail, Pickett State Park: If you are continuing on to Pickett State Park, or beyond, follow the Rock Creek Loop description to mile 6.0 (JMT mile 41.3), then come back to this paragraph. At the intersection, turn right (west) onto Rock Creek Trail (the JMT in Pickett State Park); enter the State Park, descend and ford the creek, and follow the brown blazes to a trailhead on its western boundary. The first 1.9 miles follow Rock Creek upstream along a railroad grade, go through a railroad tunnel (there is an alternative trail around the tunnel), and ford Rock Creek a few times. At mile 43.2 the JMT crosses TN 154 about 3 miles north of the State Park office then continues on the old logging road another 5 miles along Rock Creek, marked with blue-and-white blazes. It crosses Rock Creek more than twenty times, so consult a park ranger about this section while planning your trip. If you have come from the O&W Railroad Bridge, you have done 48.2 miles! Congratulations on your completion of the John Muir Trail! This trail may eventually be extended west to Alvin C. York State Park on U.S. 127 in Pall Mall, Tennessee.

44 The O&W Railroad Grade

TYPE OF TRAIL: Mountain biking, horseback riding, four-wheeling, and hiking.

TYPE OF ADVENTURE: Epic journey on a historic railroad grade deep in a creek gorge.

TOTAL DISTANCE: Up to 26 miles (one-way).

DIFFICULTY: Easy to strenuous.

TIME REQUIRED: A few hours to a full day.

SPECIAL CONCERNS: Two major and numerous minor creek crossings, deep puddles in the trail, potentially dangerous bridges; vehicle use may be heavy on weekends.

WATER AVAILABILITY: Poor east of O&W Railroad Bridge, abundant along North White Oak Creek; none along Darrow Ridge Road or at either trailhead.

SCENIC VALUE: Excellent: dense riparian forests, huge boulders, beautiful creeks, and great view from the O&W Railroad Bridge, but section on the plateau in rural area.

USGS MAPS: Oneida South, Honey Creek, and Stockton.

BEST STARTING POINTS: Toomy, O&W Railroad Bridge, Zenith, or Darrow Ridge for bikes and off-road vehicles; horseback riders should use either Bandy Creek, Cumberland Valley, or Mt. Helen Trailhead.

Overview: This fantastic trail should be high on your adventure list, regardless of your mode of travel. The treadway lies on the grade of an old logging and coal mining railroad constructed by Oneida and Western between 1913 and 1930. The railroad was abandoned in 1953, and the rails and most of the ties were eventually removed. The grade runs along North White Oak Creek, one of the prettiest tributaries of the Big South Fork. Massive boulders are strewn about the sometimes blue-green, sometimes crystal-clear waters of the creek. The deep gorge, steep side slopes, primeval hemlock groves, and sooty coal pathway give this trail a remote and mysterious quality that is hard to describe.

For travel by mountain bike, two options are available: (1) shuttle one vehicle to the Darrow Ridge Trailhead, then drive back to Toomy and do a

Map 21—O&W Railroad Grade and the Confluence Trail

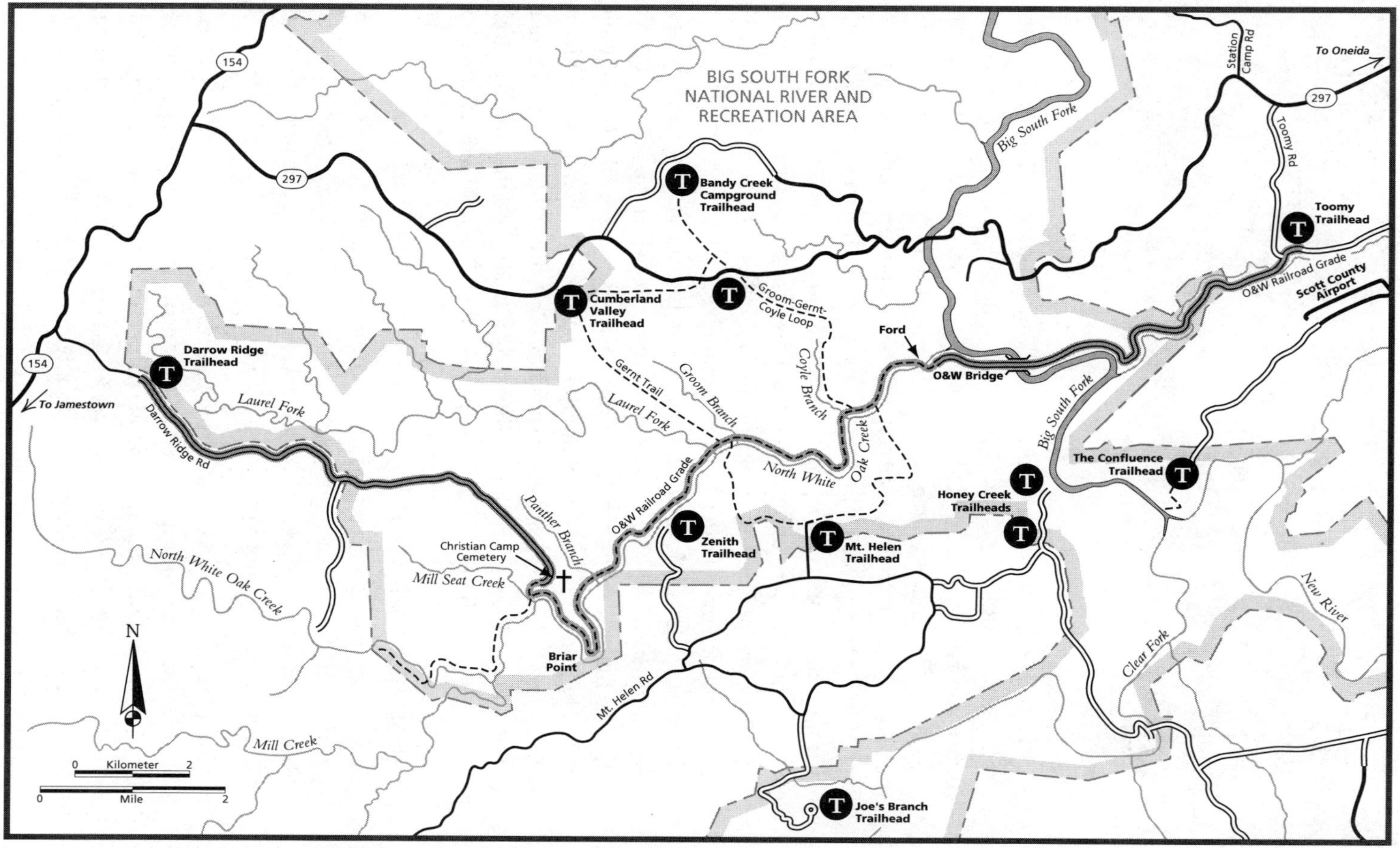

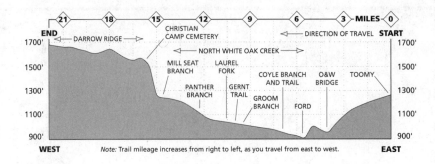

1700'   1700'

⊲— NORTH WHITE OAK CREEK —▷

1500'   MILL SEAT   LAUREL   1500'
       BRANCH   FORK   COYLE BRANCH   O&W   TOOMY
                          AND TRAIL   BRIDGE

1300'   PANTHER   GERNT   1300'
        BRANCH   TRAIL   GROOM
                    BRANCH   FORD

1100'   1100'

900'   900'

WEST   *Note:* Trail mileage increases from right to left, as you travel from east to west.   **EAST**

one-way trip going west (described below), or (2) park at Toomy, Zenith, or the Darrow Ridge Trailhead and do an out-and-back trip of whatever distance you can handle. Todd made the entire trip from Toomy to Darrow Ridge and back again on his mountain bike in about seven hours, with lots of breaks. However you go, your trip will be made more enjoyable (or possible), by carrying a water filter and using it often. It gives you an unlimited supply of potable water, with very little weight (water weighs more than eight pounds per gallon!). At the halfway point (Darrow Ridge Trailhead), you can ride a few more miles out to the T&N Grocery on TN 154 and grab a snack or a burger before heading back. What a treat!

Because of the difficult access for horse trailers at both Toomy and Zenith, and heavy vehicle use and poor access to water east of the O&W Bridge, we highly recommend that horseback riders access the O&W Railroad Grade from either (1) the Cumberland Valley Trailhead via the Gernt Trail, (2) the TN 297 Trailhead via White Pine Road and Coyle Branch Trail, or (3) the Bandy Creek Equestrian Trailhead via either of these trail systems. These trailheads and trails are described in the North White Oak Loop (Trail 30), Groom-Gernt-Coyle Loop (Trail 31), and Leatherwood Overlook Trail (Trail 32).

You can choose from a wide range of mileages—from a short afternoon jaunt to an all-day or overnight epic adventure across the entire NRRA and back again. But before you set out to tackle any or all of this level, theoretically easy trail, you should be aware of a few things:

1. All vehicles may be prohibited from this trail west of the O&W Railroad Bridge in the near future. We could not provide details in this edition, because the GMP was still in its public comment period, and off-road vehicle use was one of the most controversial issues. As of August 2001 riders of motorized vehicles could start at Toomy, ford North White Oak Creek, and travel the entire railroad grade on motorized vehicles. However, they had been prohibited from using the steep trail between the O&W Railroad Grade and Christian Camp Cemetery (at the east end of Darrow Ridge) and all other steep gorge slopes in the NRRA. Consult a park ranger or the Big South Fork NRRA Web site before making any four-wheeling plans.

2. Regardless of your mode of travel, high water will prevent you from fording North White Oak Creek during certain times of the year (winter and spring). Call the visitor center for details, but if the Big South Fork is flowing more than 1,000 cubic feet per second (cfs) at Leatherwood Ford, just assume that you cannot safely cross North White Oak Creek. This number is only a very rough guideline—if you cannot see the bottom, do not even think about crossing. Theoretically, you could start at the Darrow Ridge Trailhead or Zenith and work your way east, then just turn around before reaching this ford. However, all the railroad bridges have been removed, so you will have to cross a number of other creeks (e.g., Laurel Fork, Groom Branch, and Coyle Branch), some of which might also be dangerous during high water.

Co-author Todd Campbell crossing the O&W Railroad Bridge

3. Along North White Oak Creek, the grade lies near the water under a dense canopy of hemlock, which keeps the trail from drying out, even in late summer and fall. Numerous potholes, some of them more than 50 feet long, seem to be unavoidable without trampling through the woods. However, there is no reason for any biker, horseback rider, or four-wheeler to avoid any of these puddles; the railroad grade surface is hard, even underwater. In fact, most of the side trails made by puddle-wary users are muddier and more treacherous than the puddles themselves—and increase your risk of snakebite! Please stay on the trail and just get wet. Improper use will cause trail closures, so if you are not willing to get wet and dirty, please find another trail.

4. The trail surface is rock, gravel, dirt, and fine coal powder; you will get very dirty, wet or not, if on a bike or ATV. Bikers should wear clear or lightly tinted glasses. Sunglasses are generally too dark along this trail. Also, although the trail is nearly level along the creek, its hard, rocky surface will chatter your teeth right out of their sockets. If you have a full-suspension bike, use it!

5. The bridges along this trail are made of wood slats running parallel to the trail, with spaces between them just wide enough to grab your tires, tear up the sidewalls, and maybe throw you off your bike. Unless your balance is really good, walk your bike across these bridges. If on horseback, dismount and lead your horse across.

Finding the trailhead: Follow directions to your trailhead of choice in the "Local Directions" section (see Map 21). Toomy is the best starting spot. You can shorten your trip by more than 4 miles by parking at the O&W Railroad Bridge; however, this section of road has deep potholes and you can usually go faster on a bike than in a vehicle! It should take you just over an hour to drop off a vehicle at Darrow Ridge Trailhead and return to Toomy, including a stop for groceries or a burger. Do not plan on getting a 2WD vehicle to Christian Camp Cemetery; Darrow Ridge Road has long sections of wet sand and mud—and deep ruts from other folks getting stuck. Zenith is the best access point for out-and-back trips, especially if you are staying in Rugby, because it gets you deep into the North White Oak Creek Gorge. While it shortens the trip from Toomy by nearly 9 miles, using Zenith instead of Darrow Ridge Trailhead for the start or end of a one-way, shuttled bike trip will lengthen your vehicle trip substantially.

Trail Description

We describe this trail from east to west, from Toomy to Darrow Ridge Trailhead. Mileages for the opposite direction are provided in parentheses.

0.0 (22.0) Starting from Toomy, head west on the O&W Railroad Grade and immediately cross a bridge with widely spaced boards that run parallel to the bridge—be careful.

1.5 (20.5) Cross another bridge with widely spaced wood boards—be careful. Soon you will start descending enough to pick up some good speed, so watch for potholes and loose gravel.

2.9 (19.1) Pass the Pine Creek Access Trail leading down to the river to the left past a metal gate. You are now entering the Big South Fork Gorge, but the river lies more than 100 feet below the trail.

4.2 (17.8) Reach the O&W Railroad Bridge after about fifteen minutes of steady downhill cruising. Be very careful riding on the bridge, as the wood slats are just far enough apart to tear your tires to shreds. This unique Whipple and Truss Bridge is eligible for the National Register of Historic Places as an Engineering Structure. O&W Rapids, a Class III water, lies upstream just out of view, but kayakers might be running the rapids directly under the bridge. You can climb down to river level on the staircase on the east end of the bridge.

5.3 (16.7) Pass a road on your left (south) leading up to Hurricane Ridge. Vehicles are prohibited.

5.6 (16.4) Ford North White Oak Creek. Lots of campsites lie between the bridge and this crossing; one at the crossing itself is on a sandy beach, but it is best to get a site to the east that lies off the trail. Note the fantastic sandstone terraces in the creek just west of the crossing.

6.7 (15.3) You might notice a faint trail leading down to the creek. This is the eastern connection with the proposed Mt. Helen Prototype Trail, a multiuse trail that climbs very steeply out of the gorge above Panther Branch and eventually leads to the Mt. Helen Trailhead.

7.1 (14.9) Just after passing the intersection with Coyle Branch Trail on your right (north), cross Coyle Branch. There is no bridge, so you must ride across the creekbed. This is usually an easy crossing, but watch for large slippery rocks.

8.3 (13.7) Pass a nice campsite with good creek access.

9.0 (13.0) Pass a turnoff onto a trail that runs parallel to the creek below the railroad grade. There is a great swimming hole at the east end of this trail, with huge boulders in the creek.

9.7 (12.3) Cross Groom Branch. Again, there is no bridge, so you must ride across the creekbed. This crossing is also possible without stopping, but watch for large, slippery rocks. Just before (east of) this crossing, you will find the western connection to the proposed Mt. Helen Prototype Trail, a multiuse trail that climbs very steeply out of the gorge and leads to the Mt. Helen Trailhead in only about 2.3 miles from this spot.

9.9 (12.1) Pass the intersection with the Gernt Trail on your right. The Gernt Trail leads up to the Cumberland Valley Trailhead about 3.3 miles to the northwest. This intersection is all that remains of a mining and lumber camp where coal and lumber were loaded on trains and taken to Oneida for transfer to the Southern Railway. The camp was run by the Bruno Gernt family, German immigrants who settled the nearby community of Allardt in the 1880s.

10.0 (12.0) Pass a fabulous campsite on the left with a building-sized rock and a big pool below.

10.2 (11.8) Ford Laurel Fork, a particularly beautiful, shallow creek with a flat bottom that looks like it was paved with cobblestones. It is fun to walk up this creek and explore. Queen snakes hunt for freshly shed crayfish in creeks of this size and character. The headwaters of this large watershed cross TN 154 between TN 297 and Darrow Ridge Road. High in its watershed, the creek flows through narrow slot canyons bounded by sheer sandstone bluffs. For the next few miles you should be heading generally southwest.

10.4 (11.6) Pass a nice big campsite on your left and another shortly thereafter.

11.3 (10.7) Pass a large flat rock near a pool that is a really nice place for taking a swim. Soon afterward, a bunch of trails off to your right (north) were created by four-wheelers going off-trail ("high-marking") on red mine slag left over from the Zenith Mine.

11.6 (10.4) You can see the Zenith Mine area across the creek, which has a few unimproved campsite pads but no picnic tables. Another trail heads west along the south side of the creek, crossing Camp Branch and continuing west, but dead-ends at some more campsites. Railroad ties left in the ground in this area suggest a spur crossing the creek here, but the main grade continues on the north side of the creek. Continue southwest on the railroad grade. Shortly after Zenith, it turns northwest for a short time, then back to the southwest.

12.3 (9.7) After the trail becomes noticeably rougher, the character of the creek also changes to a narrow gorge with lots of really big rocks piled in the creek, lots of plunge pools, and small waterfalls and chutes.

12.7 (9.3) Pass a road off to the right that leads up Panther Branch, eventually reaching Christian Cemetery and Darrow Ridge Road. Shortly after, cross Panther Branch; within 0.3 mile, the railroad grade heads directly south. The trail smooths out at this point and becomes a little narrower; horseback riders might have to fight trees, but the trail surface is sandier and better for bikers here than it was near Zenith.

14.0 (8.0) Reach the southwestern tip of Briar Point and pass a trail going down to the creek on the left (south) to a nice swimming hole. Turn sharply northward through a rock cut, and continue north-northwest along the railroad grade.

14.8 (7.2) The railroad grade turns sharply left and heads generally southwest.

15.0 (7.0) Just before the railroad grade crosses Mill Seat Creek, you will reach a new trail on your right (northwest) with a NO MOTORIZED VEHICLES sign. This trail, new in 2000, heads straight up the hill to Christian Camp Cemetery.

Note: You can continue west on the railroad grade for at least 2 more miles. The trail surface is good, but the pathway gradually narrows to a tangle of briers and blackberries and downed trees. The NRRA boundary should be about 3.5 miles from where you crossed Mill Seat Creek.

15.5 (6.5) Reach Christian Camp Cemetery, a tiny overgrown plot with headstones of Earl B. Hamby, Stephen Litton, and some small, unmarked sandstone gravestones. Here the trail connects with Darrow Ridge Road, a dirt jeep trail that heads off to the northwest.

16.2 (5.8) Emerge in an open area as the road becomes wider. Continue northwest for about a mile, then veer left and head generally west for another mile along a wide ridgeline with farm fields, clearcuts, and oil exploration activities. If you find yourself descending into any deep ravines anywhere for the next 6 miles, you are on the wrong road.

18.7 (3.3) Reach an intersection. The left fork goes straight south and back down into the North White Oak Creek Gorge. Continue straight ahead (west) and immediately veer north for about 0.5 mile, then back to the west. From this intersection on, the NRRA boundary lies on this road, with the NRRA to your right (north or east) and private land to your left (south or west).

22.0 (0.0) Reach Darrow Ridge Trailhead on your right. You did it!

Mt. Helen, Honey Creek, and Rugby Areas

45 The Confluence Trail

TYPE OF TRAIL: Hiking only.

TYPE OF ADVENTURE: Short hike down to a sandy, riparian playground.

TOTAL DISTANCE: 1.2 miles (round-trip).

DIFFICULTY: Easy.

TIME REQUIRED: 15 minute hike one-way; two hours to swim, snorkel, tube, or fish.

SPECIAL CONCERNS: During high water, dangerous rapids near beach, which will be flooded.

WATER AVAILABILITY: Abundant on trail; none at trailhead.

SCENIC VALUE: Excellent: flat sandstone shelves underwater, healthy riparian forest.

USGS MAP: Oneida South.

BEST STARTING POINT: Confluence Trailhead.

Overview: The Confluence is an interesting spot where the waters of Clear Fork join the waters of New River to form the Big South Fork of the Cumberland River, hence the name of this trail. From this point north, the Big South Fork flows freely until it reaches the level of Lake Cumberland just below the Blue Heron Mine, only about 30 river miles away. This section of the Big South Fork, one of the few remaining free-flowing sections of river in the Eastern United States, was barely saved from a dam near Blue Heron that would have flooded the gorge well upstream of the Confluence.

This trail, our River Access Point #7, is a great put-in point for a float down the Big South Fork River. It is often used by Sheltowee Trace Outfitters as a raft launching site and stopover for rafters during their float through the upper gorge (Trail 49). Because it is wide and entirely downhill, this trail provides easy access for kayaks, canoes, and even large inflatable rafts. Since no motorized vehicles are allowed on the trail, you might want to use some type of handcart—but some unlucky soul will have to push it back up the hill. If you have inner tubes, there are some fun, safe rapids within walking distance of the beach; it might be fun to walk upstream on a fishing trail and float back. If you launch here, you must negotiate (or portage) the "Big Three" rapids before reaching the next take-out point, so if you lack the experience for Class III–IV white water, you should float another section of the river (see Floating the Big South Fork and Its Tributaries for details).

During summer when the water is low and running clear, this is a fantastic place to go swimming, snorkeling, or fishing—or just plain hang out on a remote beach. If the water is clear, you will see smallmouth bass, red-ear sunfish, river redhorse, and numerous kinds of darters and minnows. Morning and evening both present great photography opportunities; the gorge is relatively open at this point, so the sun is able to reach the river at a low angle. There are no other official trails in the area, but a wet hike along the shoreline of either waterway during low water will be unforgettable, and the Big South Fork north of this point is fantastic. The "Big Three" rapids are less than a mile to the north and can be reached on foot during times of low water, but it will require some serious boulder-hopping. White-water photographers might find a hike to that spot worthwhile if a bunch of boaters are planning to run these rapids. The river runs generally east-west at that point, so the light should be better from the south bank (river left).

Finding the trailhead: Follow directions to the Confluence Trailhead (also see Map 21).

Trail Description

Head south on the wide, groomed gravel trail through dry pine woods that were recently burned, and start descending into a mixed forest along the east slope of a ravine of a small stream that empties into the river just below the Confluence. Simply curve west at the bottom and follow the trail down to the beach. You will likely hear red-eyed vireos, hooded warblers, nuthatches, pileated woodpeckers, and wood thrushes on the way down. If the water is low enough, you should be able to cross either river freely and continue on narrow fishing trails along either bank of either river, but be very careful—and don't push your luck.

46 Honey Creek Loop

TYPE OF TRAIL: Hiking only.

TYPE OF ADVENTURE: Technical hike in a beautiful "Pocket Wilderness."

TOTAL DISTANCE: 6.1 miles.

DIFFICULTY: Strenuous.

TIME REQUIRED: Half day for experienced hikers, full day for novices.

SPECIAL CONCERNS: Stairs, ladders, slippery roots and boulders, deep mud, tight squeezes, lots of scrambling and possibly crawling in a creek bed; particularly dangerous during or shortly after a rain.

WATER AVAILABILITY: Abundant on trail; good at trailhead (a small spring).

SCENIC VALUE: Spectacular: large rock walls, great overlook, and five waterfalls.

USGS MAP: Honey Creek.

BEST STARTING POINT: Honey Creek Trailhead.

Overview: This remote area was originally set aside as a Pocket Wilderness by the Bowater Company, which owns and manages large tracts of land in the South to supply trees for their pulp and paper mills. The biological diversity along this trail is reflected in the many types of geological features you will encounter. Six great waterfalls, each one slightly different from the other, seem to have been placed along the trail at strategic spots to keep your interest: Hideout, Cold Springs, Ice Castle, Boulder House, Moonshine, and Honey Creek Falls. The view from Honey Creek Overlook has become

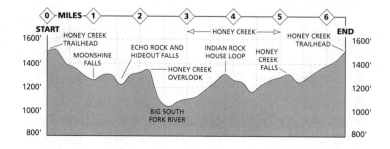

Map 22—Honey Creek and Burnt Mill Bridge Loops

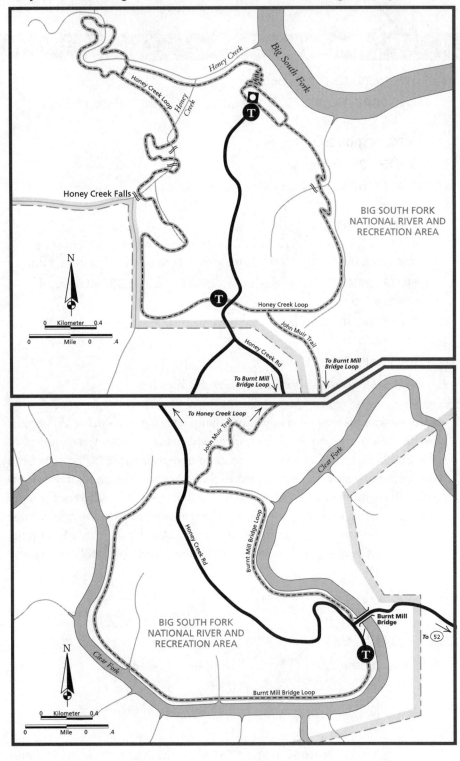

Honey Creek

Big South Fork

Honey Creek Loop

Honey Creek

Honey Creek Falls

BIG SOUTH FORK
NATIONAL RIVER AND
RECREATION AREA

N

0   Kilometer   0.4

0   Mile   0   .4

Honey Creek Loop

John Muir Trail

Honey Creek Rd

To Burnt Mill
Bridge Loop

To Burnt Mill
Bridge Loop

To Honey Creek Loop

John Muir Trail

Clear Fork

Honey Creek Rd

Burnt Mill Bridge Loop

BIG SOUTH FORK
NATIONAL RIVER AND
RECREATION AREA

Burnt Mill
Bridge

To 52

Clear Fork

N

0   Kilometer   0.4

0   Mile   0   .4

Burnt Mill Bridge Loop

somewhat restricted by trees, but it still provides a nice view of one of the most remote and violent reaches of the Big South Fork River. Up in the headwaters of Honey Creek, you will scramble (and sometimes crawl) along the creek bed itself in a deep box canyon and enter spectacular rock shelters. This trail is great!

Although we were warned by locals that Honey Creek Loop had broken many a strong hiker, we believe that to be an exaggeration. Although it involves stairs, ladders, and scrambling up a creekbed, this trail is relatively short and *not* strenuous from an endurance standpoint. However, while experienced hikers and rock climbers might find our warnings silly, check your ego at the trailhead; there are some precarious and slippery spots, and it is easy to twist an ankle or stray from this remote and sometimes poorly marked trail. You should definitely avoid taking young children on this loop.

Our rating and frequent warnings are directed mainly toward less experienced hikers, who should allow at least six hours for the hike. In some places you can "hoof it" at 4 mph, but in most you will be lucky to average 0.25 mph. The average person hikes about 1 mph over the 6-mile trail, so assess your abilities and do the math. If it rains, this hike will be dangerous—could even be deadly—because of slippery boulders and rising waters in the creekbeds up which you will be hiking. Absolutely never hike this trail during or soon after a rain, regardless of your level of experience. Also, this trail is remote; if you get hurt you may spend a long time alone in the woods. Never hike it alone without leaving a detailed itinerary with someone who will actually come look for you if you do not return on time.

While most trail guides put the loop at less than 6 miles, we include mileage on a shorter loop near the overlook, requiring some backtracking that adds about a half mile to this 5.6-mile loop. As of August 2001 this trail was not backpack-friendly because of ladders and difficult scrambles up the creek, and there were no plans to render this trail good for backpacking per se. However, you could set up a base camp near the confluence of Honey Creek and the river (mile 2.5) and spend the next day exploring the tough parts of the trail. The southernmost portion of the John Muir Trail (JMT) provides a direct connection between this loop and Burnt Mill Bridge Loop (Trail 47). However, the trail is not very scenic and may be overgrown, blocked, or even rerouted; you will be better off driving between these trails and spending your extra time swimming or fishing. We do not describe the trail in this edition.

Finding the trailhead: Follow directions to the Honey Creek Trailhead.

Trail Description

We suggest doing this trail counterclockwise, mostly for aesthetic reasons and so that photographers have the best lighting conditions. The trail runs directly through the trailhead parking area, but the official trailhead is on the east side along the road. For safety, sign the trail log. For fun, check out the entries from other people who have done this trail. From the east side of the parking area, head up the stairs onto a dry ridge covered by small timber that was destroyed by a combination of fire, southern pine beetles, and the winter storm of 1998.

0.1 The southernmost section of the JMT turns right (south) toward Burnt Mill Bridge Loop. Stay left and continue east through a young mixed forest covering a wide ridge.

0.6 Start descending the south slope of the ridge into the wide valley of a braided stream winding its way through a forest of tulip poplar, hemlock, white pine, and rhododendron and cutting through thin soil to the sandstone surface. Watch out for ankle-twisting roots exposed by erosion along the trail. The trail turns gradually leftward and heads straight north. For the next mile or so, you will be hiking downstream along the west slope of the ravine between rock ledges on your left (west) and the creek on your right (east), crossing a number of wood footbridges over small headwaters. Turn away from the creek and come to a rock ledge with formations created by the differential erosion of soft sandstone surrounding denser iron deposits.

1.0 An orange sign points right, leading you down short switchbacks and back to the creek at a small rock ledge and waterfall. Scramble along the water's edge of the creek and cross a downed tree fat enough to require steps to be cut in its bole. Climb out of the creekbed, reach a rock house, turn right, and pass above Moonshine Falls, which free-falls over an undercut ledge. Stay right as you cross to the north side of the creek above the falls, and continue around to the base. The drip-wall is moist from groundwater even when the creek is not flowing, and the horizontal cracks provide great microhabitat for salamanders. Cross the creekbed where the creek flows underground below the falls; continue east along the south side of the creek, then cross over to the north side and immediately climb a ladder (which was broken in 2001). You will drop into a beautiful slot canyon where the creek cascades over ledges into plunge pools and walk along a very large rock wall on your left. At the north end of the wall, there is an orange arrow pointing left, up the slope.

1.5 At an intersection, the left fork heads uphill to the Overlook Trail; the right fork leads down to Echo Rock and Hideout Falls. These trails form a small loop. However, we treat the lower portion of the loop as two short spur trails and take you on both so that you do not miss anything. Go right first, and walk down to the base of Echo Rock (mile 1.6). Continue on to Hideout Falls (mile 1.7), a narrow column of water splashing hard from its 100-foot free-fall from the bluffs above, where you will be in a few minutes. There may be little or no water from July to September, especially if it is a dry year. From here you can continue straight ahead to get back on the main loop, but if you do, make sure you climb up to Honey Creek Overlook to check out the view first, and subtract some mileage from your hike. We take you to the overlook a better way, so from Hideout Falls, return to the intersection mentioned above.

1.9 Back at the intersection, take the other fork up to the top of the bluffs you have just walked beneath. Climbing two caged ladders, you may have to take your day pack off and set it on each step as you go up. Stay right above the ladders, ascend sharply to a rock ledge at the top of the bluffs, and turn right at an arrow on a white pine. You will be able to see the river below from six different side trails leading to the edge of the bluffs. This is a great section of trail, but the ledges are usually covered with loose sand and pine needles, so do not approach the edge. You were just at the base of these bluffs, so you know a fall here would be fatal. One tricky spot requires you to hop across the spot where Hideout Falls plummets over the cliff. This is an ultradangerous edge, especially when wet; think before you leap, or cross it farther upstream.

2.2 Reach Honey Creek Overlook, a protected wood platform perched above a particularly violent section of the river. The unobstructed northeast view is narrow, between zero and 40 degrees, but you can see through the trees out to about 100 degrees. Photos of this section of gorge should be possible at just about any time but will be best early or late when the sun is at an angle, providing a bit of depth. You have an unobstructed view of Honey Creek Rapids, called Surprise Rapids by river rats. A mile east of the overlook (upstream) lie the "Big Three," the biggest runable white water on the river. This section of river boasts some of the best white water in the east (see Floating the Big South Fork and Its Tributaries).

Continue on the trail west of the overlook, which curves around to the right (north) and descends to the top of a caged ladder. Go down the ladder facing the bluff as though you are using a ladder, not stairs. Descend another ladder and continue curving around to the right (east) below the overlook.

2.3 Reach another trail intersection. The right fork is the other side of the small loop, which we treat as another spur; the left fork is the remaining 3.8 miles of Honey Creek Loop. First head right on this spur for about a tenth of a mile to a huge red-rock wall, stained by iron oxide, and return to this intersection again. Sap wells caused by yellow-bellied sapsuckers riddle some large hemlock and poplar.

2.5 Back at the intersection. To continue on Honey Creek Loop, take the fork leading steeply down to the river on eight short switchbacks, rock stairs, and exposed roots; level out along the west shore of the river, walking northward about 50 feet above the water. You may hear the brief, almost forced, nasal whines of Fowler's toads, which are broadcast individually to mates and potential rivals all along the river gorge. Side trails lead down the steep slope to some nice campsites by the river.

2.7 Begin the gentle leftward (westward) turn up the beautiful valley of Honey Creek. Massive hemlock, tulip poplar, maple, white pine, beech, chestnut oak, and hickory have been saved by Bowater's designation of this area as a Pocket Wilderness. More campsites lie in the wide floodplain near its confluence with the river. If you are backpacking this loop, this is a great place to stop overnight, contemplate your reasons for doing such a silly thing, and get rested for the next day—which will be much more difficult if you continue. You are better off making camp and exploring without backpacks the next day, then hiking out the way you came.

Continuing west up the creekbed, the next mile will be the toughest part of the loop. Meet the creek at a nice pool with a river birch growing out of a rock and follow the tangle of roots on its left (south) bank. River birch is abundant here, identified by its characteristic gold, peeling bark that contains oils that allow it to be ignited when wet—a cool survival technique. Northern dusky salamanders hide in the low sandstone shelves on the north bank. Cross Honey Creek, pass a small overhang, and climb out of the creekbed on rounded rocks. Back at the creek, a small sign says FOLLOW CREEK at a sandstone shelf. Pass through a narrow crack and climb a short ladder; return to the creek in a fabulous, rhododendron-lined box canyon that will be extremely dangerous, if not impassible, during high water.

3.3 After passing through another narrow crack, reach a fork with a sign on the left suggesting a shortcut back to the trailhead. Take the shortcut if you are miserable; otherwise, turn right and begin Indian Rockhouse Loop, a short but even more difficult portion of the Honey Creek Loop.

3.4 Climb the ladder up to a hanging rock house and continue on the right (north) side of the creek, passing an immense rock house immediately afterward; then climb out of the creekbed and pass by a large but low rock house on your left. Now high above the creek, continue along an immense rock wall on your right, which opens into a massive room with a very thin roof (the "Great Room"). A fork leads left to where you were before, so continue straight ahead.

4.2 After a gradual descent back to Honey Creek, walk in the slot canyon on the right side of the creek, then cross the creek under Boulder House Falls. Climb the namesake boulders to the top of the falls and cross the creek again, then climb a few switchbacks and walk along the west side of the creek.

4.6 The left fork leads to another waterfall, Ice Castle Falls, definitely worth a visit. Back on the trail you will climb to a sandstone shelf with a lichen-moss community growing on the bare rock, called Tree Top Rock. This is extremely fragile habitat, so stay on the already-barren rock surface, blazed with arrows. Pass a small rock house and drop down to the right bank of the creek.

5.1 You will notice Honey Creek Falls on your left, below you, head-cutting into the sandstone shelf on which you are walking. You will enter the slot canyon underneath the falls in a minute, so continue along the bluff, slide down the smooth rock above the creek, and cross it on a footbridge. Turn left and follow the creek, which cuts through the thin soil and flows on flat sandstone. An intersection at a sharp right turn takes you left into the slot canyon under Honey Creek Falls—a dark, damp zone just right for salamanders. After visiting the falls, come back to the previous intersection to continue on the main trail. The next mile will be really easy to navigate and hike compared with the rest of this loop.

After passing a rock shelter, make a right-hand turn as you cross the creek yet again, and ascend the north-facing slope of a beautiful ravine. After making a gentle leftward turn at the end of a ridge, you will be walking south (upstream), ascending gently into the upper headwaters of Honey Creek. Turn gently to the east, crossing a logging road twice, and ascend to the trailhead at 6.1 miles.

47 Burnt Mill Bridge Loop

TYPE OF TRAIL: Hiking only.

TYPE OF ADVENTURE: Short hike in the beautiful riparian zone of Clear Fork.

TOTAL DISTANCE: 4.3 miles.

DIFFICULTY: Moderate.

TIME REQUIRED: 3 to 4 hours.

SPECIAL CONCERNS: A few slippery areas, rock stairs, and low ledges along Clear Fork.

WATER AVAILABILITY: Abundant on trail; none at trailhead.

SCENIC VALUE: Spectacular: riparian habitat and creek, but no big vistas or overlooks.

USGS MAP: Honey Creek.

BEST STARTING POINT: Burnt Mill Bridge Trailhead.

Overview: This is really a short hike, but Clear Fork is so beautiful, we suggest that you plan a full-day outing. By starting in the morning and going downstream, you can fish for smallmouth bass, observe rafters and kayakers starting their trips, and, if you are lucky, photograph tornado-like swirls of fog as they burn off Clear Fork. After a short climb you will return to Clear Fork just in time to eat lunch, swim, fish, or let the noise of rushing water lull you to sleep. The southern portion of this trail is spectacular in late afternoon when the sun shines directly down Clear Fork, sidelighting fish and underwater ledges—but only between rain events when the water is running low and clear. This is a perfect trail for first-time backpackers. The campsites along the southwestern part of the loop are fantas-

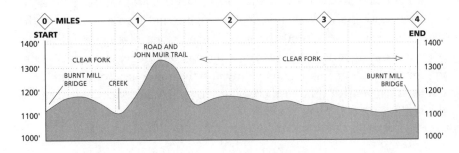

tic, and make wonderful walk-in sites. We suggest you stay overnight and hike Honey Creek Loop (Trail 46) the next day, or vice versa.

Finding the trailhead: Follow directions to Burnt Mill Bridge. As of August 2001, the bridge was slated for replacement, but the new bridge will be completed before the old one is abandoned (or removed), so traffic will not be stopped.

Trail Description

Head north just west of the western bridge abutment, down the rock steps, and begin the John Muir Trail (JMT), identified by little blue profiles of a man with a full beard. Because of flooding, the trail is perched above Clear Fork (making it a great bird-watching trail), but there are opportunities to get to the water and observe rafters, canoers, and kayakers starting their trip. The trail makes a lot of short climbs and descents, sometimes on rock or wood steps. You will pass some nice rock walls and rock shelters among the hemlock, poplar, beech, and rhododendron. Rock shelters make this section a wonderful walk in the rain. We hope you get the chance to sit out a rainstorm under a rock shelter somewhere in the NRRA—it is an unforgettable experience!

0.9 Just after passing a large boulder leaning against a rock wall, turn westward away from Clear Fork and begin a gradual ascent in the ravine of a small creek, following red arrowhead blazes. The narrow creek cuts through thin soil and flows on the flat sandstone caprock. You will cross the creek thrice on foot bridges and ascend into a dry box canyon, climbing about 220 feet in 0.4 mile. There are some singletrack switchbacks, but the trail mostly climbs up an old logging road, which becomes steep in one spot. At the top you will be walking on a ridge covered by young white oak, maple, hickory, white pine, dogwood, sassafras, and witch hazel.

1.3 At a well-signed trail intersection, the JMT leaves Burnt Mill Bridge Loop and heads north past Beaver Falls to the Honey Creek Loop (and eventually, beyond). Stay left to finish the loop. Shortly after, cross Honey Creek Road at trail signs and head generally southwest along a ridgeline under a young mixed forest with pines damaged by southern pine beetles. (See our ecology section for an explanation of why these native insects are wreaking such havoc.) At 1,330 feet you have reached the highest point on the trail. At the end of the ridge, descend some mild switchbacks into a pretty ravine, walking on the moist north-facing slope among older trees.

After the second switchback, reach a ravine lined with hemlock and rhodo-dendron, rock walls, and an extra large rock house visible along the south side of the ravine. Cross a small creek, and continue descending along the creek.

2.1 The trail comes within sight of Clear Fork again upstream of where you left it but mostly remains elevated well above the east bank, a steep outside bend lined with dense rhododendron. The outside bend of a creek or river is where erosion occurs, and outside banks are often steep and undercut. Deposition occurs on the inside bend of creeks and rivers. For the rest of your trip, you will be walking on a wide, sandy floodplain on an inside bend of Clear Fork.

2.5 Reach the riverbank at some big flat rocks hanging over the bank, where you can get your first good view of a nice pool and rapids. After this the trail follows a sweeping inside bend of Clear Fork, and the floodplain spreads out into a low, flat, sandy area. Rock walls lie far to the east through the floodplain forest dominated by dense hemlock, which makes the con-ditions ripe for ferns and many interesting herbaceous plants, including Solomon's seal and mayapple. Notice the river cane, a kind of bamboo that gave rise to the term "canebrake." You will pass some great campsites beneath hemlocks, but better campsites lie ahead. After passing the sharpest bend on the river, you follow close to a substantial, curved bluffline, requiring lots of rock-hopping and negotiating, so the hiking will not be as fast as you might expect.

3.1 The trail gets wider (an old logging road) and passes more fantastic campsites with much better access to Clear Fork. For the next 1.2 miles the trail lies close to the river and joins and leaves the old logging road many times on the way back to the bridge; just follow the red arrowheads.

Clear Fork is spectacular in the afternoon and morning sun from here to the bridge, because the gorge runs generally east-west. The clear, shal-low water flows over sandstone shelves; if the sun is low in the sky, shafts of light shine obliquely through the water and illuminate smallmouth bass, redhorse and white suckers, darters, and many other kinds of fish. We find it impossible to return to our vehicle without spending hours fishing, wad-ing around on the slippery sandstone flats, and lying in the shallow, warm water. Leave yourself plenty of time to enjoy one of the most beautiful riparian zones in the NRRA.

48 Meeting of the Waters Loop

TYPE OF TRAIL: Hiking only.

TYPE OF ADVENTURE: Short hike in the Clear Fork Gorge to a great swimming hole.

TOTAL DISTANCE: 2.1 miles.

DIFFICULTY: Easy.

TIME REQUIRED: 1 to 2 hours.

SPECIAL CONCERNS: Slippery spots and ledges, trail flooded during high water.

WATER AVAILABILITY: Abundant on trail; none at trailhead.

SCENIC VALUE: Excellent: healthy creek and riparian forest, humongous boulders.

USGS MAP: Rugby.

BEST STARTING POINT: Rugby Trailhead.

Overview: If you spent the morning touring Rugby and are itching to go swimming, bird-watching, or just walking in the woods, this is the trail for you! Clear Fork is absolutely beautiful along this trail, and there are some humongous flat-topped boulders next to the creek that make great napping or lunch spots. You are likely to see salamanders on the drip-wall above the swimming hole, lots of fish in Clear Fork, and great blue herons and kingfishers stalking their fishy quarry. You will likely see or hear at least red-eyed vireos, pine warblers, hooded warblers, pileated woodpeckers, and wood thrushes along the way. Your goal is to reach the spot where White Oak Creek meets Clear Fork, hence the trail name.

The Rugby Trailhead is only 0.7 mile from the Rugby Visitor Center,

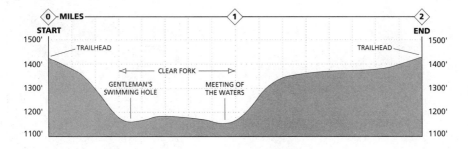

Map 23—Rugby Area

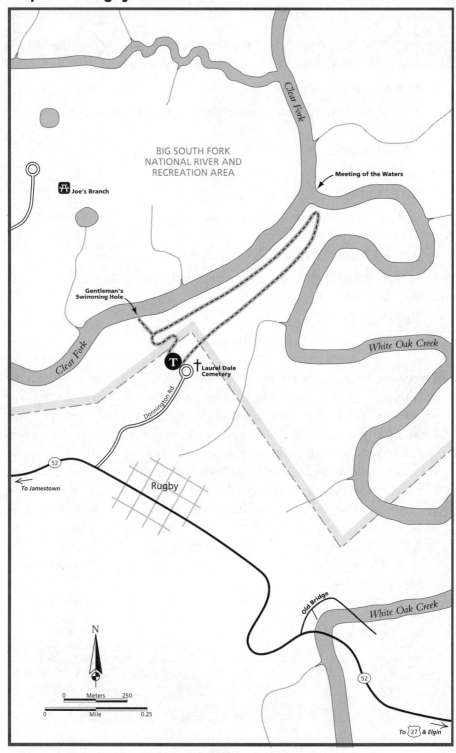

BIG SOUTH FORK
NATIONAL RIVER AND
RECREATION AREA

Clear Fork

Meeting of the Waters

Joe's Branch

Gentleman's
Swimming Hole

White Oak Creek

Clear Fork

T †Laurel Dale
Cemetery

Donnington Rd

52

To Jamestown

Rugby

White Oak Creek

Old Bridge

N

52

Meters   250

Mile   0.25

To 27 & Elgin

and the Gentleman's Swimming Hole is only 0.4 mile from the trailhead, so you could easily just walk there from town. We recommend doing this loop clockwise, going directly to Gentleman's Swimming Hole first, then hiking along Clear Fork. We say this because the lower part of the loop along Clear Fork is so much more beautiful than the upper part that you might just want to return the same way instead of doing the entire loop. Be advised that the trail lies fairly close to Clear Fork and is often underwater during high flows in spring. Check with the Rugby Visitor Center for trail conditions (see appendix). Enthusiastic kayakers can use this trail to access Clear Fork for a float to Burnt Mill Bridge or beyond.

Finding the trailhead: Follow directions to Rugby Trailhead.

Trail Description

To go clockwise and see the Gentleman's Swimming Hole first, head directly west from the trailhead on the narrow hiking trail, rather than northeast on the wide jeep trail. You will cross a dry pine ridgeline and gradually descend on switchbacks into a mixed forest in the valley of a small stream. Soon you will cross the stream and descend steeply on rock steps. The recently logged forest is young but recovering nicely, and you will see hemlock, white oak, white pine, chestnut oak, tulip poplar, maple, and magnolia, among others, some fairly large.

0.3 Reach a rock house called Witch's Cave on your left and a small cascading creek and drip-wall with lots of horizontal rock strata on your right. The combination of creek, drip-wall, and horizontal cracks makes great habitat for dusky and longtail salamanders, which are aquatic as larvae and semiaquatic as adults. Continue along the stream and in a few hundred yards reach the intersection with the spur leading down to Clear Fork at Gentleman's Swimming Hole. The trail to the right leads to the Meeting of the Waters, just under a mile away. First go left on the spur to visit the swimming hole. It is a really nice spot.

0.4 Reach Clear Fork at Gentleman's Swimming Hole. The deep pool, climbable boulders, and pebble beach made this a popular bathing place for the English gents of Rugby. Back then, women swam in the next pool upstream. This is still a great place to swim, although the water is probably not as clear, and the beach is probably underwater more often than it was during Rugby's heyday. Some walk-in, backcountry campsites can be found down here among the rocks.

0.5 Back at the loop intersection, go left to continue the loop clockwise. Along Clear Fork, the trail is elevated about 20 feet above the river and winds among huge boulders at the base of a 60-foot bluff on your right. Look for a nice rock house and odd rock sculptures, formed by the differential erosion of sandstones of different hardness; the iron ore deposits are the most resistant to erosion. Some fairly large tulip poplars, white pines, and hemlocks grow along the trail. Access to the river is difficult along here because the bank is steep and lined with dense rhododendron.

1.2 Meeting of the Waters, the confluence of Clear Fork and White Oak Creek. You can usually walk out onto a nice ledge below a massive rock wall at the very end of the trail, but during high water periods, this ledge may be underwater. From this ledge you can see the waters of Clear Fork and White Oak Creek mixing together.

To continue the loop trail, walk past the rock ledge along White Oak Creek and turn sharply uphill. The climb is steep but very short, and the trail lies on a wide, sometimes muddy 4WD road. The last 0.8-mile section of the loop is not nearly as pretty as what you have just seen, so we recommend that you return the same way you came, along Clear Fork. Trails always feel different from a different direction, and you might find different photographic light or vantage points or see critters you missed on the way to the Meeting of the Waters.

1.4 The road flattens out on top of a narrow ridge and becomes potholed and muddy. The forest is very young along this ridgeline, the tops of the trees sometimes barely above roof level. This is evidence of recent clearing for oil and gas exploration, and some oil tanks and gas wells remain in the area.

2.1 Notice Laurel Dale Cemetery on your left as you get back to Rugby Trailhead.

Floating the Big South Fork
and Its Tributaries

The best way to really experience the Big South Fork NRRA is by floating its magnificent waterways in an inflatable raft, dory, canoe, kayak, inner tube, or whatever your favorite watercraft might be. Only from the water can you experience firsthand the forces that created the deep gorges and spectacular geological features of the Cumberland Plateau. In fact, the only way to access certain portions of the river gorge and its tributaries is by water. Floatable waterways include, but are not limited to, Clear Fork, New River, White Oak Creek, North White Oak Creek, and the Big South Fork River. Because the waterways upstream of the Blue Heron area are free-flowing, paddling is seasonal and entirely subject to the whims of nature. Large inflatable river rafts are only allowed upstream of Leatherwood Ford. Motorboats in Lake Cumberland are allowed to proceed upstream to a point 0.1 mile downstream of Devil's Jump Rapids (near Blue Heron area). As of August 2001 there were no limitations on the number of boats of any kind allowed on any of the waterways and no specific rules or regulations other than the personal flotation device requirement, a backcountry permit for staying overnight on the river, and a valid Kentucky or Tennessee fishing license if you want to fish.

Novices can leave all the logistics to a commercial outfitter. As of this writing, only one permitted outfitter, Sheltowee Trace Outfitters, ran regular float trips on the Big South Fork and its tributaries. They run a great white-water rafting trip on the upper gorge and also rent canoes, kayaks, and tubes; provide shuttle trips; and help you design your own adventure in the lower gorge. The Life Development Center, operated by Anderson County Health Council, offers customized rafting or canoe trips for groups on an as-needed basis. (See appendix for contact information for both outfitters.) More-experienced boaters and "river rats" can design their own trip using the general information below and the two river chapters that

Canoeing on the Big South Fork

follow. The eighteen river access points are shown on Map 2, and directions to and descriptions of each launch/load site are provided in the "Local Directions" section in The Basics chapter.

General River Safety

Safety should be your primary concern when you plan your adventure in this riparian wonderland, since water-based activities can be dangerous. To make your trip enjoyable—and avoid having to be rescued—please review the Safety and Etiquette section for all users in general and for boaters in particular (see pages 39–47). We also provide specific tips for improving your safety and comfort for each of the trips described below. Always consider safety first when you plan your adventure in this riparian wonderland! The following information will help you assess which runs you can handle safely—the first step in planning a safe trip.

River and Tributary Run Data: The table on page 307 presents basic data on each "run," or section of river or tributary, modified or taken directly from the NPS pamphlet entitled *A Guide to Paddling in the Big South Fork* (www.nps.gov/biso/river.htm), and USGS 7.5-minute series quadrangle maps. First we explain in detail what is meant by each column in the table:

Run Rating indicates the difficulty of the overall run and particular rapids using the standard river rating system, followed by the total drop in elevation of each section (in feet).

- Class I denotes moving water with a few small waves but few or no obstructions.

- Class II requires some maneuvering through waves less than 3 feet high; scouting of the course is generally not required for safety.

- Class III describes rapids with high, irregular waves and narrow passages that require complex maneuvering; scouting from shore may be required.

- Class IV rapids are long, difficult, constricted passages and turbulent waters that require precise maneuvering; difficult rescue conditions necessitate frequent scouting from shore. Open canoes should not be taken through Class IV rapids, and those using kayaks or decked canoes should be very comfortable performing an Eskimo roll in difficult conditions. The Big South Fork reaches an overall Class IV rating at about 2,500 cfs at Leatherwood Ford.

- Class V waters exhibit extremely difficult, long, and violent rapids and congested passages that should always be scouted from shore. A mistake in a Class V rapid may lead to significant injury or even death, and rescue may be very difficult. The Big South Fork reaches an overall Class V status only when it is running more than 10,000 cfs at Leatherwood Ford. However, individual rapids (e.g., The Big Three and Honey Creek) will often be Class V at much lower flow rates.

Keep in mind that low flow does not automatically mean easier rapids. In fact, some rapids are much more technical during low flow periods, and it may be easier to become pinned or trapped underneath rock ledges, boulders, and logjams that are deeply submerged during normal flow, probably the most dangerous aspect of floating the Big South Fork. That said, rescue will nearly always be easier during low flow periods.

Min/Max Flow shows the suggested range of flow rates for safely and enjoyably floating each waterway section in inflatable rafts (R) or canoes and kayaks (C&K). Numbers are in cubic feet per second (cfs) and always indicate the flow rate of the Big South Fork River measured at the Leatherwood Ford gauge. Minimum flow simply indicates the lowest possible level at which it is possible to run a given section without having to get out and drag your boat. Lowest flows are usually in late summer and fall. Maximum flow is an upper limit of safe navigation for a given waterway segment—above which even the most experienced river rats, professional boaters, and rescue units are likely to encounter serious trouble. These values are meant only as a general guideline and are in no way absolute. Very dangerous conditions can be present in all of these waterways under much lower flows. Maximum flows are generally the highest with snowmelt and spring rains, between February and May. During periods of high flow, these waterways can be deadly, if only because of the vast amount of large, floating woody debris that will be running the river with you. Always check the gauge at Leatherwood Ford or call the visitor center before attempting to float the river, and consult a park ranger for advice.

Best Season takes into account all the above information and indicates when these waterways are generally navigable (not too low, but not too high). During the driest periods in late summer and fall (July through October), these waterways may not be a pleasant place to paddle—unless you enjoy dragging or even carrying your boat. If you paddle during flow periods lower than suggested, you should double your anticipated trip time.

The table on page 307 shows river runs in the Big South Fork NRRA, in order generally from south to north, with numbered access points keyed to Map 2.

The Best Float Trips

For those wishing to hone their white-water skills, or just play around in the water, there are a number of challenging sections along Clear Fork and the upper gorge of the Big South Fork. The runs from Peters Bridge, Brewster Bridge, or White Oak Bridge to Burnt Mill Bridge, or any combination thereof, are fun and fast in times of high water, with good launches at all access points and shuttle trips of less than thirty minutes along TN 52. Once you combine any of these sections with any access points on the upper gorge of the Big South Fork River to the north, the trips become more intense and spectacular (Class IV), but vehicle shuttling times increase substantially.

The most action-packed white-water adventure lies between The Confluence and either Pine Creek or the O&W Bridge. This fantastic stretch

River Run (with access points)	River Miles	Run Rating (Class/Drop)	Min/Max Flow (cfs)	Best Season*
1. Peters Bridge to Brewster Bridge (41–40): Clear Fork	6.0	I–II/40	R: 1,200/10,000 C&K: 600/3,500	W, Spr
2. Brewster Bridge to Rugby (40–38): Clear Fork	3.9	II–III/50	R: 1,200/10,000 C&K: 600/3,500	F, W, Spr
3. Rugby to Burnt Mill Bridge (38–36): Clear Fork	6.3	II–III/75	R: 1,200/10,000 C&K: 600/3,500	F, W, Spr
4. White Oak Bridge to Burnt Mill Bridge (39–36): White Oak Creek to Clear Fork	11.4	II/140	R: 2,000/10,000 C&K: 1,000/3,500	W, Spr
5. Burnt Mill Bridge to The Confluence (36-34): Clear Fork	3.8	III/80	R: 1,100/10,000 C&K: 600/3,500	F, W, Spr
6. New River Bridge to The Confluence (35–34): New River	9.0	I–III/85	R: 1,200/10,000 C&K: 600/5,000	F, W, Spr
7. The Confluence to Pine Creek (34–28): Big South Fork River	3.2	III–IV/75	R: 1,100/10,000 C&K: 600/3,500	F, W, Spr
8. Pine Creek to O&W Railroad Bridge (28–29): Big South Fork River	1.5	III–IV/40	R: 1,100/10,000 C&K: 600/3,500	F, W, Spr
9. O&W Railroad Bridge to Leatherwood Ford (29–23): Big South Fork River	2.2	III/25	R: 1,100/10,000 C&K: 600/3,500	F, W, Spr
10. Zenith to Leatherwood Ford (31–23): North White Oak Creek to Big South Fork River	7.6	II–III/185	R: Too narrow C&K: 2,000/3,500	W, Spr
11. Leatherwood Ford to Station Camp (23–11): Big South Fork River	7.6	I–II (IV at Angel Falls)/40	R: 400/20,000 C&K: 150/5,000	F, W, Spr, Early Sum
12. Station Camp to Bear Creek (11–8): Big South Fork River	12.2	I–II/60	R: 400/20,000 C&K: 150/5,000	F, W, Spr, Early Sum
13. Bear Creek to Blue Heron Mine (8–6): Big South Gap Fork River	4.7	I–III (IV at Devil's Jump)/35	R: 400/20,000 C&K: 150/5,000	F, W, Spr, Early Sum
14. Blue Heron Mine to Worley (6–5): Big South Fork River	2.3	I–II/0 C&K: 150/5,000	R: 400/20,000 C&K: 150/5,000	F, W, Spr, Early Sum
15. Worley to Yamacraw Bridge (5-4): Big South Fork River	2.3	I–II/0	R: 400/20,000 C&K: 150/5,000	F, W, Spr, Early Sum
16. Yamacraw Bridge to Alum Ford (4–3): Big South Fork River	5.4	I–II/0	R: 400/20,000 C&K: 150/5,000	F, W, Spr, Early Sum
17. Alum Ford to Big Creek (3–1): Big South Fork River	3.8	I/0	Lake Cumberland	All

*F = fall   W = winter   Spr = spring   Sum = summer

Inflatable kayaks are a great way to see the Big South Fork.

has the best Class IV rapids on the river; the shuttle trip is not too long, but you will have to carry your boat and equipment down to the launch on the Confluence Trail (Trail 45) and up a short hill at either take-out.

The shortest white-water trip lies along a reach of the Big South Fork called "The Narrows," in which you float through Jake's Hole and O&W Rapids (Class IV). To do this section, put in at Pine Creek and float to the O&W Bridge. The shuttle is only 1.5 miles along the river, so you can either walk it yourself or trade shuttle duties with a buddy so that you can repeat the short, intense trip numerous times.

A similar adventure with a canoe, kayak, or inner tube is available along North White Oak Creek between Zenith and the point where the O&W Railroad Grade fords the creek (Map 21). The railroad grade lies within 50 feet of the creek along this entire stretch, so you can scout the creek on the way up, but you will need a competent off-road vehicle. As of this writing, you could shuttle between Zenith and the ford. However, all motorized vehicles may be prohibited west of O&W Railroad Bridge in the near future, so check with a park ranger before you make plans. The best way to do this section in an inner tube is to park near the ford and walk upstream, rolling your tubes along the flat railroad grade, and float back.

Less than 8 miles long, the canoe trip between Leatherwood Ford and Station Camp is an easy half day in a kayak or a nice, lazy, full day of fishing and swimming from a canoe. Both access points have decent hand-launches and good vehicle access, and the vehicle shuttle between the two access points will take only about thirty minutes (one-way). That said, be advised that you will have to portage Angel Falls—a very dangerous, technical Class IV chute only 2 miles into your trip. Refer to our description of the canoe camping trip (Trail 50) for details.

A similar canoe adventure is possible between Station Camp and Blue Heron, but at nearly 17 miles, it will be a long day, and the shuttle trip will be substantial (about an hour, one-way). Also, you will have to portage around Devil's Jump at the very end, so watch your time. Refer to our description of the canoe camping trip (Trail 50), starting at mile 7.6. You can shorten the trip to just under 5 miles and cut the shuttle to a mere twenty minutes by starting from the Bear Creek Trailhead. You will have to lug your boat and equipment down a fairly steep hill at the put-in (see Trail 8), but the shortened trip and shuttle might be worth the effort.

All the trips below Blue Heron can be made as out-and-back trips, as the river is nearly at the level of Lake Cumberland, and flow is slow. In the summer you can even canoe upstream from Blue Heron to a wonderful garden of massive boulders around Devil's Jump, spend part of the day swimming and fishing there, then canoe downstream to the quiet waters below Blue Heron before returning. We highly recommend cruising the river in this area. The same can be said for the river near Alum Ford, where the river is basically a lake.

49 White-water Rafting in the Upper Gorge

TYPE OF BOAT: Inflatable river raft, wood dory, decked canoe, or white-water kayak.

TYPE OF ADVENTURE: White-water extravaganza on Clear Fork and the Big South Fork River.

TOTAL DISTANCE: 10.5 miles.

DIFFICULTY: Class III overall; at least five Class IV rapids.

TIME REQUIRED: Full day for the entire trip, including the shuttle, preparation, and lunch.

SPECIAL CONCERNS: Class IV rapids, large boulders, suck-holes, hydraulics, logjams; many remote sections with difficult rescue opportunities.

SCENIC VALUE: Spectacular: free-flowing river among building-size boulders within a deep gorge blanketed by dense, uninterrupted riparian forest and capped by massive, sheer rock walls.

USGS MAP: Honey Creek.

START-END POINTS: Put-in at Burnt Mill Bridge; take-out at Leatherwood Ford.

Overview: If you want to float the Class IV sections of the Big South Fork but require an outfitter to float Class III or above, the best trip is a one-day rafting trip on Clear Fork and the upper Big South Fork River Gorge (Runs 5, 7, 8 and 9). This trip is among the best in the East. Sheltowee Trace Outfitters runs this stretch of river nearly every day in spring. All you have to do is make reservations (see appendix), then meet the shuttle bus at the Leatherwood Ford parking area at the specified time. The float takes a full day, including the shuttle trip and a stop at either The Confluence or Pine Creek, where they will stuff you full with sandwiches, snacks, and lemonade. This trip is best done in April or May, when the flow rate is around 3,000 cfs at Leatherwood Ford. The trip consists of some fairly long stretches of quiet water where you can fully enjoy the beautiful scenery of the river gorge, punctuated by some adrenalin-inducing rapids!

Rafting Safety and Comfort: You will get very wet floating the gorge and might get cold in the early spring water, but a few simple items will make your trip comfortable. At the very least, bring a rain jacket and rain pants. They may not keep you dry, but they will conserve your heat when you do get wet. Do not bring a poncho—it will just get in the way and could be very dangerous under certain circumstances. A wet suit is advisable if the water temperature is below 70 degrees Fahrenheit. Your feet will definitely be wet the entire day. A combination of neoprene socks and river sandals works fine, but because you will have to shove your feet between the boat tubes to stay firmly anchored, old sneakers (over neoprene socks) will be much more comfortable.

Sheltowee Trace Outfitters provides the mandatory life jackets and river helmets. They have wet suits for rent and neoprene socks for purchase if you don't have your own. Bring a baseball cap or bandana to wear under your river helmet to make it more comfortable. Avoid wearing cotton shirts and blue jeans, which just hold water; go with synthetic fabrics. Definitely bring sunglasses with a good strap. If you bring a camera, it should be waterproof and small enough to fit in a pocket or fanny pack. Backpacks or other large carry-on items are not allowed. On rafting trips we prefer to carry our personal items (keys, wallets, lip balm, sunscreen, gum, etc.) in three Ziploc bags inside a small fanny pack so that they are secure, yet easily accessible.

Trip Description

The shuttle from Leatherwood Ford to Burnt Mill Bridge takes about an hour. At the bridge, the guides will give you detailed safety instructions and a brief paddling lesson, and put you in the boat. All rapids require serious paddling efforts on the part of the guide and participants to get through without swamping the boat, but the experienced guides should make you feel safe and comfortable. Team participation in paddling is fun and a great life experience for kids. You will really get to know the guides, the folks in your boat, and the safety kayaker, who floats alongside and instigates hilarious splash fights.

Clear Fork is a beautiful stretch of water, and the gorge feels very remote. Within an hour, after some warm-up rapids, you will reach First Drop, the first real rapid on the trip. Soon after that you will reach The Confluence, where Clear Fork and New River meet to form the Big South

Fork of the Cumberland River. You may stop there for a quick break and explanation of what lies ahead. Very soon after pushing off, you will reach the three biggest rapids of the trip: Double Falls, The Ell, and Washing Machine—all Class IV rapids within a few hundred yards of one another. By themselves, these rapids are challenging and fun, but the fact that they lie so close together adds another dimension. If you fall out of the boat early in this set of rapids, there may not be enough time for a rescue between rapids; you may have to swim through a Class IV rapid or two.

If you "become separated" from your boat in a rapid, there are a few things you should do to ensure your safety. First, hang on to your paddle if possible; it adds 5 feet to your reach and may help you get back in the boat quickly. If you end up far from your boat, immediately signal to your guide that you are OK by touching the top of your head to show that you are conscious. Look for the throw-bag rope, which the guide will have tossed to within an arm's length of your head even before you have recovered from the shock of the cold water. If you end up in the water at or immediately upstream from a rapid, you might not want to swim back to the boat (unless the guide tells you to), because you could be pinned between the raft and a rock. Instead, quickly float on your back with your feet pointing downstream, toes out of the water, and just ride it out, using your feet to push off any rocks you encounter. If you find yourself beside your boat while going through a rapid, move to the upstream side of the boat and extend your paddle so that someone can grab it and haul you in, or grab a safety line on the raft and keep your legs out from under the raft. Never allow yourself to float downstream of a boat! Your guide has to think about the safety of the people remaining in the craft as well as those separated from it, and sometimes it is safer just to ride it out alone and regroup below the rapid.

After the "Big Three," enjoy some quiet water, tell some stories, and look for the Honey Creek Pocket Wilderness on your left—a beautiful area with an overlook high above the river. The gorge walls are very high along here, and you will notice some fantastic sandstone walls far above you on either side of the river as you head directly north. Get ready for Rion's Eddy, another fun Class IV rapid. Soon after, you will encounter Pine Creek. You will see the river access point on the sandbar on your right just downstream of Pine Creek. This may be your lunch stop.

For another 1.5 miles the railroad grade lies about 40 feet above the river on your right. Now heading directly west, you are floating in "The

Narrows," where the gorge is somewhat constricted. Here the river flows among massive, building-sized boulders that broke away from the spectacular sandstone walls above you, creating interesting pools and eddies. Jake's Hole is a particularly large, beautiful pool that ends with a trip through the Class III-plus O&W Rapids, the last rapid on the upper gorge of the Big South Fork. Soon afterward, you will round the bend and see the massive O&W Bridge looming nearly 80 feet over the river. You might be able to "cowboy" the rapids directly under the bridge and may be caught on film at the only easy access point for white-water photography on the river.

The bridge is only 2.2 miles from Leatherwood Ford, and the rest of your trip is relatively slow and beautiful. Look up to your right for the East Rim Overlook, to get a different perspective on the river gorge. As you complete this wonderful trip, remember that had it not been for the establishment of the Big South Fork NRRA, this river would have been dammed just 20 miles downstream, flooding the gorge you just floated with water to a depth of a few hundred feet above your head. Thanks to the hard work of the many people involved, this is one of the last large free-flowing rivers in the eastern United States! Please enjoy it, but also respect it and protect it.

50 Canoe Camping in the Lower Gorge

TYPE OF WATERCRAFT: Wood dory, decked canoe, open canoe, or any type of kayak.

TYPE OF ADVENTURE: Relaxing and remote river camping adventure.

TOTAL DISTANCE: About 25 miles.

DIFFICULTY: Class II overall, numerous Class III rapids, and two Class IV-plus that must be portaged around.

TIME REQUIRED: 2 to 3 days.

SPECIAL CONCERNS: Large boulders, suck-holes, hydraulics, and log-jams; remote stretches of river in a deep gorge with no road access and few rescue opportunities.

SCENIC VALUE: Spectacular: This wide, free-flowing river flows around building-size boulders within a deep gorge blanketed by forests and capped by huge rock walls.

USGS MAPS: Honey Creek, Barthell SW, Oneida North, and Barthell.

START-END POINTS: Put-in at Leatherwood Ford; take-out at Blue Heron Mine.

Overview: This must-do trip rivals any other canoe camping trip in the eastern United States. The 25 river miles between Leatherwood Ford and Blue Heron contain some of the oldest and healthiest riparian forests, the biggest boulders, and the highest sandstone bluffs in the NRRA. Your trip ends at the most significant historical site in the NRRA, the Blue Heron Mining Community. Along the way, you will see signs of mining impacts on the gorge slopes and in some of the tributaries, but you will also see how the area has recovered.

Fish and wildlife are abundant in the river and surrounding riparian forests. Freshwater mussels are abundant in shallow gravel shoals, and the Big South Fork contains among the most diverse mussel fauna on the plateau. Unfortunately, the most common species, the Asian clam, is an exotic, invasive species, and you will see the small shells of dead ones in nearly every shoal. A number of species of darters (tiny fish in the perch family) can be seen in the clear, shallow waters of fast-flowing riffles. Look for tiny fish that behave almost like little underwater lizards by using their expanded pectoral (front) fins to plaster themselves against the rocks in fast water. Bluegill, long-ear, red-ear, and green sunfish and channel catfish are abundant in pools and eddies. Smallmouth bass are the most popular quarry in the river and are easily hooked in flowing waters of wide raceways and just downstream of the point where raceways enter deep pools.

Map turtles are fairly abundant downstream of Station Camp but are very difficult to approach. Have binoculars ready if you want to see turtles before they dive off their perches. Water snakes (not poisonous) are very abundant in the river but feed on fish at night, so the best way to see them in action is to search along the shoreline at night with a flashlight. There are absolutely no cottonmouth water moccasins in this waterway, or in the entire region. The nearest populations are in midwestern Tennessee and Kentucky. However, be very careful walking around at night, because copperheads and timber rattlesnakes are nocturnal hunters, and could be near water, especially if the river rocks are warm.

Kingfishers and great blue herons hunt for aquatic quarry and will give you a great show if you approach slowly. The songs of riparian forest birds will provide better entertainment than any radio station, and you may see swallows "dipping" for a drink on the wing. River otters were reintroduced at Leatherwood Ford after being trapped out long ago but still seem to be very rare. Beaver are abundant, especially near No Business and Troublesome Creeks, and you might get to see a deer wading for a drink or even swimming across the river.

Even beginners should be able to do this trip in two full days of steady paddling, but we strongly recommend staying on the river no fewer than three days and two nights. You will not want to rush this trip. We prefer to spend four very enjoyable, lazy days—getting up late, fishing, napping, and puttering around—and three wonderful starry nights on the river. Nice rest rooms, changing areas, and showers are available at Leatherwood Ford and Blue Heron. However, the only facilities between are a few portable toilets at Station Camp.

Canoe Camping Safety and Comfort

Although the Big South Fork is only an overall Class III river from this point downstream, there are two Class IV rapids, and you will be floating in an extremely remote section of the river. Because of the steepness of the gorge and surrounding rock walls and the limited number and wide spacing of trails that reach river level, there is virtually no possibility for a quick rescue, even near Station Camp or Big Island. For these reasons alone, you should take no unnecessary risks. In addition to the precautions mentioned in the "Safety and Etiquette" section (see The Basics chapter), we recommend at least the following things to make your trip safe:

1. While planning your trip and getting your backcountry permits, be sure to ask someone at the NPS Visitor Center about water levels. Flow rates of 600 to 800 cfs (at Leatherwood Ford) are not so high that you are likely to swamp and not so low that you have to get out and drag your boat through every riffle. You do not want to get caught in a flood on this river, so check the weather forecast. Be familiar with your route and the general area where you want to make camp each night. In summer someone else might float by, but few people float the section north of Station Camp. Never assume that someone will float by and be able to help you.

2. Respect this river. Leave your "river ego" at Leatherwood Ford for a few days. Being humble about your paddling ability is much better than being humbled by this river. Your partners will be more impressed with your cool head and dry sleeping bag than an arrogant attitude and wet or missing gear—especially if it is theirs!

3. Although it may be hot and uncomfortable in summer, wear your life jacket. This is not only smart, it's the law.

4. Carry a knife or multipurpose tool in your pocket or fanny pack so that it is easy to reach in an emergency where ropes or bungee cords might have to be cut quickly.

5. Scout any rapids that give you even the slightest pause on their approach. Steer your boat through the V created by the water hitting the rocks. It is like a directional arrow telling you the best way to go.

6. Carry your gear in rugged waterproof containers and secure them to your boat for improved stability, better flotation, and quicker retrieval. "Batten down the hatches" through all rapids, no matter how small.

7. Watch your step when getting out of the boat. The river bottom is covered with really slippery, large, and odd-shaped boulders that can catch your foot and twist an ankle.

8. If someone gets hurt very badly, it might be worth paddling to the nearest major river access point and having someone climb out of the gorge on a trail to try to get help or see if their phone works from the top of the plateau, while others tend to the injured party. Although the strenuous climb will be around 500 vertical feet, you can generally reach the plateau rim in less than a mile.

On river camping trips, we recommend carrying at least the following:

1. A forty-eight-quart cooler (block ice lasts longer). Fasten the lid with rope or bungee cords.

2. A tent, sleeping bags, and sleeping pads stuffed first in plastic trash bags and then in their own nylon stuff-sacks or river bags, tied individually to the canoe. These are great flotation devices.

3. Two small waterproof river bags with clothing and towels and personal items, preferably distributed among the bags in case one bag gets lost or punctured.

4. Two large, rugged plastic bins with locking lids fastened with rope or bungee cords for camping and cooking gear and dry food, first stuffed into plastic trash bags. Plastic bins will balance nicely in a canoe and are great for short trips but are difficult to portage. If you can afford them, get heavy-duty, waterproof portage packs. Bring lots of extra trash bags, too.

5. A rugged waterproof case for your camera gear, electronics, and/or binoculars.

6. Fishing poles (and licenses), snorkeling gear, binoculars, field guides, and other fun stuff that you just can't live without.

Trip Description

The launch site at Leatherwood Ford is convenient, but be ready to carry your stuff down a few stairs. You will encounter a small rapid immediately after pushing off and a few potentially canoe-swamping Class II rapids in the first few miles, so be ready!

2.0 Reach Angel Falls after about an hour of paddling. Look for a gravel/cobble bar on your right on a right-hand bend just after Fall Creek empties into the river, followed by flat sandstone shelves near water level.

Caution: Be extremely careful not to get sucked into Angel Falls, which was once a small waterfall with a plunge pool below. Locals blasted some rocks away to make it navigable but just made it worse. Although not really a waterfall, it is an extremely dangerous, nonnavigable chute with scoured, undercut walls that only an expert with a white-water kayak or decked canoe would dare try. A trip through Angel Falls in an open canoe will at the very least ruin your trip and could easily end in serious injury or even death. Even the most experienced boaters portage around this powerful chute.

The Angel Falls portage is on the right. There are many take-out places, your choice being influenced by water level, safety, and the distance you are willing to carry your stuff. The first take-out lies on the gravel/cobble bar on the inside bend directly across from the PORTAGE RIGHT sign and makes the portage nearly 0.2 mile. You should always stop here and scout the shore for the shortest but safest route. At normal water levels, you can proceed another few hundred yards to where the portage trail ascends to River Trail East. At lower water (less than 600 cfs), you can safely proceed or bank-line your boat to within 100 feet of Angel Falls.

Lug your boat uphill on the portage trail to River Trail East; pass the small wood platform overlooking Angel Falls, then look left for the trail returning to the river over some big boulders about 100 yards below the falls. Unless you are traveling light or in a hurry, plan about an hour for the portage, including a swim and a snack afterward. There's no need to rush. There are some good campsites in this area, and camping near the loud roar of Angel Falls is great if you have three days to spend on the river. If you only have two days, however, you need to move on. This is your last chance to recover forgotten items easily.

Be sure your gear is fastened tightly to the boat before you shove off. There are a few really fun Class II rapids within an hour of Angel Falls, some of which you might want to scout first if you lack experience. It will take about an hour to get through the big horseshoe bend in the river, which will be obvious by your frequent change in direction. After that, the river runs generally north-northwest and widens into large, quiet pools; you will have to paddle a lot to keep your momentum. Watch for huge spotted gar lurking at the surface of these pools.

7.6 Reach Station Camp Crossing less than three hours after leaving Angel Falls. This is the first of only three places in the NRRA where multiuse trails cross the river. Station Camp Road reaches the river level at this spot, and there are pit toilets and plenty of campsites here. There will surely be other people, dogs, horses, and vehicles; we suggest that you move on if you really want to experience the remoteness of the river gorge. The historical Station Camp area is located in the lower reaches of Station Camp Creek about 0.2 mile west of the west bank of the river (see Charit Creek Lodge section for a historical overview). The one-hour stretch between Station Camp and Big Island (heading generally northeast) consists mainly of quiet pools, but you will encounter a couple of good shoals and some fun, non-threatening rapids.

10.9 Reach Big Island about an hour after leaving Station Camp. Big Island was formed by the deposition of gravel and cobble from No Business Creek, which enters the river from the west. The island is interesting, and a short look around will really give you a feeling for the erosive power of water. The shoals on either side of the island are great for wading and look-ing for darters, clams, and other interesting river dwellers. The riffles, pools, and eddies directly below Big Island are good fishing spots and are just plain beautiful.

You are nearly half done with your trip and can easily make it to this point in the first day if you leave early, portage efficiently with a short swim and lunch, and paddle steadily in the quiet water sections. There are plenty of campsites on Big Island (try the downstream tip), along No Business Creek, and along the right (south) side of the river just below Big Island. For the next few miles, the river runs nearly east-west, providing fantastic evening and morning sunlight that shines obliquely down the river and reflects off river redhorse suckers and other fish. You should start seeing map turtles basking on logs. In the morning, shafts of light shine through the river fog in a golden glow that is unforgettable.

We highly recommend camping somewhere along this great stretch of the river, whether you are doing the trip in two, three, or four days. The next east-west running section of river, between Troublesome Creek and Bear Creek, is just as spectacular, but is more than 5 miles downstream on quiet water. You might want to plan your trip so that you can camp some-where along that stretch of river on your second night. Numerous multi-use trails lead down to Big Island, but downstream of this point trail access to the river is sparse. For the next 13 miles you will be paddling in a very remote section of the gorge.

13.0 About an hour from Big Island, pass Williams Creek and turn sharply north. Williams Creek receives water from Puncheoncamp Fork, which has a history of coal mining impacts. As a result, the water quality in Williams Creek is somewhat degraded in terms of pH, and the diversity of fish and aquatic invertebrates is depressed. However, the creek is pretty, the water generally runs clear, and there is no need to be concerned about health risks. The gravel bar and huge eddy on the outside bend of the river on the right just past Williams Creek is a good place to stop and swim. You may encounter some horse tracks or people here, as horseback riders doing the Pilot-Wines Loop (Trail 10) often stop at this spot for lunch and a swim. However, this is not a good safety access point, as the trails leading out of the gorge are rough, steep, and long; one trail is not even a maintained NRRA trail. There are plenty of campsites along the horse trail above the swimming hole, but they are all situated well above river level.

Heading north, the nearly 4-mile section between Williams and Troublesome Creeks has at least a few campsites; a couple are really nice. Possibly the best river campsite in the lower gorge lies on the left immediately downstream of the chutelike rapid created by Difficulty Creek. Be ready to eddy-out to the left just after the rapid, or you will have to paddle back upstream. The site is covered by large river birch that eerily lean at about the same angle toward the river; it has plenty of flat spots to pitch tents, a good fire pit, and water sounds that will lull you to sleep. Gardens of massive boulders grace this section of river, and the braided rapids that flow between them provide regular opportunities to test your steering skills.

17.0 Round the gradual right-handed bend at the point where Troublesome Creek empties into the river from the west. You should now be facing directly east. There are a few good campsites in the Troublesome Creek drainage, but you may want to hold out for something better. This is the beginning of a nearly 5-mile section where the river is oriented east-west. Our favorite campsite is on a gravel bar on the south bank of the river near Annie Branch. Like the east-west section of river you floated the previous day, this is a spectacular reach, with great light bouncing off the water in the morning and evening. The Kentucky Trail (Trail 23) runs along the north side of the river for nearly 2 miles, then turns and climbs out of the gorge about a mile past Oil Well Branch. Should major problems arise, you could climb out of the gorge and even reach Ledbetter Trailhead relatively quickly.

19.8 Pass the point where Bear Creek empties into the river on your right at a gaging station, and turn sharply northward. During low water, a small island will have emerged at this spot. Bear Creek has been severely affected by acid mine drainage, and a whitish precipitate covers the rocks of the creek (see ecology section). The only living things we have ever seen in the creek were some minnows, and they were near its confluence with the river. If you need to filter water for the rest of your trip, take water from the river *above* Bear Creek—or wait until you pass another tributary.

This is a potential access point for those inclined to carry boats down (or up) the hill to the Bear Creek Trailhead—a 0.5-mile, groomed gravel trail ranging from 760 to more than 1,200 feet in elevation. It could also serve as a crucial take-out point in an emergency. However, do not expect anyone to be at the trailhead, as it is relatively remote and infrequently used. The trail is gated near the trailhead, so you will need to get someone to open the gate before a rescue can be made with a vehicle.

21.0 Just over a mile below Bear Creek, you will encounter Big Shoals, a Class III rapid. This narrow stretch of river has lots of huge boulders to negotiate around, followed by some fairly flat sections. Note Blair Creek on your right about a mile below Big Shoals. This small drainage was severely affected by acid mine drainage, to the point that the rocks are bright orange-yellow. We have never found signs of life in this creek. Soon after, you will pass Laurel Branch, a relatively healthy creek.

23.0 Pass a number of reclaimed mine areas on your right just before a gentle westward bend in the river. These open areas and young forests are fading reminders of the vast coal mining operations that occurred in this area. The largest reclaimed area is directly below Devil's Jump Overlook. You should be able to pick out the railing and pavilion at the overlook from your position. At this point start looking for Devil's Jump, another extremely dangerous Class IV rapid that you should portage around. Devil's Jump comes soon after the first indication that you are heading southwest on the river, so get out your compass and be ready.

24.0 Enter the large boulder garden and start looking for the Devil's Jump portage. Do not wait until you can hear the roar of this rapid or see the chute, because it will be too late. The portage on the right begins on a large sandbar. Some folks take out here because the sandbar is more obvious and the portage seems shorter. However, you will have to carry your boat and equipment separately over numerous large, widely spaced boulders. The portage on the left across from the sandbar, although slightly longer, is much easier. Take out on the left and scramble up the riverbank to a wide trail that leads to a spot just below Devil's Jump.

Devil's Jump is a narrow chute between three massive boulders, with a sharp turn and a spot where water "pillows" up on one of the rocks, then cascades down into a plunge pool. It is extremely dangerous to run this chute in an open-decked canoe—or any boat, for that matter. People have been pinned underwater in a logjam beneath these rocks. After Devil's Jump, traverse a large number of building-sized boulders in the river, and run one more very small rapid.

24.5 Look to the right for the concrete slab at Blue Heron that marks the end of your trip. Take one last look at the river, and ponder what it would look like with a high dam at Devil's Jump. From here north, this raging river slides into the quiet waters of Lake Cumberland, created by Wolf Creek Dam on the Cumberland River. Although it is a staggeringly beautiful reservoir, it totally lacks the character of the wild waterway you just floated.

Picnicking, Swimming, Fishing, and Hunting Adventures

Developed picnic spots are not widely available in the NRRA, so we help you locate the nicest roadside spots with at least picnic tables, garbage cans, some type of toilet facility, and usually barbecue grills (see next page). In 2001 the best picnic spots were at Yahoo Falls Scenic Area, Blue Heron, Leatherwood Ford, and the big pavilions at Bandy Creek area. Consult a park ranger for the newest information about additional spots. Most of the picnicking spots are also good swimming spots, and some of the swimming spots provide at least marginal opportunities for fishing.

Bandy Creek Campground has a nice, clean swimming pool with lifeguards. It has pool chairs, rest rooms, showers, soda machines, drinking water, a playground, vast grassy fields, a volleyball court, and picnic tables. It is a great place to picnic or relax on a hot afternoon.

Although the pool is nice, we prefer swimming in the Big South Fork River and its tributaries. Swim in the river and creeks only when the water levels are low—luckily, during summer and fall, when it is hot enough that jumping in the river will be irresistible. Since the water is clear during low water, it is fun to go snorkeling and watch the fish and invertebrates. The pools below Angel Falls and Devil's Jump Rapids are our favorite places to swim, and the huge boulders along the shoreline make a great place to sun yourself.

You will be swimming at your own risk, so be extra careful. Never swim alone, and never swim above rapids. In the river, pay attention to your surroundings; watch out for people boating or fishing. Be aware of deep pools, holes, rocks, ledges, strong currents, and underwater objects—all can be dangerous. Avoid jumping from boulders. If you must jump, make absolutely certain that the water in your splash-down area is deep enough and free of underwater objects or rocks.

The following table shows, from north to south, areas that as of summer 2002 had nice picnic areas (P) with direct vehicle access, picnic tables, garbage cans, rest rooms, and usually a place to grill some burgers. The swimming areas (S) are places with direct vehicle access or a reasonable walk to a safe place to wade or swim. The fishing holes (F) we list have easy access so are probably not the best fishing spots in the NRRA, but they are wonderful places to have some family fun, worm some hooks, and maybe let the youngsters land their first fish. Flip to the "Local Directions" section for directions.

Although there are lots of places to bobber-fish and fool around at a relaxed pace, with a little effort some great fishing opportunities are available within the Big South Fork NRRA. You will need a canoe to get to the best fishing spots, such as river pools, boulder-lined runways, and the confluence of creeks and the river (see Chapter 50).

Fishing regulations within the Big South Fork NRRA follow the guidelines established by the states of Tennessee and Kentucky. Check with the visitor centers, the Tennessee Wildlife Resources Agency, or the Kentucky Department of Wildlife Resources regarding information on fishing regulations (see appendix). When fishing in the NRRA you must have a valid fishing license from the state in which you are fishing. Fishing licenses from either state are valid when fishing in the Big South Fork River from the Leatherwood Ford Bridge (TN 297) to the Yamacraw Bridge (KY 92), but this rule does not apply to tributaries. The Big South Fork NRRA does not sell fishing licenses, but they can be purchased from many locations in the surrounding area. Fishing and hunting licenses also can be purchased over the telephone for Tennessee and over the Internet for Kentucky (see appendix).

The Big South Fork NRRA allows hunting of both small and large game during the regular state seasons. Since Tennessee and Kentucky do not have reciprocal hunting agreements, a valid state license is required when hunting in the portion of the NRRA in each state. Hunting regulations within the Big South Fork NRRA follow the guidelines established by the states as well as some additional NPS regulations. A complete list of NPS hunting regulations can be obtained from the visitor centers. Check with the Tennessee Wildlife Resources Agency or the Kentucky Department of Wildlife Resources regarding information on hunting regulations and seasons (see appendix).

Place	Activities	Location / Comments
Big Creek River Access	S, F	See "Local Directions," 1.
Yahoo Falls Scenic Area	P, S, F	Trail 1; superb picnic area and forest, "Local Directions," 2.
Alum Ford River Access	P, S, F	Trail 2; see "Local Directions," 3.
Blue Heron River Access	P, S, F	See "Local Directions," 6; has snack bar.
Devil's Jump Rapids	S, F	Trail 5; requires 0.8-mile easy hike (round-trip); only swim below these rapids.
Station Camp	P, S, F	See "Local Directions," 11.
Twin Arches Trailhead	P	Trail 16; nice, but no water available.
Charit Creek Lodge	P, S	Trail 22; remote, peaceful, and gorgeous.
Bandy Creek Area	P, S	See "Local Directions," 20; many spots, but usually busy.
Leatherwood Ford	P, S, F	Trail 36; wonderful area, but often busy.
Angel Falls Rapids	S, F	Trail 37; requires 4-mile easy hike (round-trip); swim only below these rapids.
O&W Bridge	S, F	Trail 44; access by long stairs or rocky climb; swim only below rapids under bridge.
The Confluence	S, F	Trail 45; incredible spot for both activities but requires 1.2-mile hike on steep trail.
Burnt Mill Bridge	P, S, F	Trail 47; superb spot, easy access, not deep, but great for wading with kids.
Rugby Trailhead	P	Trail 48; nice, but few picnic spots.
Gentlemen's Swimming Hole and Meeting of the Waters	S, F	Trail 48; requires 0.8-mile hike on steep trail, but great swimming and fishing.
Brewster Bridge	P, S, F	See "Local Directions," 40; beautiful area, rarely used, but great access.
Peters Bridge	P, S, F	See "Local Directions," 41; not very scenic.

Rock Climbing and Rappelling Adventures

Excellent rock climbing and rappelling opportunities are available in the Big South Fork NRRA on spectacular sandstone bluffs that line the gorge. As of this writing, a Climbing Management Plan is still under development but will not be part of the GMP. Our information comes from the *Code of Federal Regulations* (Title 36, Chapter 1, Section 1.5), a memorandum to the NPS staff from the chief park ranger dated July 25, 1996, and interviews with NPS staff.

Since protection of natural and cultural resources is a primary concern, certain areas and formations are closed to rock climbing and rappelling. They include all arches, Chimney Rock in the No Business area, Chimney Rocks in the Station Camp area, Devils Cave, Yahoo Falls, Maude's Crack, and any fragile natural geological feature posted as off-limits to climbing. Climbing and rappelling are not permitted within 100 feet of developed or undeveloped overlooks, or waterfalls. Bolts, pitons, spikes, or nails must not be pounded into any rock wall, and the rock face cannot be damaged in any way. Power drills are not permitted in the gorge or nondeveloped areas. Consult a park ranger for a complete list of the most current rock climbing and rappelling rules and regulations.

Except for those areas listed above, the NRRA is generally open to rock climbing and rappelling. The most popular locations include the big wall below the O&W Overlook, a long wall at Crack in the Rocks above the Blue Heron Mining Community, two areas east of Coyle Branch Trail, and the walls above Station Camp Creek and No Business Creek.

Crack in the Rocks lies on the upper gorge slope between the Blue Heron Mining Community and Blue Heron Overlook. More than forty-two pitches rated between 5.6 and 5.12 have been established, with very few bolts. The wall is between 30 and 60 feet tall and has cracks of all sizes and angles, even some overhangs. To get there, take the Blue Heron Loop (Trail 5) or the Blue Heron Overlook (Trail 3).

The Bowl lies on the rim of the North White Oak Creek Gorge just east of the Coyle Branch Trail. To get there, drive west from the intersection of TN 297 and Bandy Creek Road for 1.5 miles and turn left on White Pine Road (no sign), a gravel road that enters a large field at an angle. This is part of the North White Oak Loop (Trail 30, miles 1.8 to 2.7). Measured from TN 297, head southeast through a number of pretty farm fields and make a sharp right (south) turn at mile 0.8. Pass the turn for the North White Oak Loop on your right (west) at mile 0.9, pass the intersection with the trail leading to Leatherwood Ford Overlook on your left at mile 1.5, pass the intersection with Coyle Branch Trail at mile 1.6, and enter a long, grassy field on a narrow ridge line at mile 1.7. This Y-shaped field forks at mile 2.0, with climbing areas at the end of each fork. Simply follow the network of trails that head south from a bunch of primitive campsites just inside the wood line.

Due to the long history of climbing on the O&W Wall, a big wall below the spectacular but as yet undeveloped O&W Overlook, climbing and rappelling will be allowed at least until a developed overlook is built. This massive wall provides an uninterrupted 300-foot climb on five consecutive pitches, each rated 5.12—making it one of the biggest climbs in the eastern United States. The best way to access this wall is from below. Follow directions to the O&W Railroad Bridge on page 34. At the east end of the bridge, look for a large, overused campsite flanked by a massive boulder spray-painted with local "artwork." Walk north around this campsite and past the large rock on the John Muir Trail, and look for a faint trail on the right that takes you very steeply uphill (about 200 feet in elevation) to the base of the wall.

Since climbing and rappelling are potentially very dangerous activities, safety should come first. You should be properly trained and under the watchful eye of experienced climbers. Obviously, proper equipment and knot-tying expertise are essential. As with any other outdoor activity, never climb or rappel alone and let someone know your plans. The Life Development Center offers customized rock climbing and rappelling adventures for groups (see appendix).

Big South Fork National River and Recreation Area

Headquarters
4564 Leatherwood Road
Oneida, TN 37841
(423) 569–9778
www.nps.gov/biso

Bandy Creek Visitor Center
(423) 286–7275
8:00 A.M. to 6:00 P.M. Eastern Time
(June through October)
8:00 A.M. to 4:30 P.M. Eastern Time
(November through May)
Open every day except Christmas.

Bandy Creek Campground
(423) 286–8368
Blue Heron Campground
(606) 376–2611
Reservations for both campgrounds
through Spherix, Inc. (from April 1
through October 31):
(800) 365–2267, code 244
Internet reservations:
reservations.nps.gov or
www.nps.gov/biso

Kentucky Visitor Center, Stearns
(606) 376–5073
9:00 A.M. to 5:30 P.M. Eastern Time
(May though October)
Hours vary November through April.

Blue Heron Interpretive Center
(606) 376–3787

State Agencies That Regulate Fishing and Hunting:

Kentucky Department of Fish and Wildlife Resources
#1 Game Farm Road
Frankfort, KY 40601
(800) 858–1549 or (502) 564–4336
www.kdfwr.state.ky.us/

Tennessee Wildlife Resources Agency
Cumberland Plateau–Region III
464 Industrial Boulevard
Crossville, TN 38555
Information: (800) 262–6704 or (931) 484–9571
Poaching Hotline: (800) 241–0767
Purchase Fishing and Hunting
Licenses: (888) 814–8972
www.state.tn.us/twra/index.html

After-Hours Emergency
Tennessee

Highway Patrol
(800) 792–1033

Fentress County General Hospital
West Central Avenue, Jamestown
(931) 879–8171

Fentress County Ambulance
(931) 879–8147

Fentress County Sheriff
(931) 879–8142

Scott County Hospital
Highway 27, Oneida
(423) 569–8521

Scott County Ambulance
(423) 569–6000

Scott County Sheriff
(423) 663–2245

Poison Control (Knoxville)
(865) 544–9400

Veterinarians:

Cumberland Animal Clinic, Oneida
(423) 569–5243
(423) 569–4384 (Emergency)

Dogwood Animal Clinic, Jamestown
(931) 879–1111

Upchurch Animal Clinic, Jamestown
(931) 879–7357

Horse Trailer Repair:
Bowman Service Center
4535 Highway 127 North (close to
intersection of I–40 and U.S. 127)
Crossville, TN 38555
(931) 456–2397
(931) 456–9332

Kentucky

McCreary County Ambulance
(606) 376–5062

McCreary County Sheriff
(606) 376–2322

Poison Control
(800) 772–5725

Great Places to Stay

**Miner's Houses at Barthell
Mining Camp**
K.B.M.T.
P.O. Box 53
Whitley City, KY 42653
(888) 550–5748
(606) 376–8749

**Bear Creek Campgrounds and
Equestrian Area
Station Camp Campgrounds and
Equestrian Area**
*Exclusively for those with horses
Bernard Terry
P.O. Box 4411
Oneida, TN 37841
(423) 569–3321 (reservations)
(423) 569–6108 (after hours)
(423) 569–7501 (beeper)
www.nps.gov/biso/bear_ck.htm
www.nps.gov/biso/stn_cmp.htm

**Big South Fork Cabins, Bar BEE
Ranch**
*Bring your horse
3090 Leatherwood Ford Road
Jamestown, TN 38556
(931) 879–0707
Fax: (931) 879–0878
E-mail:
sunshine@bigsouthforkcabins.com
www.bigsouthforkcabins.com

Big South Fork Motor Lodge
HC 69 Box 335
Stearns, KY 42647
(606) 376–3156
(606) 376–3861
Fax: (606) 376–3008

Big South Fork Wilderness Resorts
*Bring your horse
Route 2, Box 169-A
1463 Big Ridge Road
Oneida, TN 37841
(423) 569–9847
E-mail: alax@highland.net
www.wildernessresorts.com

Charit Creek Lodge
*Bring your horse
250 Apple Valley Road
Sevierville, TN 37862
(865) 429–5704
E-mail: reservations@charitcreek.com
www.charitcreek.com/home.html
www.nps.gov/biso/cclodge.htm

Grey Gables Bed & Breakfast Inn
Bill and Linda Brooks Jones,
Proprietors
Highway 52, Post Office Box 52
Rugby, TN 37733
(423) 628–5252
E-mail: greygables@highland.net
www.rugbytn.com

Laurel Fork Rustic Retreat
*Bring your horse
1364 Oby Blevins Road
Jamestown, TN 38556
(865) 281–7495
Fax: (865) 281–8357
E-mail: laurelfork@laurelfork.com
www.laurelfork.com

**Newbury House, Pioneer Cottage,
and Percy Cottage in Historic
Rugby**
P.O. Box 8, Highway 52
Rugby, TN 37733
(423) 628–2441
E-mail: rugbytn@highland.net
www.historicrugby.org
www.nps.gov/biso/rugby.htm

**Oneida Guest House Bed &
Breakfast**
103 Shepherd Road
Oneida, TN 37841
(888) 834–4525
(423) 569–3898
E-mail: OGH@highland.net

Pickett State Park
4605 Pickett Park Highway
Jamestown, TN 38556-4141
(931) 879–5821
(877) 260–0010 (cabin reservations)
www.state.tn.us/environment/
parks/pickett/

Williams Creek Retreat
*Bring your horse
Lillard Miller
Station Camp Road
555 West Third Avenue
Oneida, TN 37841
(423) 569–6323
(423) 569–8694

**Wildwood Lodge, Bed and Break-
fast, Stables, and Cabins**
*Bring your horse
3636 Pickett Park Highway
Jamestown, TN 38556
(931) 879–9454

Zenith Stables and Campground
*Bring your horse
Gary Matthews
1001 Range Cemetery Road
Allardt, TN 38504
(931) 879–5252

Great Places to Eat

Bacara's Family Restaurant
*Closed Sunday through Tuesday
*Do not take credit cards
Sharp Place
329 Wheeler Lane
Jamestown, TN 38556
(931) 879–7121
E-mail: bacaras@twlakes.net

**Coal Miner's Diner at Barthell
Mining Camp**
(888) 550–5748
(606) 376–8749

**Harrow Road Cafe in Historic
Rugby**
Central Avenue and Harrow Road
5545 Rugby Highway (Highway 52)
Rugby, TN 37733
(423) 628–2350

J.C.'s Cafe Take-out
Main Street
P.O. Box 1356
Whitley City, KY 42653
(606) 376–1455

Mark Twain Family Restaurant
104 South Main Street
Jamestown, TN 38556
(931) 879–2811

Preston's Loft Steak & Pizza
19787 Alberta Street
Oneida, TN 37841
(423) 569–4158

Rancho Grande Mexican Restaurant
18148 Alberta Avenue
Oneida, TN 37841
(423) 569–2104

Stearns Restaurant
*Do not take credit cards
Henderson Street
Stearns, KY 42647
(606) 376–5354

Activities, Attractions, Concessionaires, and Outfitters

Barthell Mining Camp
K.B.M.T.
P.O. Box 53
Whitley City, KY 42653
(888) 550–5748
(606) 376–8749

Bandy Creek Stables
*Horseback riding
1845 Old Sunbright Road
Jamestown, TN 38556
(423) 286–7433
E-mail: Bandycreek@twlakes.net
www.nps.gov/biso/bsf_stab.htm

Big South Fork Outdoors
*Hunting and fishing licenses, supplies, and information
North Highway 27
Whitley City, KY 42653
(606) 376–5057

Big South Fork Scenic Railway Enterprises LLC
*Train to Barthell and Blue Heron
21 Henderson Street
P.O. Box 368
Stearns, KY 42647
(800) 462–5664
(606) 376–5330
www.bsfsry.com
www.nps.gov/biso/bsfrr.htm

Breakaway: The Wilderness Experience
*Backcountry experience including rappelling
Dallas Stults, Director
Anderson County Health Council
P.O. Box 570
718 Charles Seivers Boulevard
Clinton, TN 37716
(865) 463–8870

Buck Horn Hunting and Fishing Supply
*Hunting and fishing licenses, supplies, and information
533 Industrial Lane
Oneida, TN 37841
(423) 569–9452

Earth Traverse Outfitters
*Complete outfitters for camping, hiking, backpacking, mountain biking, rock climbing, canoeing, and kayaking (sales, service, and rentals)
2815 Sutherland Avenue
Knoxville, TN 37919
(865) 523–0699
www.earthtraverse.ws

Historic Rugby
P.O. Box 8, Highway 52
Rugby, TN 37733
(423) 628–2441
E-mail: rugbytn@highland.net
www.historicrugby.org
www.nps.gov/biso/rugby.htm

Life Development Center
*Rock climbing, rappelling, river floats, and backcountry adventures
P.O. Box 570
Clinton, TN 37717
(800) 532–1123
(865) 482–7375
E-mail: ldc@icx.net

McCreary County Museum
P.O. Box 452
Stearns, KY 42657
(606) 376–5730

Pickett State Park
4605 Pickett Park Highway
Jamestown, TN 38556-4141
(931) 879–5821
www.state.tn.us/environment/
parks/pickett/

Sheltowee Trace Outfitters
*Guided rafting and tubing trips; canoe
rental and shuttles
P.O. Box 1060
Whitley City, KY 42653
(800) 541–7238
(606) 376–5567
E-mail: fun@ky-rafting.com
www.ky-rafting.com

Southeast Pack Trips, Inc.
*Horseback riding
299 Dewey Burke Road
Jamestown, TN 38556
(931) 879–2260
E-mail: horseride4u@aol.com
pegasusweb.com/bsf/southeast/

**Sundowner Trailers of
Tennessee**
*Horse trailers
Gary Cox
263 Pressley Road
Vonore, TN 37885
(423) 420–0500
www.trailerwarehouse.com

Tally Ho Stables
*Horseback riding
6334 Grave Hill Road
P.O. Box 4773
Oneida, TN 37841
(877) 300–7438
(423) 569–9472
E-mail: tallyho@nxs.net
www.tallyhostables.com

Regularly-Scheduled Special Events

**Big South Fork Adventure
Challenge**
Life Development Center

P.O. Box 570
Clinton, TN 37717
(800) 532–1123
(865) 482–7375
E-mail: ldc@icx.net

**Big South Fork Competitive Trail
Ride**
Lucy Scanlon
P.O. Box 7
35 Dairy Pond Road
Norris, TN 37828
(865) 494–7654
E-mail: merrymount@naxs.net
www.natrc.org

**Big South Fork Triathlon and Ride-
and-Tie**
Joanne Grimes
9013 Coburn Drive
Knoxville, TN 37922
(865) 693–4308
www.blueridgetrailriders.com

Big South Fork Endurance Ride
Karen Clark
154 Noah Taylor Road
Elizabethton, TN 37643
(423) 474–3024
www.aerc.org

**Big South Fork 17.5-Mile Trail
Race**
Knoxville Track Club
P.O. Box 967
Knoxville, TN 37901
(865) 673–8020
E-mail: knoxtrac@bellsouth.net
www.ktc.org

**Big South Fork Nature
Photography Workshop**
Friends of the Big South Fork
(423) 569–1599

Check with the visitor centers for
information on regularly-scheduled
programs and events, such as Pioneer
Encampment, A Haunting in the Hills
Storytelling Festival, and Cumberland
Heritage Day.

Bibliography

Allawos, J. G. "The Vascular Flora of North White Oak Creek Gorge, Scott and Fentress Counties, Tennessee." M.S. Thesis, University of Tennessee, Knoxville, Tennessee, 1994.

Bailey, C. J., Jr. "The Vascular Flora of the Riparian Zones of the Clear Fork and New River in the Big South Fork National River and Recreation Area." M.S. Thesis, Tennessee Tech University, 1998.

Baker, H. H. and J. Netherton. *Big South Fork Country*. Nashville: Rutledge Hill Press, 1993.

Campbell, T. S. "The Reptiles and Amphibians of the Big South Fork National River and Recreation Area." Unpublished report to the National Park Service, 2002.

Caplenor, D. "Woody plants of the gorges of the Cumberland Plateau and Adjacent Highland Rim." *Journal of the Tennessee Academy of Science* 54(4) (1979): 139–45.

Comiskey, C. E. "The Fishes of the Big South Fork of the Cumberland River System." M.S. Thesis, University of Tennessee, Knoxville, Tennessee, p. 92, 1970.

Comiskey, C. E. and D. A. Etnier. "Fishes of the Big South Fork of the Cumberland River." *Journal of the Tennessee Academy of Science* 47(4):(1972): 140–46.

Deaver, B. G., J. A. Smith, and H. R. Duncan. *Hiking the Big South Fork, 3rd Edition.* Knoxville, Tennessee: University of Tennessee Press,1999.

Goodson, B. E. "The Vascular Flora of the Clear Fork and New River Gorges of the Big South Fork National River and Recreation Area." M.S. Thesis, Tennessee Tech University, 2000.

Howell, B. J. "A Survey of Folklife along the Big South Fork of the Cumberland River." Report of Investigations No. 30, Department of Anthropology, University of Tennessee, Knoxville, Tennessee, 1981.

Leary, M. C. "The Effects of Abandoned Coal Mines on Stream Water Chemistry in the Big South Fork National River and Recreation Area,

Tennessee and Kentucky." M.S. Thesis, University of Tennessee, Knoxville, Tennessee, 1991.

McDade, A. *The Natural Arches of the Big South Fork: A Guide to Selected Landforms.* Outdoor Tennessee Series, J. Casada, Editor, Knoxville, Tennessee: University of Tennessee Press, 2000.

Manning, R. *Exploring the Big South Fork: A Handbook to the National River and Recreation Area.* Norris, Tennessee: Mountain Laurel Place, 1994.

————. *The Historic Cumberland Plateau: An Explorer's Guide, 2nd Edition.* Knoxville, Tennessee: University of Tennessee Press, 1999.

————. *100 Trails of the Big South Fork Tennessee & Kentucky, 4th Edition.* Seattle, Washington: The Mountaineers Books, 2000.

————. *An Outdoor Guide to the Big South Fork National River and Recreation Area, 2nd Edition.* Seattle, Washington: The Mountaineers Books, 2000.

Manning, R. and S. Jamieson. *Trails of the Big South Fork National River and Recreation Area: A Guide for Hikers, Bikers, and Horse Riders.* Norris, Tennessee: Mountain Laurel Place, 1995

Mitchell, D. G. *Horsin' Around East Tennessee: A Trail Guide for East Tennessee, Southwest Virginia, Western North Carolina, and Southern Kentucky.* Jefferson City, Tennessee: Jefferson City Printing Co., 1994.

National Park Service, U.S. Department of the Interior. Undated brochure. *A Checklist of Birds of the Big South Fork National River Area.*

————. Undated brochure. *A Guide to Trees along the Angel Falls Trail.*

National River and Recreation Area, National Park Service, U.S. Department of the Interior. Undated brochure. *A Guide to the Oscar Blevins Loop Trail.*

————. Undated brochure. *A Guide to Paddling in the Big South Fork.*

O'Bara, C. J., W. L. Pennington, and W. P. Bonner. *A Survey of Water Quality, Benthic Macroinvertebrates and Fish for Sixteen Streams within the Big South Fork National River and Recreation Area.* Tennessee Cooperative Fishery Research Unit, Tennessee Technological University, Cookville, Tennessee. Submitted to the U.S. Army Corps of Engineers, Nashville, Tennessee, Contract Number DACW62-81-C-0162, 1982.

Safley, J. M., Jr. "Vegetation of the Big South Fork Cumberland River, Kentucky and Tennessee." M.S. Thesis, University of Tennessee, Knoxville, Tennessee, 1970.

Shaw, J. T. "The Woody Plants of the Big South Fork National River and Recreation Area (BSFNRRA)." M.S. Thesis, University of Tennessee, Knoxville, Tennessee, 2001.

Stephens, D. E. "A Survey of the Amphibians and Reptiles of McCreary County, Kentucky." M.S. Thesis, Eastern Kentucky University, Richmond, Kentucky, 1985.

Summers, C. 1999. *A Year in the Big South Fork National River and Recreation Area*. Jellico, Tennessee: Contemplative Images, 1999.

U.S. Army Corps of Engineers (USACOE). *Inventory and Evaluation of Architectural and Engineering Resources of the Big South Fork National River and Recreation Area, Tennessee and Kentucky*. Prepared by Environmental Consultants, Inc., under Contract No. DACW62-81-C-0013 for the U.S. Army Corps of Engineers, Nashville District, 1982.

————. *An Endangered Species Survey of Abandoned Mine Shafts in the Big South Fork National River and Recreation Area, Kentucky and Tennessee*. Prepared by L. A. Barclay, Jr., and D. R. Parsons, U.S. Fish and Wildlife Service under Order No. 83-11 for the U.S. Army Corps of Engineers, Nashville District, 1983.

U.S. Department of the Interior, National Park Service. *General Management Plan, Environmental Impact Statement, Big South Fork National River and Recreation Area, Kentucky and Tennessee (Draft)*, 2000.

Van Manen, F. T. *A Feasibility Study for the Potential Reintroduction of Black Bears into the Big South Fork Area of Kentucky and Tennessee, Final Report*. Tennessee Wildlife Resources Agency, University of Tennessee, TWRA Technical Report No. 91-3, A Contribution of Federal Aid to Wildlife Restoration FW-6, 1991.

About the Authors

Despite his roots in the suburbs of Chicago, Todd spent his early years camping and fishing in the North Woods with his family, and most of his adult life exploring natural areas all over the United States. Todd was awarded a bachelor's degree in zoology (1984) and a master's degree in zoology (1986) from Eastern Illinois University, then worked as a professional field biologist in Florida and Nevada until 1993. He received his Ph.D. in ecology and evolutionary biology from the University of Tennessee in May 2000. Currently, he is a postdoctoral fellow at the University of Tennessee's Institute for Biological Invasions, studying the ecology, evolution, and environmental impacts of introduced species. Along with his training as a naturalist, Todd is an experienced writer, an award-winning nature photographer, a sport-class mountain bike racer, an experienced horseman, a river-rat, and general outdoorsman.

The love of the outdoors and adventure was instilled early in Kym. She was raised in sunny South Florida where she spent lots of time boating, fishing, scuba diving, and riding horses and bikes. Her love of the outdoors led her to pursue a career in biology, earning bachelor's degrees in biology (1985) and limnology (1986) and a master's degree in biological sciences (1993) from the University of Central Florida. Working in Oak Ridge, Tennessee for the past nine years, she has studied the effects of pollution on the environment and has published numerous articles. She spends every moment possible trail-riding with her horses in the mountains of East Tennessee and (with Dakota) has completed five consecutive years of endurance rides at the Big South Fork NRRA. She writes a monthly column about places to trail-ride in the Southeast, as well as other horse-related subjects, for *Southeast Equine Monthly* magazine.

Todd and Kym live on a small farm outside Maryville, Tennessee, with their two horses and three cats. They spend a lot of time camping, hiking, backpacking, mountain biking, boating, fishing, and rafting in East Tennessee, in the western United States, and in the Caribbean. Their favorite place in East Tennessee is the Big South Fork NRRA, and they have spent countless days exploring it on horseback, on bikes, and on foot since 1994.